210 —

D1013149

Nuclear
Diplomacy

George H. Quester

The First
Twenty-five
Years

Sponsored by
The Center for
International Affairs
Harvard University

Nuclear Diplomacy

The Dunellen Company, Inc., New York

International Standard Book Number 0-8424-0016-8.

Library of Congress Catalogue Card Number 78-132979.

Printed in the United States of America.

Designed by University Press of Cambridge, Inc.

To Aline

Acknowledgments

I owe many debts to those who helped in the writing of this book. Special gratitude goes to the Harvard Center for International Affairs and its directors, Robert Bowie, Thomas Schelling, and Raymond Vernon, for generous financial and intellectual support for my research. Participation in the Harvard-MIT Joint Arms Control Seminar, and in Henry Kissinger's Seminar on National Security Policy, proved particularly stimulating. Helpful criticisms and suggestions on various portions of this book were received from Morton Halperin, William Harris, Robert Jervis, James King, Thomas Schelling, and Jeremy Stone.

I am deeply grateful for the many substantive and editorial suggestions of my wife, Aline. Her encouragement has been as indispensable as ever.

Contents

List of Figures

Preface

What will follow is an account of international relations since 1945, as determined or influenced by weapons inventories and deployments. It is not contended that all of the cold war can be explained by the ebbs and flows of the arms race; but too much of it perhaps can.

With the appearance of weapons of mass destruction, peacetime defense strategy has become a bargaining or blackmail process of "deterrence," a process which must consider the motives and expectations of opponents far more carefully than ever before. In effect, peace depends on each side's using a rational model to analyze the other, even when contemporary social science remains very much undecided about its faith in such "rationality." This author's bias toward such rational models should thus be stipulated.

The distinction between sociological and economic analysis has sometimes been portrayed as follows: that sociologists are intent on describing the unanticipated or unconscious consequences of human interaction, while economists are describing that which was anticipated, sought after, or schemed for. An economic bias applies here. If some would thus portray the 1945-1968 Soviet-American arms race as a string of aimless and blundering accidents, this study generally attempts to view it quite differently, as a series of deliberate engagements. If such engagements have often wasted tax dollars on useless weapons, or brought the powers unhappily close to war, it may yet have been that each side clear-sightedly anticipated such harmful results as "prisoners" in a game-theoretic prisoner's dilemma, and simply could do nothing about them.

The account here is therefore generally nonpathological; it is reluctant to condemn policies, or to denounce error, or to suggest alternative reforms. Where error and miscalculation seem indispensable for explaining some particular decisions or policies, the bias is that some concrete, perhaps unavoidable, source for such error will be identifiable. For example, it is obvious that most strategic analysts in 1944 would have underrated the future striking power of the U.S. Air Force, simply because wartime secrecy would have kept them from knowing about nuclear weapons. Where such clear cause cannot be adduced for unavoidable miscalculation, however, simple foolishness will not so quickly be introduced into the record.

The sequence is largely chronological, alternating between strategic and tactical weapons issues. Concrete confirmation is available and noted for deliberations assumed in a number of the cases presented, but in others the reasoning must be determined by inference, and the reader must decide for himself whether or not he sees the inference to be valid. The methodological point is basic. One can assume that what men have (sagely or ignorantly) said about military strategy straightforwardly establishes what was believed. Alternatively, one can assume that the statesmen involved all knew most of what they had to know, and then decided to pretend ignorance wherever such a pretense was strategically appropriate. This book seeks to test the latter trial assumption; generally correct conclusions about the weapons environment are assumed for Soviet, American, and other decision-makers wherever the contrary is not explicitly stipulated. For at least some of the cold war, the actors of international decision-making had to be precisely that—"actors"; what will follow is a description of their stage as it actually was, as they all knew it.

To assume that statesmen were more intelligent than they have seemed may appear a somewhat radical or perverse approach to any area of social science. Yet a straightforward defense for this assumption might argue as follows. Statesmen will often find it to their interest to pretend to be what they are not; to feign nonexistent ignorance is easier than to feign nonexistent intelligence; hence statesmen will generally seem more ignorant than they are. A second argument would be that we can indeed account for one major persistent error amongst strategists, namely, underrating the intelligence of other strategists. Adhering to the earlier stipulation that all serious miscalculation must be explainable, one would have to cite the ego-gratifying benefits for an intellectual of the "out" party in believing that the "ins" are simply stupid.

Indeed, it may seem to the reader at points that the only error repeatedly identified in this account is one man's assumption that another has made erroneous assumptions.

An advantage of this sort of analysis is that it seeks the environmental factors which produce mutual disadvantage even when all the actors are pursuing fully rational policies. The prisoner's dilemma matrix of game theory indeed accounts for a great deal of political life, domestic and international, but it leaves fewer grounds for criticizing the "prisoners" trapped in it. Ideological fanaticism (of whatever variety—Stalin, Dulles, or later) can have caused conflict as easily as foolishness, but neither of these may have been necessary, when military technology could provoke suspicions amongst even the more moderate and reasonable of men. Throughout this account, therefore, heavy stress is placed on the political problems presented by material arrangements and technology themselves. Some kinds of missiles make political understanding easier, others do not; defeating one enemy can change an ally into another enemy; an enclave with a high wall around it may be very different from one without; one megaton of explosive power may have a political effect much greater than 50 times that of 20 kilotons.

By focusing so heavily on objective environment, this account can be accused of ignoring the nonrational internal workings of the states involved. Few can deny that the intranational characteristics of the super powers, bureaucratic or ideological, have been significant; the U.S.S.R. today is not that of Stalin, and the United States of the 1960's differs much from the McCarthy era. Yet one must also concede that the international range tolerated by any given domestic structure seems to be quite wide. It was Khrushchev in 1962, and not Stalin, who brought us all closest to World War III; and when was the U.S.S.R. ever friendlier to the United States, at least superficially, than it was in 1943?

A second advantage of the rational bias is that it allows us to judge rationality by its own standards and thus to question the value of clarity and explication in strategic thinking. If some of the premises articulated above are correct, less credit goes to the strategist or statesman who indulges in the luxury of publicly and clearly displaying his full perception of an issue in military strategy; such displays can easily be counterproductive in a world where most points already are implicitly well understood, where the other actors are playing a delicate game of feigning only a partial understanding.

Third, this "rational" focus may require a reexamination of the immediate military facts of life for each year since 1945, and of what we have known as the facts over this time. We may be deeply impressed by prophets who in 1946 seemingly foresaw the strategic environment of 1956; such prophets are with less honor or significance, however, if they were assuming such conditions to exist already in 1946.

Since this is a study of the impact of weapons, the prime case in point will of course be the atomic bomb. Many of us today might too readily credit the atomic bomb with decisively influencing the world, ever since the first nuclear device was detonated at Alamogordo, New Mexico, in June of 1945. The new weapon has been seen as facilitating horrendous inflictions of destruction on civilian populations, or as making possible extremely rapid and effective attacks against enemy military forces. It might then be presumed that the post-1945 military and political balance of power would have been substantially different if nuclear fission had never been discovered; territory might have changed hands, wars otherwise avoided might have broken out.

Yet much of this importance for nuclear weapons may be premature for 1945 or 1949, and we might be exaggerating how much we have agreed over the years on assessing this importance. Whatever the weapon's capabilities as measured by knowledgeable technicians, widely varying premises seemingly were adopted amongst analysts of the bomb's political significance; one can find examples of seriously inconsistent strategic theories stated for each and every year of the post-1945 cold war, theories not always very well correlated with the immediate objective weapons environment, or with any environment that could even be imminent. As in earlier periods of air strategy, therefore, some strategic arguments have been largely speculative, while others have been more immediately serious; one must also recognize, however, that earlier speculations may be responsible in some untraceable way for more serious operational analyses when they later occur.

The most important concept normally thought to have emerged after World War II is that of "deterrence." The exact origin of the term itself remains obscure; ordinary dictionaries in the later 1940's did not yet contain it. The concept involved an assumption that one's atomic weapons had raised the cost of all-out war enough to dissuade any aggressive opponents from launching it, even where military victory could be theirs, i.e., even if they controlled all the territory in question at the end. It is clear that similar arguments definitely had been presented for nonatomic air weapons prior to 1945, at times in very operational contexts, and that the later hydrogen bomb would conclusively validate such arguments. What is not so clear is whether the pure concept of deterrence as stated here was operationally effective over the period from 1945 to 1952; while arguments are to be found articulating a notion of deterrence in this form, Western hopes for a military balance may have been considerably more complicated, even into the hydrogen bomb era.

A second major theme repeatedly sounded through the cold war has been that of secrecy or deceit, the notion that trusts have been violated on one side or both, that a fulfillment of such trust would have been crucial to the avoidance of hostility. Much of the American argumentation on disarmament and arms control has seemingly depended on such assumptions, but it may be appropriate now to question whether mutual trust could have made all that much difference in the evolution of postwar military balances. Revisionist interpretations today cite some interesting examples of Western failure to adhere to obligations, thus presumably inducing Soviet distrust and perhaps launching the cold war in a direction opposite to what is normally supposed. A more accurate interpretation may yet be revisionist in a very different sense, concluding that trust and mistrust in either direction played a much smaller role than one might assume.

A third recurrent theme that will be confronted is that of détente, periods when the hostilities of the cold war were presumably lessened. A consensus may be difficult to establish on the chronology here, for some periods are clearly subject to dispute on whether they showed greater conflict amongst the major powers. Above all, a major definitional problem exists on what we mean by "détente" or "better relations," for some of the objective indicators may be quite misleading. Additional difficulties emerge on whether to regard the postwar years as a serious arms race, or perhaps instead as an "arms walk," and on whether the increasing affluence of the major powers does not make military expenditure a less reliable index of political hostility.

The cold war has a military history, although, unlike other military histories, weapons have rarely been used. Because they have not been used, the activity surrounding weapons has been much more speculative and theoretical than it otherwise might have been; to have realized one scenario would have been to cancel many others. The attempt here is to identify the events, the thinking and speculation, as they were.

George H. Quester

Ithaca, New York
August, 1970

1   The U.S. Monopoly: 1945-1949

The Impact of Nuclear Weapons

The years from 1945 to 1949, the years of the American nuclear monopoly, are too often depicted as an example of special Western moral restraint. When asked to explain why preventive war against the U.S.S.R. was not launched with this American monopoly, or why the threat of such war was not used to force concessions of more permanent significance, we often refer to American traditions of "never striking first," or to American short-sightedness and naiveté. On closer examination, however, one might identify more concretely counter-deterring factors sufficient to preclude any strong Western attack or pressure on the U.S.S.R. In particular, it seems that the United States doubted whether atomic weapons could even guarantee a containment of Soviet influence, and that it was dissuaded by such doubts from pursuing any policy more ambitious than containment.

However much significance we might attach today to the American nuclear monopoly from 1945 to 1949, it is remarkable how little military and political importance was attached to the early atomic bomb by many Western observers at the time. Much of this skepticism stemmed from interpretations of the conventional bombardment of Germany and Japan in World War II. These bombardments had proved disappointing in terms of forcing a capitulation, and the impression was widespread, in academic as well as popular circles, that Germany could never have been brought to surrender by bombing, and that Japan had surrendered only after undergoing a most prolonged suffering.[1] The facts were often cited that more people had died in the conventional bombings of Hamburg, Dresden, or Tokyo than at Hiroshima or Nagasaki.[2] Many commentators thus implicitly or explicitly assumed such ghastly conventional attacks to have been common in World War II, although they had in fact been quite rare, depending on fortuitous combinations of correct bomb load choice, meteorological conditions, breakdown of civil defense, refugee overflow, etc. (If Germany had had to endure a raid of the magnitude of Dresden or Hiroshima on a regular once-a-week basis, she might not so clearly have been able to refuse to surrender; as it was, however, any such regular destruction would at least have required nuclear weapons, so that the experience of World War II still left many observers quite skeptical of the terror efficacy of strategic bombing.)

Even analysts focusing on the Hiroshima and Nagasaki atomic bombings might attribute their high civilian casualty figures in part to the absence of any warning inducing people to take shelter. If even the same civil defense procedures specified for an ordinary 200-bomber raid had been implemented, the casualties from blast, heat, and radiation might have been significantly reduced, so that deaths might have been less than on many ordinary World War II raids.[3]

In the last months of World War II, as decisions had to be made on the use of the first production run of nuclear weapons, it had not been clear that American planners expected the bombs to force a surrender by themselves. Three amphibious invasions of the Japanese home islands were planned for late 1945, presumably invasions which would take a great number of American lives. It is reported that three atomic bombs were to be detonated to support each landing[4] —the first tactical use of atomic weapons, some six years before the concept would undergo wide discussion as a revolutionary idea. Assuming that American nuclear production for 1945 was not much greater than the total of 12 bombs thus to be expended (Alamogordo, Hiroshima, Nagasaki, plus nine),[5] this reflected a basic skepticism about the terror impact of such weapons, a skepticism that would persist.

Skepticism on the power of nuclear weapons was also fortified by some optimistic trends for air defense which had emerged from World War II. Had the war gone on in Europe without the atomic bomb, it seemed very plausible that a combination of radar and jet fighter-interceptors (plus the decisive innovation of the proximity fuse if the Germans had ever gotten around to inventing it) would make continuous manned-bomber raids impossible, since American bomber losses would have become prohibitive.[6]

During the war, there was of course a certain amount of enthusiasm also on the offensive weapons side, especially with the breakthroughs in guided missilery seemingly accomplished in the German V-2, against which no defense was in sight. As many German missile engineers as possible were collected into American custody at the end of the war (with the U.S.S.R. taking similar steps), and such scientists, for various reasons, made the offensive missile sound promising, especially now that the nuclear warhead was available. A study (MX-774) was conducted in the United States from 1945 to 1947 on the possibilities of an intercontinental missile, but it was terminated in July of 1947 on pessimistic assumptions of the thrust required to propel a warhead any long distance, and on the poor accuracies that seemingly could be achieved.[7] The accuracy of German missiles indeed had been atrocious in World War II, with a CEP (Circular Error Probability, a radius within which half the missiles fall) of about 25 miles,[8] and scientists hence could remain generally conservative on the "inherent" limitations to such firing accuracies. As a replacement for the manned bombers that had leveled Hamburg and Dresden, the V-2 thus seemed hardly adequate, since it appeared too wasteful a delivery vehicle for the expensive and precious atomic bomb.

A considerable number of American scientists not privy to the development of the atomic bomb in 1945 had thus come to see time running out for the strategic air offensive; such an impression, accumulated in months of experimentation in the laboratories, would not now be immediately expunged by the attacks on Hiroshima and Nagasaki, or by the V-2. If there were objective reasons to expect that atomic bombs could inflict greater destruction than the mass air attacks of World War II, or that a few such bombs would be much harder to stop with air defenses, there were subjective factors to keep many observers from accepting such conclusions. As long as the atomic bomb seemed to embody the upper limit of destructive weaponry, hope persisted that defensive advances would reduce the total destruction inflicted in war, perhaps even below World War II levels. The number of bombers that could slip through could be progressively reduced; the missile's accuracy would be too poor to allow it to take the bomber's place. Dispersals of new industry and housing might further reduce the damage that an atomic attack could inflict.

Some of the skepticism on nuclear weapons would thus be justified, at least for the short run; other parts of it, however widespread, might already be outmoded and invalid. There could be a debate on the destructive impact of atomic bombs themselves, or on the efficacy of

3

the delivery systems carrying such bombs to their targets. Yet a third uncertainty remained about the significance of nuclear weapons for the strategic balance, namely, the production rate for such weapons. If the production of atomic bombs was to be as slow and costly as many assumed, the military "nuclear age" might not be so revolutionary, because simple economy would still require a great reliance on conventional weapons.

To establish even an order of magnitude for the American nuclear stockpile of any particular year—say for 1946, or 1948, or 1950—is extremely difficult, and this difficulty is not a little surprising. It is surprising precisely because so much of the strategic speculation of this period may have been crucially dependent on whether the United States possessed 25 or 250 or 2,500 bombs of Hiroshima size. How "impossible" would a preemption of Soviet nuclear development have been in 1948, or a "taking out" of the development in 1950?

This secrecy does not seem to have been limited to lay strategists generally denied access to classified information, but may have restricted information flows even within the classified circles of the government itself. President Truman, for example, notes that stockpile numbers were never written into government documents he was given, but were cited orally for him to fill in for himself.[9] George Kennan, who as Chairman of the Policy Planning Staff of the State Department might well have had occasion to count his bombs, never seemed to get a chance to do so.[10] Senator Brien McMahon, Chairman of the Congressional Joint Atomic Energy Committee, would publish an article in 1949 asking for an end to stockpile secrecy, asserting that at least some strategic questions were being discussed incorrectly in public for lack of accurate information.[11]

Some of the continuing secrecy on the exact size of the 1945-1950 stockpiles may be due to the disclosure of too much else about the American nuclear program in those years, including broadly the types of production facilities, the cost of production, and the electrical consumption. Thus an aspiring "nth" power today might use military stockpile figures to deduce the most effective production processes from the early American experience.

Much of the vagueness on bomb numbers at the time stemmed from the intricacies of weapons assembly, since fissionable materials could be assembled in various ways, making inexact any translation of component material amounts into bomb totals. Yet again this illustrated a tendency to stockpile components in the broad sense, still some time-consuming stages away from assembly into usable military weapons. Shortfalls in bomb production over the 1945-1947 period also contributed to the reticence in circulating total figures. If one were proud of his achievements as a weapons manufacturer, one would be more tempted to stretch the margins of security in presenting detailed portrayals of growing weapons stockpiles. If the stockpiles were disappointingly or shockingly small, smaller than every newspaper columnist was blithely assuming them to be, then tighter security and technological obscurity might be convenient covers to fall back on.

It is reported that the United States had exhausted its immediate supply of nuclear weapons after the attack on Nagasaki, with a number of bombs, however, in the production and assembly pipelines.[12] From what can be pieced together about the stockpile thereafter, weapons production clearly lagged in 1946 and 1947; some of the facilities erected in the World War II crash program proved to be either inefficient or not very durable, while large numbers of skilled physicists (whose day-to-day presence was still required even for fissionable materials production) left government service.[13] Great amazement and concern were now several times expressed within the government on the small size of the stockpile, and this perhaps explains why only two bombs were detonated in tests in 1946 (at Bikini) and none in 1947.[14] At various points between 1946 and 1949, moreover, the uranium ore required for nuclear weapons production seems to have fallen into short supply, as arrangements for delivery of such material from the Belgian Congo and from Canada ran into difficulty.[15]

If the three-a-month production figure that seemed to apply in late 1945 had been projected, it would have given the United States some 36 bombs a year thereafter. Production apparently did not keep up to this pace, however, in 1946 or early 1947. New facilities were put into use in 1948, but a really significant expansion of nuclear weapons production still did not occur. In the fall of 1948, warhead output apparently had not yet hit the one-a-week rate a newspaper columnist had conjectured,[16] which meant that the American stockpile might still be well under 150 warheads, and perhaps under 100. Some might have argued that even 100 warheads would have been a decisive force against an enemy that possessed no nuclear weapons at all; but others could have responded with calculations that these 100 weapons could do no more damage than had been inflicted on Nazi Germany in conventional air attacks[17] (when the Germans also had no retaliatory air strength remaining and did not surrender).

The more sizable breakthrough in nuclear weapons production was to come only in 1950 and 1951, with a new series of tests demonstrating that fissionable materials could be more efficiently used, so that twice as many bombs might perhaps be produced from a given amount of uranium or plutonium.[18] By 1951, estimates at last were circulated that the United States stockpile had grown to 750 or more weapons,[19] which represents a considerable rise over the 200 a steady three-a-month production rate after 1945 would have turned out.

Prior to 1949, therefore, nuclear weapons would seem costly and scarce for an extended time into the future. This might preclude any tactical use of nuclear weapons, and in effect any use by the Army or Navy. It also made dubious any air war fought with nuclear weapons alone, or any attempt to wipe out the enemy's air force in a single "splendid first strike." Progress was also slow in the expansion of bomb potency. The Eniwetok series of tests in 1948 produced some very useful information on the feasibility of new bomb designs, designs already more reliable and efficient in consumption of fissionable material, with a test detonation now almost reaching 50 kilotons. Yet by 1948 the AEC had still not produced the ten-fold increase in explosive power over that at Hiroshima which some newspaper accounts claimed; the most powerful available bomb would presumably yield only about 100 kilotons,[20] with a destructiveness perhaps three or four times that of the Hiroshima bomb. This might still not be a decisive or ultimate weapon, in the view of those close to the military problem.

The widespread skepticism about atomic weapons' potency is illustrated by a poll taken as late as November of 1950, in which American interviewees were asked to predict the impact of nuclear weapons on any future war with the Soviet Union. Of the entire population, only 22 percent agreed that the bomb would allow the United States to win the war easily, while 37 percent merely saw the bomb as significant in a long and hard struggle comparable with World War II, and 18 percent thought the bomb would make "no difference at all"; amongst college graduates, moreover, only 13 percent saw the bomb as making victory easy, while 47 percent saw it as important instead for a long struggle, and a full 22 percent thought it would make no difference.[21]

A number of possibilities for war would exist after 1945: The Soviet Union might blunder into some sort of accidental war, or decide that it should no longer be inhibited by American air power, and deliberately begin a move westward into Europe. Conversely, the United States might generate such a war through some accidental process of escalation, or might even consider launching some deliberate preventive or preemptive war to keep the Soviet Union from reaching its maximum of power.

For each of these possibilities, the United States leadership saw no clear guarantee of victory in its sole possession of the atomic bomb, and a preventive war deliberately launched by the United States therefore became much the least likely of the possibilities listed above. American Air Force planners could not surely expect to cripple the Red Army before it overran Western Europe, although they might try. The prospect of outright terror attacks, or of the collateral damage from counterindustry air raids, would perhaps be sufficient for the time to deter the U.S.S.R. from crossing the Elbe, but not to force any further concessions, or to force a surrender if war had already broken out for any reason. The Soviet capability for occupying Western Europe, and the American capability for air attack, thus might seem to be of the same order of magnitude, and hence mutually deterrent.

The strategic form anticipated for any United States-Soviet Union war from 1945 to 1949 thus might seem somewhat peculiar today. The periodization of air strategy can perhaps be summarized in terms of what targets one will aim at, and what targets the enemy is expected to aim at. If war did come, the prime target for the bombs of the United States Air Force was not to be the Soviet Air Force, but rather Russian military support facilities and industry in general, in a repetition of the slow-but-sure industrial attrition process of World War II. In this campaign, atomic bombs would be used, as well as mass flights of conventional bombers, since atomic bombs might be in short supply,[22] and ill-suited to certain kinds of targets in any event. Striking at the other side's air forces, if such forces were at all dispersed, did not seem cost-effective as long as nuclear warheads were scarce; such forces might be hard to find as targets and contributed less to the enemy's military position than more traditional targets did.

For the early period from 1945 to 1950, the target complex the U.S. Air Force expected to hit, and to have to defend, amounted thus to a cross between the RAF and U.S. Air Force programs of World War II. In World War II, the RAF had assigned a significant portion of its bomb tonnage to an "area bombing" campaign essentially designed to destroy the housing and morale of German workers, in low-accuracy night raids. The U.S. Army Air Force, priding itself on greater accuracy until the final air offensive against Japan, had professed to be aiming at industry and communications centers. The atomic bomb clearly did not lend

7

itself now to any pinpoint accuracy in which one city block was destroyed while the next one was left unscathed. While recognizing that whole cities and their civilian populations would have to suffer, as industry, military arsenals, and political command posts were destroyed, the U.S. Air Force nonetheless continued to describe its attack plans as countercapability rather than countermorale attacks.

In part this was because studies of World War II seemingly (somewhat misleadingly) showed that countermorale attacks could not work. Air Force planners may have come to share this view, or if the public seemed to share it, may at least have felt themselves forced to endorse it publicly; American doubts about the morality of deliberate destruction of civilian residential areas would in any event militate against any explicit countervalue strategy. Finally, there was some sense of a race that would be run against the Red Army's advance on Paris, which might require that military attrition be undertaken as early as possible, that all available bomber resources be devoted to it. Yet a great number of Russian civilian casualties would be inflicted as a necessary adjunct to military or industrial attrition, and such casualties still plausibly contributed to weakening Russian resolve for any drive westward across the Elbe.

When the U.S.S.R. at last would have the atomic bomb, it would presumably aim at a similar target complex, again not rationalizing this in terms of outright terror bombing, but rather as interdiction blows at the urban centers that made an American war effort possible. Presumably the thought of Soviet acquisition of nuclear weapons should have upgraded Soviet air bases on the American target list; yet any notion of atomic bombs being in short supply—i.e., more bombers than bombs perhaps being available on both sides—might still make this seem a waste of resources, except when intelligence spotted an unusual target of opportunity, as perhaps in a large assembly of bombers and bombs on a single airfield.

If the industrial potential of the United States were at all vulnerable to atomic weapons on these war-of-attrition calculations, passive defense measures, such as dispersal of new construction, might significantly lengthen the time it took an enemy to cripple the United States, either industrially or demographically.[23] As part of the longer-duration interpretation of general war thus adopted, great emphasis was to be placed on the repeatability of air strikes, disparaging any aircraft capable only of one-way missions. Soviet bombers would seem generally incapable of striking at the United States and then returning to bases in Russia, and "suicide" use of such bombers (although it must have seemed clear that one-way bail-out missions by no means required actual human suicide) was treated as a bizarre expedient not in keeping with modern technology or morality. This interpretation, like several others, might persist beyond its actual relevance. (The possibility should not have been overlooked, for example, that a single "suicide mission" might, even in 1947 or 1948, have interfered with American nuclear weapons production.)

Exploitation of the American Strategic Position

Turning to some of the specific East-West issues of 1945, one can see how the retrospective interpretation of the atomic bomb as an ultimate weapon is related to complimentary self-evaluations very widely held amongst Americans. If asked to give an example of a nation which possessed absolute military superiority over its potential political rivals, and chose not to exercise it, many Westerners would cite the United States in the autumn of 1945. Not only had the United States demonstrated the atomic bomb, a supposedly most awesome weapon now presumably being produced in quantity, but there still remained also the large American, British, and French armies, which, together with the Russians, had just defeated Germany.

The explanation therefore offered for the failure to impose territorial demands on the Russians (e.g., demands for the democratization of Poland and the Balkans, for a corridor to Berlin, or even for substantial political changes in the U.S.S.R. itself) is that the West "trusted" the Soviets in a mood of magnanimity or naïveté unprecedented in international politics; the West's trust was then presumably betrayed. If the weight of the atomic bomb is downgraded, however, then all this period does not seem so stupid or paradoxical. An honest explanation of these events probably will have to be more complicated, less flattering to the generosity of the West, more flattering to the strategic sensibility of the American leaders involved.

The "origin" of the cold war is too often phrased as an issue of who betrayed whom in breaking up the grand alliance. Did Russian failure to tolerate Polish non-Communist political forces constitute a betrayal of the Yalta understandings, or was it American negotiations with surrendering German commanders in Italy? Such analyses probably overrate international trust as a binding force between the United States and the U.S.S.R. during World War II, and blame too much of cold war hostility on 1945-engendered "distrust." Claims of betrayal by the

9

opposition made good propaganda for both the United States and the Soviet Union after 1945, but the real significance of all this might be challenged.

An avoidance of the counterproductive activities of the cold war would have required a substantial shared interest between the two super powers, or a shared outside threat. As the shared outside threat of Nazi Germany was eliminated, one could hope, but not expect, that conflicts of interest would not be too serious. If they did turn out to be very serious in Germany, in Poland or Italy, or in strategic or tactical weapons, then betrayals of trust would play only a marginal role in making them so. If this is correct, the issue of who started the cold war becomes almost meaningless, for both sides simultaneously start a disagreement by disagreeing.

It is not clear what the American governmental vision of the future balance of power in Europe had been as victory against the Axis hove into sight. Optimism about a community of interest after the war might have dissuaded many individuals from engaging in such speculation; little evidence exists, for example, that President Roosevelt had given the problem much thought yet.[24] The hope was sometimes expressed that the United States might not have to maintain occupation forces in Germany for more than two years after the war, and this presumably hinged only on the process of de-Nazification in Germany itself. A traditionalist view might have expected an assertion of British influence on the Continent, and perhaps a resurrection of France; such a balance of power hopefully might be much more implicit than it had been in earlier decades, so that general goodwill and agreement would leave considerations of economic or military strength only the most residual of roles.

Whether it was the death of Roosevelt and the advent of the Truman Administration that induced a more realistic concern for the exact mechanics of postwar stability, or the external events of 1945, may never be clear. Yet the way in which World War II was terminated in Europe almost inevitably affected the interests and strengths of the Allied powers, and several sorts of conflicts thus emerged in 1945, conflicts which might force Americans and Russians to race to preempt each other. First, there was the question of which army occupied and controlled what territory at the end of the war. While occupation zones had been agreed to for Germany, and more vaguely for Austria, some time necessarily had to elapse before all forces were moved into their assigned zones, if they in fact moved at all. For countries such as

Czechoslovakia or Denmark, where no postwar occupation was envisaged, the temporary administration of liberating armies might decisively alter the future political tone of the territory in question. The prestige of being first to reach Berlin or Prague might, moreover, establish other indelible impressions of the relative military prowess of the powers, even if such cities were then speedily evacuated by the conquering forces.

A second question related to the physical custody of war prisoners and refugees; every half-million of such persons crossing the Anglo-American lines rather than the Russian represented a significant loss of potential political adherents to the Communist cause. If Poland or East Germany could not be made free, at least some Poles or Germans could.[25] Related to this were the casualties still being imposed by Germans on the Russians by Germans who were surrendering to American and British forces, thus leaving these forces more intact and militarily viable. The Soviet leadership might well suspect that mass local surrenders in Italy and the Netherlands proved Western acquiescence in a German policy of selective attrition, aimed at weakening Soviet forces only, and at shifting territory into Western control.[26]

American and British decision-makers thus had to decide how their troops should react to the disintegration of German forces, a disintegration which almost inevitably bred conflict with the Russians. Humanitarian considerations would induce acceptance of mass surrenders even when such surrenders were not occurring on the Russian front, and the acceptance of streams of refugees fleeing the Red Army, with occasional threats to the German command that this policy would be reversed if it was exploited too extensively. Similar considerations sanctioned local surrenders or even de facto truces, as in Holland.

With regard to racing for territory which ultimately would have to be relinquished, British pleas for such action were generally rejected by the U.S. Government, by both President Truman and General Eisenhower, on the grounds that casualties might thus be needlessly incurred. While this gave some territory to the Red Army by default, it had the compensating power effect of reducing U.S. Army losses, while presumably subjecting the Russians to greater casualties in subduing German units not engaged by Americans. No move was made to go deeply into Czechoslovakia, or to try to reach Berlin before the Red Army, although British forces did race into Denmark in response to false rumors that Russian paratroops were landing there.[27]

American and British forces did, nonetheless, penetrate into the future Soviet occupation zone in Germany, and a third question arose on whether such territory should be held as a bargaining counter until Soviet policies in Eastern Europe, especially in Poland, were accommodated to the preferences of the West. British Prime Minister Churchill indeed advised that such territories be held, and that the Russians be summoned to an early conference while Western forces were still at their peak of effectiveness in such forward positions.[28]

For the Western powers not to have withdrawn into their occupation zones in 1945 would have been a clear violation of prior agreements, perhaps comparable with certain contemporaneous Soviet practices in Eastern Europe, or to the Soviet policies that might have applied if Russian forces instead of Western had overrun the demarcation line in Germany. It presumably would have resulted in a denial of access to West Berlin and, if made permanent, would have produced some increment of mutual bad feeling, together with a cleaner and more convincing division of Germany into two distinct regimes. If, however, one retrospectively considers the discord caused by the geographic anomaly of West Berlin since 1945, one might well argue that the West (and the whole world) would have been better off if it had reneged in 1945, scooping up an area geographically larger and militarily more defensible than West Berlin, if not as valuable. Conversely, the enclave in West Berlin has contributed significantly to undermining the legitimacy and stability of the East German regime, and thus to keeping hopes of German unification alive, perhaps to some eyes a gain for the West.

President Truman had decided, however, that a refusal to pull back the forces would needlessly provoke the Russians, and that the Potsdam conference should be held some weeks later, after American and British forces had withdrawn to their zones (while simultaneously being admitted to their sectors in West Berlin). The card of forward troop deployment having thus been given up somewhat gratuitously, the President picked up another in his atomic bomb as the Alamogordo test was carried off successfully, the news in fact reaching the President at Potsdam.[29]

The most plausible instance of real American leverage against the U.S.S.R. thus emerged only in the late summer of 1945, with the American conventional forces still on the continent of Europe and on the oceans of the world; these forces at least balanced those of the Soviet Union, and presumably thus precluded any balance after the United States had acquired its atomic bomb in addition. If the

12

confrontation of such forces with the Soviets had been inadvertent, it nonetheless might now tempt the American leadership to exert these forces' power, and might induce matching fears in the Soviet leadership. If they were kept intact beyond their usefulness against the Germans, they might have illustrated a proclivity toward "toughness" in the Truman Administration. Without nuclear weapons, the objective strategic situation would perhaps have been a standoff. As it was, the Soviets for the time had no counterthreat which could clearly deter the threat of American nuclear attack.

With regard to countries liberated by the U.S.S.R., American and Soviet preferences might now conflict both on the internal regimes of each state and on the external power implications of such regimes. Communist governments might please the U.S.S.R. for their own sake, and/or because they could be counted upon to help defend the Soviet Union against any external attack. Nondictatorial regimes, conversely, were preferable to Washington and London, again for their own sake, and/or because they made it easier for neighboring states to the west to remain non-Communist.

A similar Soviet-Western conflict of interest could of course have been defined for the governing of Italy, France, or Belgium (where Communist resistance groups were not allowed to gain power), but this would not be as openly argued now, while the aggregate balance of power seemed tipped even slightly in favor of the West. American demands in August of 1945 for changes in the political administration of Bulgaria and Rumania thus were surprisingly met by the Russians, and the process of Communization in these countries and in Hungary was held back.[30] For a period of months a position of real American strength seemed to exist, coupled with an American willingness to cash in on this strength. A Foreign Ministers' conference for the first time was allowed to adjourn in September of 1945 without enough accommodation of the U.S.S.R. to facilitate a declaration of agreement.

But this strength was not to be maintained, for the United States removed a large part of its armed forces from Germany in late 1945 and early 1946, so that the Red Army soon would seem capable of sweeping west to the Bay of Biscay. The decision to bring home and disband this ground army is perhaps crucial, but it is not as irrational in terms of American national interests as it has sometimes been made to seem. If nuclear weapons seemed to balance Soviet land power, they could not cripple it or eliminate it. A large American Army in Europe might have been able to save or influence Czechoslovakia and Bulgaria, but could not have fought its way to Moscow at a bearable cost (or perhaps at any cost, given the Russians' probable fervor in defending their own territory). Merely to achieve at most the marginal liberation of one or two European states would not have justified keeping a larger army in being, in terms of American national preferences. This American disinterest in maintaining a substantial counter-Soviet leverage probably must be traced back through Truman's tenure in office; the President could probably have allowed and occasioned himself to maintain a large American army in Germany, but only by keeping the zonal occupation issue open. Perhaps even more was required—an American dash for Berlin, Vienna, and Prague—really to involve forces in enough confrontations with the Red Army to make early demobilization seem inappropriate.

Alternative interpretations have been offered of the autumn of 1945, contending that the United States was indeed going quite far with policies consciously hostile to the Soviet Union. (Whether this constitutes our starting the cold war is left open to the definitional quibbles cited above.) Observers holding this view implicitly agree with today's consensus that the atomic bomb was already decisively significant; but they construe the Anglo-American exclusion of Russia from nuclear technology, and the very use of the atomic bomb against Japan at Hiroshima and Nagasaki, as deliberately anti-Soviet gestures, thus exploiting the bomb's power and initiating the cold war.

Having been forced to devote resources to the resistance of the German advance after 1941, the U.S.S.R. had not conducted any serious program of nuclear weapons development prior to 1943, although a body of capable physicists was indeed at hand.[31] After 1943, research in nuclear physics had been resumed, but in the absence of Anglo-American confidences, there was still no firm ground for any Russian belief that a bomb was feasible. Indeed, there had been little assurance in the United States as late as 1944 that the bomb could in fact be exploded.[32]

The American test at Alamogordo in late July of 1945 proved forever that the bomb would work, but the reporting of this event to the U.S.S.R. by Soviet espionage nets was apparently slow, so that Stalin may not yet have had the news when Truman advised him of the bomb at Potsdam.[33] In any event, someone like Klaus Fuchs would, prior to Potsdam, have reported that the bomb might never be used because of moral opposition within the scientific community. When this possibility was disproved at Hiroshima, a more severe shock may have been inflicted on the Soviet sense of security.

14

The public disclosure and use of the bomb was now quickly accompanied by statements declaring the United States government unwilling to share possession of the bomb with other powers.[34] A very short time thus had elapsed for the U.S.S.R. to consider several alternative postwar strategies with regard to nuclear weapons. Hardly had it been established that bombs were feasible before the United States had used them and announced an intention to monopolize them. Within this brief period the Russians could have decided to suggest a total sharing of scientific laboratories and weapons research, giving Russia a bomb but substantially opening Soviet society; alternatively, they could have embarked on a secret program of their own to break the monopoly. It is thus sometimes argued that the first option expired before the Russians could have moved to suggest it, and that the second had to be the one chosen.

Pressures for greater sharing of information did, however, exist in the United States. Since the existence of the A-bomb project had been known to so few individuals in the United States prior to Hiroshima, it would take some time for Congressional and popular attitudes towards such weapons to form, especially since the pleasant surprise at the early termination of World War II had to be digested as well. The most immediate reaction, supporting the stand announced by President Truman shortly after Hiroshima, was that the "secret" of this weapon, like that of other weapons in the past, ought to be kept; but such a policy would be adopted in any event for an interim period of debate, for a shift to any other position was irreversible.

Two strands of argument soon emerged to challenge any American policy of secrecy. First, atomic energy was quickly advertised as having enormous potentials for peacetime use, a picture which had a considerable factual backing but which illustrated also a certain penchant of the physicist, and of the taxpayer who had supported him, for seeking long-run human benefits to erase the moral stigma of super bomb production.[35] Within a few months such hopes had occasioned an internal debate in the United States on the future administration of atomic energy, with fears expressed that noncivilian control would hold back human progress and impose unnecessary military censorship or, worse, that it would lead generally to undue military influence in the government.

While this argument perhaps was directed mainly to the domestic sharing of nuclear information, it related to other concerns expressed within the government, even prior to Potsdam and Hiroshima, that secrecy might in several ways alienate the Soviet Union.[36] For the

United States to share at least the "nonmilitary" technology of atomic energy, or perhaps all of the technology, would in any event be a magnificent sign of trust. If bombs were not already meaningless, the trust demonstrated here might induce a reciprocation which in fact made them meaningless. A variant on this argument, not so often presented publicly or discussed within the government, might have been that Russia's possession of a stockpile of bombs would ensure her against attack, thus stabilizing world peace and easing tensions which otherwise would have a real base; it was presumably arguments of this sort that had in fact moved Klaus Fuchs to transmit information on bomb manufacture and design from New Mexico to the Soviet Union.

Throughout the pre-Hiroshima development of the A-bomb, the American government had generally been more reluctant than the British to disclose information on the project. Yet American attitudes were not so crystallized, as illustrated by the sudden bursts of information disclosed in the Smyth Report,[37] published shortly after the Nagasaki raid and Japanese surrender, over the misgivings of British officials and of Secretary of War Stimson.[38] The Smyth Report spelled out in considerable detail the basic principles on which the bomb had been developed, and was generally acknowledged afterwards as being of real assistance to any aspiring nuclear power, in that it could steer research away from certain dead ends and indicate where progress was to be made. The issuance of the Smyth Report thus demonstrated something of an American hope that disclosures of information, if packaged dramatically and demonstratively enough, might earn dividends of goodwill, perhaps leading to an easing of tensions with the U.S.S.R.

The American intention to maintain a monopoly on atomic weapons can, of course, be interpreted as a recognition of some great potency for such weapons, and as a brandishment or exploitation of that potency. Yet it was not normal for any nation to share its weapons technology with other nations, and the Soviet Union had not been especially open in giving its Western allies access to technical details and plans of the World War II weapons it was developing, even during the period of American and British lend-lease aid. Straightforward secrecy on the techniques for producing fissionable materials thus could hardly be a hostile initiative coming as an unexpected shock to the U.S.S.R. in the postwar world. Secrecy, at any rate, could always be lowered after it had been raised, but never vice versa, and it was only prudent for a nation with even the most friendly intentions to go slowly about releasing such secrets.

The American use of the atomic bomb in August of 1945 had demonstrated two things to the world: first, that such a bomb was possible, and second, that the United States could be willing to employ it in wartime. Interpretations of the bombings of Hiroshima and Nagasaki as consciously anti-Soviet gestures, or as evidence of an American sense of enormous postwar power, are very difficult to verify, if only because of the vagueness of the recorded deliberations on these bombings' postwar significance.[39]

The use of the bombs can be seen equally validly as a brandishing of American potential in the face of the U.S.S.R. as an adversary, or as a friendly demonstration that the United States had done its part in sacrificing resources and generating weapons for the war against the Axis. With regard to demonstrating the existence of the new weapon, both arguments vis-à-vis the Russians could in fact apply simultaneously. Some American commentators even feared later that the exhaustion of the American nuclear stockpile after the bombing of Nagasaki—when the United States had publicly promised to maintain the pace of such attacks—might have shown that the United States was given to bluffing, to making threats and promises it could not fulfill, so that the Russians might draw a very different "dangerous lesson" from the events.[40] The development of nuclear weapons, moreover, was much more inevitable (and therefore perhaps less tragic or mistaken) than a nonphysicist might sometimes suppose: such weapons would in any event have emerged, and necessarily been used or tested, fairly soon. Even had the United States not used the bombs against Japan in the expectation that they would shorten the war and thus on balance save some lives, such bombs would necessarily have been "brandished" in tests in the following year, if only, perhaps, to forestall Congressional investigations of the large expenditures involved.

The bombings have also been described as a frantic attempt to preclude Russian entry into the war against Japan, to avoid sharing the prestige and spoils of victory with the U.S.S.R. On this line of reasoning, the United States no longer desired the Russian participation it had been urging for so long, since the war would be over very quickly. A problem arises with this interpretation, however, in that few Americans really were certain that a Japanese surrender was imminent; even postwar research into the papers and deliberations of the Japanese leadership cannot guarantee that the atomic bomb was bound to force a surrender.[41] If the war would go on for even another year, Russian entry would assist the United States in balance-of-power terms, taxing Russian manpower and material resources and easing the strain on those of the United States.

A more sympathetic interpretation of American relations with the U.S.S.R. in 1945 thus could contend that American nuclear secrecy during World War II was natural, necessary, and without any substantial malice toward the U.S.S.R. and that the decision to drop the bombs on Hiroshima and Nagasaki was made primarily in the context of World War II, on balance with intentions friendly toward the U.S.S.R. Neither of such actions can really be accepted as a conscious launching of the cold war by the United States, if only because the atomic bomb could not yet be cashed in for that much political return. Cold war issues had in fact emerged between the West and the Soviet Union in 1945, but any tough line on these depended on American troop strength on the Continent, and this very necessary strategic input was to dwindle away as Americans did not yet find the costs of the cold war worth paying.

If the American atomic bomb and the Soviet Army now could plausibly be paired as mutually effective deterrents to each other's use (but as less-than-absolute guarantees of victory in a war in which both were used), then the addition of an Anglo-American Army to the equation might just possibly have deterred the Red Army more surely, or have promised some liberation of Eastern Europe. These two probabilities were low enough, however, to make such an Anglo-American force seem too costly to the publics involved. Unless a violent confrontation with the U.S.S.R. could be made to seem inevitable, or the toppling of the Soviet regime made to seem easy, it would be difficult for any administration to induce the American Congress to agree to a prolonged deployment of sizable ground forces in Europe.

What conventional military strength existed on the Allied side was thus almost entirely a by-product of the campaign against Germany. It retained much of its strength as long as the shipping was not yet available to return great numbers of troops to the United States, or to transfer them to the Pacific. If any German underground operations had emerged, this would have supplied an excuse for maintaining an effective force of U.S. troops in Europe, but no such resistance was to occur. As shipping space became free, therefore, troops returning from Europe were reassigned on the basis of personal considerations or length in service, with little or no concern for the damage done by such individual discharges to the combat effectiveness of the units involved.[42]

The Baruch Plan

The United States ended the year 1945 as party to a strategic balance which might maintain the existing division of Europe, but which would

18

seem unsatisfactory in many other respects. First, the balance might persist only until the U.S.S.R. or some other nation broke the American monopoly and manufactured atomic weapons of its own, probably sometime in the mid-1950's. Second, the threat of destruction posed by existing atomic weapons stockpiles might induce widespread popular neuroses, thus warping the normal flow of civilian life or even leading to aberrant governmental behavior; more directly, the threat of nuclear air attack might force threatened nations to adopt postures of political hostility, and forward military deployments, to establish some counterweight in the diplomatic exchange. One could not even be certain that neutrals or anti-Communist American allies would not undergo a moral revulsion to bombing in general, and to atomic bombing in particular, which might estrange them from the United States. If it was obvious, moreover, that nuclear physics also had civilian uses, these could not indefinitely be withheld from the world.

The United States government thus came forward in the spring of 1946 with a proposal to alter the nature of the military balance so as to retain the existing power distribution, but in a form less objectionable from a humane point of view and more stable for the longer run. The Baruch Plan for international control of atomic energy, arising out of the Acheson-Lilienthal Report, embodied two divergent strands of reasoning about the possible coexistence of the United States and the Soviet Union; it can be defended as showing an analytical awareness of the "prisoner's-dilemma" relationship between the major powers, or as illustrating the normal and understandable reaction of a "prisoner."

The proposal involved a supervised abolition of nuclear weapons, to be accomplished by an international monopoly of nuclear research, and of nuclear production for civilian purposes, the monopoly to be free of any national veto; it thus seemed responsive to the argument that the threat of imminent atomic attack might otherwise drive nations into aggressive postures designed to deter such attacks.[43] The Acheson-Lilienthal Report, as first drafted, thus made relatively little mention of any American need to retain asymmetrical advantages vis-à-vis the Soviet Union, concentrating instead on the bilateral advantages that would accrue to all the world in the sharing of nuclear information and the scrapping of nuclear weapons stockpiles. Fearful, however, of the reaction of Congress and the American public to any plan which seemed strategically naïve, the authors of the report decided to add a final section spelling out in greater detail some advantages the United States would retain through a transition period inevitably extending for four or five years.[44] Such advantages were quite real, and were seen by

19

the authors as quite important, but the constraint perhaps remained that Congress and the Soviet Union could not be reassured simultaneously.

One could have assumed, of course, that the internationalization of atomic energy proposed in the Acheson-Lilienthal Report would inevitably have produced an equalization of latent military potential amongst all the great powers, especially after some years. The termination of American bomb production and development, however, was to be deferred for at least several years under the Baruch Plan, as the international authority was established; until bombs would be destroyed and factories dismantled, an even greater American backlog of experience in efficient and rapid production of fissionable material, and in advanced weapons design, would thus be accumulated. Any Soviet aggression or violation of the nuclear agreement, after it was at last fully implemented in the scrapping of the American stockpile, would find the United States easily winning the race to reconstitute a nuclear force. All the world's bomb-production experience and expertise would remain intact in the minds of American scientists, an advantage which it might take decades for the U.S.S.R. to equalize; by that time some irreversible amelioration of American-Soviet relations might have begun.

Had the amelioration not begun, the United States itself might have elected, towards the end of its technological superiority, to terminate the agreement (even escaping legal sanctions if it controlled a majority in the U.N.) and to re-establish a large nuclear force before the U.S.S.R. had a chance to match it. In effect, the Acheson-Lilienthal proposals, as first published as well as in the version presented to the U.N. by Baruch, served to freeze American nuclear superiority for some extended time into the future, while bringing the potential of a quickly unfrozen superiority to bear as an equalizer in Europe. The clear advantage offered the U.S.S.R. was relief from the threat of an "out of the blue" American atomic air attack, but at a price of forgoing any early move towards nuclear equality.

The Acheson-Lilienthal Report was modified by Baruch and his staff, chiefly in that clear sanctions were specified against violators of the bans on weapons manufacture, such sanctions to be applied independently of any U.N. veto.[45] One could argue after the fact that these demands for explication, and fears of the veto, were unnecessary from the U.S. point of view, representing a costly accommodation to the formalism of the American Congress or of Baruch himself. Any violation of an agreement this important was a probable cause for war, explicit legal sanction or no, and the real significance of the internationalization plan hence would lie in the warning it gave countries (especially the United States) of any moves to develop another national nuclear capability. If such moves were detected or suspected, all nations would race to establish precautionary nuclear capabilities of their own (a race which the United States would presumably win, even beating the violator who first induced the race), or at least to take defensive measures to disperse population. For any such scenario the veto might seem unimportant.

But the demands for legal specificity and U.N. majority rule may have been more necessary for the intent of the Acheson-Lilienthal proposals than Baruch's critics assumed. Warning depended on some continuity of international inspection and positive management, and the United States might be reluctant to break off the agreement and initiate a nuclear arms race whenever some dispute arose as to management or inspection procedures. To avoid repeated dilemmas in face of Soviet obstinacy on the inspection question, the veto might have to be erased at least on such marginal procedural issues. To justify a relaxation of the veto on inspection, legal neatness might require a relaxation on the more "substantive" issue of whether bombs in fact were being manufactured.

The Soviet counterproposal to the Baruch Plan called simply for a ban on the use or manufacture of nuclear weapons under any circumstances, and for the destruction of existing stockpiles of weapons, without any serious system of inspection or surveillance to monitor and induce compliance with these provisions.[46] The proposal of course may have been offered merely to reduce any propaganda advantages the United States might win in Soviet rejections of the Baruch Plan. If the United States had agreed to the Soviet Plan, a question remained on whether the U.S.S.R. could have dared to comply with the ban on weapons production itself, dared to trust that the United States would completely destroy a stockpile which had perhaps been accumulating steadily since the end of the war. Even if the United States destroyed its stockpile completely, could it be trusted not to renounce the agreement if war were to break out, not to rush to produce bombs and not to use them again in combat? Pressure of civilians outside the government might constitute a more effective conscience in the United States, forcing adherence to treaties signed, but if a war were to break out, such inhibitions would be much weaker; a nation always could feel legally justified in abrogating a treaty if the original environmental conditions were no longer present.

The Soviet proposals offered what appeared to be concessions to international control, in complex schemes which under close examination, however, always involved some ultimate Russian veto over controls, e.g., requiring an affirmation by a positive vote of the U.N. Security Council, or a respect in doubtful cases "for national sovereignty."[47] Similarly, the Russians now pushed a campaign questioning the moral legitimacy of atomic weapons, culminating in the 1950 Stockholm Peace Petition, thus psychologically undermining the relative American strength in such weapons.

Had the Russians accepted the Baruch Plan, the postwar balance in Europe might have taken a new form. Neither side would have possessed nuclear weapons for as long as the international agreement was in effect. Fearing no immediate threat of bombardment, the Russians might have felt themselves able to relax the forward troop deployments within striking distance of Paris. The American ability to terminate the international control agreement, to produce and use nuclear weapons in the event of a Soviet attack on Western Europe, might still have served in turn to deter such an attack. Hence in the Baruch Plan the United States seemed to be retaining its deterrent while removing its immediate threat. The situation, moreover, would be stable over time, if an international monopoly of nuclear development could keep the Russians from ever matching the American technological background in weapons manufacture. Because of aversions to inspection per se, or because the plan presumably would thus deny the Russians a try at an "equalizer" at the strategic level, it was unacceptable.

Plans for the Bikini A-bomb tests of June and July of 1946 seem to have originated with the U.S. Navy's curiosity on the effectiveness of such weapons against naval vessels.[48] In any event, the tests were now viewed as a demonstration of an American capability for continued bomb production, or at least were so construed by critics of American policy, especially in the undiplomatic proximity of the tests to the presentation of the Baruch Plan to the U.N. General Assembly.[49] Yet tests of the Bikini type might have had a drastically different impact if the atomic bomb had not already been used publicly in World War II. Had the war with Japan been terminated without any introduction of nuclears, the world would not have seen the remains and survivors of Hiroshima, and might never have become so acutely conscious of the nuclear threat. The Bikini test in fact seems to have convinced (or reassured) many observers that the atomic weapon was still of finite magnitude; 53 percent of the public interviewed found the Bikini bombs to have been less powerful than expected, while only 18 percent found them more powerful.[50] Conversely, an American decision to detonate an entirely new and untested weapon under peacetime circumstances might have been viewed as a very threatening act.

A common observation of the late 1940's was that the U.S.S.R. naturally desired disarmament at the nuclear level, while the United States instead desired reductions of conventional forces; each side would straightforwardly try to cancel out the category in which it was behind. Yet this might be a misleading simplification, for each power could easily enough compose self-satisfying proposals in either category of weapons. If the United States was reluctant to give up nuclear weapons, it nonetheless had managed to author the Baruch Plan, which many neutrals might find reasonable and appealing. Similarly, the U.S.S.R. probably desired to retain its conventional advantages, but it could rebut American demands for conventional disarmament with its own superficially appealing proposals in this category. The Russians in 1948 proposed proportional reductions based on existing levels of forces;[51] herewith their advantage might well have been enhanced, since two-thirds of the Western ground force might resist two-thirds of the Red Army even less well than the entire existing Western force could resist the entire Red Army. Disarmament proposals could thus be written to eliminate some category of weaponry from power calculations, if one felt behind, or to freeze one's superiority when one was ahead.

A Postwar Balance

Having implicitly decided in 1945 that any real rollback of Russian influence was not feasible, the Truman Administration remained determined to resist Soviet expansion, but unsure as to how much expansion there was to resist. If large ground forces had been readily available, as in the summer of 1945, perhaps a challenge would have been addressed even to some of the Eastern European territory over which Russian influence was now seeking consolidation, but the costs of maintaining such forces had proved unacceptable to the West after the defeat of the Axis, and deployment of the U.S.S. *Missouri* and other naval units to the Mediterranean in the spring of 1946 could not really suffice as a substitute. American influence might thus have occasioned delays in Communist assumption of control in Eastern Europe, but any line of containment was drawn further west. Similarly, the Azerbaijan dispute occurred before the completion of all American demobilization, at perhaps the height of Russian recovery problems, and at any rate over relatively unimportant segments of territory in the north of Iran.

It is often remarked that American postwar foreign policy first received definition with the 1947 "Sources of Soviet Conduct" article by George Kennan, known more familiarly for its "containment" thesis.[52] Yet while the definition provided here was valuable to both observers and participants, the substance of containment was not entirely new to American policy in 1947. The doctrine essentially noted that American interests would pertain more intensely to territory not yet under the control of a foreign power than to territory already under its control. While one might in the abstract identify equally with the freedom and well-being of all peoples, one in fact identified more strongly where there was an ongoing attachment, and where liberty could more easily be defended, not having first to be restored. The territorial status quo could also serve as a psychological bench mark or guarantee that progress was indeed possible as defined by American values, for only a loss of territory would offset the gains otherwise expected from economic recovery and expansion, and from political modernization and reform.

On the spectrum of American interests, the current division of territory thus defined a substantial discontinuity; defending the last piece of one's territory might seem rational even if no liberation of Communist-held territory could be under consideration. As part of this satisficing point, there might additionally have to be an absence of military operations, for the suffering of human casualties touched on another discontinuity in the American value scheme. A stable status quo without physical hostilities thus represented the most natural plateau. Kennan's argument suggested that containment would be a natural cutoff, moreover, in that it would induce a softening of Russian attitudes toward the world as visions of world conquest progressively became more clearly unrealistic, as fears of external attack faded.

A question remains on whether containment therefore represented anything new for American policy in 1947. For much of its history the United States had been a status quo power, in that it preferred to develop the territory it controlled rather than to expand it. If one focused on one's own territory, this was labeled self-defense; if one focused on likely threats to one's territory, it could be labeled containment. If there were but a single threat, then the containment side of the coin was most likely to be in view; when there were several threatening powers, these might conflict with and cancel each other out, in a "balance of power" obviating the need for great American defensive vigilance. Clearly the postwar situation thus was peculiar for the United States, in that the threat to the American-influenced land area was single and identifiable, in that American effort had to be expended to defend the perimeters, in default of any power rivalries on the other side to sap the aggressor's strength.

Yet the United States might have preferred to expand its influence rather than settling for the status quo, as when in 1945 it had gone on into Germany in quest of unconditional surrender, rather than contenting itself with pushing the Nazi regime back within its own boundaries. The end of World War II may or may not have illustrated a transcendent American desire to "liberate" Germany from the Nazi regime, but it at least demonstrated a preemptive fear that future military attacks by such a regime could not be deterred or easily warded off. The 1947 American containment statement thus expressed and formalized the most significant conclusion of 1945: that Russia was not yet so obnoxious or so aggressive that preemptive operations would again be required.

For six months after the Japanese surrender, Soviet conflicts with the United States had appeared most clearly on concrete questions of policy, rather than in proclamations of grand philosophy. Disputes on marginal questions had been seen as likely for the postwar settlement in any event, and such evidence might still be more disappointing or ominous than definitive of an intense cold war. Stalin's speech of February, 1946, however, might have been thought to signal a salient shift toward greater hostility and more militant confrontation with the West,[53] being described by U.S. Supreme Court Justice Douglas as a "Declaration of World War III."

Stalin's speech was followed by Winston Churchill's Fulton, Missouri, "iron curtain" speech of March, 1946, but much of the public in the United States and Great Britain was still not prepared to increase military preparedness on the assumption of any imminent conflict with the Soviet Union. American newspaper editorials in many cities denounced Churchill for premature hostility or for a resurrection of traditional and outmoded "balance of power" politics.[54] For as long as the United States still remained appalled by the costs of World War II (costs which had not been so excessive for the United States), no arms augmentations would be launched to improve the Western military posture in opposition to that of the U.S.S.R. Anglo-American military forces, having been rapidly demobilized after the Japanese surrender, reached their nadir about 1947 and then gradually began to sort themselves out of the chaos of the reduction process.

A Soviet forward strategy, maintaining an army poised to drive for Paris, might have seemed necessary after 1945 on either or both of two stability arguments. Since the United States had just clubbed a nation into surrender by strategic bombing, with a finale of two atomic bombings, American leaders might feel that they could exercise a similar leverage over the Soviet Union, with little or no ground effort required to complement the atomic attack. While scoffing at American "air power" theorists, the Russians may have taken them to be very influential, so that a visible counterthreat to Paris had to be maintained to deter air attacks on Moscow. Alternatively and more deliberately, the United States might at some point have elected first to resurrect a large ground army in Western Europe, which together with an atomic bomber force would then threaten or invade the U.S.S.R. To deter such ground force expansion, a preemptive threat against Paris might similarly be effective. The Red Army thus served both as balancing counterweight to the U.S. Air Force and as preventive to a potentially unbalancing U.S. Army expeditionary force. Significant efforts, moreover, were expended to acquire a Russian nuclear "equalizer" that might once and for all prevent the reassertion of the 1945 Western superiority, even were the West to rearm conventionally.

Had the United States maintained its ground forces on the European continent continuously after the defeat of Germany, the confrontation might have been different; as it was, at least some possibility existed that the Russians would try to preempt any American attempt to restore such forces to Europe, when the decision to do so had been announced but not yet implemented. If aggression were not launched with an American decision to deploy ground troops, at least some great Soviet hostility would be induced, greater than if the troops had been in Germany all along. Fears of inducing such hostility or preemption in fact remained persuasive for some years, until the Korean War made Russian hostility and proclivities toward armed aggression seem so great as to render continued American restraint less advisable.

The exact size of Soviet conventional armed forces after the German defeat has been a subject of some dispute. It is clear that the Russians could not have maintained the standing army they had put into combat by V-E Day, not if any economic recovery at all were to be achieved. While this Soviet force seemed quite formidable, moreover, it must be remembered that it had not defeated the Germans easily, even with an Anglo-American army in France. An estimate of 175 divisions for the Soviet Army seems somehow to have remained in general circulation from 1945 until as late as 1962. While it was widely recognized that Soviet divisions had perhaps half the manpower of American divisions, and that heavy equipment and firepower were likely to be deficient, it was also widely assumed that Soviet soldiers were less dependent on "frills," so that a larger percentage of the individual soldiers in each division actually were manning weapons. This assumption may have been wrong.

The Russians may have slashed their ground forces by late 1946 to 25 percent of their World War II maximum, while the United States reduced to 13 percent of its maximum, which had been slightly lower than the Russians'.[55] Nonetheless the estimate of "masses of Soviet manpower," and of 175 divisions, continued to be widely accepted. While it can be argued that this represented some chronic misapprehension in Western circles, one must concede that the Soviet reserve mobilization system, at least for the time, was likely to be far more efficient than any in the West, given the nature of Soviet society; in as little as three or four months this might indeed have allowed the Russians to generate 175 divisions.

To maintain a deterrent to American air attack, the Russians had to keep some significant standing force in East Germany, a force faced by no significant opposition in the Western zones. The 175 division figure was not relevant here, except in that it might discourage any American effort to build a defense against the Russian forces already in place, since these could potentially be augmented on so vast a scale. If one expected Soviet economic recovery to be complete within a few years, moreover, the Russians might indeed then mobilize the much larger force, capable of sweeping over Europe all the more quickly.

The demands of a deterrent "forward strategy" thus might force the U.S.S.R. to dominate Poland, Hungary, and Czechoslovakia (but not, perhaps, Finland or Yugoslavia, off the main road to Western Europe). A distrustful observer of Soviet foreign policy might, however, have counted the ideological commitment to Communist political expansion as sufficient incentive for Stalin to seek control of Europe, even if no springboard was needed to maintain a deterrent to American air attack.

We may never know whether the U.S.S.R. ever greatly desired territorial acquisitions in Eastern or Western Europe for their own sake. If it was likely that the option of such a seizure was important, as a deterrent to air attack, this still does not prove that Stalin ever thought digestible the larger morsel of Western Europe's humanity and industry. Stalin certainly seemed cautious enough in his pre-1939 decisions as to the manageable extent of Soviet political control, and the post-Stalin experience of the U.S.S.R. in Eastern Europe and elsewhere might suggest that no such effective control was possible where Russian nationalism did not supply the bond necessary to overrule other nationalisms. If Stalin's assertion of control over the East European satellites were seen as a departure from earlier caution, this departure would still come fairly timidly and gradually over the 1945-1948 period, and could be construed as illustrating some special fear of a resurgence of Nazism in Germany, although closer cooperation with the West might then have been appropriate.

Yet the industrial potential of Western Europe would have been of great value to the U.S.S.R. even if full political control had not been achieved, and even a very short-term program of dismantling and looting might still have contributed to Soviet postwar recovery and industrial growth. As long as Western Europe was not destroyed in the process of the Russian takeover, the military position of the U.S.S.R. could be significantly strengthened thereby. The political problems thus created for the Soviet leadership, in the exposure of large masses of Soviet military personnel to Western society, might have outweighed the industrial or military benefits; yet such exposure to East Germany, Poland, and Czechoslovakia in 1945 had not proved so disastrous for Stalin, and the industry and military manpower of these countries remained fairly surely available to the U.S.S.R. for a long time to come.

A Russian deterrent to any U.S. nuclear assault on the Soviet Union thus plausibly existed after 1945, in the vulnerability of Western Europe to Soviet ground force attack; yet a balance had to prevent attack in either direction, and here uncertainties could certainly arise. Soviet acquisition of an atomic bomb by itself made the balance of deterrents seem impermanent, even if this acquisition was never to be imminent; American nuclear stockpiles and delivery systems would then remain greater than those of the Russians, but an American reluctance to use nuclear weapons might become evident once the monopoly was broken, leaving the Russians free to roll westward.

But aside from prospects of Soviet nuclear weapons, the American deterrent might be short-lived on other arguments. A danger existed that the Russians were not really deterred by the American monopoly of nuclear weapons (and not really provoked by it), but rather that they were only taking some time to repair the damage suffered in World War II before rolling west again. Before Russian industry had recovered in the areas ravaged by the Germans, before communications and transportation had been reestablished, it would be much more difficult for the Red Army to make rapid forward progress; after such recovery, the 175 divisions might indeed be called up and war might break out.

If the Russian threat to Western Europe were thus poised despite the American air nuclear threat, rather than because of it, an augmentation of Western ground forces would make war less likely, rather than more so. Perhaps a European economic recovery could have generated this force buildup naturally; if not, an American deployment might again have to be considered (yet the danger always would remain that the above assumptions were wrong; the United States, in preparing ground forces to resist a Red Army attack, might simply be forcing the Russians to generate that attack preemptively).

Marginally related to the Soviet recovery from the war was the consolidation of military control over territories that had been occupied by the Germans. Forms of guerrilla resistance persisted into 1947 in Poland and in the western Ukraine, by groups of non-Communist partisans which presumably had originally emerged to fight against the Germans.[56] While any outside material assistance to these groups seems quite implausible for this time period, émigré groups sympathetic to such causes existed in Britain and in the United States, and some liaison might fairly easily have been established in the event of war.

With regard to political control over the future "satellite" states, even here the Russians had to move slowly, for several reasons. Open domestic resistance presumably was less likely if the Communist takeover progressed only gradually, from a coalition government in which Communists were represented, to a "patriotic front" in which other parties were forced to run on a single slate with the Communists, and then finally to definitive control over the state. If open domestic resistance could be avoided, there would be less risk of outside alarm or outside interference. For the first few months after the war, while large American and British armies were still on the Continent, the threat of such interference might have been thought considerable, so that caution would be important.

Policies would differ from country to country. In former Axis coalition members, the right wing could be immobilized on charges of fascism, so that no early Soviet move was required. In Yugoslavia and

Albania, Communist partisan control was already a fact, and it would have seemed foolish to surrender it (although fear of the West might still require some show of conciliation, as in Yugoslavia, where Tito was required to conduct negotiations with Dr. Subasic, representing the royal government-in-exile in Great Britain). In Poland, where neither of these conditions applied, early action was required to forestall the development of any non-Communist political force, and it was thus in Poland that the earliest and most open defiance of Anglo-American desires came. In Czechoslovakia the Communist Party was legitimately strong, enough so to allow the Soviet leadership to leave the political system substantially alone until 1948, when the non-Communist forces moved to drive the Communists out of sensitive Cabinet positions. The ensuing Communist coup was to serve as a yet more decisive trigger to Western suspicions on Soviet totalitarianism and expansionism.

It was therefore perhaps only in 1948 that Russian political and military control over Eastern Europe might facilitate an early move westward. If Russian economic recovery were proceeding apace, Americans might soon no longer feel so confident of a balance of power holding the line at the Elbe.

There was also, however, the question of economic and political recovery in Western Europe. Any rapid economic recovery here might have established enough latent military potential to block the Red Army from Paris; one could have feared that this would be as threatening to the U.S.S.R. as any return of substantial American ground forces to West Germany, in eliminating the Soviet deterrent to nuclear air attack. One could even argue that Communist obstruction of economic recovery in Western Europe now would derive largely from such a fear.

Yet European recovery might on several grounds be less threatening to the strategic balance required by the U.S.S.R., even if it had not taken longer than expected. Economic recovery was, first, desirable in its own terms, so that any latent military potential developed thereby would not be a sign of hostile intent, as an American deployment might be; indeed, the evidence was that full economic expansion conflicted with the maintenance of standing armies in Europe, as it did in America. If the European defensive potential were thus to remain largely latent or in reserve, it at least did not threaten an imminent move eastward across the Elbe, as might 15 active American divisions in West Germany; the Russians might yet have been really more concerned about a Western ground attack supported by atomic bombing than about atomic air attacks per se. Finally, European military potentials would be less easily allied or coordinated in any move against the U.S.S.R. than a force with a dominant American ground force component; simple balance-of-power considerations might make France or Britain reluctant to support the United States in some grand move to overrun Eastern Europe and wipe out the Soviet Union.

Yet it was not certain that a European recovery had even begun by 1948, so that a threat to the U.S.S.R. could arise; it was also still not clear that Communist designs on Western Europe were only defensive or preemptive. One can perhaps note two distinct peakings of Communist potential here, the economic crises of 1946 and 1947, and the political crises of 1948. The decline of European economic production as a result of World War II (and severe climatological conditions which followed) had not been expected in 1945. The wartime American hope and expectation had been that Britain and France would revive economically and generate a natural military resistance to any Russian pressures, while the whole of Europe, Germany included, would soon be able to feed and maintain itself. Actually, much greater economic assistance was required, as shortages of food and of all economic necessities persisted through the winters of 1945, 1946, and 1947, shortages which Communist parties might expect to facilitate their own takeover of power.[57] The Western response had come in stages, with the cutoff of reparations deliveries from West Germany in 1946, and the termination of industrial dismantlement and the economic unification of the British and American zones of West Germany in 1947.

Uncertain as to whether and when challenges would come from the U.S.S.R. in the face of the atomic bomb, the American government and people had remained reluctant to stampede the Russians into aggressive action by too early adopting a tone of conflict or preemptive endeavor in Europe. It was thought that a premature commitment of American resources against Russian expansionism might simply stimulate such expansionism. It was thus in a sense unfortunate that the most pronounced occasion for American intervention, albeit only with material and training assistance, arose in February of 1947, with a very sudden British inability to continue supporting the governments of Greece and Turkey. The proclamation now of an "anti-aggression" Truman Doctrine, with its generality of tone, in many circles was thought needlessly provocative to the U.S.S.R., especially with Secretary of State Marshall still in Moscow at the time, taking part in what was to be an unsuccessful Foreign Ministers' Conference.[58] Convinced now that a more substantial European economic recovery, requiring substantial American assistance, was necessary to head off nonmilitary forms of Communist expansion, the United States went on to formulate the Marshall Plan, seeking, however, a phrasing less probably offensive to the U.S.S.R.

Even then, the process of Congressional approval for such aid, and the organization of its delivery and distribution, would take time; the Soviet leadership might thus feel itself driven to move while economic distress was generating real Communist political strength, for the Italian and French Communist parties in particular. Communist attacks on the Marshall Plan (a plan which had been defined in a deliberately nonanti-Communist declaratory style, and theoretically was available even to countries in Eastern Europe) were thus launched immediately, and Czechoslovakia was directed not to participate in it. Tensions mounted in the spring of 1948 as the first such American aid was sent on its way, and Communist-led trade unions in France launched a series of strikes verging on guerrilla warfare, with similar outbreaks in Italy.

Whether or not 1948 thus represented a peaking of Soviet military strength, in terms of strategic weapons or ground forces, a peaking of paramilitary strength had to be taken into account; Russia's political control over Eastern Europe was consolidated just as its potential for political disorder in Western Europe seemed to be approaching a maximum. At the least, the Russian leadership might be tempted to use this strength to head off an American economic presence for a while longer, and the American-controlled resurgence of conventional strength in Europe that it might imply. If Communist control over one or two more nations in Western Europe could be accomplished in the process, this might be desirable also. For various reasons, therefore, a crisis seemed at hand by 1948.

The Fragile Monopoly

Debate on the power of the U.S. atomic monopoly had to be logically subsidiary to a debate on its duration. If one argued that the monopoly would almost immediately be broken, a discussion of its exploitation might seem irrelevant. If, conversely, one expected that it would last for some extended time to come (estimates continually stated that the Russians were at least three years away, the same estimates being repeated and updated until actual detection of a Soviet blast in 1949), then one might also be less concerned that the bomb monopoly soon be used to preserve itself. Only if an end to the monopoly seemed soon, but not immediate, could interest be roused in any preemptive or preventive war to preclude the Soviets from acquiring their bombs.

There were in fact two separate scenarios under which the United States' monopoly of nuclear weapons might be brought to an end. There was the ever-present expectation that the Soviet Union would at some point develop its own atomic weapons; but there was also a possibility that the Russians, without developing their own bomb, might cripple or eliminate the American nuclear force or some ingenious use of nonnuclear weapons, thus restoring the world to the preatomic confrontation.

For some of the post-1946 period, the U.S. stockpile of nuclear weapons apparently was kept concentrated in a single location at Los Alamos, New Mexico, outside of Albuquerque, with the bombs left unassembled as a collection of components in the custody of the Atomic Energy Commission.[59] With the supply of bombs already produced being very small, the facilities required to produce more fissionable material were also few in number—each, moreover, occupying a large land area and hence relatively open to air attack. Under such circumstances, therefore, Soviet conventional bombers operating even on a one-way mission in early 1949 might have been able to cripple further production of bomb components, and perhaps to interfere with the assembly of those already produced. The possibility thus existed that the United States atomic advantage might be erased, or substantially erased, so as to restore the conventional bombing conditions of World War II, at least for a time.

The possibility of a primitive, complicated nonnuclear preemptive strike at American nuclear production facilities had not gone entirely unanticipated in the United States; the summer of 1948 saw several sabotage alerts called by AEC security officers, in one case after an anonymous letter listing critical installations indicated the possession of such information outside of classified channels.[60]

Despite the postwar optimism that had been generated regarding active defenses, however, next to nothing was done prior to 1948 to build an air defense system for the United States.[61] Apparently in an attempt to state its ideal where no economic constraints would be imposed, the Air Force in 1947 had put forward a "superiority" plan which called for 411 radar stations, 374 of which would be in the United States, at a cost of some $400 million. But approximately four radar stations, left over from World War II, were all that were in operation at the time, and these only on a less than full-time basis, without connection to any interception system. Congress failed to act on the large-scale proposal. It was only in response to the crisis of 1948, after the Communist coup in Czechoslovakia and the Berlin blockade, that Air Force Chief of Staff General Spatz ordered the Air Defense Command to deploy more air raid protection for the northeastern and northwestern United States. After the crisis had eased, protection was also provided around Albuquerque and the U.S. nuclear stockpile.

While it is normal to discuss radar warning systems in conjunction with the interception systems of active defense, the extreme potency and high cost of nuclear weapons might by 1947 and 1948 have made the evacuation and dispersion of American strategic forces the crucial consideration in the event of an enemy air attack, thus focusing far more attention on the maintenance of radar per se than on interceptor fighters' destroying some indecisive percentage of the attacking force. The fact that radar stations were not operated except on an occasional training basis over these years is thus especially curious, perhaps based simply on assumptions that a Soviet acquisition of weapons and delivery systems in the immediate future would be impossible.

Regardless of one's theories on the potential and application of air-delivered atomic weapons, there had to be some sort of delivery vehicle or strategic air arm to put any such theories into effect, and here skepticism on the value of nuclear weapons, or complacency on Soviet programs, also constricted the standing offensive strength of the U.S. Air Force. The Air Force that was expected either to win a general war against the Soviet Union by itself, or to help the other services in a prolonged war, emerged from World War II with no greatly urgent program. The Strategic Air Command, established in 1946, still relied on B-29's; only a few crews were trained to deliver nuclear weapons, and standards of training and vigilance were not unusually high.[62] While some other bombardment groups of B-29's were kept going apart from the Strategic Air Command, SAC itself in 1946 possessed only nine bomber groups, of which some were still equipped with B-17's; only the 509th Composite Group, veteran of Hiroshima and Nagasaki, was equipped and trained to carry nuclear weapons. It was stationed at Roswell Field, New Mexico, close to the weapons stockpile at Albuquerque.[63]

By 1947 SAC had expanded to 16 groups, all equipped with the B-29, with the slow process still under way of equipping more of these aircraft to carry the atomic bomb. The B-29 did not really have the range to strike at the U.S.S.R. from North America and return; but any war was expected to come slowly enough to allow for a deployment overseas, and in fact to allow for the assembly of bombs and their final transfer from the custody of AEC to that of the Air Force, which as yet had none in its possession.

While a spectacular and well-publicized Guam-to-Washington B-29 flight was presumably intended to demonstrate bombing range to the Russians (albeit the bomber used was stripped down and could carry no bomb load this distance), the long-range potential was less impressive. In 1946 it required four days to fly a small force of B-29's from Arizona to Germany.[64] In a maximum effort in 1947, SAC was able to put only 101 B-29's over New York as part of an air show; 1947 saw practice deployments to Yokota Air Base in Japan and to bases in Germany, with visits to other countries in Europe, thus hinting at overseas deployment if not quite accomplishing it.

It may have been highly improbable that the Soviets would have tried to take out the American nuclear capability with their conventional air force; yet the American failure to guard against the preemptive strike still seems surprising, if one considers that the Russians might have satisfied themselves at some point that they had a nuclear weapon without testing it—and perhaps then tried a nuclear grand preemptive strike against SAC or Albuquerque. Whatever the other possibilities, Russian progress in nuclear weapons would thus certainly be crucial, and even here the United States seemed somewhat overconfident.

Serving as a catalyst to force the United States into more realistic estimates of Soviet prospects was a series of espionage cases, beginning with the Gouzenko case in February, 1946; these proved not only that the Russians were interested in getting a bomb, but also that they might be able to take advantage of Western progress to date to speed up their development process.[65] Yet it was still apparently only the urgings of Admiral Strauss on the AEC that forced the United States even to begin a program of reconnaissance flights to monitor any Soviet nuclear testing, and this only in 1949.[66] At the extreme we have estimates that the Russians would take until 1970 to detonate their first bomb, or that they might never obtain it. Vannevar Bush had the misfortune of having his book *Modern Arms and Free Men* in page proofs at the time of the first detection of a Soviet detonation in 1949—with a prediction that the Russians would require another 10 years to achieve such a detonation.[67] (Able to remove this prediction, Bush left in another that ICBM CEP's would probably never get below 10 miles, or at best one or two miles.) As early as November, 1947, Soviet Foreign Minister Molotov proclaimed that the atomic bomb was "no longer a secret" for the Soviet Union, but this vague claim for a Soviet nuclear capability was not taken very seriously in the West.[68] A world-detected nuclear detonation thus may have been necessary, as well as sufficient, to convince the world of a capability.

Alternative Strategic Analyses

On various grounds, it seemed generally plausible from 1945 to 1949 that the atomic bomb would not be a decisive weapon or absolutely reliable deterrent; not even the leaders of the Air Force itself were yet prepared to stake everything on the intimidating effects of terroristic air attacks alone, or to assume that such air attacks could easily cripple opposing air or ground forces. The report of the President's Committee on Air Policy, otherwise known as the Finletter Report (for its chairman), should have presented the "air power" view most strongly, but nonetheless it left basically unsettled the nature of any immediate or future air war.[69] It did commit itself to the sober prediction that the Soviet Union would have a significant nuclear force by 1953, and that strategic planning had to focus on that likelihood. Yet the report at points seemed to indicate a counterindustry offensive as still being the most important air operation, and at other points discussed the need to attack the Soviet Air Force.[70] It was still uncertain, therefore, that counterforce missions were so practicable or important as to be worth pursuing (or so practicable for the Russians as to require preemption by the United States). And there was as yet no conclusion that air attack had become too horrible for anyone to be willing to bear.

Yet the possibility could no longer be totally excluded that the atomic bomb might immediately or soon become a weapon so horrible as to provide an ignorable deterrent threat, rather than a simple weapon of attrition on the style of World War II. At least a few planners of the American government, or in the U.S. Air Force in particular, would already attach such a countervalue significance to the nuclear bomber, and draw some more daring conclusions. Perhaps the mere threat of an atomic bomb raid on Moscow and a few other cities could indeed decisively influence Russian behavior, or at least deter aggression, even where such raids could not be maintained over some length of time in an industrially meaningful offensive. While no American bomber could yet fly round-trip missions between North America and Russian cities, the threat of an intercontinental one-way "suicide mission" might thus at least be articulated, as in the 1946 demonstration flight from Guam to Washington. While few would feel comfortable relying upon it, even a limited-duration American countercity threat might thus be useful, for political or military circumstances which might someday deny overseas bases to the U.S. Air Force.

The minority believing in an immediate or imminent decisiveness for atomic weapons in the later 1940's could have come to this position on several arguments. Some, of course, were still believers in "air power," having been enthusiastically in favor of a strategic air campaign throughout World War II and continuing as a matter of faith. A second group included people who had read the U.S. Strategic Bombing Survey more closely than most, noting its conclusions that strategic bombing had not in fact brought the German war machine to a halt, but that it would have done so within a matter of weeks, even if the German Army were not decisively beaten by Allied ground forces.[71] These same observers, moreover, would find the Survey's conclusions plausible with regard to the war in the Pacific: namely, that Japan would probably have surrendered even in the absence of the atomic bomb,[72] simply under the prolonged conventional bombing by B-29's from island bases in the Pacific.

A third inducement for some analysts to be more revolutionary in their interpretation of the strategic problem came with increasing expectations of A-bomb explosive power. Any detailed comparison of the conventional destruction inflicted on Axis cities and the potential destruction inflictable by atomic bombs, even of the prehydrogen bomb variety, suggested that a significant step-up in destruction had indeed been achieved, at least on psychological grounds. Even if many of the World War II conventional raids had inflicted destruction equivalent to the 1945 atomic bomb (which was not the case; only a few memorable raids had), a tremendous difference in psychological impact might now have been expected in the perceptible ease of the delivery of the new weapons. To be bombed by 1,000 enemy bombers, over a period of hours, in a raid which obviously taxes the resources of the attacker, clearly is different from having one city leveled by one bomber in a matter of seconds.

To such observers of the strategic picture, the atomic bomb and its American monopoly had indeed now given the United States a decisive weapon, which perhaps might even have been used to establish world peace and to impose disarmament on the Soviet Union. It might be noted in passing that the substance of the Baruch Plan would not differ very substantially from the substance of any demands which the United States could logically have made as part of a preventive war policy. In fact, had the United States gone to war with nuclear attacks on Soviet cities, if only to demand Soviet acquiescence in the Baruch Plan, this might well have been a very consistent national policy. In effect, the United States in 1946 was making the very demands that it might logically have backed up with military force, except that it proved unwilling to try using military force to back them up. Perhaps the latent possibility of an American use of nuclear weapons might yet have been enough to induce the Soviets to accept such a policy, but after American ground forces were withdrawn from Western Europe, it no longer sufficed.

While one often today expresses great skepticism about the possibility of a Pax Americana being enforced through the American nuclear monopoly, it may be that the possibility has been too much dismissed. At the very least, a preventive military campaign had to seek to preclude any Soviet acquisition of nuclear weapons. American nuclear weapons therefore would have been used against any identified Soviet installations large enough to be diffusion plants for uranium production. A countercity threat might additionally have been presented, requiring that Russians surrender all their prominent physicists, and submit themselves to unlimited inspection, if they were not to have three cities a month destroyed by nuclear attack. Once a sort of Soviet capitulation had been achieved, it might only have been necessary for the United States to keep small teams of inspectors wandering about the Soviet Union, ensuring that no attempt was made to revive a Soviet nuclear weapons or nuclear research program.

Perhaps an additional demand would have been enforced, as a condition for the sparing of Soviet cities, that the Russian army be reduced in size and that no military action ever be taken against Russia's neighbors. At the early stage, it certainly should not have been necessary for the United States to demand a change in the political system of the Soviet Union, or any occupation on the pattern of Germany and Japan. Yet the American experience in Germany and Japan may also have shown the occupation and political remolding of a foreign country to be less strenuous than had been supposed. It is often contended that the United States had to shrink from such a preventive war policy because the political tasks of governing the world would have been unbearably difficult, perhaps leading to a military dictatorship in the United States itself, but this could not be so clear.

A more certain explanation of the American failure to discuss, consider, or initiate a preventative war must therefore go back to the limitations on the potency of the American nuclear stockpile; it was not widely expected that the Russians would surrender, even if their cities were regularly being hit by nuclear weapons, as long as they could install themselves in the cities of Western Europe. If atomic bombs had seemed to be available to the United States in the hundreds before 1949, and if enough governmental planners had known of them, and if the political impact on the Soviet Union of the destructive prospect of 100 Dresdens or Nagasakis had been differently (perhaps more correctly) perceived, then the temptation to preempt the Soviet achievement of a nuclear force (in effect, perhaps, to force a Baruch Plan on the Russians) might have been much greater. As it was, the nuclear weapon was more widely interpreted instead as a menace (in other people's hands) for the future, but as not yet enough of an American menace to coerce the Soviets into giving up this future.

Among the minority of observers who saw any real and immediate political advantage to the atomic monopoly, most normally had thus to interpret the American moral or analytical mood to be such that the monopoly would not be exploited before it had been lost. Crediting the atomic bomb with more significance than most Americans did, they had thus to look glumly ahead to the analysis of wars in which both sides would have nuclear weapons. But if they were thus forced to look ahead, it was possible that they would too early be discussing the implications of stockpiles and weapons magnitudes which did not yet exist. If the world would be unpleasant when each side possessed 500 bombs of 200 kilotons explosive power each, one might consider heading it off, if one already had a monopoly which consisted of 500 bombs of 200 kilotons each. But if tomorrow's duopoly stockpiles did not yet exist in today's monopoly, if one instead had only 100 or so bombs of 20 kilotons, then it might be difficult to assure the feasibility of a preemptive application of monopoly powers, and the cautious might reject the possibility outright.

Russian Strategic Analysis

The public pronouncements of the Soviet Union on nuclear weapons in the period from 1945 to 1949 consistently labeled them as useless and militarily insignificant, incapable of reversing the outcome of any war.[73] It was conceded that there would be a great deal of human suffering in nuclear attacks, perhaps as much as there had been in the ordinary air raids of World War II, but this in the Soviet version was incapable of forcing any government to surrender, and was therefore irrational and purposeless. The Soviet interpretation of the Allied World War II conventional air offensive was in fact generally to scoff at it, and in the case of Dresden, to denounce it as useless butchery. In public, the atomic bomb was generally given no credit for the Japanese surrender, this being ascribed instead to the Russian entry into the war. If the Soviet leadership wanted to discourage the United States from seeing any advantages to starting a war, or more immediately, if it wanted to escape being pressured on smaller questions, such a professed skepticism about nuclear weapons was advisable, regardless of whether or not it was genuine. Pursuing the theme of the irrationality of nuclear war, the Soviet Union continued to stimulate petitions for an absolute ban on the use of nuclear weapons, coupled with an uninspected ban on their manufacture.[74]

The Soviet Union had acquired little direct experience with strategic bombing prior to 1945; it had never undergone Luftwaffe assaults comparable to the London blitz, and had not conducted serious strategic bombing campaigns of its own.[75] That Stalin and his advisers nonetheless attached at least some significance to strategic bombing is supported by repeated Soviet requests for B-17 bombers on lend-lease in World War II, requests always denied.[76] The Soviet failure to return three B-29's interned in Siberia after raids on Japan in 1944 may similarly be significant, especially since a Russian copy of this bomber went into serial production within two or three years.[77] The conquest of eastern Germany also allowed Russian officers to examine at first hand the conventional destruction of German cities, most saliently of Dresden. Yet the Russians must also then have been impressed by the failure of the Germans to capitulate under such bombing, perhaps reassuring the Politburo that a Russian population might stand up as well. However much the Russian leadership may have seen a propaganda advantage in claiming that nuclear weapons were incapable of reversing the outcome of any war, some of such skepticism may yet have been genuine.

The pattern of Soviet military procurement in the later 1940's may also indicate that the Russian leadership—like the American leadership—in truth did not find the atomic bomb yet to be a psychologically decisive weapon. The decisions to be considered here include a massive investment in air defenses, the procurement ultimately of about 1,000 Tu-4 bombers (carbon copies of the American B-29),[78] and finally the development of the atomic bomb.

The Russians over this period had begun allocating considerable sums of money to an air defense radar warning system, largely dependent at first on captured German technology, and to a force of jet interceptors (ultimately some 15,000 of the Mig-15 type).[79] If the Russians had invested only in radar, this might have conformed to a belief in the short-war surprise attack, or in the awesome nuclear deterrent; radar warning would have been required to detect an American surprise attack, to get the Soviet Air Force evacuated or on its way on retaliatory missions against Western cities. The addition of an interceptor force, a force which could never be of even near-perfect effectiveness, suggested a belief, rather, that the war would continue for some extended time, with a need for repeated air strikes on the pattern of World War II, and a slow attrition of American bomber strength by Soviet active air defenses.

The investment in Tu-4 bombers can be interpreted in several ways. The bombers might be able to reach United States cities or air bases on one-way missions, or to bomb cities or bases in Western Europe on round-trip repeatable missions. If the Russians did not possess atomic weapons, the one-way intercontinental mission would not be very profitable, unless the United States were extraordinarily lax in dispersing and protecting its strategic attack force. Repeated strikes against air bases or other targets in Britain and Western Europe made sense, however, if the United States were dependent on such bases to maintain a prolonged air offensive against the Soviet Union, and this is again consistent with the prolonged-war hypothesis. If American atomic bombs were still limited in number and explosive power, then a combination of air defenses and medium-range bombers might still help the U.S.S.R. to survive the extended war of attrition that would be waged.

The Russians of course were expending considerable efforts over this period to develop the atomic bomb, and the Tu-4 force must be interpreted also in the context of Russian hopes that such bombs might soon be available. Even if one doubted that atomic bombs were the ultimate weapon, they certainly were powerful and efficient strategic weapons, and it would be no waste of effort for the Soviet Union to acquire them. Yet the 1,000 Tu-4's purchased by the Soviet Union still shed doubt on any Russian inclination to regard ordinary atomic bombs as a reliable deterrent once they had them, since nuclear weapons production would probably not come near to supplying one bomb for every bomber produced.

The large quantities of Tu-4's acquired may thus have been a hedge against a total failure of the Soviet nuclear program or, more probably, a recognition that a Soviet-American air war would be prolonged whether or not the U.S.S.R. acquired nuclears. If the first 100 Tu-4's purchased plausibly offered the Soviets a try at nuclear strikes at the North American continent on one-way missions, the other 900 showed the Russians not yet ready to bank on this option. The advent of the hydrogen bomb, for which development of atomic bombs was a necessary first step, might change this interpretation, but this would not come about for another four years.

Another possible explanation for the Soviet production decisions is of course that Russian industry was incapable of producing anything bigger or better for the time, so that the Soviet leadership settled for less than the best, with which perhaps to develop some air-crew experience. Yet the U.S.S.R. has never lacked for alternative uses for its industrial potential, and it is thus not so likely that it was simply producing Tu-4's or Mig-15's for lack of a better weapon to produce.

The Soviets unveiled the Tu-4 at the 1948 May Day flyover,[80] in the first of what over time became a series of upsetting air shows for the West. Having no atomic bomb at the time, the display of such a developing delivery capability could perhaps now be seen as provocative, and even as inviting preemptive air attack by the United States. Of course the Soviet government had already begun to hint that it possessed nuclear weapons, and this faint untested possibility might have been enough to deter preemption, as soon as the long-range bomber was deployed. In any event, the Russians apparently did not see their decisions to invest in air defenses or medium-range bombers as likely causes for an American preemptive attack, which doubly confirms the impression that air power was not yet seen to be militarily decisive; Russian preparations would not be so significant as to give the American overwhelming cause for alarm, and whatever the alarm, the United States would not really have any means for definitive preemptive action.

If a nation could not be beaten into surrendering by terroristic air attack, and if a prolonged air offensive still seemed necessary for crippling a nation's war industry, then Soviet medium-range bombers might (by bombing forward bases) preclude such an offensive by Western air forces, but they were incapable of conducting such an offensive themselves. In a narrow sense, the Russian bombers could therefore be labeled as "defensive," serving to factor air power out of any war, rather than bringing it to bear. Either of two developments could have served to reverse this interpretation of the Soviet force: explosive power of bomb loads might have been increased to make repeated strikes unnecessary (to make one-way missions militarily or politically decisive), or the Soviet bomber force might have been augmented in range to make round trips possible. One or both of these factors would seem to appear in the mid-1950's, but for the time the Soviet Air Force could be credited with remaining within a certain primitive "arms control" restraint; it served to prevent or reduce prolonged inflictions of destruction on Russian cities, without threatening similar inflictions on American cities.

Since it was unlikely that the Soviet Union contemplated a politically or militarily decisive air attack of its own, at least until into the 1950's, it was perhaps thus also less surely deterred by U.S. air power from launching a ground attack. One might then try to assess the implications of Soviet strategic weapons investments for whether the Russians were now in a defensive mood, or prone to take the offensive on the ground into Western Europe.

Soviet air defense preparations could easily be rationalized as preparing for an offensive move. Radar warning was still academic as a trigger for Soviet retaliation, since a warning of three or 10 hours made less difference in dispatching the Red Army toward Paris; radar thus served primarily to help jet interceptors wear down attacking bomber forces day after day. The fact that the Soviet interceptor system was primarily a daylight system might, however, occasion great suspicion of Russian intentions, since its effectiveness would be far greater in the summer, when daylight persisted on the polar approaches to the U.S.S.R., than in the winter. A system that varied so much in effectiveness suggested that the Russians would choose the time at which it would be brought into play, i.e., that the Russians would be launching an attack themselves some summer, rather than sitting in fear of an unpredictable American air attack.

Yet the Mig-15's might still have some value even if the U.S. had chosen the season for war initiation. Any poor weather or darkness keeping the Mig-15 from finding an American bomber in winter also made it difficult for that bomber to find its target, and large inaccuracies of bomb delivery were not yet so tolerable for the offensive side before the hydrogen bomb had been developed. A combination of surface radar and visual sighting by Mig-15 might still, moreover, have achieved some success in interception attempts, enough to cut down the American strike force of B-29's especially.

While the Mig-15 deployment may not have been such a malevolent gesture, therefore, it at least inadvertently gave the U.S.S.R. an incentive to choose the time for any crisis, and hence was disturbing. Perhaps less of a clue as to Soviet intentions could be drawn from the Russian Tu-4 bomber deployment, which would be almost as effective in response to American attack as it would in a Soviet-launched attack, especially for as long as the Russians had no, or only a few, atomic bombs. If one assumed that many airstrips could survive for months of air war, then Russian bombers could keep on striking at American bases in England, if the American Air Force had still not become a meaningful intercontinental force.

The Crisis of 1948

While an argument could be made that American defensive preparations might stampede the U.S.S.R. into some preemptive move on Western Europe, it would not always be clear that such a ground attack on the West was not already underway; 1948 in particular was to be a crucial year, as indigenous Communist forces, with the latent threat of the Russian army behind them, staged a coup to seize power in Czechoslovakia. With Communist labor unions and other organizations similarly sabotaging and harassing the governments of Italy and France, fears were expressed in Washington that American ground forces might soon have to intervene to prevent a coup in those two countries.[81] The defection of Yugoslavia also seemingly suggested military action by Russian or satellite forces to remove Tito from power and bring Yugoslavia back into the Stalinist fold. In 1948, therefore, the prospect of Soviet aggression in Europe did not seem so very remote, given the many assorted forms it might be capable of taking, and any decision on a United States force buildup required a very delicate balance of judgment.

While the Czech coup and the disruptive activities of the French and Italian Communist parties thus gave the United States enough cause for concern, the Berlin blockade, with its involvement of American forces, provided the most direct threat. Western observers often interpret the interference with Allied access to West Berlin as a militant initiative timed deliberately by the U.S.S.R. in terms of its own purposes; yet it may as much have come as a Soviet response to a seemingly unacceptable process of events in Germany. If the U.S.S.R. was unprepared to see the economic recovery and political independence of West Germany proceed at the rate it was approaching in 1948, it may well have felt itself forced to raise the level of tension in an attempt to head off these developments, an attempt which was to prove unsuccessful. The Soviet authorities had ignored or rejected many aspects of four-power control in Germany which did not suit their interests. Yet there were formalistic aspects of German unity and four-power control in 1948 that the Russians were still interested in maintaining or expanding, including the extraction of reparations from the Western zones and some influence in the Ruhr.[82] The blockade of 1948 thus could be seen as an attempt to deter or prevent the Western Allies from further "splitting" Germany economically, by using Berlin as a lever to be bargained against events in the rest of Germany. Alternatively, if the Allies persisted in going ahead in tidying up the partition, the Russians could hope to round it off by drawing all of Berlin into the Soviet segment.

Whether the U.S.S.R. ever favored a more genuine reunification of Germany after 1945 is open to real question. Several gains could be cited. Presumably such a unification would reduce the threat of a clash between Communist and NATO forces, as in the disengagement argument later credited with inducing the toleration of Yugoslavia and Finland and the termination of the occupation of Austria. Reunification with military neutralization, moreover, meant a greater concession of manpower and industrial potential by the West than by the East, and might remove certain German political frustrations which otherwise would induce a new revanchism. Finally, some forms of unification might retain the Communist base in East Germany long enough to facilitate a Communist take-over of the entire country, perhaps a clear gain for the Soviets.

The last possibility, of course, posed the dilemma, for the Western powers would reject unification plans posing any large chance of Communist domination of the whole. On balance, it was all too probable that the U.S.S.R. would reject all plans which did not offer this chance; a bird in the hand was worth two in the bush, and even a part of Germany would constitute a valuable economic and military asset. If international morality were to favor the reunification of countries, then the Russians would have to pay some lip service to the possibility, but little more.

The eternal question would then arise for the West of what could be done to make a non-Communist reunification more acceptable or necessary to the U.S.S.R. (given that a Communist reunification was unacceptable to the West). While a maximum of formalistic pretense at four-power control might strengthen the pressures and inducements to such unification, endowing the three Western sectors and West Berlin with self-government and "sovereignty" might ultimately exert even greater pressure, with fewer costs and risks for the interim. In effect this was the approach adopted by the Western allies by 1948, and the approach against which the U.S.S.R. mobilized itself.

The suggestion has been advanced numerous times that the Soviet action around Berlin in 1948 was really only a probe of Western resolve, and that the Russians would not have resisted an armored column moving down the Autobahn to Berlin to reassert the Western rights of ground access.[83] As it was, the failure to adopt this line of action is thought to have given the Russians a permanent option of ground blockade, which can be reasserted from time to time in the future.

It should be noted, however, that the Russians did not need to resist the passage of the column violently at this stage, but could have been content merely with putting bridges along the Autobahn out of commission, by legal pronouncement or simple sabotage. Unless the West had been prepared to seize and assume permanent control over a corridor zone to Berlin, secure ground access would have been very difficult to establish. The Soviet threat of forcing the West to an airlift operation, moreover, has lost some of its potency over time, given the tremendous expansion of air transport capabilities in the next decade and a half. If the maintenance of the West Berliners was feasible in 1948, it became far easier for the West in the 1960's, even ignoring the stockpiles of coal and other essentials that have always been maintained within Berlin since the first blockade. Thus any real Russian or East German threat to the existence of West Berlin required a challenge to the air corridors as well, making the "precedent" of 1948 less effective.

The option of giving up West Berlin was apparently raised but not discussed at the outset of the Soviet blockade. A quiet withdrawal might have solved the enclave problem before each side became enmeshed in it, but it now seemed to President Truman that Western rights in Berlin had already been defined too clearly to make a unilateral Russian abrogation of them acceptable. Too many West Berliners had already been induced to come forward and declare themselves against the Communists, and the spectacle of these people being thrown to the wolves could hardly bolster the pro-American factions in Italy, or in France, or in the rest of Germany. Whether or not the Berlin enclave should have been liquidated on its merits, the danger was too great that Communist forces would be intent on, or tempted into, some exploitation of the momentum thus created.

46

The coup in Prague and the ensuing Berlin blockade thus induced the first significant postwar expansion of American defense effort; a much greater one would follow in 1950, with the onset of the Korean War. In losing certain options at perhaps quietly surpassing the United States, the Russians in the Berlin crisis set the postwar arms confrontation onto a distinctly different course from what it would have followed otherwise. A question remained on whether the American response should now be a conventional force augmentation back towards 1945 levels, so that Europe could be defended at its frontiers, or whether some other adjustment would be made in the American posture.

In March of 1948 President Truman went before the Congress to request conscription legislation and the inauguration of the Universal Military Training Program. But the budgetary proposals submitted thereafter could hardly be described as closely tailored to such steps.[84] The determination of the form and amount of the ensuing increase in defense expenditures did not amount to a very clear process. For the next two years such policy would be contested actively by the three armed services, by competing committees in both Houses of Congress, by the Secretary of Defense, the Bureau of the Budget, and the President himself. The outcome can be summarized as follows: a continued lid on total military spending, now hovering at about $15 billion a year for defense, instead of $11 billion, with President Truman several times declining to spend amounts appropriated by Congress in excess of this figure; second, a persistent stress in both Congress and the Executive on the Air Force as the highest-priority weapon, often without any clear vision of exactly what kinds of air units would be in question in the difference between 48 and 70 groups, but with a consistent conclusion that the strategic bomber force was the highest in priority for modernization and regular reequipment; and third, a sense that a very large potential reserve of ground forces was preferable for several reasons to any sizable standing army, with no actual progress, however, being made on generating such a reserve potential.

Several factors explain the Truman Administration's preference at this point for strategic force augmentation rather than buildups in ground armies. The argument arose repeatedly (as it did later under Eisenhower) that the American economy was not capable of supporting large military expenditures, and that the Soviet Union was deliberately luring the United States into such outlays on larger standing armies and naval forces in order to force the American economy into collapse.[85] Whether this collapse involved rapid inflation, or a severe shortage of physical resources, or unemployment and depression, is not always clear in these somewhat simplified discussions of macroeconomics; but the effect was to support the idea that reserve forces, to be mobilized when war was immediately threatening, should be substituted for established armies in being, at least until a Soviet threat of an armed invasion of Europe was immediately at hand. Universal military training rather than extra divisions, lower taxes and a balanced budget rather than arms production harnessed to the number of Soviet divisions— these were to be stipulated as program goals, for domestic as well as external reasons.

Nonetheless, this economic analysis was not absolute or all by itself now in precluding an expansion of the American Army, since other, more interesting, arguments also still seemed relevant. At the time of the 1948 Berlin blockade, the possibility was considered of raising larger ground forces for a defense of Western Europe which would be sufficient unto itself; but Secretary of State Marshall declined to support Defense Secretary Forrestal on his request for such force expansion, on the grounds that it would drive the Soviets into military action.[86] Large American forces on the Continent might or might not be seen as a threat to Eastern Europe: yet if they seemed only about to eliminate Soviet access to Paris, this might still be enough to drive the U.S.S.R. into snatching Western Europe before it could no longer be snatched.

However unacceptable a Soviet seizure of West Berlin might be now, it was still plausible in 1948 that Russian intentions would not extend west of the Elbe if provocation were not supplied from the West. The seizure of power in Czechoslovakia, and even the agitations in France and Italy, had reflected at least some indigenous Communist sentiment, so that it did not necessarily presage an imminent resort to the force of the Red Army. Under such assumptions, there might thus be an additional argument for holding off on any augmentation of Western ground forces on the European continent, especially while preliminary negotiations were under way on a NATO mutual-defense treaty, negotiations which might already be thought provocative east of the iron curtain.

One could of course argue that any universal military training (UMT) program would inherently seem just as threatening to the U.S.S.R. as a straightforward ground force expansion, since the training of reserves indeed might facilitate a speedier resumption of the two-handed American superiority of 1945. But at least the program did not yet accomplish such a resumption, or make it seem immediately imminent; the prospect of a reserve force mobilization thus might come to serve instead as an added unexecuted deterrent to any Soviet move across the Elbe, while such a Soviet move remained feasible as the deterrent to an air strike on Moscow. If force mobilization ever became a matter of days, and if air transportation ever made feasible an overnight trans-atlantic deployment of 20 American divisions to Europe, then the erection of large reserve programs might have the impact of a deploy-ment of standing armies; but no such prospects were in sight in 1948.

As it was, no vast reserve program was really in sight either, since both Congress and the President proved somewhat halfhearted about going ahead with any UMT program.[87] It may well be that the very prospect of UMT was serving as the deterrent, to be raised when Soviet action indicated possible imminent aggression, and to be shelved when such actions abated.

The American military response to the Berlin blockade thus came instead at the Air Force level. An "airlift" of transport aircraft was maintained to supply West Berlin, and three nuclear-capable squadrons of B-29's were dispatched to bases in Great Britain;[88] the military bomber force that had been stationed in Germany was also expanded, the implication being that a Soviet seizure of West Berlin would be met with bomber raids into the Soviet Union. It is interesting that proposals for an expansion of ground forces in Europe at this point were vetoed, at least in part because they would be threatening to the Russians, while bomber deployments were not. The first step might have denied the Soviets access to their hostages in Western Europe; the second merely confirmed and strengthened U.S. access to its hostages in Russian cities.

Flights by B-29 bombers had been staged over most of the cities of Western Europe in the postwar period, as friendly demonstrations, as parts of air shows or courtesy visits. Some B-29 bombers had been stationed in West Germany, and B-29 missions had been flown into and out of West Berlin before the blockade.[89] Yet most or all of these were B-29's that had not yet been fitted to carry the nuclear weapons of the time, still fairly large and bulky bombs. While the distinction was not clearly publicized, the Soviet government most probably knew that such a technical distinction existed, and that the nuclear-capable bombers of the United States Air Force were not generally deployed forward, but rather were based in the continental United States. The deployment of such bombers to Britain during the Berlin blockade thus was the first explicit forward movement of what amounted to the American nuclear strike force. While the long-range demonstration flights of the B-29 in 1946 could be seen as airpower-rattling, as could many offhand statements by Air Force generals, "air power" advocates, etc., this bomber deployment clearly constituted a step upward in brandishing what was still the American nuclear monopoly.

If 1948 was not the ideal year for the Russians to apply pressure from strictly military considerations, it would not either be such a very poor year, if one maintained the assumption that American atomic air power was overrated. If the paramilitary advantages of the West European Communist movement would otherwise be dissipated, the military power of the United States thus might at least be challenged as it was around Berlin. But the American failure to buckle in Berlin may thus have illustrated somewhat greater reserves of military power than the Russians had anticipated. The effectiveness of the "gimmick" of military air transport in the Berlin resupply problem came as a surprise to the Russians, such that they seemingly decided to wait for it to fail, and were disappointed when it did not. The deployment of B-29's to Britain should, moreover, had convinced the Russians that the Americans attached more significance to atomic bombing than had been supposed (and/or were less inhibited from having recourse to it), with the implication that such bombing indeed was more significant. With the potential impact of strategic bombing a matter of some doubt on all sides, the apparent willingness of the United States to brandish it, and to rely so exclusively on it, would move the analysis in one direction.

Whether any nuclear weapons were in fact dispatched to the United Kingdom in 1948 with the atomic-capable B-29's has not yet been disclosed. Defense Secretary Forrestal, supported by his Secretary of the Air Force, Stuart Symington, at this time apparently did urge President Truman to release nuclear weapons into the physical custody of the Air Force, and to make the decision in principle that such weapons would be used in the event of war.[90] Truman apparently declined on both counts, leaving his Secretaries with the fear that an American hesitancy to use nuclears might become visible abroad.[91] The deployment of B-29's to Britain, which Truman had approved, thus was accompanied by a fair amount of lower-level publicity disclosure that the bombers were atomic-capable,[92] implicitly hinting that they were accompanied by nuclear warheads when very possibly they were not. Truman's aversion to the nuclear option at this stage may have illustrated some fear of American public opinion on the issue, but probably was also a function of his own feelings on the subject, feelings which might persist for as long as the United States still held a monopoly on such weapons.

The custody issue did not definitely settle the question of whether bombs were moved forward, and it seems likely that weapons were deployed to Britain before the Eisenhower administration took office. (The Navy's aircraft carriers apparently began carrying nuclear weapons in February of 1950,[93] and SAC probably should also have received its allotment of warheads by that date.) It would in any event have been easy to retain AEC custody by placing an AEC officer on the crew of each bomber, and even less stringent physical control might still have been consistent with nominal or legal AEC control. Conversely, AEC control might have been relinquished without any forward deployment to Britain. The simple fact that the Soviets still were not credited with any nuclear weapons presumably eliminated any need for rapid activation of nuclear weapons stockpiles in the event of war; one could consider retaining all warheads on the North American continent instead of deploying them forward to Britain or to Guam.

Air defenses also were to be augmented in the United States. Late in 1948 Congress had approved a scaled-down Air Force proposal for an $86 million air defense program, with 75 radar stations to be operational by 1952. Since this still left the United States unprotected for the interim, a temporary "Lashup" program utilizing obsolescent World War II equipment was extended to fill the gaps left in the deployment of 1948.[94] The system called for radar warning and interception by jet fighters of the F-80 or F-84 caliber, vectored from the ground and sighting their target visually. After 1948, however, Air Defense Command was merged with Tactical Air Command to form Continental Air Command, which left uncertain the exact force available for defensive purposes at any particular time, a situation not relieved until 1951. On the civil defense side, the memory of rudimentary preparations for the threat of German air attack during World War II ensured that the psychological groundwork would not have to be developed all over again, but next to no preparations were yet undertaken.

As a corollary to any theory of deterrence, observers might introduce the concept of limited war, i.e., the notion that some upper spectrum of violence would reciprocally be deterred on each side, even while smaller wars continued to be fought. The possibility of such imperfect deterrence of Soviet aggression had now emerged in 1948, even before the advent of a Russian nuclear capability, with Communist-sponsored military insurrections in Greece, Malaya, Burma, and the Philippines. But as long as the United States alone possessed nuclear weapons, it might not have been thought so logical that a major armed conflict between Russian and American armed forces would have to be kept local or nonnuclear. If the atomic bomb did not yet provide that much destructive capability, any large conventional war would already approximate an "all-out" war, by definition; if the atomic bomb did make a difference, moreover, there might be little to stop the United States from using it, as it had against Japan.

But it was also not obvious in 1948 that American escalation to nuclear warfare would be certain, even while the Russians did not yet have an atomic bomb. President Truman's reluctance to commit himself on this question, when pressed by his subordinates, at least cast some doubt on his intentions. The Russians, perhaps while attacking only one country, might signal that greater aggressions would come if and only if the United States might then be deterred into accepting a "limited war" by this prospect, just as surely as it might later have been deterred by a Soviet atomic threat against American cities. Truman's statements on the undesirability of using nuclears may thus have illustrated a moral reaction to the aftermath of the Hiroshima and Nagasaki raids, but they also may have shown an awareness of the Soviet options described above. If the deployment to Britain was intended to couple an escalation threat to Berlin, doubts might remain; such doubts might have been even stronger for a Soviet assault only on Yugoslavia.

The deployment of B-29's to Britain, whenever it was at last to be accompanied by a physical deployment of atomic bombs, constituted another significant precedent in that atomic weapons for the first time were located in an area not under American physical and legal control. While the prospect of a British seizure of such weapons in a sudden coup was understandably remote, the physical circumstances surrounding the deployment of weapons were not unimportant, for later years demonstrated certain natural tendencies toward nuclear-sharing in such contexts. The B-29's had been stationed in West Germany earlier, but it seems less likely that nuclear weapons accompanied them, and no German assertion of sovereignty was possible in any real sense until the 1950's, by which time the "strategic bomber" was no longer to be based on German territory. The bombers that had similarly been flown in and out of various western European countries in the later 1940's, on "courtesy flights" and aerial demonstrations, almost certainly carried no nuclear weapons.

The Détente of 1949

How domestic developments within the U.S.S.R. influenced Russian military policy in the later 1940's is still not perfectly clear.[95] Stalin's control over the Communist Party seems to have faced no serious challenge, but some prominence for subordinates was nonetheless almost inevitable. One such subordinate, Zhdanov, died mysteriously in 1948, just before the purge of the Leningrad Party, which had been somewhat dominated by his protégés. This "Leningrad affair" of 1948-1949 was seen in some ways to have been connected with the ostracism of Tito in 1948, and it is plausible that links between Tito and Zhdanov had indeed existed. Yet the defection of Tito was often seen as a victory for more liberal independence, while Zhdanov was remembered as the deliverer of some of the more bellicose anti-Western speeches of 1947 and 1948, thus making the "Leningrad affair" interpretable also as a softening towards the West on the part of Stalin himself.

It is indeed likely that Tito was as militant vis-à-vis the West as Stalin, or more so, until his defection, and there are reports that Stalin pressured Tito to terminate the Greek Communist insurrection, rather than vice versa.[96] If the failure of Communist military and paramilitary pressure in 1948 thus showed Stalin that this particular peak of Communist power would not lend itself to expansion, or to inhibition of West European recovery, then the demise of Zhdanov may in fact have been an objectification of this, not necessarily contradicted by the alienation of Tito.

Outside of Central Europe, the American problem of containing Communist expansion had not yet become so burdensome. It was clear after early 1947 that China was no longer in danger, but this seemed to be more the result of the local political situation than of any U.S.S.R. military force deployment beyond its borders. Most colonial areas were not yet directly threatened, and American naval superiority could easily prevent the Russians from skipping across continents to Latin America or Africa. The insurrections in Indochina after 1946, and in Malaya and the Philippines after 1948, were potentially troublesome, but still manageable as long as massive aid was not available from privileged sanctuaries immediately across a border. The termination of Yugoslav aid in 1948 seemed to have solved the American problem in Greece, and in the end the balance sheet in Europe would show only that the free world had "lost" Czechoslovakia and "gained" Yugoslavia in that year.

As the Berlin blockade ended in the spring of 1949, American leaders could conclude that the brandishing and upgrading of SAC had indeed deterred an approaching Soviet aggression, and that the now-jelled strategic balance might remain essentially acceptable for the Western position. Yet the issue of reliance on nuclear weapons was not yet totally settled in military or civilian circles, in either practical or ethical terms.

The political significance of the B-29 deployment as a gesture had not been limited to the Soviet Union. The psychological aftermath of the Hiroshima and Nagasaki bombings, exploited and amplified in the presentation of the American Baruch Plan, had left somewhat unclear whether the public opinion of the United States itself would sanction strategic bombing (nuclear or otherwise) under any circumstances, particularly in defense of as minor a territorial morsel as West Berlin. There was the danger that the United States had played on the world's revulsion toward nuclear warfare too strongly in presenting its Baruch Plan, so that American and other public opinion might not allow a government now to deploy, brandish, or use such weapons. Perhaps publicity of the horror of Hiroshima and Nagasaki was inevitable and unavoidable; perhaps it was to the U.S. interest in building up the awesomeness of the American weapon, necessary to give the weapon the deterring reputation it needed, even if that reputation threatened to become an inhibitor of its application. To the satisfaction of the American administration, no extreme opposition to the use of deployment of nuclears seemed to have emerged by 1948, since the deployment of bombers to Britain was well received and the American Congress and public continued to sound very air-power-minded.[97] Yet the issue was far from settled.

The effort to brandish a real American strategic air potential now began to show some results, as General Curtis LeMay, assuming command of SAC late in 1948, strove to make it an elite service conscious of a special importance for its mission. Augmented budget allocations accounted for only part of the increase in potential, since the new deployments and alert psychology of 1949 by themselves significantly upgraded SAC as a striking force.[98] Technological progress also offered some new weapons. The B-50, a substantially improved version of the B-29, yet approximately of the same class, was now delivered to the Air Force, while the very-long-range propeller-driven B-36 was procured amid great controversy; simultaneously, the B-47, an all-jet medium-range bomber was gotten under development.[99]

Yet arguments on the immorality of all-out strategic bombing might still draw some response from the American community. There emerged at this point a vehement U.S. Navy opposition to the Air Force's B-36 program, contending that such weapons, intended and suited solely for the leveling of cities, were immoral, and that the Army and Navy should be given the appropriations and nuclear material to put military technology to a more civilized use. The bitter dispute erupted in 1949 after the cancellation of the first of the Navy's jumbo aircraft carriers, which had been intended, among other things, to carry bombers capable of delivering nuclear weapons. The attack on the strategic bomber program did not in any event prove convincing amongst the American electorate or Congress, in part because the Navy had assembled too long a series of objections, perhaps hoping that one would prove convincing if another did not.[100]

Leaving out the charges of political influence in the B-36 procurement decision (charges which came forward only in an anonymous document prepared by a civilian official in the office of the Secretary of the Navy, and which were speedily enough dismissed), the Navy, in the "admiral's revolt," contended that the B-36 could not penetrate a screen of jet interceptors to reach its target, and that it would have to attack from too high an altitude for precision bombing, hence leading to "area bombing," which had supposedly been proved ineffective in World War II. Even if bombing could be executed from lower altitudes, it was argued that the atomic bomb would not lend itself to precision bombing, thus forcing a reversion to repeated conventional strikes, which the B-36 purportedly could not carry through by itself. Such strikes would require advance bases (Navy carriers, perhaps) for fighter escorts, and also high-speed medium bombers capable of striking from low altitudes. Finally, the Navy argued, even if atomic bombing did prove effective, it would be immoral because of the number of civilian lives it took, perhaps thus making a permanent peace impossible.

It may have been that none of these arguments could have stood by itself as a valid objection to the B-36 program (or as support for the Navy's super-carrier program). In any event, stringing all the charges together gave the impression that they might not stand by themselves. The Navy's antiatomic bomb arguments seemed to be belied by Navy requests for access to the weapon, and for a super carrier which could launch heavier aircraft capable of delivering the weapon. The objections to the immorality and military ineffectiveness of "area bombing" tended to assume that wars would occur and have to be fought, ignoring Air Force arguments that wars might be deterred in advance by a reliance on retaliatory air power. Here, after the war scares of 1948, the Navy might have found greater support, but the arguments were articulated on a moral plane, rather than on the practical level that the U.S.S.R. might soon get its own bomb and no longer be deterred. The attacks on the penetration capability of the B-36 in particular might also have been more convincingly presented, but for the fact that no other long-range bomber option was at hand, and that even a small percentage of B-36's penetrating to Russian cities might plausibly suffice as a deterrent.

For a Congressional committee at this early stage, such an argument between military services may have seemed too technologically profound to be intelligible. Yet the technical exchange between Navy and Air Force was very unsophisticated and unresponsive by modern standards; the Air Force, for example, seemed to be banking on nighttime penetration of Soviet air space, while the Navy continually assumed that the Russians would begin a war in the summer, when there would be no Arctic darkness.[101] Faced with such a large barrage of Navy arguments against strategic bombing as it would be conducted under SAC auspices, the Air Force presented its general claim carefully, lest it be caught overstating its case, as the Navy had contended it had. The responsive testimony nonetheless illustrates well the limits to Air Force capability claims as late as 1949, limits perhaps crucial to the nature of the strategic balance:

> The anonymous document accuses the Air Force of fostering the idea that an atomic bombardment offensive "can reduce warfare to a clear, quick, inexpensive and, to our side, painless procedure," and that the B-36 could wage this type of warfare. This has now become a familiar charge. . . .
> We can hope, but no one can promise, that if war comes the impact of our bombing offensive with atomic weapons can bring it about that no surface forces ever have to become engaged. Disregarding such an illusory hope, we do know that the engagement of surface forces will take place with much greater assurance of success, and much fewer casualties to the United States and its allies, if an immediate, full-scale atomic offensive is launched against the heart of the enemy's war-making power.[102]

Since the decision was made to procure additional B-36 bombers for the Air Force, the general augmentation of SAC capabilities continued, but no other bomber was capable of striking at the U.S.S.R. from bases in the United States itself. Through 1949, SAC's operational units still largely consisted of B-29's and B-50's, for which bases presumably had to be at hand in Japan and the United Kingdom if war were to break out. To demonstrate the possibility of a pure intercontinental strike, a round-the-world flight was conducted in February of 1949 with a B-50 refueled four times in flight by B-29 tanker planes, using a relatively primitive hose-coupling system for refueling, a system which was not, however, widely installed in SAC units.[103]

An absence of urgency in procurement of B-36's as bomb carriers is suggested by General LeMay's conversion of some early deliveries to reconnaissance aircraft.[104] The need for target intelligence about the Soviet Union now apparently would lead to overflights of the U.S.S.R. by RB-36's, perhaps by RB-47's, and by camera-equipped unmanned balloons (this was before the commencement of the U-2 program in 1956).[105] (British RAF overflights have also been reported.) Given the general laxity of American preparations for strategic air war between 1945 and 1948, it is possible that a shortage of intelligence existed on the location and vulnerability of target systems in the U.S.S.R. With the restricted access to foreigners offered by Stalin's regime, and the extent to which much of the Soviet industrial complex had had to be rebuilt since 1945, the information available through normal intelligence necessarily had to be somewhat limited. Nonetheless, at the time of the B-36 hearings, civilians in the office of the Secretary of the Air Force had leaked a list of "70 major targets" in the U.S.S.R.[106] which, if struck by the American Air Force, would supposedly cripple Russia's ability to fight a war. When the program of reconnaissance overflights of the U.S.S.R. was actually begun may always be difficult to establish, but 1949 saw a definite increase in the number of American aircraft reported attacked or shot down along the peripheries of the U.S.S.R.[107]

In summation, the strategic balance with which the United States passed into the summer of 1949 was not such an unsatisfactory one. Concern might be expressed about its ultimate termination with the arrival of a Soviet nuclear capability, or with Soviet aggression even without a nuclear umbrella to shield it, but the crises of 1948 had passed well enough from an American point of view, and the responsive augmentation and brandishment of nuclear weapons might again keep the Russians deterred.

2   The Monopoly Eliminated : 1949-1953

The New Soviet Threat

A major problem for American defense policy emerged in August of 1949, naturally enough, with the detection of a Russian A-bomb test. Pessimists ever since 1945 had warned that the asymmetrical postwar military balance (American ability to bomb and destroy Russian cities, Russian ability to occupy and hold West European cities) would not last much longer. But for the majority of Americans, any decision on appropriate responses to such a Soviet offensive weapons breakthrough had been easily enough deferred, on an assumption that the Russians would not discover the "secret" of the atomic bomb for some time yet. Now the Soviet breakthrough was at hand.

Paradoxically, American defense planners at this point seem just to have made their most optimistic assumptions of a decline in Russian hostility, or of a deficiency in Soviet nuclear achievement, since Secretary of Defense Louis Johnson had drastically stunted appropriations for the Army and Navy, and even somewhat for the Air Force. Secretary Johnson now professed not to believe, even on the basis of the evidence supplied by U.S. Air Force flights, that the Soviets really had acquired a bomb.[1] He suggested instead the possibility of an accidental explosion in a Soviet laboratory. The bulk of the American decision-making community, including the President, however, accepted the assumption that the Soviets indeed had a bomb and that American policy would have to adjust to it. Detection of the Russian detonation in fact had been quite fortuitous, coming first in the radiation shown on photographic plates of a cosmic-ray research aircraft, and only then being confirmed by air samples from a flight dispatched specifically to monitor potential Soviet nuclear testing.[2]

The unexpected Soviet nuclear achievement might be interpreted as evidence on sincere Russian strategic theory. Even if one wished to credit espionage with having offered certain shortcuts to the Russians, the U.S.S.R. seemingly had expended a great deal of effort to achieve a bomb as early as 1949, and it was plausible that the Soviets had in fact begun their project before the announcement of the American bomb in 1945. Given the relative poverty of the Russian economy, a decision to expend such resources on nuclear weapons perhaps indicated much greater Soviet concern in this area than had been admitted, treating the atomic bomb as a very significant weapon in itself. Since the American monitoring system was established so late, with the actual detection in 1949 coming almost accidentally and fortuitously, it cannot be certain that this was indeed the first Russian test, and that no Russian bomb had been detonated earlier in 1949, or in 1948. In any event, the Russians seemed somewhat reticent about publicizing their progress, hardly discussing the test even after the U.S. announcement of the detection of 1949.[3] If Stalin indeed had any "sneak attack" hopes of using his nuclear weapons, hopes of leaving the United States in a false security perpetuating the small and poorly dispersed postwar American A-bomb stockpiles, then it might have made sense for him to forgo announcing Soviet weapons tests in 1949, or in 1948. As it was, President Truman had expected a public sense of panic in response to his own announcement of the Russian bomb,[4] but no anxious American response emerged at the mass level.

If instead the Russian leadership were still seeking only to de-emphasize nuclear weapons and to debunk the notion that such weapons made any difference, while slowly allowing an impression to emerge that the U.S.S.R. was not without such weapons itself, then the Soviet public posture also made sense. Once Russian weapons were available in quantity, with delivery systems also fully established, then some more attention could be allowed to focus on nuclear weapons, but such a shift in Soviet public stance would not come until after Stalin had left the scene.

The Soviet atomic bomb might indeed have served mainly as the necessary prerequisite to the "ultimate weapon" of the hydrogen bomb; it is plausible, in fact, that the U.S.S.R. intended all along to go directly on to the hydrogen bomb, given the small number of Soviet

A-bomb tests which ensued—only the one in 1949 and then two in 1951—and given the Soviet H-device detonation in 1953. The sincerity of the earlier Soviet nuclear skepticism might thus still be supported, both by the investments in weapons systems which would respond with TNT up to 1949, and by the apparent rush to an H-bomb after 1949. There would be some point to establishing an A-bomb capacity to strike at the United States, but it might yet be foolish to rely upon it, or to surrender to the Americans without it.

Thus even after the first Soviet A-bomb test, the Russians would not brandish their ability to strike at the United States itself. If the Russian leadership had been monitoring American public opinion closely, perhaps a panicky reaction to the Soviet test might then have occasioned a claim for a great countervalue capability, but no such panic occurred. Until an H-bomb could be tested, therefore, it was at least good propaganda to leave the impression of war-fighting exchanges of bomber strikes, exchanges which atomic bombing would not terminate in any matter of days. The real facts of the case, moreover, may have made this more than a propaganda position.

For psychological purposes, it might have seemed advisable for the United States to test several nuclear weapons soon after the detection of the Soviet test, in order to restore or maintain the aura of American superiority. Nevertheless, the United States did not stage any tests again until the series of 1951. Such testing would have been seen as provocative by those who were reconciled to Soviet accomplishment of some sort of parity, and hoped that further stages of an arms race might now be averted. Perhaps more significantly, the United States stockpiles might yet have been small enough to make American planners reluctant to waste warheads on simple demonstrations. In any event, it would have taken a little time to set up the series of tests, since the Soviet test had apparently caught the United States by surprise; the lack of any serious American reaction of fear or excitement in the interim probably made such psychological countermeasures seem unnecessary or even counterproductive.

The detection of the Soviet nuclear test came as the U.S.S.R. had seemingly just embarked on its first real postwar détente vis-à-vis the West, with the termination of the Berlin blockade and the end of the more virulent forms of Communist agitation in France and Italy. Fears of imminent war entertained in Washington in 1948 now had generally abated, and while work went ahead in establishing the NATO, it was still very unclear whether any troop augmentation would in fact be required as part of this alliance.[5] The maintenance of this détente was an important consideration for President Truman and his advisers. The possibility had been recognized at least implicitly that earlier Soviet hostility might have been exacerbated by the American nuclear monopoly; the Soviet test might have illustrated a technical progress that accounted for the apparently lessened Soviet hostility. A hostile American reaction might thus restimulate hostilities that one hoped to avoid.[6] Truman in fact was reluctant at first even to announce American detection of the test, lest the evidence of American monitoring activities be seen as provocative.

Yet because no equalization of Soviet and Western ground force strength had been achieved, the Soviet acquisition of a nuclear capability, if not preemptively disrupted by the United States, threatened to upset the entire strategic balance. If one believed that the atomic bomb had been a significant deterrent to Soviet aggression, then it could also become a deterrent to use of the atomic bomb, now that a second power had it; the possibility that the two nuclear forces would now deter each other and cancel each other out—while Soviet ground forces were free to roll westward—could not be so easily dismissed. Alternatively, the two atomic bomb forces might not be so absolutely intimidating, but would cancel each other out in terms of war-of-attrition calculations, such that the Soviets could still feel capable of going ahead. Finally, one might still believe that such weapons, if used, would have little or no impact at all, but would simply repeat the "senseless destruction" of World War II.

Whether the Russians would now attack the United States concurrently with any assault on Western Europe, or instead hold back their attack to deter the United States from intervening, was differently appraised among American observers fearing such an assault. When the Russians did not yet have an atomic bomb, the question might have been academic; all-out war simply would ensue while the Russians settled into west European cities as their own were being destroyed. Now that it had atomic weapons, the U.S.S.R. might be tempted to have a try at upsetting any U.S. strategic attacks or amphibious expeditions, by nuclear strikes at American airbases, industrial centers, ports, and cities in general. Alternatively, the Russians could, as they later did in Korea, let the local war be fought without escalation to the strategic level, calculating that the military advantage of such escalation would lie with the West, but that the United States would be unwilling to undertake such escalations because of the casualties that would result.

Even if the Russians could not reach U.S. cities with their atomic bomb in 1949, the strategic problem was at least a little complicated by the American "special relationship" with Britain. A few American administration officials were concerned that the Russian atomic threat to London would deter American use of nuclears against the U.S.S.R. while the Red Army overran the European continent.[7] Since Britain was as secure against Russian occupation as North America, for as long as Western sea and air superiority was maintained, the Russians would have less expectation of occupying British cities, and thus less incentive for otherwise holding back their air strikes at them. Similarly, if the U.S. Air Force depended on bases in Britain for its strategic operations, such bases also might come under nuclear attack if they were used for war operations.

Conventional Buildup

A first approach to the restoration or firming up of the strategic balance thus might involve a large buildup of Western ground forces, in Europe and elsewhere. A requirement for such a program was predicted in NSC-68, an early 1950 policy paper which did not, however, attempt to assess the acceptability of the economic costs involved.[8] A conventional defense offered a number of advantages. It would preclude the Russians from seizing Western Europe and holding it in another odious occupation until American air or surface power had time to liberate it. It might allow the United States to shield Europe without destroying Russian cities—a moral gain, and a practical gain, too, if it induced the Soviet government to abstain from trying to A-bomb American cities. Finally, it would allow a deemphasis of the American air-atomic threat to the Soviet Union, a threat which might have been conveyed implicitly at Hiroshima and Nagasaki, a threat which in ensuing years might have forced a forward strategy on the Russians in East Germany and Czechoslovakia.

Despite the decision to compose and sign the NATO treaty, however, several major steps toward a conventional force buildup had not been taken by the spring of 1950, and for the time it seemed to be policy that they would not be taken. No American troops, other than the occupation garrison already in Germany, had been dispatched to Europe; while the garrison could be converted into two combat divisions, it for the time remained structured for police and occupation duties rather than for combat. Second, no single command structure for the NATO military forces had been erected, and the U.S. Government's position seemed to remain that for the time being, none should be erected. Third, despite the existence of "police forces" in East Germany capable of at least some military activity, no reversal of the demilitarization policy had yet been proclaimed for West Germany.

The American military command seemed to favor German rearmament (while opposing the commitment of additional American divisions to Europe), but this view continued to be overruled by the State Department and by the Truman Administration as a whole.[9]

Similarly, European NATO signatories were not yet really being pressured to augment their conventional military capabilities. At least until the Korean War, conventional augmentations would be seen as a generally undesirable financial burden, which might postpone European economic recovery and might even disrupt the American economy. The cutback in American military spending launched just prior to detection of the Soviet atomic bomb test was thus continued through the spring of 1950, despite the suggestions of NSC-68, as the détente with the U.S.S.R. seemed to persist until the invasion of South Korea. Strategic air forces might be maintained or slowly expanded, but little preparation was in evidence for any conventional ground war.

The North Korean attack across the 38th parallel in June of 1950 was almost unique for the postwar world, a case of explicit aggression with no more of a cover story than Hitler had used in his invasion of Poland in 1939. Simultaneously it would become the clearest model of "limited war," illustrating that the U.S.S.R. might launch (and the Western bloc resist) such attacks without escalation to wider hostilities. For the direct purpose of operations in Korea, and because of the plausibility of the Korean precedent recurring elsewhere, American conventional forces were now indeed augmented, although still not enough, perhaps, to fulfill the functional requirements suggested in NSC-68.

The more immediate United States response brought conventional land, sea, and air forces to Korea to stop the Communist advance, and then to drive into North Korea itself; repulsed by the entry of Communist China into the war, the American forces withdrew to a stalemate on a front close to the original 38th parallel demarcation line. In the fighting itself, an archetype of limited war emerged, as sanctuaries were reciprocally respected in Manchuria, Japan, and Okinawa, as well as on the shipping lanes used to resupply the American effort in Korea.[10] Communist air forces were generally confined to air defense of North Korea, although varying explanations of this refer to American suppression of forward bases, or reliance on Russian pilots who could not be allowed to be captured, rather than some sort of mutual defense trade-off for the sanctuary in Manchuria.

The Korean War served also as a minor watershed on the plausibility of the introduction of nuclear weapons, at least into such peripheral arenas; none were used, and when President Truman tried to leave open a possibility that they might be used where appropriate, Prime Minister Attlee forced him to make a more explicit and reassuring promise of abstention.[11] The explanations offered for the nonuse of nuclear weapons in the Korean War have been various. The persisting shortage of nuclear weapons in the American stockpile may itself have been decisive, especially if further Russian attacks were expected elsewhere in the near future. The use of nuclear weapons in tactical situations had not been very thoroughly researched; one piece of conventional wisdom even asserted that nuclears might be ineffective in such situations—for example, that nuclear weapons were incapable of destroying bridges.[12] The Russian possession of a nominal nuclear capacity may also have brought into play arguments of symmetrical mutual deterrence, as had been foreseen in NSC-68.

The invasion of South Korea had seemingly made it more plausible that Communist military potential was not merely intended to deter American air attack, but that it might be used even despite the retaliatory threat of such attack. Czechoslovakia and Berlin in 1948 might yet have been interpreted as defensive consolidations on the Soviet side, making any American conventional force augmentation perhaps unnecessary and provocative. Korea, however, seemed to foreshadow a Soviet move on Paris for its own sake, such that Western augmentations would not be responsible for Soviet aggressions, but might be essential to preventing them.

Whether or not the brazen but limited Korean pattern was really intended for extensive repetition may never be known, for the Western reactions to the Communist initiative, in Korea and in Europe, may have disrupted any schedule once and for all. The Communist leadership might indeed still have seen Korea as a special case. Perhaps the open aggression came before enough impressionable "new nations" had emerged to make the illusion of "internal revolt" seem worth generating. Perhaps the American intention to defend Korea had been too vaguely stated, so as to convince the Communist leadership that no propaganda spotlight was focused on that particular country, especially given the advantages of getting the seizure over with in a great hurry; a slow guerrilla war preliminary might have alerted the United States enough to increase its commitment, presumably an unwanted development. South Korea, moreover, may not have lent itself geographically or politically to guerrilla war, since some Communist efforts in this direction had proven unsuccessful prior to 1950.

The expansion induced in Western forces nonetheless went beyond Korea, extending also to Europe, since the plausibility of Russian limited aggressions also seemed greater there. American fears for the safety of western Europe could be supported by other developments now, besides the war in the Far East; from 1948 to 1954, a sizable augmentation of ground forces occurred in the Balkan satellites of the U.S.S.R., as well as in Poland and East Germany. Several explanations for the buildup were possible, aside from the scenario of a move westward across the Elbe, but none of these could perfectly reassure the West. Stalin may have retained hopes of reconquering Tito's Yugoslavia, to erase an example of deviationism that might otherwise undermine the Russian position throughout Eastern Europe (rigorous efforts to purge potential Titos were in progress over the period). Alternatively, Stalin may have desired large forces merely to intervene to preclude anti-Communist rebellions or coups in the satellites, although the buildup of satellite forces might have seemed the greater threat to Russian hegemony.

Fear of American land invasion also may have played a role. As late as 1951, according to the testimony of Col. Wennerstrom, Soviet intelligence services were uncertain that an American assault on the U.S.S.R. in the event of war would come entirely by air.[13] The American decision to build up NATO ground forces might thus have amplified this latent fear of a land invasion—somewhat paradoxically, in view of Western images of an enormous Russian army of 175 divisions. The Soviet propaganda stress on permanently operating factors and conventional armies, rather than miracle weapons and surprise attack, may account for what otherwise would seem to have been a serious doctrinal lag.

A question would remain, however, on whether the precedents and policies of the Korean defense could continue to be very appropriate for an area much larger and more valuable to the United States, specifically Western Europe. The American military budget now shot to an annual level of $50 billion by 1953, more than three times what it had been prior to the war. Part of the expansion simply reflected the costs of the Korean War itself, which was prolonged far beyond the optimistic expectations of the fall of 1950. Some of the extra appropriation went to accelerating the expansion of SAC, still regarded as the primary component of the American military establishment. The remaining budget accretions went to conventional forces outside the Korean theater, with four additional American divisions deployed to Germany in 1951,[14] over the strong objections of isolationist Republicans in the Congress. The decision was also made to begin a push for German rearmament, and for an ambitious and costly expansion of West European land armies in general, to a point where their chances of holding back a Soviet invasion would be greatly improved. In these discussions of a conventional buildup, there was generated the concept of a "year of maximum risk," i.e., the year in which Soviet economic recovery would combine with the earlier Western neglect of arms expenditures to offer the most favorable opportunity for Soviet aggression.

Yet, however menacing the Red Army now seemed, it was still thought by Democrats in 1950, as by others for the rest of the 1950's, that the financial costs of any self-sufficient conventional ground-force buildup would be too high for the economies of the West, high enough, perhaps, to bankrupt the democracies and enable Communism to make gains without recourse to military weapons. As the war in Korea seemingly became stalemated in 1951, with the launching of peace talks at Panmunjom, the Truman Administration thus in fact began a "stretchout" of the sizable military augmentations it had programmed at the start of the war,[15] in both tactical and strategic weapons. The year of maximum risk would be reidentified several times, so that by the end of the Truman Administration it had been shifted back to 1954.[16] While it thus might seem normal to charge the succeeding Eisenhower Administration with reducing Western conventional forces, there was in fact no such clear discontinuity. Even if the Russians' new A-bomb seemed to have given them an "umbrella" of sorts, the temptation was great to seek some cheaper way of deterring or preventing a Soviet seizure of Western Europe, and the Lisbon Goals' ambitious schedules for NATO conventional buildups were subjected to wide criticism and doubt within months after they were proclaimed in February of 1952.

Preventive War

A second option could not be debated so openly. Preventive or preemptive war might have been on many observers' minds ever since 1945, but it had hardly broken into public discussion, either because the U.S.S.R. had not seemed so vulnerable to the atomic bomb, or because preventive war seemed incompatible with American traditions and American democracy. Presumably one might be more tempted to suggest the possibility if a clear and relatively costless military victory against the U.S.S.R. could be expected, or if one perceived an imminent Soviet threat of great damage to the United States.

After 1949, considerations of the preventive war alternative could not be easily postponed on optimistic estimates of Soviet nuclear incompetence. The Soviet capability might still be denied in some relatively uninformed circles which refused to credit the Communist system with a real scientific prowess, which could even believe that the Soviet bomb had been put together from components stolen from the United States. Yet most of the American public did not feel driven to believe this. Other self-satisfied Americans might credit espionage with having given the Soviets great assistance, with the implication that a general tightening of security would serve to slow further Soviet nuclear progress, but with the acknowledgment that the Russians now indeed had the bomb. (Most surprisingly, President Truman, on leaving office in 1953, professed to believe that the Russians in fact had not yet developed the bomb,[17] a viewpoint at odds with that of most of the scientific community.)

Either because the Russians would soon acquire and/or use nuclear weapons and should best be denied them, or because they were about to commence a series of conventional wars to sap the strength of the free world, it might thus be preferable to initiate the war earlier, on terms more favorable to the West. Hence the Soviet A-bomb test produced a small flurry of preventive war discussion, and the Korean War considerably more, in the fall of 1950 perhaps most memorably in a speech by Secretary of the Navy Francis Matthews suggesting that Americans become the first "aggressors for peace."[18]

Militarily, the Russians should by 1951 have been able to hide away at least a bomb or two, which might then somehow be delivered to New York or Washington in retaliation, perhaps by suitcase. But it still should presumably have been possible for SAC to catch and destroy most Soviet reactors, diffusion plants, and bomber bases, perhaps even more easily in 1951 than earlier, because the United States had more nuclear warheads to direct against them; a greater availability of nuclear weapons in an "atomic plenty" might indeed now make counter-Soviet Air Force operations generally more appropriate.

Yet the NATO treaty had only just been ratified, with no military ground force expansion program yet showing results, and the likely result of any American preemption would still have been a Soviet occupation of Europe. Again the nuclear question by itself could not be decisive. In such preventive war discussions as emerged after the Korean War, the scenario thus was not so typically one of American nuclear weapons easily preempting and wiping out Soviet nuclear forces.[19] Rather, the suggestion was for earlier initiation of the very long drawn-out war that had been feared before, on the assumption that since it was likely to come anyway, it should better be fought before the "year of maximum risk."

The Hydrogen Bomb

A third means of restoring the pre-1949 balance was for the West to go on to the next higher weapons generation after the atomic bomb, to the hydrogen bomb or "super," and it is clear now that the most significant effect of the Soviet atomic detonation was in fact the stimulus it gave to the American proponents of such a program. President Truman's "decision" to go ahead with the hydrogen bomb, albeit then far from decisive in impact, was thus proclaimed in January of 1950,[20] even before the Korean War. Yet the option of the bigger bomb occasioned a major debate within the American decision-making community.

Many of those who had been skeptical of the deterrent power of the atomic bomb (or of strategic bombing in general) were impressed now by the apparent thousandfold increase in power of the hydrogen weapon, reasoning not only that first possession of such a weapon would give any major power a real political advantage over its rivals, but also that it would deter aggression more absolutely and certainly than had the atomic bomb. The hydrogen bomb clearly might make comparisons of nuclear war with World War II bombing obsolete, enough so to remove all skepticism, enough so to supply a sure deterrent, regardless of who "won" any war.

This strategic significance of the hydrogen bomb was, however, subject to some dispute. At least some of those opposed claimed now to see the step-up from A-bomb to H-bomb as we often see the 100-megaton bomb today: as being a physically greater accomplishment, but as only adding destructive power where sufficient quantities already existed for all human purposes. If a mutual minimum deterrence was supplied by two opposing A-bomb forces, in this view, the H-bomb would not upset it, but would, rather, be quite redundant. Yet the world could hardly be sure that a Russian A-bomb would deter use of an American H-bomb in defense of Europe, if it had been unsure that an American A-bomb could deter a Russian seizure of Paris; the "super" might thus be a lot more than a redundant addition to a preexisting balance of terror. In any event, it seems likely that simple redundancy does not account for the energetic opposition of some scientists to an H-bomb program.

For much of the American liberal community, a reliance on such a "super" countercivilian threat was very undesirable, even if it for a time restored the balance between the Soviet and Western blocs. The contingency of war could never be ruled out completely, and the physical prevention of H-bomb development, or removal of incentives thereto, could very much reduce casualties and physical destruction if war were ever to come. But the issue involved much more than this. The threat of mass destruction seemed obnoxious in itself even if it were never realized. Political leaderships would be driven to precautionary countermeasures in face of such threats, to ever-higher levels of hostility, and perhaps even to rash preemptive ventures. The effects on the individual would be similarly severe, as lifetime planning became more tentative in face of the prospects of all-out war, as pedestrians flinched at every sudden flash of light.

The reestablishment of a balance, to prevent the outbreak of war and the loss of significant amounts of territory to Communism, was thus not the only consideration for such points of view, for it was important that such a balance this time be reestablished without deleterious side effects. A balance of containment which led to a diminution of hostility and of human fear would be preferable to a balance of containment which did not, and a way thus had to be sought to pull or push war "back to the battlefield."

Some Americans now proposed negotiations with the Soviets in advance of any American H-bomb program, to achieve some mutual abstention from such programs, and thus to reassure the Russians of their physical security; the State Department had vetoed this proposal, however, for fear that the U.S.S.R. might prolong such discussions once the United States was engaged in them, to immobilize the American program and thus to leap ahead.[21] (Subsequent events seemed in fact to indicate that the Soviet Union had already launched its H-bomb program before the United States had begun its own.)

Little would be tried or achieved now in disarmament discussions with the Soviet Union. Discussions were carried on in two separate agencies, the U.N. Atomic Energy Commission and its Commission for

Conventional Armament, until January, 1950, when the Soviet Union left the deliberations of both bodies; in July, 1952, the General Assembly created a single Disarmament Commission, and talks were resumed in the context of the Korean negotiations and projected NATO ground force buildups. Throughout this period the United States still had clung to its Baruch Plan, largely for the propaganda value that could be extracted from persistent Soviet rejections of the proposals, although the plan might no longer leave the United States in all the positions of advantage it had held in 1946; international control and inspection, if accepted by the U.S.S.R., might still have imposed a political constraint on the Soviet leadership, perhaps enough even to compensate for an erosion of American nuclear superiority.

Tactical Nuclear Weapons

A fourth possibility, a variant on the conventional buildup to hold territory by defense on the ground, emerged with the battlefield application of nuclear weapons, especially after a 1951 breakthrough in nuclear warhead production.

The possibility that weapons might be available for all three military services almost inevitably had induced the Army and Navy to request tactical nuclear weapons for battlefield contexts outside the exclusive preserve of the Air Force. The extent to which the parochial considerations of the separate military services determine the nature of the American defense debate is always a little difficult to determine, because one must judge the good faith of the proponents of the various arguments. It may well be that officers of the particular services in fact come to believe the strategic arguments which bolster the role of their services, and that the distortion of the objective arguments is therefore much more subtle. At any rate, the services' particular interests have played a role, at times inducing a debate on strategy itself, at other times producing a debate instead on which service was best able to execute an already agreed-upon strategy.

It was of course clear from the start that custody of the atomic bomb would add glamour and status to any of the military services. Rather than leaving the bomb to the Air Force alone, therefore, it was important for the Army and Navy to carve out some nuclear role for themselves. For the Navy, the choice might lie between asserting that it could duplicate or improve upon the Air Force's strategic attack mission, and claiming that some oceanic or amphibious tactical mission also required the use of nuclears. For the time, the Army had little option but to stress tactical uses of the atomic bomb, at least until one of its allotted tactical delivery systems could be stretched to reach strategic-weapons ranges, a development which did not occur until 1957.

General Omar Bradley, then Chairman of the Joint Chiefs of Staff, had as early as 1949 urged the development and acquisition of tactical nuclear weapons, on the assumption that they would increase the firepower of Western forces, and therefore presumably balance the superior numbers of the Russian Army.[22] The assumption seemed implicit that nuclear weapons would favor the smaller forces, presumably finding the larger masses of the enemy easy targets. Such weapons also possibly favored the defense, since aggressive forces would have to mass to penetrate and break through the defensive line. Bradley's article, published at almost the time of the first Soviet nuclear test, conceded that the Russians might indeed design and test a bomb, but was skeptical as to whether they could mass-produce such weapons. Bradley also doubted, however, that nuclear weapons could be decisive in any strategic sense, and argued that their very best use was directly on the battlefield, to win the military victory.

Yet there were other commentators equally intent on inducing a shift of the dominant American strategy from the strategic air offensive to battlefield victories. In a summer study series of conferences under the title "Project Vista," a group of scientists presented strong recommendations for tactical nuclear weapons development rather than an H-bomb program.[23] For the time, it seemed that simultaneous research on both the hydrogen bomb and tactical nuclear weapons would be impossible, and since a choice had to be made, that the H-bomb should thus be avoided. This later proved to be largely untrue, but Americans of a liberal persuasion could hope that tactical nuclears might yet eliminate any feeling of need for an H-bomb, even if the big bomb was not eliminated as a practical option. The "Vista" proposals in fact included an American announcement that SAC would not be entered into a war unless the Soviets had used their long-range bomber force first against U.S. civilian targets.[24]

Tactical weapons, when combined with ground-force buildups, might establish a new balance on the continent of Europe itself, a balance which presumably favored the defense, a balance which would remove much of the need for large-scale destructive capabilities aimed at the homelands of the major powers. This latter destructive capability once having been relaxed, the need for the Soviet Union to menace Western Europe might also recede, with a general relaxation of tensions.

It is interesting that those favoring tactical nuclear weapons here apparently did not fear that such use would induce escalation to all-out war by crossing the conventional-nuclear firebreak and eroding a well-understood distinction. It was, after all, only five or six years after Hiroshima and Nagasaki had seen the use of nuclears in combat, and a longer period of complete nonuse of nuclear weapons might have been required before the distinction would become so salient.

There had not been many nuclear weapons tests throughout the world prior to 1951, reflecting in part the limited stockpiles available. There had been two U.S. detonations in 1946 and four in 1948. The Soviets had exploded a bomb in 1949, and two more in 1951. In 1951, however, there came a series of U.S. nuclear weapons tests which both supported and undermined the "liberal" position on defense.[25] One series demonstrated that atomic bombs could be made with only half the fissionable material previously required, thus in effect doubling the American stockpile and opening possibilities of tactical weapons previously rebuffed on the argument of scarcity. The other test, "Project Greenhouse," demonstrated, however, that the hydrogen bomb was more surely feasible, and that its development would require less time and effort than its opponents had supposed.

In an attempt to enlist further military support for tactical nuclear weapons development, a delegation of scientists went to Paris to present the program to NATO headquarters. While the proposal might have been accepted straightforwardly by a theater commander as a valuable addition to his tactical arsenal, it was interpreted by opponents in the U.S. Air Force as a diversion from the strategic arsenal. Given the scarcity still assumed of nuclear material and production facilities, there might not have been enough to produce both tactical nuclears and hydrogen bombs. Air Force warnings thus were dispatched to NATO headquarters, in what was seen to be a plot to weaken the strategic deterrent, and the "Vista" proposals were not endorsed in Paris.[26] At about the same time, an Air Force colonel attempted to brief General LeMay on the implications of nuclear plenty—that weapons might now be shared for tactical purposes with other American military agencies besides SAC; General LeMay apparently became very angry and refused to allow the briefing to be completed.[27]

Active Air Defenses

Yet a fifth mode of response to the Soviet progress in atomic weapons remains to be considered, one that also might figure in the general debate if it tended to move war "back to the battlefield," and here we come to the 1950 air defense issue. One of the recommendations of NSC-68 had been for a larger American program of active anti-aircraft defense; this was now endorsed by some of the scientists who had opposed the hydrogen bomb, and was outlined in great detail in "Project Charles," an MIT-sponsored, Air Force-contracted study group of 1951.[28]

If air defense could be improved to impose high enough casualties on an attacking bomber force, it might make such air raids militarily unattractive. If an attacker lost more of his forces-in-being in such a raid than he destroyed on the territory being bombed, the urge to "strike at the enemy's heartland" might be relieved. If the prospect of killing or terrorizing large segments of a civilian population were diminished or eliminated, offensive air weapons would perhaps no longer be brandished about.

It was true, of course, that an air defense program would be expensive and might well draw funds away from American offensive weapons programs. But if air defenses delayed or precluded any new American strategic offensive force, they would also shield the United States from any similar Soviet force. The Russians had an atomic bomb now, but their development of a hydrogen bomb did not have to be accepted as probable or imminent. Under such conditions, a moderately effective active defense program of dispersal and shelters might significantly reduce wartime damage. If no defensive effort was made against A-bomb carriers (or against conventional bombers), these would still be intimidating weapons; but active defenses, at least in the absence of the H-bomb, could erase much of the threat of extreme civilian destruction.

Any large American effort in air defense technology might, moreover, induce Soviet reciprocation. Emulation of military development was, after all, the normal pattern of arms races in the past, since an opponent's effort to make progress on a certain weapons system logically suggested that there was progress to be made. Any technological breakthroughs generated in active defenses would inevitably leak out sooner or later, so that Russian air defenses might ultimately be strengthened also through the cullings of Soviet scientific intelligence and espionage. American concentration on population defense thus might induce a similar Russian concentration, not only because the morality of the shift was convincing, but also because of the rules of military arms races in general. Technology, moreover, still seemed to be coming to the side of the defense. The Korean War reinforced earlier

74

expectations of air defense efficacy, since the U.S. Air Force was obliged to curtail its daylight B-29 raids over North Korea in face of the effectiveness of Russian-built Mig-15 jet interceptors.[29]

Any large allocation to weapons intended for use against some particular foreign country would normally imply an increase in hostility toward that country, since the expenditure of money reflected on the reliability and friendliness of that power. Implicitly, therefore, an arms race was in part a propaganda exchange, unless some very sophisticated and complementary explanation of arms expenditures could be circulated to take the sting out of their publicity impact. It could be claimed, of course, that defensive weapons required less expenditure over time than would massive offensive strategic weapons programs based on the hydrogen bomb; but while this might help sell defensive programs, it was not likely to be true. Yet one might still hope that greater expenditures on air defense would seem less provocative to the Russian leadership than would smaller expenditures on air offense. The general Soviet willingness to debunk nuclear weapons, to disparage offensive bomber campaigns, and to label weapons as "offensive" and "defensive" might thus have allowed the United States simultaneously to spend great amounts on weapons systems, albeit defenses, and to achieve some détente.

The air defense proposal might divert the emphasis from offensive to defensive weapons in still another way. Any large anti-aircraft radar program would cost a great deal of money, and money could be just as scarce a resource as uranium. At least some of the supporters of air defense must have noted that such programs might induce the United States to dispense with any tremendous bomber buildup, and thus (if the Soviets were driven to match U.S. defensive development) to a general situation in which the offensive strength of both sides remained quite low relative to the defenses to be crossed. Even if these possibilities had not been obvious to the air defense advocates at first, they were pointed out almost immediately by opponents of active defenses in the Air Force,[30] who accused the defense proponents of being guided by such considerations, considerations quite parallel to the earlier supposed incompatibility between H-bomb and tactical nuclear weapons development.

Motivation is always difficult to prove, even for those motivated, but it would have been fruitless for an air defense program to be enacted only to be beaten down by new generations of offensive weapons. If the U.S. Air Force merely expanded to offset Soviet air defenses, it was likely that the Russians would reciprocate. The advocates of civilian security for the United States (or for the whole world) could thus not easily be indifferent to American Air Force planners' desires for long-range jet bomber procurement; the opposition expressed to the hydrogen bomb applied logically also to the B-52.

Today's inverted logic of deterrence, that larger destructive capabilities mean less risk of human suffering, had thus not yet become so plausible for many Americans. Life might be considerably more pleasant on each side if weapons of mass destruction did not seem primed for use all over the world, or if the effectiveness of such weapons was substantially and clearly lowered by defensive counter-measures. A straightforward morality here disapproved of weapons that could kill people, but approved of interceptor weapons that destroyed any incoming weapons that could kill people. Returning the war to the battlefield would be a two-part effort, giving the free world some tactical tools so that it could hold its own on the battlefield, and perhaps denying the whole world the weapons that were intended for use off the battlefield, on the cities and homes of nations at war.

Russian and American behavior before 1949 might show that air power had given the United States a unilateral advantage of only moderate strength; the hydrogen bomb could now conjure up a more symmetrical distribution of enormous destructive strength. If symmetry was inevitable, or if it wasn't, the procurement policies of the early 1950's might also now be manipulated to keep this enormous destructive strength from emerging, i.e., to keep the skeptical assumptions of the late 1940's from losing all their validity. At least some participants in the American decision-making process now had seen this to be desirable.

The Technologically Determined Decision

Some additional measures had now indeed been taken to bolster American air defenses. An agreement was negotiated with the Canadian government for the "Pine-Tree" line of radar stations ranging along the U.S.-Canadian border. Newer radar-equipped jet interceptors were procured, an Anti-Aircraft Command was organized in the Army, and an Air Defense Command was reestablished separate from the Continental Air Command in the Air Force. Work was under way on the development of the Nike interceptor missile and, late in 1950, President Truman for the first time authorized the actual interception of unidentified aircraft.[31] The danger that Soviet bombers might penetrate at low altitudes, shielded from such radars by the earth's curvature, required the establishment of a Ground Observer Corps in the United States and Canada—which, however, never drew enough volunteers to become really effective.[32]

Yet such American air defense as was provided might never be effective enough to satisfy the population-protection goal outlined above. Until 1950, air defense plans had still been based on radar warning and aircraft guidance, as in Great Britain in 1940, with visual target identification by the intercepting aircraft, and the use of anti-aircraft artillery around immediately defended sites.[33] The development of high-speed jet bombers, comparable with the American B-47, would raise difficulties for this form of defense, requiring much more reliance on radar and rocket-powered interceptor missiles, rather than artillery, for making the kill. If insufficient countermeasures were taken, Soviet strategic strike capabilities would inevitably increase. In support of its arguments for population defenses, an American Civil Defense Summer Study of 1952 conjectured that the Russians would have over 130 nuclear warheads by 1953, 200 by 1954, and about 270 by 1955;[34] another estimate published in 1951 credited the U.S.S.R. with an existing stockpile of 60 weapons.[35] A program of population warning and preparations for mass evacuation was thus urged, since Soviet bombers presumably would be aimed at American cities, at least as collaterals to industrial targets and perhaps as prime targets.

Much larger programs, involving multibillion-dollar radar nets across the northern reaches of Canada, coupled to sophisticated communication and interceptor guidance systems, were thus urged now by air defense proponents.[36] But any appropriation of funds for such programs would inevitably come more slowly, perhaps too slowly to beat the offensive capabilities being developed. Civilian scientists were often reluctant to commit themselves to any high effectiveness figures for their proposed air defense systems, accusing their opponents of falsely asserting that unrealistically high protection rates had been promised. Yet the implicit tone of their arguments was that some significant portion of incoming bombers could be detected and intercepted, for anything less than 70 percent interception would have made little difference to the populations of cities under attack, if the Soviets programmed more than one bomber for each major American city. Air Force officers charged with air defense typically offered a far lower interception rate, in the neighborhood of 25 to 30 percent,[37] thus implicitly suggesting that the major value of the system was in generating warning to get SAC bombers aloft (and perhaps to accomplish some city evacuation), rather than actual interception.

If the retaliatory force on an American bomber base would someday become absolutely significant, then that very base would become an absolutely significant target. There were thus already some analysts within the Air Force to argue that the primary, or perhaps only, object for air defense might soon become the alerting and protecting of the American retaliatory nuclear strike force itself.[38] Advocates of population defense, such as J. Robert Oppenheimer, castigated this as an inhuman or foolishly pessimistic position:

> A second example may illustrate further. A high officer of the Air Defense Command said—and this only a few months ago, in a most serious discussion of measures for the continental defense of the United States—that it was our policy to attempt to protect our striking force, but that it was not really our policy to attempt to protect this country, for that is so big a job that it would interfere with our retaliatory capabilities. Such follies can occur only when even the men who know the facts can find no one to talk to about them, when the facts are too secret for discussion, and thus for thought.[39]

If the full-scale air defense system were to produce the benefits its proponents sought, it thus had to be implemented before H-bomb forces had been deployed. In effect, there was a race between the funding and deployment of population-protecting air defense equipment, on the one hand, and Soviet and American progress in the development of the hydrogen bomb and jet bombers, on the other. The President's decision to go ahead with the bomb in 1950 had not been a final defeat for the defense advocates; but the "Greenhouse" preliminary nuclear tests of 1951 and the actual H-bomb detonation of 1952 were more serious setbacks,[40] showing perhaps that "nature" was on the offensive-weapons side, since any big program of early-warning radar and jet interceptor protection had still only reached the proposal stage.

The Korean War, which had highlighted the feasibility of air defense, now also served for the short run to weaken the continental air defense programs, perhaps for both the super powers. The commitment of Soviet air defense aircraft to the Korean theater grew quite large after the winter of 1950-1951, nominally because part of the Communist Chinese Air Force, based in Manchuria, was flying air patrols over North Korea. This commitment of aircraft had the apparent intention of forcing American bombers out of their long-range missions, thus allowing an establishment of Communist advance bases in Korea, from which then to achieve a tactical air superiority over the front lines. The Russians may thus have been reducing the defensive capabilities of their protective net for the U.S.S.R. itself; in any event, the Soviet commitment to Korea forced the United States to reciprocate, and air defense fighters programmed for continental defense several times were dispatched instead to the Far East to forestall the establishment of a decisive Chinese force there.[41] By draining off interceptor fighters, the Korean War thus might temporarily extend existing bombers' effectiveness on both sides, making the American B-36's penetration problem easier in 1951, as well as that of the Russian Tu-4.

The Soviet Union of course had begun a massive air defense program first, perhaps supplying some of the stimulus for the American scientific community's interest in such a program, and some of the hope that the Russians might be induced to shift their military emphasis still further in this direction (apparent parallels to the present of course come to mind). Yet if anyone had suspected that offensive military establishments would not hold themselves back, as defensive walls were erected against them, he could confirm this now in the anxiety of the U.S. Air Force leadership to get a second generation of jet bombers (and the hydrogen bomb) to reinsure its destructive capabilities. In the race to head off a reliance on overkill, perhaps the most direct and threatening opponents for the defense-minded scientists would be the U.S. Air Force planners themselves. If the Administration could be won over, such opposition could be overcome, for the military determined weapons policy no more independently in the United States than in the Soviet Union; but if the Administration were more ambivalent, no move towards an all-defense posture was possible.

American opponents of H-bomb strategic forces might logically have approved the erection of a Soviet air defense screen, presumably parallel in time and in effectiveness with that advocated for the United States; such a screen would have been somewhat unsettling, however, for those charged with maintaining the American deterrent. The very long-range B-36 did not differ drastically from the B-29 in speed and altitude capabilities, and its ability to penetrate fighter defenses had been challenged in 1949 in the "revolt of the admirals," with the suggestion that Navy jet interceptors be given a chance to demonstrate their superiority over the B-36. The news of the B-29's vulnerability in Korea thus reflected on the B-36, confirming the fear that a bomber of much superior performance would soon be required, with a coupled sacrifice of range.

If the United States had looked forward, on various arguments, to expanding its strategic force on a substantially North American basing, the obsolescence of the B-36 frustrated such plans. Russian air defenses would threaten all the propeller-driven bombers of SAC, the B-29 as well as the B-36, but a substitute for the medium-range B-29 promised to be available in the all-jet B-47. The addition of four jet engines to the six piston engines of the B-36 might serve as an expedient to maintain its intercontinental-range penetration capability for a short time, but after some time no viable long-range bomber would be at hand, and (at least until the B-52 was developed years later) overseas bases would again be required.

A continued or expanded reliance on overseas bases for the augmentation of SAC's capability had its difficulties too. An increase in the number of such bases might be psychologically threatening to the U.S.S.R., and would require greater Western activism to insure the acquisition and control of such bases. Neutral or moderately pro-Russian regimes otherwise tolerable in North Africa or Asia might now raise new dilemmas for the United States if they withheld the bases upon which the prevention of a Soviet take-over of Europe seemed all the more to depend. Even bases in Britain might have their cost, in requiring greater concern for British desires on various issues; for better or worse, the United States' hands might thus be tied by the absence of an intercontinental delivery system. For better, the U.S. commitment might be clarified for some areas it desired to shield in any event; for worse, it might become committed to less apparently valuable areas, merely to hold on to necessary air bases.

If the Russians had been interested in an acquisition of Europe per se, they might thus have been well-advised not to challenge the efficacy of American intercontinental weapons systems, as they did by erecting air defenses in the late 1940's (or again by outflanking the B-52 in the late 1950's move to missiles). There was clearly a latent American aversion to commitments to Europe, reinforced slightly by an American Air Force relish for the technological elegance of weapons not requiring overseas bases. Other factors of course fostered an American attachment to Europe, and any Soviet forward progress would have required great subtlety, in addition to recognition of the military factors cited above; but the American need for air bases in and around Europe may yet have fortified a commitment that otherwise could have come into doubt.

Yet there were also rational arguments for the Soviet air defense deployment. If air defenses now cast doubt on the penetration capability of American intercontinental-range bombers, this presumably enhanced the significance of Soviet Tu-4 medium bomber strikes against B-29 and B-47 bases in Britain, even if only with conventional weapons. Aside from the political aspects of American bases in Europe, Soviet interference with intercontinental options could thus be explained and defended as further reducing the American ability to attack Russia, while not augmenting the Russian ability to attack the United States. Again, this presumed that many repeated air attacks were required in either direction for any politically or militarily significant results. If the United States believed that only a few nuclear attacks could be decisive, or thought that the Russians believed this, then Soviet air defenses would be less significant, while the Soviet Tu-4 intercontinental "suicide mission" might be a serious "offensive" threat. If skepticism were more general, then Soviet air defense would be important, at least because it gave the Soviet bomber force an important "defensive" role.

If the Russians were insecure, moreover, as to their ability to deter American air strikes against the U.S.S.R., it might have been to their interest to enhance American commitment to Western Europe, either by making the United States dependent for its own purposes on military bases there, or in less military ways. To hold a hostage in Western Europe, the Soviets presumably had to keep the United States committed to, and in interaction with, that hostage. It is thus difficult to isolate any clear Soviet attitude over this period on the American presence in Europe; Soviet propaganda attacking this presence is by itself not definitive, since embarrassing the Americans may have seemed very tempting once they seemed surely committed.

An American crash program of overseas base construction was thus initiated after the outbreak of the Korean War, with bases opened in French Morocco during 1951 and in Spain by 1954, while runways were lengthened in Britain and Guam.[42] Negotiations for bases in other countries were not always successful. The random B-29 deployments to Europe now were replaced by more regular deployments of B-36's (and after 1951, of B-47's) to bases less immediately vulnerable to the ground forces of the Red Army. Air refueling techniques were introduced after having been tested experimentally from 1948 to 1950, and a fleet of KC-97 tankers was procured; perhaps this would enable some B-47's to reach Soviet targets directly from the United States, or at least would facilitate penetration of Soviet defenses from all geographic directions.[43] The American reliance on potentially neutralizable overseas bases could not be seen simply as a temporary stopgap now, for the bases and B-47's to use them cost a great deal and might hold back expenditures on parallel intercontinental systems. Projects for the B-52 long-range jet replacement for the B-36 thus were not to be accelerated,[44] but were still approved only as a backup, in case the B-47 should prove incapable of carrying the H-bomb.

The objections of the Air Force command to proposals for an American air defense system thus came at several levels. First, the likely conflict between future expenditures for air defense and for strategic offensive vehicles was clear to Air Force planners, as it would have to be to anyone familiar with the workings of the American budgetary process. If an extensive air defense system thus soaked up funds and further delayed production of the B-52, the Air Force would generally oppose it. Second, the psychology which the defense advocates hoped to instill, involving mutual physical security against attack, was not very congenial to Air Force officers, especially if they were not convinced that Europe could otherwise be held on the battlefield. The Air Force referred here to a Maginot Line psychology,[45] implying both that the air defense might be as unreliable as the Maginot Line and, more subtly, that as France had neglected to protect its allies, so the United States might also fail to protect its associates, even if the air defense system were effective.

As the hydrogen bomb seemed more imminent and feasible in 1952, hopes faded that such bombs would prove impossible or infinitely delayable; yet it seemed that an addiction of the two political publics to overkill might still perhaps be forestalled. Opponents of the offensive air emphasis at this point urged a "no-first-test" policy, in which the United States would promise not to test any fusion bombs unless the Russians did.[46] In such a moratorium, the prospect of overkill might still be left in some doubt, and the hope of population defense kept alive, with the rush to large counterpopulation offensive forces thus being forestalled.

The Truman Administration rejected the no-first-test proposal, as the AEC moved ahead with its plans to detonate the world's first hydrogen device in early November. It did make a point, however, of not announcing the first hydrogen-bomb test to the world,[47] and several explanations are possible for this. The closeness to the 1952 election was of course significant (the test was in fact executed three days before the election, but the exact date necessarily had to be determined by meteorological considerations); any announcement just before the election might have seemed to be politically inspired, while an announcement immediately after might also have seemed intended to draw attention away from the Republican victory. Yet other possibilities remain. The Truman Administration had been under pressure not to develop or produce the bomb, then not to test it, and now perhaps not to make a big splash in publicizing the test; it may at last have partially accepted the argument that world public opinion would not view great destructive capabilities as part of the natural order of things. Perhaps the Soviet Union thus could also be dissuaded from development, or from tests, or from provocative publicity.

Yet the test of a weapon of such magnitude was inevitably difficult to conceal, and the news in fact leaked out within a few weeks.[48] In his final State of the Union Message, therefore, President Truman cited the new bomb as opening a qualitatively different era of destructive power.

The Proliferation Issue

Few Americans would propose a deliberate development or stimulation of friendly national nuclear forces, now that the Russians had broken the monopoly; yet the issue of nuclear proliferation would arise at least tangentially, since additional American bomber bases were required on foreign territory abroad. Bringing Allied governments into the process of nuclear decision-making might, moreover, have some desirable effects, as well as undesirable.

If one assumed that substantial conventional efforts were required as part of any extended war or confrontation with the U.S.S.R., then Allied participation in such efforts might be more likely if Britain or France were already involved in the nuclear portion of the confrontation as well. If repeated air strikes, even with nuclear weapons, were required as part of a long attrition process, then the participation of British air crews (flying British or American bombers, perhaps carrying American atomic bombs) might also be welcome, as would the availability of additional air bases in East Anglia or French Morocco. The proximity of other governments to American nuclear equipment might thus serve as a token of commitment in both directions, while also offering practical advantages for the more plausible war scenarios.

Objections to proliferation of course dated from the Truman secrecy statement of 1945 and the Atomic Energy Act of 1946, so that the legal obstacles to any outright sharing of nuclear weapons or technology would be difficult to overcome, even where various echelons of the American government were so inclined, as in the case of Great Britain. Denying access to all foreign powers had seemed wise in 1946, for it apparently raised American foreign policy to a level of abstract principle which did not have to distinguish between friend and foe when denying nuclear weaponry to the U.S.S.R. or other powers. Even if the Russians had now broken the monopoly, it might be too early for the United States to adopt a more flexible standard; aid to Britain but not to France, for example, might cause more alliance problems than total denial of aid. In September of 1949 some 81 percent of Americans polled opposed deployments giving allies access to U.S. nuclear stockpiles.[49]

The American dependence on British and French bases might of course induce certain tendencies toward de facto proliferation, as well as suggesting some veto by foreign governments on American recourse to its own national nuclear capability. Psychologically, at least some of the American yearning (particularly in the Air Force) for an intercontinental delivery capability may have stemmed from the latter consideration. While the use of such weapons against targets in the Soviet Union would be largely acceptable to Britain and France in the event of a Russian attack on Western Europe, such countries might not approve nuclears for more marginal cases—for example, in Korea or Indochina. Vestigial remnants of a "no first-use" agreement existed in the Churchill-Roosevelt understanding initialed at the Quebec conference of 1943, which pledged the United States and Britain never to use atomic weapons against each other, or against any other power without each other's consent.[50] While the British government had naturally enough been reluctant to declare such an agreement obsolete, since it included other provisions for the sharing of gains from nuclear research, the 1948 Truman-Attlee air base agreement had given Great Britain a veto only on operations from British bases,[51] thus by implication excluding the more general veto; consultation on any question as important as the initiation of nuclear warfare nonetheless was understood.

American attitudes on a British acquisition of nuclear weapons were influenced by several factors which confused any parallels with later cases of proliferation, or with the Soviet acquisition of nuclears. Aside from the "special relationship" thought to exist between the two English-speaking powers, an impression was widely held (if perhaps somewhat inaccurately) that British physicists had made significant and indispensable contributions to a joint 1940-1945 effort producing the first American bombs. If the United States had decided to hold the bomb as a national asset after the war, it might thus have been simply to avoid precedents justifying the Russians in asking for the bomb also. Justice, in this view, entitled the British to share in this weaponry, since only political realities had precluded the United States from repaying British scientists with American assistance; if the United Kingdom had gone ahead to get the bomb (perhaps even before the Russians got theirs), this would be just and perhaps desirable, as long as no form of internationalization was likely to be adopted.

The chances of a British nuclear force being seen as a threat to the United States were also enormously lessened after 1948 with the stationing of American bombers in Britain, thus for the time making the scenario of a war between the United States and the United Kingdom ludicrous. American support for a British nuclear capability, at least at the administration level, was now illustrated, moreover, by a decision to give some 70 B-29's to the RAF after 1950,[52] bombers which probably would have less real value if they were not to carry nuclear weapons. Prospects emerged in 1949 for a formal agreement assigning Britain a supply of nuclear weapons in the event of any war fought jointly by the United States and Britain,[53] but Congressional objections, stimulated again by espionage cases involving scientists resident in Britain, made difficult, for the time being, the necessary amendments to the Atomic Energy Act. Nonetheless, the implication was that means would have been found to deliver some nuclear weapons into the custody of the RAF, for use by the B-29 bomber force, if a war involving Britain against the Soviet Union had become imminent.

One of the more persuasive arguments against assisting or tolerating a British nuclear capability had perhaps disappeared in part with the 1949 Soviet test. Many Americans had argued straightforwardly that Britain was not objectionable per se as the second nuclear power, but that the risk of nuclear espionage and security leaks would then be substantially greater, so that the Soviets might acquire the bomb sooner thereafter. Similar arguments would be extensively cited against sharing nuclear information with France in the late 1950's, even after the Russians had tested atomic and hydrogen bombs, and espionage would be an objection to proliferation within the alliance for as long as there still seemed to be some nuclear discoveries for the U.S.S.R. to make.

Another factor legitimizing British nuclear progress to American eyes was the ownership by British companies of much of the Belgian

Congo's uranium supply, upon which the United States found itself significantly dependent during the later 1940's.[54] While the desire for a sharing of nuclear information at first glance seems to place the United Kingdom in a supplicant role, the apparent shortage of weapons in American stockpiles in fact may have placed the United States in this position; if Britain did not voluntarily relinquish a substantial portion of the Congo's production, the American stockpile might not grow to anything adequate for the strategic burdens it had to carry.

Rather than bargaining closely on the exchange of uranium for nuclear technology, the British chose instead to acknowledge a "public interest" for the West that the American stockpile be augmented as expeditiously as possible, for the protection of all the Western powers. By assuming such a posture, the British not only fortified their own claim to an ultimate nuclear capability, but reinforced the sense that the United States was already reciprocally committed to the defense of Britain and of Western Europe.

While the British Labour Party's handling of nuclear questions was several times criticized by Winston Churchill as leader of the opposition prior to 1951, after assuming office Churchill stated that he was quite satisfied with the Labour Government's efforts.[55] Yet it is not clear that the British Government had done all it could to produce an independent nuclear stockpile, given the expertise at its disposal after World War II. It could be argued, moreover, that British slowness to generate an independent program was a political and strategic mistake, such that Churchill's 1949 lamentation of Britain's failure to beat the Russians to the second nuclear power slot was well taken.

Britain, of course, may have had good reason to expect to share in American weapons capabilities on the basis of World War II arrangements, so that the American Atomic Energy Act of 1946 had come as a shock in its clear exclusion of Britain from access to weapons or data. For Britain to acquire weapons next after the United States might have been politically unwise, moreover, simply because it might have phrased too many hypothetical discussions of nuclear duopoly in terms of wars or confrontations between the United States and Britain. Abstract discussions of this sort might always be taken too seriously, as the Anglo-American "naval arms race" of 1918-1922 had proved. Yet it might at least have been to Britain's advantage to be prepared to detonate one or several bombs immediately after the Russians tested theirs first, to undermine the Russian accomplishment on behalf of the West and on behalf of Britain. Here again, overly sanguine estimates of the slowness of any Russian program may have led the British to expect a Russian test perhaps only in 1951.

Finally, the British slowness in nuclear weapons development after 1945 was due largely to economic burdens, in real and balance-of-payments terms, that Great Britain would have to bear at least until 1949. Even if no American assistance whatsoever had been alienated by a British move towards a nuclear capability at this time—and indeed such alienation may have been unlikely—national economic priorities might require that the weapons program should wait a while—quite a different set of priorities from those seen in the U.S.S.R., presumably also under economic constraints. As it was, then, the British nuclear energy project succeeded in setting off its first A-bomb detonation on October 13, 1952, as the Truman Administration was drawing to a close. The British entry into the nuclear club did not draw any large or adverse reaction from the two previous members; such a reaction would in any event have been overshadowed by the world's first hydrogen bomb test, which occurred a little more than two weeks later.

3   The New Look: 1953-1957

New Opportunities and Preferences

The Republican Eisenhower Administration brought in a preference for fiscal economy in 1953, a preference to be both furthered and frustrated by advances in weapons technology. The acquisition of the hydrogen bomb might at last have constituted the absolute weapon: its use possibly could cripple any opposing military force, and it certainly might impose such awesome suffering as to deter any aggression, or even to force any surrender. When coupled to the tremendous expansion in American stockpiles of ordinary atomic bombs, to the development of small tactical nuclear explosives, to the augmentation of NATO forces, and to the continuing American superiority in nuclear weapons delivery systems, it might have generated a peak of politically negotiable military power, just as the new Administration was coming into office.

One could thus have cashed in on the power position of 1953 in different ways. As one possibility, taxes and defense expenditures might be reduced in an absolute reliance on the new deterrent, perhaps establishing a psychological climate of balance to persist even after the U.S.S.R. had acquired H-bombs also. At the opposite extreme, a series of ultimata might have been presented to the Soviet Union, designed to force a rollback of the Red Army's advanced position, presumably thus freeing the satellites and reunifying Germany, with a threat of preventive war if the ultimata were not obeyed.

The Eisenhower Administration rejected the latter alternative and moved toward the former. The 1952 election campaign had been phrased in terms which seemed to require an early review of American defense policy as a whole, with consideration even of the more drastic alternatives. At the "Solarium Conference" convened in May of 1953, three broad possibilities were thus presented for consideration, while a fourth was raised but quickly dismissed.[1] The three were (1) containment as practiced in the Truman years, (2) massive retaliation to be invoked automatically if a certain line were crossed, and (3) active liberation operations to foment insurrection in the Russian satellites. A fourth alternative called for intense negotiations with the Russians during the anticipated period in which they would not have their own H-bomb, with a firm deadline and a threat of drastic action thereafter if Western demands were not met; this proposal, coming closest to the preventive war arguments, was rejected, while the other three were left open to further discussion.[2] The expectation behind the toughest proposal, of another two-year grace period in which the Russians would not acquire thermonuclear weapons (and would not acquire large stockpiles of ordinary atomic bombs), would, moreover, be proved overly optimistic.

American embarkation on a preventive war campaign was unlikely in any event, since President Eisenhower persistently refused to permit open governmental discussion of the option, characterizing it as contrary to all American principles and traditions.[3] Whether or not such statements served as reassuring signals to the Russians, the Republicans' special attachment to constitutional procedure, and to an Executive sharing of power with the Congress, presumably also precluded the quiet planning and secret coordination of a preventive strategic first strike. A Congressional declaration of war, and an escalation to all-out war, might be fairly likely in the event of a major Russian incursion into Europe, but in the absence of a provocation as salient as this, the need for formal constitutional processes precluded any drastic action. Thus in the Quemoy-Matsu crisis of 1954-1955, President Eisenhower went to the trouble of securing a Congressional resolution authorizing some defense of the islands,[4] in part in an implicit criticism of Truman's failure to take similar steps in the Korean War, but also in part because of genuine constitutional scruples. The stiffness of Republican constitutionalism thus might combine with the inflexibility of massive weapons to reinforce a single message: that the United States would not initiate violent attempts to alter the territorial status quo, but might react with instruments as extreme as an H-bomb if the Soviet Union initiated such attempts.

It is possible that no serious consideration had been given to the operational mechanics of a preemptive or preventive first strike at the U.S.S.R. prior to 1949. With the buildup of SAC after 1948, however, and the accumulation of target intelligence and maneuver experience, such planning almost inevitably had to come forward, since SAC's duties in the event of war would include at least some strikes at its Russian equivalent. If any reliable intelligence about Soviet nuclear weapons production and storage facilities was at hand, the ideal time for such a preventive war presumably might thus have emerged about 1953, perhaps just before the Russian H-bomb test, when little or no damage could have been inflicted on the United States in retaliation, despite the lack of active defenses in North America. General LeMay states in his memoirs that this possibility was salient at SAC head-quarters at the time, as well as at Air Force headquarters, but that as far as he knows, no clear proposal of this option was conveyed to the President.[5]

Yet the American hydrogen-device test of 1952 had not established any immediate capability for inflicting high levels of destruction in a general war. The first bomb small enough to be delivered by the B-52 would not be tested until 1954, with the first test actually using a B-52 coming only in 1956.[6] Even here, the bomb presumably had not yet been miniaturized sufficiently to fit the bomb bay of the medium-range B-47, which still constituted the bulk of the U.S. strategic delivery force.[7] Production of hydrogen bombs still came slowly in the early stages, moreover, although after a time a process was begun of converting atomic bombs already in existence to hydrogen bombs.

While the hydrogen bomb clearly would ultimately give the United States a convincing massive retaliation instrument, the A-bomb might have sufficed for this purpose. John Foster Dulles had talked of massive retaliation as early as February of 1952, before the H-bomb had been tested anywhere in the world, before the presidential election campaign had in fact really been launched in the United States.[8] The production of atomic bombs had of course been stepped up substantially in 1951, and impressions of nuclear scarcity were being replaced by images of large stockpiles with thousands of bombs, each considerably more powerful than those dropped on Hiroshima and Nagasaki. Yet the hydrogen bomb program had officially been launched in the United States, and reports had already been circulated on how large an explosion one might expect from such devices. Americans in general expected that such bombs were feasible, and that it would be only a matter of time before they were developed. Had the possibility of such weapons not been leaked in 1949, it perhaps would have been more difficult for the future Secretary of State to begin talking in terms of massive retaliation as early as he did.

Yet if preventive war had been at all in the air, the U.S.S.R. would quickly enough have its big bomb also. The Soviet Union carried out its first H-test, but apparently of a more plausibly deliverable bomb than the United States', in August of 1953. The first American test of what was plausibly a deliverable bomb came in 1954, followed by the first Soviet air-dropped test in November of 1955, and then the first American air-dropped test in May of 1956.[9] The closeness of this race, which the Soviets in some sense "won," could have been quite upsetting. At any rate it was surprising.

While the Soviet A-bomb test detected in 1949 convinced the bulk of the American scientific and political public that a Russian nuclear capability existed, no more Russian tests were detected until 1951, when two more explosions were recorded, and then again no more until the test of the Russian hydrogen device in late 1953. The small number of Soviet atomic bomb tests recorded in these first four years (Great Britain, with two, had almost caught up, while the United States had already set off 42)[10] might be explained several ways. First, the Russians may have tested more devices or bombs that were undetected by the United States; such a view is consistent with the possibility that the Russians had already developed and tested a bomb earlier than late 1949. Second, Stalin may have desired to lull the West into inactivity while he accumulated a larger stockpile of A-bombs or developed the H-bomb, and he may thus have withheld approval of weapons tests. Third and conversely, the Russians may have been experiencing difficulty in mass-producing nuclear weapons, perhaps having chosen inefficient production processes, as had the United States at times during the World War II crash program. The last explanation perhaps accounts for the persistent willingness of many Americans to deny any real weapons accomplishment on the part of the Russians, and even for President Truman's mysterious skepticism upon leaving office in 1953;[11] but the early Soviet possession of the H-bomb seemingly makes it far less satisfactory as an explanation today.

It was of course not obvious that the Soviets could have "won the H-bomb race" in any significant sense. If the Russians were seeking a dominant countervalue instrument, the significant variable might be the number of delivery vehicles, multiplied by the destructiveness of the warhead attached to each vehicle; here the United States always had to seem in the race, given the post-1951 nuclear plenty and a far larger round-trip delivery capability. With regard to the option of a significant counterforce capability against U.S. bombers on their bases, the Soviets would have had to produce enough deliverable hydrogen bombs to scatter across these bases; given all the uncertainties involved, and the fact that the United States was not very far behind the Soviets in packaging its hydrogen bomb into a deliverable form, it is not clear that the Soviets could have achieved anything substantial here either. Yet similar considerations in reverse had quickly kept the new American Administration from giving serious consideration to any preventive war solution.

The three major "Solarium" proposals had been delegated to separate task forces which submitted reports during June and July of 1953.[12] The Planning Board of the National Security Council was then charged with sifting the strongest ideas out of the three reports and combining them into a single policy paper. The final outcome, NSC-162, settled for a continuation of containment (i.e., giving up ideas of liberation and rollback), but with a shift towards massive retaliation as the means of thus holding the line.

With regard to stabilizing territorial tenure against the general threat of Soviet ground aggression, the solution proposed in NSC-68 was of course still available: namely, to buy a defense of Europe and Asia by augmented conventional ground forces, to complete the balance at the tactical level, since the Soviets now might match the United States at the strategic level. Yet the financial cost of such a program was extremely distasteful to a Republican Party just elected on a platform of reducing government expenditures. Hence the new administration became not a little enthusiastic about applying the nuclear weapons unveiled in tests since 1951. The awesomeness of the hydrogen-bomb stockpile now to be assembled promised to stabilize the tactical balance as the atomic bomb never had. It certainly seemed more plausible that the Soviet Union would in the future be deterred from seizing Europe or other vulnerable and valuable portions of the world by the knowledge that hydrogen bombs delivered in any escalation to all-out war could kill a large part of its population.

The willingness to rely on less expensively procured massive-retaliation weapons to stabilize the containment of Russian power was not only to be found among American Republicans, however. In 1952, the British Government had reached the very similar conclusions that the massive destructive power of the new thermonuclear weapons should allow a lowering of NATO force goals, since Russian ground force aggression could be deterred by prospects of battlefield defeat.[13] While the American Joint Chiefs of Staff under President Truman had apparently rejected this as rationalization for a British reluctance to meet commitments (General Bradley especially seems to have accepted this interpretation), the idea was parallel to arguments already finding their way into speeches of John Foster Dulles, and then of the Republican presidential candidate Dwight Eisenhower.

The new "massive retaliation" doctrine has often been portrayed simply as a misguided extension of Truman's European deterrent policies to areas of Asia where they might not be as plausible. Yet the doctrine in fact may have been presented primarily for its relevance to Europe, for it now coincided with the more explicit suspension of the Lisbon Goals, which would have provided far larger reserves of conventional forces for NATO. To the extent that the doctrine owed anything to the British military leadership for inspiration, it was thus focused on Europe more than on peripheral areas. The relationship to Asia is perhaps more easily derived from Secretary Dulles' address of January, 1954, which included the phraseology of the doctrine's label.[14] Yet the defense procurement policies implemented by the Eisenhower Administration in the summer and fall of 1953 were already fully consistent with this new reliance on the strategic level to balance the tactical; one could as easily argue that the doctrine had been defined then.

If the world had come to know the hydrogen bomb as a weapon that made general war unbearable, then the United States might hope (and offer) to stabilize the world's political complexion by citing the threat of escalation to such unbearable war. A logical problem would remain, however, of how American escalation to such war could be credible, if the war were presumably now as unbearable for Americans as for anyone else.

Even if the U.S.S.R. had bombed American cities, some might argue that a full-scale American counterattack could no longer be rational. It would do the United States little or no good to kill millions of Russians just because millions of Americans had been killed; perhaps it would bring increased harm, since Soviet cities might be the primary source of relief supplies for the American survivors. How much more, then, would such a response lose its credibility for a Communist attack on Berlin, or Hamburg, or Indochina?

Some such external credibility might be retained in a doctrinal lag, feigned or real. The shift from "long war of attrition" calculations to "horrendous spasm war" was desirable in that it might conclusively frighten the Russians on the size of an American attack; but some continued discussion of wars of industrial attrition (with hydrogen bombs slowly doing the attrition) might make attacks on Russian cities seem still purposeful and rational for Americans, and thus credible. For deterrent purposes or otherwise, American descriptions of future wars thus continued, even after the H-bomb tests, to talk of destruction of enemy war production.

Vehement assertions of American moral commitment, "to carry through one's word," etc., might similarly make American retaliation more credible, even where such retaliation would never physically benefit the United States. The mere presence of American young men in the area, potentially to be involved and wounded on the battlefield, might promise to excite a maximum military effort by the United States. Treaties formally negotiated and ratified similarly could couple American escalation to the defense of less crucial areas.

A third major possibility involved the further development and deployment of tactical nuclear weapons. Less doubt might arise over time about an American administration's willingness to initiate the use of such "local war" weapons, and this had in part been one of the arguments offered for their development in studies such as "Project Vista." The use of tactical nuclears would seem immediately rational if they were assumed to favor the defense. Hence they might balance the tactical battlefield situation as much as large NATO conventional force buildups. Admittedly they would destroy a larger part of the territory being defended, but this made the prospect of territorial gain less attractive for the Soviets. Battlefield casualties would be greater, moreover, with a concomitant reduction in Soviet willingness to attack. Yet the threat of escalation from local tactical-nuclear war to general hydrogen bomb war would be considerable, as intended targets were missed and new land areas or categories of targets were blighted, as the qualitative firebreak of nuclear weapons was crossed; and this served thus to make an American "massive retaliation" additionally credible for the defense of any area to which tactical nuclear weapons had already been deployed.

While all such explanations of America's likely escalation to nuclear war would be valid, it would have been counterproductive for the United States to advertise a full and sophisticated understanding of them. The Republican Administration did not therefore, in this period, ever really confess that its commitment to Europe was in any doubt, or that tactical nuclear weapons were required as some sort of trip wire for a doomsday machine. Rather, tactical nuclear weapons were interpreted as contributing to holding the Russians out of Europe, presumably while the SAC assault equally straightforwardly held up its end on war-of-attrition arguments.

Secretary of State John Foster Dulles in January of 1954 thus presented what has become known as his "massive retaliation" doctrine, making explicit what had purportedly become policy for the American defense of Europe and Asia. Without specifying whether the American willingness to do so depended on operational considerations of military superiority or on moral commitment, Dulles asserted that conventional attacks on allies of the United States might be met by nuclear air strikes at the countries originating these attacks. This presumably was intended to prevent future Koreas and to inhibit the Chinese Communists from active intervention in Indochina, as well as to shield the NATO countries and West Berlin. The attempt to extend the deterrent had in fact emerged in 1953, with warnings to the Chinese Communists that nuclear weapons might be used if they did not terminate the Korean War,[15] and with the deployment of missiles to Okinawa capable of delivering nuclear warheads to Chinese targets.

The status quo thus would presumably be crystallized, but now perhaps for both sides. Although the Republican Party had alluded to "liberation of the satellites" in its successful election campaign, no significant move now came in this direction. The earliest test came with the riots in East Berlin and throughout East Germany in the summer of 1953, shortly after the death of Stalin. While the Western powers might have threatened to intervene militarily in East Germany under various circumstances, the United States was careful to assure the Russians that nothing of the sort was in question,[16] and to discourage West German or West Berlin assistance to, or participation in, the rioting. If later evidence that Soviet Secret Police chief Beria had suggested abandoning East Germany to the West at this point is to be believed,[17] the Republicans may possibly have missed a significant opportunity; but the risk of war in any real American attempt at interference would then have seemed great.

The one force deployment that might have seemed consistent with a "liberation" policy after 1953 was the administration's tolerance of Nationalist Chinese forces on various islands off the Chinese mainland.[18] The Nationalist hold on these islands had gone essentially unnoticed in the last years of the Truman Administration, and was now tolerated by the Republicans, as Chiang was ceremoniously "unleashed." Yet it is doubtful that any serious thought was given to assisting a Nationalist landing on the mainland, especially after the Korean War was terminated. Quemoy, Matsu, and the Tachens may thus have had only the symbolic value of West Berlin (with some of the ensuing threat of armed hostilities).

The "massive retaliation" balance of power the Republicans now claimed to be establishing might thus be politically smoother than the asymmetrical pre-1949 balance. Stabilizing the confrontation at the tactical level itself had been rejected because of its great economic costs. But a more intensive bomber and missile race, as urged by some other segments of the Democratic opposition, was also rejected. At all levels, the Republicans now would express contentment with the power of their new weaponry and a willingness to forgo arms races.

The Republicans chose at first to attack Truman's defense planning as having aimed at a single "year of maximum risk" while ignoring the "long haul," but there was not much substance to this specification of the issue. The Democratic program for arms augmentation had not been planned to peak and then fall off in terms of defense effectiveness, but rather was intended to reach some high level of military power which would remain stable thereafter.[19] The year of maximum risk had somewhat fortuitously coincided with the projected completion of the most important buildup programs, which may indicate that Russian intentions were publicly being assessed with a view to selling these programs to the Congress, rather than on any simple objective analysis of available evidence.

Yet there may have been more than a political campaigner's difference between the Eisenhower "long haul" and Truman "year of maximum risk" concepts, for the Republican interpretation credited the Russians with more patience, and hence less immediate disposition toward violent alterations of the status quo, than had that of the Democrats. Wittingly or otherwise, despite its talk of liberating satellites, the Republican message of 1952 and 1953 could therefore serve as a signal to the Soviet Union that immediate aggression was not anticipated, and that the arms race (in terms of level of expenditures) might be slowed for the present. Similar signals, always couched in terms of reiterating the Republicans' firm opposition to Communism, continued to be transmitted to the Soviets for almost the entire Eisenhower Administration, perhaps primarily as part of the domestic political debate, but always radiating beyond it.

The Response to Hydrogen Weapons

Apart from the operational realities of strategic weapons, both the United States and the Soviet Union had to attach great significance to the responses of their publics, and of other publics, to the reported awesomeness of the new hydrogen bomb. The H-bomb might be interpreted as making war unacceptable, and therefore unlikely, in a sense in which Dresden and Hiroshima had not yet been interpreted; conversely, the H-bomb might upset all hopes and plans for civil defense issued on any side since 1945, making publics all the more frightened. For purposes of coupling or uncoupling strategic and tactical situations, such public attitudes might be crucial.

Early in 1953, before the Soviets had tested their own hydrogen bomb, pressure was exerted on President Eisenhower to acquaint the American people with the awesome destructive capabilities of the new hydrogen weapons, some of the pressure coming from various portions of the press, and some from scientists who had opposed the bomb's development from the beginning.[20] Time was running out, but in the liberal view the American public might yet be shocked out of a reliance on super weapons, before the second-generation delivery systems required to beat down Soviet air defense systems were fully procured, before the Russians got their H-bomb, before the political publics had accepted the threat of mutual annihilation as an unpleasant but necessary status quo.

But the new administration saw the problem differently. The world had to be shocked and convinced of the power of hydrogen weapons, but it would be most important that Americans did not become more obsessed with nuclear destruction than were Russians or others, and that they not seem more obsessed. The whole world, including the Russians, must be convinced that war was too horrible for the Soviet Union to contemplate, with any similar American horror coming along behind, hopefully never being quite as explicit.

Perhaps if Adlai Stevenson had won the 1952 election, greater weight might have been given to the argument for avoiding dependence on weapons of mass destruction. Perhaps the Truman Administration's failure to announce the hydrogen bomb test immediately might have held open for Stevenson an option of "no super-bomb legitimacy," an option which might yet be entered into with the Soviets. As it was, information leaks, for whatever reason, had within a matter of weeks eliminated this option, and the Eisenhower Administration now coming to power would probably not have used it anyway.

Drafts of a presidential speech on the hydrogen bomb were prepared and revised numerous times, as the news came in of the first Soviet hydrogen device test in late 1953. In September, Eisenhower apparently turned to the idea of peaceful uses of atomic energy, which might serve as an antidote to the disquieting impact of weapons research.[21] "Operation Candor" thus became "Operation Wheaties," as the full disclosure of hydrogen bomb capabilities was allowed to trickle out only very slowly in the United States, with a less jarring impact on the American public. This "Atoms for Peace" proposal, formulated perhaps as much for its psychological impact as for its substantive value, in fact created other problems for the future by suggesting a more rapid spread of potential for nuclear weapons.

The Soviet H-bomb test, and then the news of a spring, 1954, test of the first American dropable bomb, with its tremendous explosive power and unexpectedly large amounts of radioactive fallout, nonetheless created a certain stir in the United States despite "Operation Wheaties," as when Admiral Strauss told a press conference that one bomb could destroy any city in the United States.[22] Color films of the first U.S. H-device detonation in 1952 were distributed for public showing in April of 1954, but were quietly and quickly called back when American reactions were not as composed as had been hoped;[23] while only 19 percent of Americans interviewed in 1950 had expected man to be wiped out in a future war, 27 percent expressed this view in 1955.[24]

"Atoms for Peace" did not lack a more general substantiation, however, for scientists now saw real economic prospects for peaceful nuclear development, such that underdeveloped nations would be anxious to receive technical assistance. Under such circumstances, the United States might realize at least two immediate foreign policy gains by stimulating national research and power reactor programs. Such programs would tend to legitimate the existence of things nuclear in general, and the American dependence on nuclear weapons in particular. For as long as the U.S.S.R. could not produce nuclear materials as cheaply, moreover, the United States would hold the advantage in trading reactor fuel for neutral nations' friendship. It was recognized that the distribution of such plutonium-producing reactors might allow even backward countries someday to produce atomic bombs; simple prudence, and Congressional pressure, therefore made the American government require bilateral safeguards to control the disposition of nuclear materials, at least until an international body such as the International Atomic Energy Agency (IAEA) could be assigned the task of implementing safeguard procedures.[25]

99

But just as it was to the propaganda advantage of the United States to stimulate demands for nuclear materials, materials the U.S.S.R. could not compete in supplying, it was now to the Soviet advantage to support smaller countries in resisting American or international inspection, even if such inspection inhibited weapons proliferation. Thus, after initially endorsing the principle of IAEA inspection, the Russians supported Indian opposition to such safeguards, and for a time generally deprecated the status of the IAEA.[26] Similarly, when Euratom after 1957 threatened to become a self-sufficient nuclear operation if the safeguard requirement were not relaxed, the United States had to suspend its principle for the European case, perhaps in hopes that less explicit controls might evolve if the NATO alliance fabric were kept whole.[27]

Aside from "Atoms for Peace," another approach to quieting American fears of Soviet H-bombs now arose with population defense. Confronted with the proposals for a large air defense program passed on from the Truman Administration, President Eisenhower had for the time withheld any decision. Three different committees were commissioned over the spring and summer of 1953 to examine the proposals.[28] The Kelly Committee in May seemingly sought to take the wind out of the defense advocates' sails by endorsing a defense program costing considerably less money and by supporting it as a component of a military posture that relied most heavily on retaliatory strength. It condemned overly optimistic estimates of the degree of protection provided by any population defense system. The Bull and Edwards Committees, reporting over the summer, endorsed programs costing considerably greater sums, but the National Security Council again did not endorse any action for the time.

It was not until the Russian hydrogen bomb test of August, 1953, that the administration committed itself; in an apparent paradox, the Soviet hydrogen bomb seemed to decide the Eisenhower Administration on an expanded program of air defense,[29] even though most pre-1953 population defense planning seemed to have been undone by the advent of hydrogen weapons.

First, if the Eisenhower administration wanted to bank on a balance of terror to balance the territorial status quo all around, it would still be important that Americans seem no more intimidated by the H-bomb than Russians were. Since the Soviet Union could control the dissemination of data on the bomb's destructiveness more effectively than the United States could, it was necessary for the United States to engage in some population defense program, if only to reassure Americans and prevent any domestic hysterics (while to some extent hoping for overseas "hysterics"). Honestly or otherwise, the Eisenhower administration now desired (as had the Soviet leadership) to retain some impression that air war could go on for months before it became unbearable. Ideally, it should seem to be unbearable for the other side, but not for one's own, and investments in air defense might serve this purpose at least until H-bombs, or missiles that could surely penetrate any defensive system, were freely available.

Many in the administration were, moreover, sincerely concerned to reduce casualties if war were to come in the immediate future, even if millions of casualties remained. The argument could always be cited (as it is today) of the irrational or undeterrable nation which would attack U.S. cities soon after it became able to do so; to avoid "missing any bets," a certain amount of population defense was thus always "desirable." Active defenses similarly received a boost because dispersal and shelters had been discredited, so that whatever political energy the nation had for the protection of life would have nowhere else to turn. (Even against hydrogen bombs, moreover, air defenses might still be effective for a time to spare a large portion of the American population, given the fact that American bombers might destroy much of the back-up Soviet bomber force in a second strike at its bases; the Russians similarly might not launch a countercity hydrogen bomb attack without programming some weapons against the SAC bases, which could otherwise devastate them in retaliation, and only a portion of the Soviet bomber force might therefore be aimed at U.S. cities.)

Other areas of policy can be cited to support the conclusion that the Republican Administration was burdened by a doctrinal lag in prolonged general wars of attrition, and/or that it was feigning such a lag to maintain American confidence as the world adjusted to a balance of terror. The Department of Defense in 1955 would attempt to force a dispersal of the American aircraft industry away from the Atlantic and Pacific coasts, implying that the fate of American industry was still of significance in the conduct of a future war.[30] Industry spokesmen rebutted such suggestions with reference to the forces-in-being arguments now often emerging from Air Force spokesmen seeking a large air force. Regardless of whether the Defense Department was guilty of a doctrinal lag here, or whether the forces-in-being position was premature, any policy of dispersal would have taken some years to have effect, and by that time might have become useless. Moreover, outside analysts, including several from the RAND Corporation, were prepared to argue that dispersal could make American industry even more vulnerable to air attack,[31] since communications links between various portions of the country would be most vulnerable.

Similarly, the Eisenhower Administration seemed still to be anticipating a prolonged war of attrition in its stockpiling of strategic raw materials. For the first five years of the administration, substantial quantities of certain materials were accumulated, until in 1958 the policy was subjected to review.[32] Faced at last with substantially conflicting estimates of the length of any future war, the administration in effect averaged an extremely short Air Force estimate and the long Army estimate into a compromise prognosis of three years, which made much of the inventory that had been built up immediately surplus and subject to disposal.[33] It is clear that some of the momentum for such a stockpiling program had come originally from raw material producers and the Congressmen representing their districts. The longer estimates of war duration reflected limited-war arguments that Army spokesmen would have difficulty in getting the administration to accept; yet limited wars presumably would not have been so intense as to require the raw materials stockpiled in any event. A substantial part of the American impetus for the program thus stemmed from another source, the priority that President Eisenhower himself had seemed to attach to the program. This may have illustrated a genuine doctrinal misinterpretation, as with the dispersal program; but it may also have been intended to convince the American economic and political public that the relative security of the days of war-of-attrition calculations had not yet been undone.

Air defense systems would now finally be put into place. In 1954 the U.S. Army began to deploy the Nike-Ajax system around American cities, offering some likelihood of intercepting Soviet bombers as they approached their final target. Construction began on the DEW (Distant Early Warning) line across Canada at the beginning of the summer of 1955, to be finished by the end of the 1957 summer, a crash program with the attendant inflated costs and mobilization of public attention.[34] The DEW line would give three hours' warning of a bomber attack, thus allowing the SAC bombers to get aloft before they could be destroyed. After 1958, it was also intended to be plugged into a SAGE system guiding American jet fighters to intercept Soviet bombers at some distance from the target. A seaward extension of the DEW line, composed of radar picket ships and Air Force search radar planes, was also introduced, combined with three "Texas towers," semipermanent radar platforms located off the Atlantic coast.

The expansion of air defenses constituted the Eisenhower Administration's largest and most voluntary augmentation of defense expenditures. Yet any population protection achieved here would necessarily be incomplete and short-lived, with the danger that American resolve would again be cast into doubt once such protection had obviously and dramatically been undone; for research and progress on intercontinental missiles, against which no defense was likely, now seemed very promising.

As in the Soviet Union, the explosive power and fallout of the hydrogen bomb had led scientists in the United States to reexamine the option of the intercontinental missile as a rough countervalue weapon, if not as a precise counterforce instrument. An Air Force Advisory Committee headed by Dr. John von Neumann now concluded that missile CEP's might be brought down to less than five miles;[35] this was acceptable for a counterpopulation retaliatory weapon, and held the advantage that such missiles would be most certain of penetrating Soviet defenses. By 1954 a certain amount of money had been allocated to development of a liquid-fuel missile, the Atlas, as the first intelligence reports of Russian missile experiments began to arrive; but the funding in the United States still did not amount to any crash program, or to what advocates of missile development in the Air Force and in Congress had come to demand.[36]

Given the imminence of moves to missile delivery systems, and given even the likely failings of any antibomber defenses, the effective function of an air defense system thus could no longer be population protection; the most important real contribution of the expanded programs of the Eisenhower Administration would, a little later, become the alerting and protection of the SAC bomb force. While some of the continuing advocates of air defense contended that this had been given a high priority throughout all the agitation for defenses, in fact it represented a substantial reversal of the situation for which many of the original proponents of active defense had been striving.

Disarmament Negotiations and Détente

After the Soviet rejection of the Baruch Plan, the United States had become less hopeful on the prospects of disarmament, but had continued to press basically similar proposals for their propaganda value: pillorying the Soviet Union as the nation which in pathological secrecy continually had to reject disarmament. The inspection and monitoring aspects of the Baruch Plan indeed won some considerable approval for the United States amongst Western European and even neutral publics, since such publics wanted to be assured, not merely promised, that nuclear exchanges would not erupt in a Russian-American war.[37] Russian counterproposals for uninspected bans on use and possession of nuclear weapons might in turn serve to ward off some of this propaganda pressure, but over the long run such an exchange settled to the West's benefit, as third parties took the time to examine the merits of the inspection issue and found it reasonable.

Some other inherent aspects of disarmament psychology did not help the West as much. The logics of nuclear and conventional disarmament were perhaps too often thought parallel by Western commentators, with the assertion that the United States naturally would favor conventional arms reductions, while the U.S.S.R. would always demand nuclear disarmament first; the two questions did not lend themselves to such a parallel format. Proposals on nuclear weapons normally suggested total bans on the use or possession of such weapons, i.e., reductions to zero in inventories, on the assumption that any partial reductions were too difficult to police or even to negotiate. "Nuclear weapons are a bad thing, and should be abolished straightforwardly." With regard to conventional weapons, the stress was rather on reductions according to some fairly precise and elaborate formula, because the process here had to be slower, and because some military or police forces would always be required. A sense of fairness thus often hit here upon proportional reductions as a proper first step, or at least upon a parity of substantial ground forces for East and West.

But the above proposal on nuclear weapons would have completely erased the American strategic advantage in that area, while the "fair" proposal on conventional weapons might very easily have enhanced the Soviet advantage in that area, given that the Russians were starting with larger military forces, and that direct access to Western Europe gave even a numerically equal force on their side an advantage. There may thus have been a redeeming logical equity in later American attempts to reverse this asymmetry by suggesting freezes or proportional cutbacks in nuclear stockpiles, but these could too easily be labeled as deliberate efforts to gain an advantage at Soviet expense, rather than as the natural conclusions of a fair-minded reasoning process. Similarly, Western negotiators continually had to devise alternative formulas and ratios for conventional disarmament in order to counteract the propaganda appeal of Soviet proposals, perhaps thereby skating close to the margin of what NATO could really accept without a dangerous increase in its own vulnerability.

The Truman Administration and its NATO associates still were seriously contemplating a defense per se of Europe in 1952; serious proposals for ground force disarmament could thus be addressed to the U.S.S.R., with a view to making such a traditional balance of power feasible at lower costs for all concerned. The rigid Soviet demand for a flat one-third reduction of all forces would have to be rejected, because it would maintain or amplify Russian advantages on the NATO central front; the Soviet demand for a prior and uninspected renunciation of all use and possession of nuclear weapons was similarly rejected. But American, British, and French proposals had been advanced for some more reasonable schedules of ground force reduction, both for their impact in appeasing neutral audiences, and in the hope that the full-scale European rearmament envisaged in NSC-68 and the Lisbon Goals might yet be made unnecessary.[38]

But if the "new look" had itself now made the Lisbon Goals unnecessary, some of the conventional disarmament proposals receiving Western endorsement might be irrelevant, while others might even have become detrimental to the Western position. Reliance on tactical nuclears, "tripwires," and threats of escalation indeed obviated the need for large NATO reserve forces, or for 40 or 50 standing divisions, but it might now require an irreducible minimum of standing forces, considerably more than had been at hand from 1945 to 1950, to remind the U.S.S.R. that aggression across the Elbe could lead to horrendous consequences. Before such obsolescent Western proposals could be withdrawn, however, the U.S.S.R. moved to endorse them.

One often speaks of periods of good or bad relations, of moves toward and away from détente, in chronologies of international politics, but there is a danger that such terminology can be vague and misleading. If pressed to define their concept of détente very precisely, most American commentators would probably have reference to a diminuation of counterproductive activity between the United States and the foreign power in question, as with disarmament. No longer is each side purchasing weapons to undo the effect of the other side's weapons, no longer is each writing uncomplimentary prose to reduce the credibility of the other's prose. Presumably the world would be getting closer to some Pareto optimum, one reached when all powers avoided activity intended to reverse the impact of other powers' activity.

But to most observers the areas of prose and of weapons procurement are not so distinct, for the prose after all purports to describe weapons procurements, among other things. As each side injures the other a little less by its defense expenditure decisions, by its "economic warfare" decisions, the exchange of news releases and radio broadcasts presumably comes quite naturally to reflect this; each side, in expressing its acceptance of the other's new conduct, will thereby compliment the other in neutral eyes, i.e., will fairly automatically cease counterproductive activity on the publicity front, too.

Interpreting the prose exchange, therefore, as a reflection of the entire spectrum of exchange, rather than as a secular addition to it, commentators have tended to identify certain periods of American relations with the Communist powers as periods of "détente," and others as periods of "worsened relations," "increased tension," or "intensified cold war." A major move toward such détente presumably came with the "spirit of Geneva," extending from the spring of 1955 to the fall of 1956; the Russian verbal portions of this détente included de-Stalinization and the more sympathetic view of the West it implied, the general cordiality implied in statements on "peaceful coexistence," and apparent concessions on the subject of disarmament. Concrete manifestations included the Austrian peace treaty and the Soviet withdrawal from Porkkala, Finland. At the verbal level the Chinese at this point joined in (in fact having first proclaimed the modern slogan of "peaceful coexistence"), with participation in the Bandung Conference and the opening of the Ambassadorial talks with the United States.[39] More concrete was the settlement in Indochina and the termination of the Quemoy and Matsu crisis.

Yet one can express some doubts about whether a real détente at the arms control level had occurred, to justify the sense that an overall détente was in progress. The first signs of a shift in Soviet disarmament policy came with a statement of Andrei Vishinsky in September of 1954 to the U.N. General Assembly, to the effect that an unconditional ban on the possession or use of nuclear weapons would no longer be insisted upon as a preliminary to conventional disarmament, and that certain ground force reduction schedules proposed by Britain and France in 1953 and 1954 should now be implemented.[40] While the Soviet willingness to stick by this modification of position was unclear for a period of some months, in May of 1955 the Russians presented a long and detailed proposal confirming the change.[41]

If the Soviet Union no longer demanded an immediate ban on

nuclears, this might be seen as a concession to reality, or to the West, or as a recognition that nuclear legitimacy now served Russian interests also, since the U.S.S.R. had some of the biggest and best of such weapons itself. The growth of weapons inventories had probably made such demands far less significant in any event; absolute destruction of even American stockpiles would become increasingly uncertain and unmonitorable in the most tension-free times, as the U.S.S.R. was almost to admit. The U.S.S.R. thus would now presumably escape the onus of continually having to reject Western proposals found attractive by neutrals, and in exchange had eased its own propaganda pressure for a priority ban on nuclear weapons.

The Soviet endorsement of force reduction proposals did not reduce propaganda pressure all that much, however, for the West would now be embarrassed by its own proposals, premised as they had been on earlier propaganda considerations and 1951-1952 strategic assumptions, especially since they suggested a dilution of NATO tripwires. The Russians may never have seriously hoped that the United States would now agree to conventional reductions that would boost relative Soviet power, but at least the onus of "blocking disarmament" would for a time fall on the West.

To skeptics it seemed that the Soviet leadership had sensed the obsolescence of the Western position and had now decided to surprise and embarrass the United States by endorsing it. Some important Soviet qualifications still were imposed, for the Russian statements did not really propose substantial inspection in the U.S.S.R., and still at least hinted at an immediate ban on the employment of atomic weapons, in that Security Council permission might be required for any nuclear military operations; the Russian proposals also required a ban on nuclear testing and a liquidation of "overseas bases." Yet the United States nonetheless felt itself embarrassedly forced to qualify its endorsement of all earlier conventional force reduction proposals, in view of the changed military environment.[42]

The Russian failure to offer real inspection was still quite important. It would have been a mistake to assume that the real impact of any postwar nuclear or conventional disarmament treaty would correspond to the specified terms of that treaty. More realistic observers would have contended that the precise terms of an arms reduction agreement would be executed only as far as could be monitored and demanded by an adversary power, by neutral nations, or by individual citizens conscientiously desiring the disarmament of their own country. If this

107

were true, the ratio of real to agreed arms reduction for each country was a function of the initial openness of that country, and of any additional inspection to which it submitted itself. The real impact of any disarmament agreement was therefore indeterminate unless the information flow accompanying it were also specified. Over the years after 1945 there were many proposals for bilateral disarmament; a literal implementation of some of these would have been preferred by both sides to the existing situation. Unfortunately, either side probably preferred still more (if it were able to escape detection) to cheat somewhat while the other fully executed the agreement. Even if the United States were sure that the Russians straightforwardly preferred joint disarmament to a joint arms race, some mechanism had to be present to dissuade the Russians from cheating into the rationally still more preferred option, that of unilateral U.S. disarmament.

In the post-World War II world, however, any inspection would give the United States a political advantage by opening the U.S.S.R. to foreign influences and thereby undermining the regime. The Soviet leadership may thus have several times felt itself driven to reject otherwise desirable disarmament schemes, simply because its system could not stand the inspection required to make credible and necessary the execution of its half of such schemes.

There were many cases, of course, where the neutral world strongly favored the literal content of a disarmament proposal. If either major power felt that such an implemented program would work to its disadvantage, it might nonetheless be reluctant to accept the onus of having rejected it. Since neutrals might not so clearly understand how information flow was casually related to the degree of implementation of an arms reduction agreement, each side might phrase its objections in this hazier realm.

Thus the Russians have probably several times endorsed schemes they would have found undesirable if fully implemented, knowing that their refusal to accept inspection would force the United States to accept much of the onus of rejecting them (or if the United States were foolish enough to accept such programs without inspection, that the U.S.S.R. would be able to cheat and thus in practice apply a much more acceptable and favorable mutual disarmament exchange rate). Conversely, the United States may have feigned acceptance of schemes (such as conventional disarmament) to which it was actually opposed, escaping implementation because the Russians could not bear the inspection required to facilitate such a scheme.

108

The United States would continue to demand some inspection of the Soviet Union, for the realization of any arms reductions, throughout the Eisenhower Administration. Partially as a counter to the propaganda coup achieved in the Soviet disarmament proposals of 1955, the United States that summer had proposed what was labeled the "Open Skies" plan[43] for mutual aerial inspection of the United States and the Soviet Union, presumably to guarantee each power against the possibility of surprise attack, against the use of nuclear weapons rather than against their existence.

The Soviet rejection of the "Open Skies" proposal was based on several grounds: that it entailed a compromise of national sovereignty, that it proposed inspection without any disarmament, and that aerial inspection was not really appropriate to the question of surprise attack. The last objection to the proposal was not so badly taken, for the American plan after all was formulated to some considerable extent for its propaganda impact, and may not have been adequately staffed in advance. Preparations for a surprise air attack might well not involve enough kinds of activity visible from the air to give any clear warning of aggressive intention. As a guard against ground attack, aerial inspection was useful, but here the Soviet proposal for ground inspection posts, if defined without too many inhibiting jokers, might have worked even more surely. Regular aerial inspection of the United States by the Soviet Union might, moreover, have made SAC even more vulnerable to a Soviet first strike, at least until completion of reforms worked into SAC procedures in 1955 and 1956. The United States persisted after 1955 in putting forward its "Open Skies" proposals, even when some observers had concluded that it was essentially a propaganda gimmick not very well related to the disarmament schemes to which it was coupled. A more unilateral version of "Open Skies," with no Russian reciprocation, was undertaken with the United States U-2 flights commencing in 1956,[44] although the purpose of these flights was more clearly to establish Soviet force strength and location, rather than any imminence of a Soviet attack; overflights with other aircraft had reportedly occurred even earlier. Since the Russians might suddenly become capable or desirous of downing such reconnaissance aircraft, it was perhaps wise for the United States to remain strongly on record as to the general legitimacy of overflights, in order to weaken international recriminations once the Russians did shoot down one of the aircraft.

Observers have generally assumed that the Russians were not able to down a U-2 until they did so in 1960. Perhaps one should not dismiss the possibility, however, that the Russians were deliberately tolerating the overflights as the minimum of inspection upon which the Eisenhower Administration was basing its own arms economies. Alternatively, at a less sophisticated level, the hopes of some détente with the West may have been seen to depend on no such American planes being shot down.

Both the United States and the Soviet Union have been criticized since the 1950's for having tied disarmament and arms control steps into unrealistically large packages, requiring massive reductions in weapons stockpiles and substantial changes in the international system. While there may have been some naïveté on the part of the proponents of such schemes, an important consideration in the framing of such proposals still had to be the impact of naïve third parties, amongst whom serious propaganda benefits might yet be gained. The general disarmament catalogue framework might thus allow each nation to suggest partial proposals implicitly, without yet publicly committing itself to such items. In retrospect, the partial proposals all seem to be the most interesting, if only because some might possibly have been implemented without a drastic and unpredictable upheaval of the strategic balance.

If grand disarmament proposals were put forward to embarrass the opposing side in what was essentially a barrage and counterbarrage of propaganda, modifications and concessions within this general framework would conversely serve more positive propaganda purposes. Amended proposals, accepting items from the plan of the other side, might be a means of launching a détente by implicitly hinting at the reasonableness of one's adversary, declaring a truce to the propaganda barrage, and restoring each side's prestige in neutral eyes. Proposals and counterproposals of amendments thus might be composed quite independently of substance, since disarmament schemes would not be seriously considered but would serve instead as gestures attacking or supporting the image of the opposing side, as periods of "tension" and "détente" alternated.

The "spirit of Geneva" détente extended from late 1954 to the crises of the fall of 1956; in this period, Russian pronouncements on disarmament could be interpreted as partially consistent with the general relaxation of propaganda pressure. The apparent modifications of substantive position coincide with a domestic de-Stalinization, with a large opening of cultural and personal exchange with the West. Tensions remained, since the West could have avoided embarrassment at some points only by acceding to potentially dangerous Soviet disarmament proposals; yet the Soviet proposals, coming as apparent acceptances of prior Western positions, did not per se have to suggest hostility, and might themselves be interpreted widely as reinforcements of rather than inhibitions to détente.

The Special Problem of Central Europe

It was thus unlikely that the NATO allies could have been tricked or fooled into accepting substantial conventional or nuclear disarmament arrangements putting them at a major disadvantage; it is similarly unlikely that the Soviet leadership expected the NATO powers thus to be fooled, or that this was the primary intent of the U.S.S.R.'s new disarmament proposals. The 1954-1955 shift in Soviet disarmament policy, like other shifts, was probably molded, rather, largely for its propaganda impact, designed in this case both to accommodate the West in détente and to rebut some of the West's propaganda pressure.

NATO military preparations would thus be molded substantially along the lines envisioned by the Republicans early in 1953.[45] While some scientists in the United States had urged a combination of tactical nuclear weapons and air defense in 1950 as an alternative to the H-bomb, American defense policy now had come to depend on a combination of tactical nuclears, air defense, *and* the H-bomb.

Signals of the greater American (and NATO) reliance on tactical nuclear weapons, in lieu of larger conventional forces, had not been long in coming after 1952. In April of 1953, provision was made for the first training of NATO officers in the handling and use of tactical atomic weapons.[46] In September of the same year, the first artillery capable of firing atomic shells, large and unwieldy 280-millimeter cannon, was deployed to Europe, to be followed in 1954 by short-range rockets which could carry smaller and more fully developed nuclear warheads.[47] In the fall of 1953, appropriations for programmed expansions of conventional army units were canceled.[48] In October, President Eisenhower approved a National Security Council decision that nuclear weapons be included in all contingency planning, even for smaller aggressions in Europe.[49] Admiral Radford virtually announced this decision in December,[50] and Secretary Dulles delivered his "massive retaliation" message in January of 1954.

European endorsement of the strategic shift was inhibited a little by the terms of the 1946 U.S. Atomic Energy Act, which denied allies

111

information on American nuclear stockpiles, denying it even to potential European commanders of American forces equipped with such stockpiles.[51] The amendment of these restrictions in the 1954 Atomic Energy Act released information on weapons availability and characteristics while withholding information on manufacture, and the West European powers now accepted a strategic shift which presumably rationalized their failure to fulfill the Lisbon Goals. The North Atlantic Council in late 1954 formally endorsed military contingency planning on the basis of nuclear weapons, thus hoping, like the Americans, to avoid the more onerous burdens of high taxes and long conscription periods.

While it is common to describe the NATO powers' failure to implement the Lisbon Goals in terms of divisions-in-being, this is somewhat inaccurate, since the high figures adopted at Lisbon in 1952 referred to all fronts, not just to the front in Germany, and included reserves.[52] In terms of forces-in-being, NATO has in fact come close at various times to meeting the Lisbon Goals; it was in terms of reserves to be mobilized over a short period of time that the goals went drastically unfulfilled, and this was quite consistent with the new emphasis of American strategy. For on the central front, the United States still might need ground forces-in-being, equipped with tactical nuclear weapons, as a tripwire to make escalation to all-out general war credible as a deterrent to Russian aggression; but reserves would play no part in this, for only some modicum of ground forces would be required. Even after the 1956 NATO Council reendorsed its earlier approval of a reliance on tactical nuclear weapons, the NATO Military Committee, at American urging, adopted a five-year MC-70 plan specifying 30 divisions for the central front, a standing force larger than had been proposed in the Lisbon Goals,[53] but without any significant reserve back-up.

Many of the changes thus introduced in NATO defense posture would draw a pro forma Soviet propaganda attack. If the West normally would accept such propaganda losses ahead of disarmament disadvantages, however, it might elect the reverse by adjusting its decisions on some more marginal instances, thus still giving the U.S.S.R. some leverage over Western policy. Yet the purposes for which the U.S.S.R. would exploit this leverage hardly seemed consistent or clear, especially in and around Germany.

The unification or continued division of Germany could be of value on its own terms, to Germans who cherished reunification, or to other

Europeans who might prefer permanent division for the sense of security it offered. But the conditions under which any reunification were to be executed would be crucial to most parties, especially to the U.S.S.R., whose control over East Germany established a veto over any scheme. Several explanations can be offered for why that veto was continually exercised, indeed why it was likely to be exercised over almost any arrangement acceptable to the West. These would include a fear of Germans in general, hopes for an ultimate Communization of all of Germany, and a sense of the economic and military value of East Germany by itself. Hopes for a neutral non-Communist reunification might still arise because the Russians in 1955 had indeed agreed to an end of the Austrian occupation, but the Soviet vested interest there had been much less; Austria by itself was less of a threat, and no Communist regime had ever been established separately for the Russian occupation zone.

To win sympathy among its World War II associates, or to stimulate suspicions within the new NATO alliance, the U.S.S.R. now referred very often to the first of the above-listed rationales, to a fear of Nazi resurgence. It was quite plausible after 1945 that the average Russian had nurtured a dislike and fear of Germans, a fear that might even be independent of, and prior to, considerations of ideological competition with capitalism. Presumably the Soviet fear might have focused especially on a resurgence of German conventionally armed military forces, or worse, on a German acquisition of means for mass destruction by nuclear weapons.

Yet Russian choices of policy over this period hardly support any single-minded fear of German revanche or military resurgence. If Americans were being asked to share a Russian distrust of Germans, they also were being asked to withdraw their troops from Europe, in effect to reduce their influence over events in Germany. It might be that the propaganda opportunities for embarrassing the West just were too inviting, when it seemed that the Allies were sure to maintain a forward deployment in Germany anyway: yet even the more discreetly and seriously offered Soviet proposals of the 1950's seemed designed to reduce the American potential for conventional operations on the continent of Europe. Similarly, quotas were presented to reduce British and French armed force levels in 1955, while limits on West Germany were appended later, almost as an afterthought.[54] The Russians seemingly had resigned themselves to West German rearmament in 1954 and 1955, when they began to insist that Bonn and the D.D.R.

negotiate any reunification as political equals: having thus withdrawn most options for a truly non-Communist reunification, the U.S.S.R. would still campaign for a NATO disarmament even when it made West German forces all the more significant.

If the predominant Soviet fear were indeed of a German resurgence, then the all-out Communist opposition to the European Defense Community is also a little difficult to explain; the alternative to EDC by 1954 had clearly become a German national army rather than no German rearmament at all. If the Russians felt that EDC amounted to just as explicit a German rearmament—i.e., that it was some sort of fraud—then the policy made sense, perhaps on the assumption that a delay on any pretext was desirable. Since EDC would have imposed real checks on independent West Germany military action, however, the Russian policy seems rather to have been one of weakening and delaying Western military potential in general, even at the cost of increasing West Germany military independence.

Propaganda against an American or NATO presence in West Germany thus might fan suspicions that the Russians still hoped for a Communist unification of Germany. Yet the more pressing consideration by now may have been Russian fears of a loss of East Germany; much of ensuing Soviet policy may indeed be explained more easily by this very practical fear than by dreams of Communist expansion, or nightmares of Nazi revanchism. Hopes of German reunification were kept alive by the existence of the West Berlin enclave, if by nothing else. If so, the issue was weighted against the Russians, in that they could less easily prevent reunification on Western terms than the United States could prevent reunification on Russian terms. Since many people in the world approved of German reunification per se, an exchange of propaganda proposals could go on as long as each side remained able to veto the proposals of the other; but the size and example of West Germany, coupled with the location of West Berlin, threatened that East Germany might spontaneously slip out of Russian control at some point (as the 1953 riots had already suggested). For this reason, it might soon be necessary for the U.S.S.R. to stop pretending that acceptable reunification was possible, and to begin more openly to deny the option; simultaneously it would be necessary to continue assailing the legitimacy of the Federal Republic and bolstering the legitimacy of the Democratic Republic, even if this induced more extensive West German rearmament.

Through the 1950's, the U.S.S.R. thus often had to choose between controlling the West Germans and embarrassing them. If the stability of the East German regime remained in doubt, it would be necessary to pursue the latter course even if it hastened military independence, or even nuclear independence, for Bonn. Some options did of course offer an opportunity simultaneously to hinder West German weapons acquisition and to embarrass the Federal regime. One could even argue that the Eisenhower Administration's seeming casualness on nuclear controls reduced any Soviet hopes that an American physical presence would inhibit German revanchism when it reared its head; in this case, forcing the United States to give up its bases would simultaneously help to legitimize the East German regime and to deny nuclear weapons to Bonn. Yet significant opportunities did exist for the Russians to prevent full nuclearization of West Germany, or even perhaps to have headed off Bonn's conventional rearmament, opportunities seemingly forgone because the Russians loaded their arms control proposals with explicit or implicit recognitions of the East German Pankow regime. Even if the United States' inclination to be careful about nuclears became clear only after 1960, some such inclination, some American concern to avert too full a rearmament of Germany, might have been at hand to be exploited before then.

The Soviet disarmament proposals of 1954 and 1955 in their declared substance seemed to embody grand departures from an earlier intransigence; yet it had been easy for the West to contend that these represented little or no change, since the inspection provisions were not sufficient to generate any disarmament approaching the commitments on the Soviet side. Professing a new reasonableness on the inspection issue, the Russians had included a detailed proposal for fixed ground inspection posts to warn of any surprise attack,[55] thus perhaps easing tensions enough to alleviate any need or desire for inspection of force levels. Such inspection posts were to be situated at highway junctions, railway terminals, and airports, in an agreed zone of arms reduction; while the inspecting contingents at each outpost would be quite small (smaller than corresponding contingents representing the inspected power), the proposal might yet be seen as a gratuitous contribution to Western rather than Communist bloc security. NATO presumably had most feared a surprise attack by ground forces, while the Russians presumably should have been in fear of a surprise attack by long-range strategic bombers, against which such inspection posts would give little or no warning.

The Russians, of course, may themselves still have feared a ground attack, even if such fears seem paradoxical in face of the apparent American inferiority complex on conventional force questions. Earlier Soviet strategic arguments stressing the decisiveness of conventional arms, and deprecating nuclear weapons and strategic air forces, may have been part of the cause of such fears. The German invasion of Russia in World War II also could play a role here, inevitably suggesting that such invasion was feasible, perhaps conveying an image more clearly unpleasant than air attack, with which the U.S.S.R. had had relatively less experience. Similarly effective may have been American Army and Navy officers' stating that air offensives could not win a war by themselves but would have to be complemented by naval and ground action to win and terminate wars. The United States, after all, had not relied on air attack alone to defeat Hitler, but had conducted an invasion of the European continent to depose him. The American Navy was still quite large, even aside from its air components, and prided itself on its ability to conduct amphibious operations.

For some of the inherent reasons cited earlier, however, it was not likely that fear of a superior American conventional ground force could be a dominant factor now in Soviet reasoning. Current force deployments presumably still gave the U.S.S.R. a sizable latent advantage, with the reserves it could muster; any reduction proposals, adhered to or not, might only intensify this advantage. As part of its disarmament initiatives, the Russian government now even announced unilateral reductions of active ground force troops, 640,000 in 1955 and 1,200,000 more in 1957.[56] The move could be seen as a means of applying additional pressure on the West to match such troop reductions, or as a simple propaganda move; possibly it also reflected a new confidence in the Russian hydrogen bomb as a deterrent to American air attack, perhaps making the Red Army move on Paris and fears of Western ground attack less important.

Another explanation may thus be required for the Soviet observation post proposal. The establishment of ground observer posts was seen in West Germany, and very plausibly further east, as a means of normalizing the existing division of the country, of converting the inherently "temporary" occupation status of East Germany into that of a recognized member of a regulated security system.[57] The proposed Soviet observer posts in the West could report only very noticeable force movements, movements easily monitorable by Russian espionage agents presumably already in place: thus they seemed intended to compromise the independent sovereignty of West Germany and its claim to German reunification, rather than to warn of any NATO military attack.

Western attitudes on German armaments must also be discussed. West German rearmament had been proposed in 1950, when substantial conventional force augmentations had seemed necessary to restore a strategic balance in Europe, after the Russian acquisition of the atomic bomb and, more practically, after the invasion of South Korea had seemingly made Russian aggressions more plausible. For good or ill, the mode of such rearmament had become the subject of the EDC ratification debate in the French parliament, preventing its implementation. The Republican administration had come to office in the United States, the Korean War had been terminated, and the need for large conventional forces had been debunked as part of a defensive balance, all while no Germans had yet been drawn into uniform, pending French political action. One might therefore have interpreted the French delay as beneficial, allowing the Eisenhower Administration to dispense with a force buildup which for strategic reasons it might no longer find necessary. Especially since the Soviet government still professed to be interested in a German reunification based on disarmed political neutrality, it could be argued that the one great opportunity offered here by the H-bomb was missed.

German rearmament threatened to be an irreversible process in many ways. If the Germans wanted to be rearmed, no one would easily be able to take their weapons away once they had them; a disarmed status could probably be made permanent only if it were maintained continuously from the end of World War II. In light of its own strategic theories, it is thus perhaps unclear why the Eisenhower Administration went ahead so resolutely with German rearmament from 1953 to 1955. If the NATO area could be defended without any conventional buildup to approximate the Lisbon Goals, then some of the more convincing arguments for a West German army or for EDC could presumably also have been dropped.

A continued ban on German armaments, and a removal of other "occupation" forces from Germany, might indeed have been acceptable to the United States in the context of the 1947 strategic arms balance. But if the hydrogen bomb needed some link to couple its retaliatory use to any aggressions in central Europe, the presence of at least some Western troops in Germany might be required. It would be all the more difficult to make massive retaliation credible on behalf of a neutralized disarmed Germany if no alliances could be proclaimed or troops deployed to mobilize American honor and political commitment for the more ambiguous Communist incursions. A formal alliance with West German military participation would serve domestically and internationally to legitimate the American, British, and French presence on both sides of the Rhine; if the form of the NATO alliance were thus still necessary on this argument, so might be German rearmament, if only because it had already been proposed on differing strategic assumptions, so that a reneging might impose serious strains on German sensibilities.

Yet even if the tripwire to assure American intervention were already adequate, there might be another incentive to press for West German rearmament. The Radford proposals of 1957, to rely heavily on tactical nuclears while reducing the six-division European commitment of American forces,[58] were taken seriously enough in Washington to induce considerable disquiet in Bonn. Such a withdrawal would for the time have completely countered the expansion of conventional defenses supplied by a West German Army; the American government's desire to reduce military expenditures might thus have straightforwardly looked to the substitution of German tripwire forces for American.

If the United States needed German tripwires, however, it would not do for the Bonn regime to admit that it did, since one did not openly examine the mechanics of the American commitment if one wished to maintain its credibility. When the German Bundestag was asked to give the Adenauer government the constitutional amendments and conscription laws needed to raise the conventional forces requested, American strategic pronouncements were quoted by the Socialist opposition as evidence that any future war would go nuclear so quickly as to make German forces militarily irrelevant.[59] Several maneuvers based on the use of large numbers of such weapons, most particularly one in 1955 entitled "Carte Blanche," had seemed to draw a very fearful German reaction to the damage that would be inflicted on German people and territory in the event of war.[60] The Social Democratic opposition thereafter continued to convince many Western observers that Germany, and by inference most other Western European nations, would not for long accept a strategy potentially so damaging to European territory.

The issues for West Germany, in any event, were more complicated. Since Adenauer himself could not openly justify reconstituted German military forces simply as tripwire means to reifying pledges of American support, he was thus driven to feign a questioning of the American strategic pronouncements on tactical nuclear defense and massive retaliation, hinting for a short time at a preference for a conventional defense strategy.[61] The Social Democrats now moved to make opposition to the deployment or employment of tactical nuclear weapons a major campaign issue, while Adenauer quickly shifted back to massive retaliation after his conscription bills had been passed.[62] Foreign observers began to expect that the Socialists would be able to make gains on the issue, but the provincial elections of North Rhine-Westphalia in July of 1958 gave the Christian Democrats a surprisingly decisive victory, with the result that the Social Democrats finally gave up the tactical nuclear issue, and by 1960 had in effect moved to seek coordination with the Christian Democrats on foreign policy.[63] The adverse German governmental reaction to the Radford trial balloon thus stemmed far more from the idea of an American troop reduction (which was never to occur in the Eisenhower years) than from the tactical nuclear emphasis.

Aside from tripwires for American commitments, West German armed forces may have been interpreted most importantly as solidifying Bonn's political status and its identification with the West; any foreclosure of German rearmament in principle, in response to Russian demands or promises, conversely might have been very troublesome. In 1955, relatively few Western observers would yet have felt certain that the democratic institutions of the Federal Republic had taken deep root amongst the German people. To delay the assumption of sovereignty in Bonn, of which partial rearmament may have seemed a significant part, might thus have cast serious doubts on the status and stability of the democratic regime erected. Even if the U.S.S.R. was opposed to any encouragement of antidemocratic tendencies amongst the Germans of the three Western zones, it was possible that the process of indecisive and fluctuating negotiations it was demanding might encourage such tendencies. It was plausible, moreover, that the Russians would want the Federal Republic to be beset by extremist critics from all sides as it was denied the trappings of sovereignty, in the hope that the German Communists might yet be able to pick up the pieces.

Extending the sovereignty of West Germany to include military forces might thus have defensive advantages against Communist subversion of the Bonn regime, as well as against a Russian military offensive against all of Western Europe. But the step could have offensive implications also, as part of a campaign to achieve a reunification of

Germany on Western terms. While it was often argued that the arming of the Federal Republic would make the U.S.S.R. finally unwilling to accept any democratic merger of the zones, many observers saw the Russians as unlikely to accept this voluntarily under any circumstances, even if all of central Europe were disarmed; hopes for a take-over of all of Germany, in appreciation of the economic value of the Soviet zone, or fears of ultimate German revanchism—each of these arguments would probably lead a prudent U.S.S.R. to withhold reunification if it could.

If the riots of 1953 had panicked Beria into favoring Russian withdrawal from East Germany, this may have illustrated the only avenue to a non-Communist uniting of Germany. While East German rearmament perhaps contributed to making permanent the German division and to legitimizing the autonomy of the "minority" Pankow regime, West German rearmament might further reunification, since the trappings of sovereignty for a territorial and population majority might counteract any separatist claims for Prussia and Saxony. If the Bundeswehr heightened the legitimacy and appeal of the Federal Republic for all Germans, the instability of East Germany might yet be stoked up to the point where the Russians would be forced to give up their control. Some doubts might remain on whether this process of forced liberation of the East, however democratic, could be accomplished without driving the Russians to serious steps to prevent it.

Some American participation in such pressure for unification was now assured. One immediate consequence of inviting and relying on West German participation in the defense of the NATO area was that it extended eastward the area that nominally had to be defended by all NATO forces. Prior to 1954, an acceptable NATO strategy might have been a retreat to the Rhine River, there to hold the line while nuclear bombing wore down the Russian military capability. But the raising of West Germany to the status of almost equal partner demanded greater consideration for shielding the German people and territory from the Red Army, thus requiring that any pretense at a NATO ground defense be at a forward defense. This change in strategic requirements made any de facto disengagement considerably more difficult, since American, British, and West German forces would have to be deployed substantially east of the Rhine.

The von Bonin Plan, intended to reduce the costs of large general ground forces and to provide for a more effective and credible conventional defense,[64] might have lessened the need for such a forward strategy. It called for the establishment of a large territorial militia in West Germany rather than armored divisions, on the assumption that such a militia could substantially interfere with a Soviet onslaught if it came, while the more standard divisions of NATO would hold on the Rhine. Numerous other proposals were advanced over the 1950's for regional disarmament in central Europe, to reduce tension and to preclude accidental clashes between NATO and Warsaw Pact forces.[65] Possibly such disengagement schemes would have made conventional disarmament easier for both sides, although the reverse is also plausible. An additional advantage claimed for such proposals, at least as formulated in the West by Anthony Eden and later by George Kennan and Hugh Gaitskell, was that they might allow for a democratic reunification of Germany; but the plausibility of Soviet acquiescence in a reunification under such circumstances may well have been exaggerated.

Beyond the commitment to defend all of West Germany, the United States had indeed incurred another moral debt in relying on West German troops, one probably more serious in the long run than the simple forswearing of disengagement. After Bonn's admission to NATO, it became almost impossible for the Western allies to decline to support additional pressures for German reunification. It was likely that Americans might have desired to impose psychological and political pressures on the Ulbricht regime in any event, since some of the instability was inherent in the West Berlin arrangement, an arrangement the United States might always have been reluctant to surrender. As it was, however, the aggregated Western pressures on the Russian and East German regime would now be very potent, potent enough to threaten a collapse of that regime and to tempt the Communist bloc to consider using military force to prevent that collapse. While Western statements made it clear that no initiative in the use of force would be taken, East Germany remained the one area where all of the West was clearly not to be status quo in orientation, and it is not certain that this would have remained the case without the 12 West German divisions in NATO.

If West German rearmament constituted a simple affirmation of sovereignty, sovereignty allied with the West, then Soviet military fears of a rearmed Germany should logically have been relieved by a failure to press on with such rearmament, and to some extent this is what occurred.[66] The progress of the West German buildup to 12 divisions continually lagged behind schedule, with the period of military service being curtailed in response to domestic objections in West Germany, curtailed enough to cast doubt on the military effectiveness of the Bundeswehr into the 1960's. In terms of establishing a conventional threat that the Russians would have to fear, nothing irreversible had yet occurred in the 1950's, if the Soviets had wished to negotiate to avoid it.

But, as argued above, the form of German adherence to NATO was probably already more significant than the substance of actual military preparations; enhanced West German prestige and adherence to the West were likely, such that there would be growing internal pressures imposed on the East German regime. If German rearmament had a primarily token significance for the West, therefore, then it might have a similar import for the Russian leadership.

American Commitment Beyond NATO

If the threat of escalation was now crucial to the military balance, many would find this unacceptable. Much criticism of the Eisenhower Administration in 1955 and 1956 in fact pointed to the danger of a jump from some limited encounter between Communist and American forces to an all-out, massive-retaliation war. Some critics called for a greater tactical nuclear force, to allow for an American victory within a geographically limited zone, but without great expenditures of Western manpower and resources;[67] others contended, however, that any use of tactical nuclears, even without an American intention to enlarge the war, would probably produce such escalation, for lack of a clear distinction of restraint once the nuclear-conventional firebreak had been crossed.[68]

Paradoxically, the difference between the atomic and hydrogen bombs had earlier been accepted as being of the utmost importance, for the shift from kilotons to megatons had significantly altered the late-1940's strategic balance. Thus, if the atomic bomb would not frighten the Soviets in 1948, as the H-bomb would in 1955, then similarly the first use of a small tactical A-bomb now might not so quickly make Soviet leaders forget that they had not yet been H-bombed. A threat existed, of course, of more gradual escalation, and the Eisenhower Administration was not in fact desirous of completely denying this possibility. If the continuous range of sizes of new atomic weapons seemed to leave no clear firebreak now, the administration nonetheless was stressing the very big and the very small in its atomic arsenal, which did leave some psychological prop for the distinctions of a limited war. All in all, escalation was probably not so automatic as the critics of the Eisenhower Administration contended, but was every bit as possible as the administration in fact wanted it to be; yet even this might have been unacceptable for many Americans, if another strategy of maintaining the balance were available, one that did not leave American commitments in doubt.

It could certainly be argued that dependence on an escalation threat would inhibit the United States from contesting Soviet control over unhappy and rebellious satellites. The autumn of 1956 would bring an end to the "spirit of Geneva" détente in the Anglo-French-Israeli invasion of Egypt and the Hungarian uprising. As in the East German riots of 1953, the United States did not now threaten the Soviet Union with armed intervention from the NATO area, or from the bombers of SAC.[69] The interposing positions of neutral Austria and "neutral" Yugoslavia perhaps kept temptations from arising very saliently in any event, but no Western troops appeared in Hungary, and no arms were flown to the Hungarian rebels. Western radio broadcasts, perhaps not very perfectly controlled by the governments underwriting them, could fairly be blamed by the Russians (or credited by the Hungarians) with having supplied some impetus for the attempted secession from the Soviet bloc; but the United States and its allies did little else, except to cash in on the propaganda losses the U.S.S.R. necessarily had to suffer in the process. Had Hungarian resistance to the Russian intervention persisted over a longer time, with some geographical area identifiable to the world as being under "Free Hungarian control," then American aid might have been drawn in; yet such a clear-cut situation was not to arise, and even if it had, fears of all-out war might still have inhibited any Western initiative if the territory of Hungary were not clearly divided between the forces.

The failure to threaten hostilities reflected the real preferences of the Republican Administration, thus plausibly reassuring Moscow that its deterrent against an American eastward move was sufficient. Yet the extent of the Hungarian defection, partially instigated by Western radio broadcasts, may nevertheless have reinforced Russian fears of a more political or psychological assault. As "open" a society as that of the NATO area might always threaten the Soviet position in Eastern Europe, even if the governments involved did not intend to, even if they were content to make permanent the status quo of territorial tenure.

It is unlikely that the Suez operations played any significant role in dissuading the American government from a tougher line on Hungary, although the worldwide condemnation of the Anglo-French-Israeli attack did inhibit American propaganda exploitation of the Hungarian affair. The Soviet threat to bring medium-range missiles to bear against Britain or France in fact served to pull the United States into more of a confrontation with the U.S.S.R., with American bombers alerted and deployed to forward bases. Yet even here General LeMay objected to Eisenhower's suggestion that SAC be fully mobilized, for fear that some of his war plans would thus be given away; SAC therefore, paradoxically, was the only major American military command not fully alerted during the crisis.[70] A question on the limits of American commitment might thus remain when the contested areas, as in the Middle East, were beyond the "tripwire," a tripwire which could not always be so clearly emplaced.

Doubts were expressed, moreover, as to whether the escalation threat, however dangerous it was, was really effective in deterring Communist aggressions in Asia and Africa. Perhaps because of prospects of American escalation to nuclear warfare, an acceptable Korean armistice had been signed in 1953, fairly quickly after the Republican administration had come to power in the United States. The Indochina war, however, had more clearly raised the problem of how one massively retaliates when deterrence has been only ambiguously successful, when the major party on the other side also may have some ability and inclination to retaliate. Warnings had also been issued of a move to air attacks if the Chinese intervened in Indochina with their army or air force,[71] but the Viet Minh had now gained successes relying only on massive Chinese material assistance.

As a crisis loomed in the siege of Dienbienphu, with the clear implication that the Geneva negotiations might be decisively influenced by the fall of the base, the U.S. government apparently was moved to suggest more drastic forms of American intervention to a French government markedly reluctant to enlarge operations in the theater. Air strikes were proposed, conventional or even nuclear, either on the Viet Minh forces surrounding Dienbienphu or on the border provinces of China,[72] but apparently were rejected by the French Government, in part on the basis of danger of escalation to a war with the U.S.S.R. The more clearly tactical operations were quickly precluded by the narrowing of the fortress perimeter, so that nuclear weapons could no longer have been used without damage to the French garrison.

A strategy attempting to exploit the latent threats of escalation to horrendous all-out war might thus be effective for the defense of territories already clearly held, where any Communist attempt to upset the status quo had to be very abrupt and explicit. Where the current tenure of an area was in doubt, or where the form of Communist air attack was more insidious, however, the defending United States might be embarrassed when forced to interpret its own proclamations of policy, since the initiative of subjecting the world to awesome risks would not be thrust upon the aggressor, but onto the defenders. Secretary of State Dulles, never prone to spell out the implications of his military policies too explicitly, was nonetheless now induced to qualify somewhat his earlier stress on the pure punishment aspects of massive retaliation. On close examination, massive retaliation would turn out to be a mixture of responsive defense measures plus retaliatory punishment.

> To deter aggression, it is important to have the flexibility and the facilities which make various responses available. In many cases, any open assault by Communist forces would only result in starting a general war. But the free world must have the means for responding effectively on a selective basis when it chooses. It must not put itself in the position where the only response open to it is general war.[73]

When specifically applying this stance to the Chinese case, Dulles thus shied away from any clear threat to bomb Moscow, or Peking, in response to a new aggression.

> That does not mean turning every local war into a world war. It does not mean that, if there is a Communist attack somewhere in Asia, atom or hydrogen bombs will necessarily be dropped on the great industrial centers of China or Russia. It does mean that the free world must maintain the collective means and be willing to use them in the way which most effectively makes aggression too risky and expensive to be tempting.

In the 1954-1955 Chinese Communist shelling of Quemoy, proposals to encourage and assist Chinese Nationalist air attacks on the mainland, or to add U.S. air attacks in the event of a Communist invasion attempt, were similarly vetoed by President Eisenhower.[74] But the President did request and receive from Congress authority to defend Quemoy and Matsu if the threat to the islands seemed to embody a threat to Taiwan; and statements were issued that the administration in fact did now see the threats to be so coupled,[75] so that tactical nuclear weapons would be used if needed for the defense of the islands.

Yet the number of areas with defensive positions as ambiguous as Indochina or the offshore islands was limited; for most of the areas the United States valued, a clearer line might be drawn to which an American massive retaliation doctrine could be coupled. To make American retaliatory responses even more plausible, the administration now negotiated a series of mutual defense treaties with small nations outside the European area. In addition to pledging American assistance in the event of Communist attack, the pacts presumably legitimized such American intervention and preparations for intervention, as perhaps with military bases, etc. American critics of the agreements pointed to the falsity of their "mutual security" label, since the United States would be the provider of security while the other nations were the "consumers," but in retrospect similar objections could have been made about the NATO agreement.

The degree to which massive retaliation might effectively be applied was thus probably underestimated by administration critics through the 1950's. It does not seem implausible that Communist China regarded atomic air attack as the cost of an attack on Taiwan or Korea, and was decisively dissuaded by such considerations, if by no others. For more ambiguous areas, the administration's commitment to massive retaliation, or neglect of conventional war forces, had probably not been as total as either side to the dispute liked to pretend. Too many critics pointed to Dulles' "massive retaliation" speech of January, 1954, without citing the following article which qualified its propositions. For minor skirmishes, it still was always likely that the American response would be minor and yet often plausibly sufficient; the issue was not the existence of a threshold prior to escalation to nuclear war, but rather the width of the threshold from location to location. Partially, perhaps, to take some wind out of the sails of his critics, Dulles would suggest acceptance of a need for tactical limited-war forces in another *Foreign Affairs* article in September of 1957,[76] but the impact of this article in one direction or another was quickly overshadowed by other developments at the strategic level.

The Bomber Gap

The greater number of ordinary nuclear warheads available to the United States and U.S.S.R. in the early 1950's (together with the new very-large-yield H-bomb, with which a single bomber might reliably take out an entire airfield) had now induced a number of analysts to focus more seriously on the option of striking directly at an opponent's

126

strategic force, rather than merely at his broader sources of military strength. First, the countercivilian power of the enemy's H-bomb had to be taken seriously; much more power would now be packaged at the ready-to-fire end, so that destroying the enemy's industrial backup might no longer have first priority. Second, one could now afford to aim some warheads at an enemy's air force, especially since the enemy would be doing the same to the West. The earlier assumption had more normally been that nuclear weapons and delivery systems would be few and widely scattered, so that they were not appropriate targets for each other; but economies of scale might now set up a serious strategic instability, for while 20 bombers with 20 bombs might not have been able to take out 20 bombers of the other side, 300 might easily be able to take out 1,000. If nuclear weapons were now numerous enough and powerful enough, they might thus be both worth targeting, as important parts of the enemy's military force, and targetable, since the H-bomb and more numerous A-bombs offered an effective counterforce weapon. At the worst, either side might be able to disarm the other if it struck first, absolutely in one stroke, or gradually over a matter of days.[77]

One of the more explicit scenarios came now in the form of the RAND Corporation study on SAC basing, which had gotten underway in 1951 and began to circulate its findings in 1953.[78] The RAND study concluded that the American strategic force might indeed become vulnerable to a Soviet preemptive attack by 1956, given its narrow basing structure at home and overseas and the inadequate radar warning time available for getting U.S. bombers off the ground. No Soviet numerical bomber superiority might be necessary, for the mathematics of the bomber exchange rate could be such that even a smaller Soviet bomber force would be able to disarm SAC, and thus preclude any major campaign against Soviet cities and industry. Somewhat paradoxically, the RAND study did not yet assign the same predominant mission to SAC: to eliminate the Soviet Air Force first as the highest priority target, thereby perhaps sparing the United States all the suffering of an H-bomb attack.[79] Recognizing this as an important target system, the RAND study still went along with Soviet industry as the prime target for SAC.

With the counterforce stress, as elsewhere, it is thus difficult to test the comprehension of strategic theses where the operational environment had not yet made such theses seem imminently relevant. But certain steps taken in the U.S.S.R. now served to make these issues more relevant, to the perhaps unjustified embarrassment of the Eisenhower Administration.

By 1953, the Soviet Air Force had accumulated a force of about 1,000 Tu-4's.[80] This force, presumably having only a small stockpile of nuclear warheads to deliver, could perhaps have inflicted sizable damage on as many as 40 American cities on first-strike, one-way missions through existing American air defenses. Whether this force could have done as much after any sizable American preemptive strike at Soviet air bases is not clear. Perhaps with the H-bomb the Tu-4's could even have supplied that surely unacceptable level of second-strike destruction required for mutual deterrence. For as long as the Russians did not possess a bomber capable of striking at North America and returning, less of a counterindustry or counterforce threat might be sensed.

Reports had been in circulation since 1951, however, of a Soviet long-range turboprop bomber (the straight-wing type 31, of which only a few were procured), presumably capable of round-trip missions against the United States;[81] Russian overflights of Alaska and Canada, not easily confirmed or disproved, also were reported.[82] Such a turbojet-powered bomber presumably sat between the American B-36 and B-47 in performance and in vulnerability to anti-aircraft defenses, but was nonetheless an advance on the Tu-4 in both range and performance, and thus came as a disturbing development. In May of 1954, the first medium-range jet Badger bombers flew by in the Moscow May Day air show together with a single very long-range, all-jet Bison.[83] In the Soviet Aviation Day show of June, 1955, there appeared what seemed to be a multiple flyover of Bison, together with an intercontinental-range turboprop Bear (swept-winged), although it seems now that only a small number of Bison were involved, each flying repeated passes over the city.[84]

The new Soviet bombers most appropriately alarmed those, of course, who still found plausible the earlier prolonged war of repeated strikes at an enemy's industrial base, since they clearly supplied the round-trip capability that the Tu-4 had lacked. The Bison's round-trip range was estimated at 2,000 miles, the Bear's at 3,500;[85] with the slower-flying turboprop bear as a tanker for the Bison, or as a bomber itself, the Soviet Air Force might now be able to carry through an extended war of attrition against American industry, a campaign which it could not have undertaken in the late 1940's. It was estimated that the Soviet Union by 1959 would procure over 600 long-range bombers,[86] which would have outpaced the United States B-52

128

procurement originally programmed for the same period. It is not so clear, however, why the Soviet Union would have wanted now to procure a large force of such long-range bombers, for repeated strikes at American industry were indeed becoming increasingly irrelevant as the prospect of a long war of attrition became less and less consistent with the civilian destruction or military force incapacitation that an H-bomb could inflict in a short time.

But if a Soviet assessment had now been made of the H-bomb's real power, one might yet have been able to find something foreboding in a Russian move to long-range bombers. A desire to be able to strike at the United States and return to the Soviet Union would presuppose some Soviet bases left to return to, bases which would now be few if SAC had already struck at them and the Soviet Air Force had merely been dispatched to inflict retaliation on American cities. Only a Soviet counterforce first strike, designed to take out the H-bomb stockpiles and bases of SAC, would thus enable the U.S.S.R. to recover such bombers as had survived American air defenses; this residual force could then threaten a hydrogen bomb attack on as yet untouched American cities when retaliatory destruction of the U.S.S.R. was no longer possible, thus cashing in on the grand strike politically.

Yet if this were really the Soviet motive, the round-trip capability might have seemed a secondary consideration, since a slightly larger force composed entirely of one-way vehicles might have posed the final city-busting threat as easily. As later with missiles, the addition of round-trip range was in no way crucial to the plausibility of this decisive counterforce attack. If the Russians were concerned, rather, to bolster their penetration capability for one-way retaliatory strikes at American cities by allowing for low-altitude approaches to avert radar detection, or for varying avenues of attack, then this might have been a more plausible explanation of any Soviet investment in extended-range vehicles, although procuring medium-range bombers in greater numbers might have been a more economical form of penetration insurance.

As it was, the Russians in fact procured only the medium-range Badger strategic bomber in quantity,[87] and very few of the long-range Bear and Bison bombers demonstrated at the air shows of 1954 and 1955. Several possible explanations can be found for this Soviet failure to fulfill the worst American expectations. If the Russian leadership were now interested primarily in a credible retaliatory instrument that could reach the North American continent, the medium-range Badger might have sufficed for most targets, on one-way missions, so that no more than 100 or so of the longer-range Bisons and Bears were needed. For the immediate future, the Badger would, however, still be able to strike repeatedly at the closer-in American bases from which most SAC strikes would have to be launched, and the defensive war-fighting capability thus would be maintained for as long as shortages of hydrogen bombs made long war at all a viable concept.

It was true that the United States seemed likely to acquire inter-continental-range B-52's sooner or later, but by then the H-bomb would probably make a long-war scenario meaningless, so that no requirement for repeated strikes at North American bomber bases would be generated. The Soviet decision to purchase large quantities of medium-range Badgers, and only nominal quantities of Bison and Bear (together with upgrading Soviet air defenses), thus made sense as part of a transition from the bearable scenario of medium-range atomic-bomb war to the unbearable scenario of intercontinental H-bomb war. The Badger could be used either on repeated strikes at bomber bases in Europe or on single strikes at cities in the northern United States, for war fighting or for assured-destruction (once a significant amount of destruction could be assured). The Soviet Union thus would never buy an intercontinental "round-trip" strategic capability. The "round trip" could be defensively relevant only until the H-bomb would make a single day's air assault decisive; but the United States itself had not maintained much of an intercontinental system until the B-52 was procured side-by-side with the H-bomb, and the defensive round-trip strike at American bomber bases thus did not have to be interconti-nental for the Soviet Air Force.

An ability to destroy all North American bomber bases in a "splendid first strike" (to prevent any counterattacks on the U.S.S.R.) would not be sought, at least not with intercontinental bombers, probably on the argument that the American stockpile was so large, and the Soviet bomber attack necessarily so slow, that such a perfect first strike would never be possible. The Soviet leadership also must have discovered that long-range bombers were substantially more expensive than had been supposed when the first prototypes had been built, and may thus have become satisfied with a shorter-range, purely retaliatory force. The mere hint of a longer-range force embodied in the Bear and Bison prototypes could be sufficient to accompany the real force of Badgers, and this may partially explain why the Soviet Union misled the United States on the size of its bomber program.

Development of aerial refueling techniques would possibly have augmented Soviet Air Force capabilities in a fashion similar to procurement of intercontinental-range bombers, although the fragile refueling process might have given American defenders more targets to chase. Despite demonstrations of such a capability in 1956 and 1957, however, the evidence is that the U.S.S.R. had not expended much effort in this direction either,[88] probably again because of the impracticability of any grand first strike intended to wipe out all of SAC, and because any war of attrition would be fought at shorter range. Such air refueling as was practiced presumably might help a few more Badgers reach cities in the United States, on one-way retaliatory strikes.

If the Russian leadership was less in fear now of an American attack, it may instead have been seeking the international prestige and status that would accrue to a reputed owner of powerful weapons, so that it might for nonstrategic reasons have feigned a capability it did not really have. A more diabolic explanation sometimes advanced is that the Russians hoped to divert American energies into duplicating and countering an imaginary Soviet bomber force; this would tie up large portions of American military production in jet bomber and air defense systems while the Soviet Union jumped ahead to ballistic missiles.[89]

The possibility must also be considered that the Russian leadership did not intend to mislead the United States at all on the size of its programs, but that American observers jumped to conclusions solely on the basis of one or two air shows. Few Soviet public statements are known stressing any large Soviet bomber force or imputing any great military function to bomber aircraft.[90] Rather, the Soviets at this time tended to allude more often to rockets, a field in which no American commitment had as yet been clearly made, so that the U.S.S.R. presumably might establish a reputation of being in the lead. By 1955-1956, a Soviet lead in tactical and medium-range missiles had indeed been widely recognized in the West, and fears of a Soviet breakthrough to the ICBM had begun to circulate.[91] The Russians may thus have accidentally gained their bomber reputation while intent on building a rocket reputation.

It is thus not clear what forms of imminent survival-of-forces problem could already have become impressed into the consciousness of the American strategic analyst until a real Soviet bomber force and bomb stockpile had emerged. Until very plausible scenarios were presented by which the forces of SAC might be threatened, many observers would not have given much thought to the problem, even if more farsighted speculation was already calling it to attention.

131

Attitudes towards air defense illustrated this well. With any establishment of an H-bomb force as an absolutely unignorable deterrent, radar warning might now take priority over interception, and become crucial. With the hydrogen bomb, the deterrent force of the United States might no longer be spread across its industry, but rather be concentrated on its airstrips. In one way this made the deterrent force more vulnerable, but in another, less, since air defenses plus warning and dispersal systems might keep enough of SAC (for deterrence purposes) alerted and dispersed, even if the aircraft industry could not be similarly protected. Early-warning radar thus would now be of far more use to the controllers of SAC than to the defenders of the Boeing plants (or of New York city).

Yet if early-warning radar might ultimately by itself have to keep the SAC bomber force alerted against preemptive attack by Russian bombers, the Air Force had still generally been unenthusiastic about even this form of air defense protection, for fear that it would drain away funds from offensive weapons needed to win a war.[92] If war had come in the traditionally expected form, as the result of some ongoing crisis in which the Soviets marshaled their forces over a period of weeks for the sweep across Europe, then money spent on warning radar rather than bombers would still have been wasted, at least while the Russians were short of bombers themselves. It is thus not clear whether the Air Force was guilty of a doctrinal lag, or whether the advocates of protection against preemptive attack were premature. In any event, General LeMay was to admit that he was glad to have the early-warning protection provided for SAC when the DEW line was erected,[93] but it was erected later than its proponents had advocated, which may have suited SAC's outlook completely.

The larger air defense programs that had been approved by the new administration might thus eventually have a valuable function after all. The 1950 pleas of the scientists superficially would be heeded, and some of the early advocates of air defense were praised for their foresight. But the major role of the radar warning system would now be to alert and disperse or launch an awesome American hydrogen-bomber force that had not even existed in 1950. The air defense system had originally been proposed to save American lives, and presumably to make it unnecessary for Americans to threaten Russian lives; instead, it would serve mainly to protect American weapons against counterforce strikes, insuring that these American weapons in fact could take a great toll of Russian lives.

132

Steps could be taken, in accordance with the RAND basing study, to remove the more immediate threats of strategic vulnerability, particularly with plans for more rapid evacuations of SAC bases. The number of air bases used by SAC had to be increased, and air refueling techniques had to be perfected.[94] Alternative methods of basing B-47 and B-52 American strategic bombers and of evacuating bases in the event of an attempted Soviet attack were also sought. Some esoteric possibilities emerged here, among them the use of American four-lane highways as emergency landing and takeoff strips for the B-47. This project apparently reached only the preliminary stage of calculating the cost of deploying repair and maintenance units by the sides of designated stretches of highway; yet it suggested that societies as built-up as the United States might still have some inherent military advantages over relatively less complex societies such as the Soviet Union; the possibility would be brought out more clearly some years later with the project for basing intercontinental ballistic missiles on railroad cars. American strategic forces might also be secured against Soviet preemptive strike by basing them in less vulnerable environments. The prospect of firing various sorts of missiles from submarines had already been explored by the Germans in World War II, and the United States Navy now deployed an atomic-warhead cruise missile, the Regulus, to be fired from surfaced submarines at some distance off an enemy coast,[95] perhaps serving already in 1956 as a last-ditch "ace in the hole" deterrent.

Any true war-of-attrition scenario (or the very most awesome "massive retaliation" threat) could not be satisfied with a few Regulus missiles, however, but would require the full strength of SAC. Soviet Badger medium bombers were quite relevantly threatening to the forward bases through which the B-47 would have to stage on missions against the U.S.S.R., if these were not to be suicide missions; expanded production of the intercontinental-range B-52 might thus have been made more necessary by the medium-range Badger than by the intercontinental-range Bison or Bear, by war-of-attrition scenarios rather than preemptive first strike.

President Eisenhower, at least for the interim, had seemingly been content to foster the illusion of an American "war-fighting" superiority, one that could allow the United States to bear up under a prolonged general war without unacceptable damage to its cities, one that could allow the United States slowly to cripple and defeat Soviet military power, if the Russians proved to be callously indifferent to

133

damage inflicted on their cities. Air Force officers, backed by various Congressmen, might in fact wish to pursue the reality of such a superiority, but the President now would not see this as so necessary, and would regard the possible gains of averting an expensive arms race as preferable. The enormity of projected hydrogen bomb explosive potentials probably reduced the feasibility of real American long-war protection in any event, and was similarly likely to exclude any Russian indifference to general war. With the hydrogen bomb in the U.S. arsenal, the Eisenhower Administration thus held off now for a time on any large procurement of long-range B-52 bombers,[96] given its desire for governmental economy and its decision to build air defenses. The 1951 predictions by Air Force spokesmen that active defenses would interfere with offensive weapons procurement were thus seemingly confirmed—at a point, however, where the countercivilian striking power of the two major air forces was still much greater than defense-minded scientists had wanted it to be.

Yet some procurement of B-52's had been authorized, and the 1954 and 1955 Soviet air shows served to mobilize Congress behind Air Force demands that such procurement be accelerated. To counter the supposed Soviet threat, ultimately 700 of the intercontinental bombers were procured, to replace or supplement some 1,700 medium-range B-47's, to prevent or belatedly reverse the "bomber gap" emerging with the Badger, Bear, or Bison. (Air Force acceptances of B-52's were several times delayed by technical difficulties, however, causing prolonged Congressional concern.)[97] The B-52, not yet possessing the 10,000-mile range of which the B-36 had been capable, might nonetheless be able to penetrate into the Soviet Union from bases in North America and return without refueling, should air bases closer to the U.S.S.R. ever be rendered inoperational. The impetus for augmentation of the American offensive bomber force had come now from Democratic Party spokesmen criticizing Eisenhower for economizing on national security; it is perhaps a little less likely that a Democratic victory in 1952 would have made worldwide population security so much more viable.[98]

Despite the awesome destructive power of the new hydrogen bomb, the counterindustry scenario might still be thought valid on less technical considerations. Certain Air Force officers propounded a very pessimistic view of Soviet motivation (one articulated perhaps more often in American right-wing circles): namely, that the Soviet leadership would be indifferent to and undeterred by the suffering of its own people, so long as its ability to win and hold Europe in any war was unimpaired. In this view, there was little gain in a SAC which could assuredly kill tens of millions of Russians, if it could not win the war by wiping out Russian military forces and resources. A "finite deterrent" SAC would not deter the Soviets from seizing Europe, even if American leaders were not thought to be bluffing, because the Soviet Air Force could retaliate on American cities.[99] It might not even deter an attack on the United States, since the Russians might be willing to escalate to the city-busting exchange where it made a military victory easier for them. While the American government had been concerned for the viability of a balance designed to shield Europe, this view was equally concerned for the shielding of North America, reasoning that attacks on both would come together.

As long as the Soviet leadership claimed to be unimpressed by American air attacks, as long as it invested in defensive systems which could be effective only through an extended series of such attacks, the fears of these Americans would be reinforced. If countervalue threats were not to be effective, it might thus be necessary for the United States still to play the "war-fighting" game also, to invest in systems which could not only kill many Russians but also decisively interfere with the Soviet ability to fight a war. With the move to missiles in 1957, the Russians at last would acknowledge for good that the war-of-attrition image was outmoded; but until then the danger seemed real that callous Russian leaders intended to submit their people, and the American people, to months of air war whenever they thought they could overrun Europe and Asia.

Administration opponents to B-52 procurement probably could feel that the hydrogen bomb would make all such considerations irrelevant by the time the B-52 actually reached the quantity deployment stage; either the countercity threat posed by even a few bombers would suffice to deter a Russian move against Western Europe, or all would be lost. (If the B-52's procured in 1956 would later supply a valuable second-strike insurance, when Russian missiles became threatening, neither side could yet have claimed this prescient observation as a fully developed part of its argument.)

Under the rule of Stalin, Soviet propaganda organs had fairly consistently denied any military significance for nuclear weapons, and had scoffed at any inability of civilian populations to bear up under nuclear attack. The hydrogen bomb had clearly altered such views outside the Soviet bloc, but whether it had a similar impact in Russia still could not be straightforwardly determined from a reading of Soviet statements.[100]

For as long as the Russians held no atomic bomb, or perhaps no hydrogen bomb with a sure delivery capability, it would be to the Soviet advantage to continue to shrug off nuclear weapons, lest the West be encouraged to cash in on its weapons advantage in bargaining situations. Yet deterrence of an American preventive war might not be considered secure under such conditions; it may have seemed imperative, if a Soviet H-bomb capability could be established, that the Russian leadership under Malenkov reverse its field, exaggerating instead of debunking the countervalue destruction imposed by such weapons on populations (while continuing to deny that such weapons could reverse the inevitable victory of Communism in any war). Such in fact was now Malenkov's position, in statements of March, 1954, stressing the unbearability of general war to all sides;[101] the statements were hailed in the West as proof that Soviets were no more irresponsible with their new destructive powers than they had been prior to 1953 or 1949, perhaps an important assurance for the Russians to deliver.

The Russian leadership in 1949 had not placed any stress on the atomic bomb test detected by the United States, and had persisted in playing down the significance and specifics of its acquisition of a nuclear capability; the first test of a Russian hydrogen bomb was, however, immediately publicized. This may simply have been because the larger explosion would be much easier to detect, so that any hopes of hiding the acquisition of such a weapon would prove futile. But the Soviet H-bomb test was announced publicly and often by the Soviet leadership,[102] more than it had to be and enough definitely to alert the entire American elite; the explanation probably lies, therefore, with Malenkov's desire to deter American attacks on the U.S.S.R. more securely, no longer by denying that nuclear weapons were effective as a pain-inflicting weapon, but by emphasizing and exaggerating such effect, now that the Russians had a pain-inflicting weapon of their own.

Regardless of whether the concept was ever so articulated in the U.S.S.R., it is plausible that the Russian leadership may also have seen itself imminently confronted by a "year of maximum risk," the year in which American nuclear strength and tactical defensive power would have developed enough to make an attack on the U.S.S.R. seem appropriate. If such an awesome moment could not be headed off by preemptive action, there was perhaps only the chance of hurrying on to some plateau of secure mutual deterrence.

Whether or not to make this shift, from denying countervalue damage to stressing it, related also, however, to one's estimate of exactly what would deter the United States from attacking the U.S.S.R. To assert that Soviet H-bombs could inflict great destruction on America might indeed deter the U.S. leadership, and might also serve to rebut Soviet military commanders who desired greater Russian conventional military spending. If the efficiency of Russian delivery vehicles were in any doubt, however, because military spending had not been enough, then such a Soviet message addressed to the United States might instead be seen as some part of whistling in the dark (as the Soviet military leadership may in truth have seen it), exposing Russian fears of the consequences of war while not inducing such fears in the American leadership.

Hence, when Nikita Khrushchev was seeking issues with which to depose Malenkov, he was able to criticize Malenkov's shift of military doctrine in exchange for the support of the military. Within a short time, Malenkov was forced to tone down his acknowledgment of mutual world destruction in the event of nuclear war;[103] after Malenkov fell from power, Khrushchev and his military chiefs would in fact retract the acknowledgment completely, returning for a time to the proposition that nuclear weapons made little difference at all.

The "premature" move by Malenkov to an "assured destruction" argument may simply have been an expedient issue for Khrushchev to exploit in his move toward control in the U.S.S.R., as a means of promising higher military expenditures to the armed forces in exchange for their support; there was in fact an increase in military allocations immediately after Malenkov's ouster.[104] Yet there may also have been a number of Soviet observers who sincerely interpreted the H-bomb as making an American air assault on the Soviet Union more likely. While the hydrogen bomb may have convinced Malenkov that he had a more secure deterrent than the atomic bomb had previously offered, it also seemed to be the decisive weapon for the United States which the atomic bomb had not been, so awesome and so industrially debilitating as to guarantee a victory for the United States if it were ever tempted to a preventive war. Hence the U.S.S.R. perhaps should not have called attention to the new weapon.

The argument might even have shifted from a counterindustry war of attrition to a more purely counterforce war. The opening up of the strategic discussion after the death of Stalin had allowed many officers to consider the scenario of a SAC offensive for the first time,[105] perhaps to a point where they became overly fixated on the possibility. Observers more fully informed all along might have remained legitimately skeptical about the atomic bomb, but might now also have become convinced that the H-bomb was indeed a weapon possibly capable of bludgeoning a nation into surrender, and/or of wiping out an air force in a very short time, even with near misses, etc. Genuine or manipulated, therefore, a certain concern for imminent nuclear war shows up in the Soviet strategic literature over this time, until Khrushchev's final shift forward again to assured-destruction arguments in 1956 and 1957.

While many of these strategic writings stressed the Soviet Air Force's ability to defend the U.S.S.R. by preemptive air attack, this did not necessarily set up an unstable confrontation with SAC. If an American air offensive were feared, there was less consensus on the duration and intensity of such a campaign; one could stress preemption in the context of either a long war or a short war. In a long war, preemption still suggested little more than counterairbase attacks on each side to wear down countercity offensives so that less civilian-sector damage would be inflicted. This is the mission the Tu-4's would have executed in 1948 and 1949. A matter of minutes or hours in getting one's bomber forces going would not be so crucial to the outcome of such a war, as long as the bomber forces' atomic arsenals did not constitute instantaneously effective counterforce or countervalue instruments. The counterforce exchange would serve, rather, to make air operations less than decisive, since other factors presumably gave victory, as before, to the U.S.S.R.

A vastly different interpretation emerges, of course, where bomber forces would be thought more potent. Who struck first would have been crucial, and there might well have been a clear winner of the aerial exchange, who could thereafter massively menace opposing cities without fear of retaliation. Yet there was little evidence of any general acceptance of such premises by Soviet planners. Preemptive war, on modern assumptions, would have to be completed in a day or not at all, and the Russian air force never approached a level (especially as SAC was cautiously dispersed and augmented) where it could try to wipe out the American strategic force in a day; thus, where preemption was discussed, it was just as plausibly on nonmodern premises, whereby such a campaign could be meaningful over weeks or months.

A concept of preemptive bombing campaigns could be related to the "surprise attack" discussions also emerging in some Russian strategic publications, perhaps signaling a conclusion that one should aim his major effort in a surprise first strike at opposing strategic forces, hoping thereby to emerge with a vastly superior residual air force. The ancillary discussion normally did not make this explicit, however, suggesting rather that initial surprise attacks would have to be followed up by other well-executed military campaigns, so that the initial attacks could not yet be decisive by themselves.

Rather than an endorsement of the mutual instability whereby whoever struck first would win, the Soviet stress on surprise might now simply have served as encouragement to Russian military personnel to be alert and proficient or, more importantly, as psychological reinforcement for demands for greater military appropriations. Suggestions that the enemy might "surprise" with his attack implied that one's government was not taking the threat seriously enough, not purchasing enough deterrent or defensive equipment. However real or unreal the scenario, there were thus payoffs for the Russian military in alluding to it, now that the Stalinist lid on discussions of military strategy was off.

Further Proliferation

The second generation of nuclear weapons had thus, hopefully, been molded into an enduring stabilizer in the Eisenhower years, starting with a renewal of asymmetrical balance, in which the Soviets had no hydrogen bomb force, and then sliding into a scenario in which symmetry became unimportant; a Soviet Union with an equally potent strategic force might still not dare use its conventional superiority now, if deployed tactical nuclears made escalation so likely, or if tactical nuclears equalized and eliminated the Soviet conventional superiority altogether. The program would call for some subtlety to achieve the necessary appearance of dedication; in all cases there had to be some rational motivation for the United States to retaliate but also some emotional motive in addition, and the achievement of this emotional motive precluded any full discussion of the rational motives. So far as one can tell, the transition was carried off reasonably well, from a combination of moral commitment and hydrogen bomb superiority, to another combination of moral commitment and likely tactical nuclear escalation; the strategy held on to Europe and did not cause the loss of as much of Asia as its critics had predicted. Unsettled problems may have remained, however, in the ever-dangerous anomaly of West Berlin and in the growing inducements offered for nuclear proliferation.

Extremely large cannon, capable of firing the 280-millimeter atomic artillery shell, had been deployed to American forces in Germany as early as February of 1954, with the announcement that short-range rockets with nuclear warheads would be deployed soon after. While such forward deployment might have already been seen as a slackening of American control over nuclears, it must be remembered that this was still before any particular form of German rearmament had been determined, since the French National Assembly had yet to render a decision on the EDC Treaty. With the replacement of EDC by an independent West German military force under the control of NATO and the Western European Union, German rearmament was gotten under way, but progress here would be quite slow, and it would be the later 1950's before any West German divisional units were generated as potential users of nuclear weapons supplied by the United States.

Yet the deployment of tactical nuclear weapons to the potential NATO combat zone, when at last accompanied by a buildup of indigenous West German and other combat forces in that zone, would present an issue on the sharing of access to such weapons, or in fact produce some such access even if the issue were not raised. An availability of American tactical nuclear weapons was something that European NATO members could fairly desire for a number of reasons. Being weapons which would have to be used in close proximity to friendly forces, it was only reasonable that such forces be trained to protect themselves against the by-product effects of such weapons. Next might come an equally reasonable proposal that friendly forces be able to request tactical-nuclear supporting fire when threatened by overwhelming enemy forces; if war were to break out, any delay in bringing nuclears to bear on a particular sector of the front might cause the troops defending that sector to fare less well, suffering greater casualties, surrendering more prisoners, and losing more territory.

Next there might emerge a plausible request for a physical deployment of launch vehicles and weapons stockpiles in areas assigned to West German or other forces; finally, the launch vehicles might be manned by non-American forces, with the United States retaining only a physical or legal veto over the commitment of warheads. Access to tactical nuclears would, moreover, remove any lingering doubts about whether such weapons would be used, although the Eisenhower Administration certainly had already done most of what it could to dispel these doubts; as a theoretical justification for European control, this issue of credibility might still always be raised, especially when domestic critics of the Eisenhower Administration had begun demanding that the option of a nonnuclear defense of Europe be reopened.

While the number of tactical nuclear systems was growing, the range of such weaponry was also bound to increase as systems inherently or deliberately limited to a shorter range were stretched by minor technological breakthroughs. Thus the miniaturization of the atomic warhead might adapt it to a certain cannon of fixed range, or to a short-range missile which could not easily be stretched. Yet it might also adapt it to a jet fighter-bomber which had originally not been considered a nuclear delivery vehicle at all, but which now had the range to strike far further east (perhaps on one-way missions) than most "tactical" systems. Two deterministic trends thus had emerged with regard to the forward deployment of "battlefield" nuclear weapons: first, that such weapons over time might slide into the control of the troops stationed around them (especially if it was their country in which the weapons were deployed), and second, that the range of such weapons did not prove easy to constrict.

Yet the Eisenhower Administration may well have seen the proliferation risks here as worth paying. The presence of tactical nuclear weapons reassured allies and probably deterred enemies, and if the alliance were thus kept whole, the question of a sudden coup de main might never arise (or might become irrelevant, if NATO decision-making became so integrated as to rule out independent policies on the use of such weapons). If one had faith in the efficacy of legal and treaty arrangements, moreover, then U.S.-owned nuclear weapons, even when physically surrounded by foreign troops, might yet be controlled, and repossessed if need be, so that real proliferation would not occur. An inevitable disperson of nuclear knowledge may yet make legal distinction on weapons ownership more crucial than physical capabilities; the NATO experience at least has shown no violation of American ownership rights of the weapons deployed.

Tactical nuclear weapons in any event had generally smaller yields than the Hiroshima bomb, and thus were perhaps less than unbearably threatening to the Soviet bloc, no matter how its propaganda agencies reacted. Although the hydrogen bomb already existed in some deliverable forms in 1953, any danger of this weapon working into the control of minor allies of the U.S.S.R. or United States would not arise immediately, for physical reasons if for no other. For the first years, the bomb was clearly too large to be fired by any of the tactical weapons being deployed in Western Europe: the 280-millimeter "atomic cannon" with a range of 25 miles, or the Matador, a cruise missile updated from the German V-1, with a range perhaps of 400 miles. Nor could the H-bomb be carried by any tactical aircraft deployed to the forward areas; doubt persisted for a time whether even the B-47 would be able to transport the big bomb.

With regard to nominally independent nuclear capabilities, only the United Kingdom, aside from the United States and the Soviet Union, was capable of "brandishing" a nuclear threat prior to 1960, but any application of the British nuclear force was subtle at best. Great Britain was involved in relatively little military activity in the 1950's, limiting itself to counterinsurrection operations in Kenya, Malaya, and Aden. One military encounter did stand out, however: that of Britain, France, and Israel with Egypt in 1956, with the ultimate Egyptian nationalization of the Suez Canal. It seems clear that Britain at no time directly threatened Egypt with the use of its atomic arsenal, when much of today's abstract strategic analysis might suggest some such threat in an encounter between a nuclear and a nonnuclear power. Where the issue of strategic weapons application did arise, however, was in the hints of a Russian use of "rockets" against Britain and France if they persisted in their invasion of Egypt.

It has been noticed that the decision to halt the invasion did not come from France, which had no nuclear weapons of its own, but in fact from Britain.[106] The Russian rocket threat has probably been overrated as an influence in the allied withdrawal decision, for the American withholding of currency support, in face of a run of sterling, seems to have been far more significant. The United Kingdom had its own nuclear weapons; RAF bombers had periodically been deployed to bases outside of Britain in Malta and Cyprus. Presumably this presented a sure retaliation threat against the U.S.S.R. should the nuclear question arise, and perhaps conveyed the implications of this throughout the Middle East.

The issue of the use or nonuse of nuclears was a much more complicated question in any event, moreover. For reasons of international prestige, or of the alliance with the United States, the British Government would find it impossible as well as unnecessary to brandish its nuclear force explicitly. The use of such weapons could only be hinted at, most clearly as a deterrent to massive Soviet intervention. The Russian rocket threats were further called into question at the time of Suez by the responsive American alerting of SAC, reestablishing that the American nuclear force similarly would not allow the use of Russian medium-range missiles. Whether the United Kingdom exacted any concrete advantage from its possession of nuclears during the Suez crisis is thus not easy to determine.

In the days when nuclear weapons had not seemed decisive, but rather only a marginal addition to a nation's weaponry, nuclear proliferation within an alliance might have been seen as cementing the bond rather than inducing increased national independence. At least until an H-bomb reprisal threat had come to be seen as any nation's decisive veto on aggression against itself, nuclear war might have seemed a large-scale effort requiring extensive cooperation and coordination among members of an alliance. Thus, even with the nuclear independence of Great Britain in 1956, it did not seem that atomic weapons had exacerbated the Anglo-American rift at the time of the Suez invasion, but rather that they had bonded the allies. American and British strategic forces presumably counterdeterred Soviet rocket threats together, rather than separately; as an approach to healing the 1956 differences, the United States would agree early in 1957 to deploy Thor MRBM's to Great Britain under a form of joint custody,[107] even before the United States developed a clear interest of its own in such a deployment.

There would always be limits, of course, to American willingness to diffuse nuclear weapons capabilities among its allies because of somewhat insular suspicions in Congress, or for better reasons. Taiwan and Korea would not receive such weaponry, if only because their level of industrial development never made it logical that this be their "contribution to alliance military efforts." "Communist physicists" in France and "ex-Nazis" in Germany would slow any nuclear sharing in these directions. Yet if the European NATO members were to be grafted ever more closely into an Atlantic alliance, it would not have seemed appropriate to raise an explicit issue of proliferation or nonproliferation in the mid-1950's, since de facto proliferation, at least in some cases, might have alliance benefits.

Apart from actual weapons deployments, it seems very plausible today that the American "Atoms for Peace" proposal greatly increased the possibilities of nuclear weapons production around the world. The delivery of research and power reactors to various countries, and the sharing of related technological data, at the least facilitated production of fissionable plutonium; such plutonium had constituted two of the first three atomic bombs exploded. While the spread of reactors made easier the accumulation of atomic bomb stockpiles, it did not contribute as much to the development of hydrogen-bomb capabilities, since plutonium bombs were apparently more difficult to detonate and thus less suitable as triggers for hydrogen weapons. But plutonium conversely was more suitable than uranium for certain more sophisticated forms of fission (atomic) bombs, a fact which may not have been so clear in 1954. If one accepted the analysis that atomic bombs were less significant as destructive weapons, that only the hydrogen bomb created a real "problem for civilization," then the distribution of reactors might not have been so unwise. One could have hoped that the economic benefits thus realized (apparently substantially overrated) would strengthen the economies of various nations enough to make them more viable against Communist expansion, and that this consideration would outweigh the risks of proliferation.

Yet the political transition from nuclear power to nuclear bombs might prove all too simple. Neither the United States nor the U.S.S.R. had any problems in domestically justifying their original nuclear programs. In the American case, wartime secrecy plus fear of parallel German progress removed the possibility of domestic objection, while Stalinist Russia also had no need to disclose its activities. In each case, therefore, a program providing supplies of both uranium and plutonium was carried through, capable of generating a complete and sophisticated inventory of weapons.

In the case of Great Britain, and again of France, progress of a weapons program could not so easily be justified at the outset;[108] research presumably useful for civilian purposes would have to be launched first, requiring that the initial weapons run be entirely of plutonium bombs, the "by-products" of power production and other reactor operations. Yet in each case the kiloton-range bombs generated by such processes also quickly seemed inadequate for the nation's prestige or strategic goals, so that the more costly uranium-production programs for megaton-range hydrogen weapons were then entered into. The result was that Great Britain succeeded in detonating its first hydrogen weapon (delivered immediately, in fact, by an RAF bomber)[109] in 1957, with the first French hydrogen test coming only in 1968. The British and French examples thus seemed to offer two propositions about proliferation: first, that civilian research and plutonium-producing reactors can indeed lead to an escalating program (at least in an economically able country) going all the way to the H-bomb; second, that no sense of "possessing an equalizer" adheres to the simple kiloton-range plutonium bomb (so that the economically unable country may in fact not find entry into the nuclear club so easy or so inviting).

4 The Missile Gap: 1957-1961

The Missile Issue

Fears of a Soviet bomber buildup had been substantially dispelled by February of 1957, when official U.S. intelligence prognoses of the Soviet force were reduced.[1] The U-2 flight program had commenced by now, and this presumably merged with other intelligence sources to convince the Eisenhower Administration that its original calm and confident estimates had been correct. The Russians seemed not to have produced 1,000 Bison, but only a little more than 150, and not 1,000 turboprop Bears, but closer to 100. Where the U.S.S.R. did live up to expectations, however, was in the production of the shorter-range B-47 equivalent, the Badger; some 1,000 or so were built, capable of striking at any American bases within 4,000 miles of the Soviet frontier, at European cities within the same radius, and also perhaps at the United States on one-way suicide missions.

With quantity production of A- or H-bombs, the Soviet Air Force seemed reasonably sure now of an ability to inflict great destruction on something valuable to the United States in Europe, and perhaps on the United States itself, if the threat of the advance of the Red Army was not enough. The Badger on a one-way counterforce mission might indeed take out a SAC base as easily as a Bear on a round trip, thus possibly undermining the sigh of relief emitted in 1957 at the disappearance of the bomber gap. Yet more probably it only signified that American expenditure on the almost-finished DEW Line had not been a waste of effort. Since a successful Soviet bomber sneak attack remained implausible, additional U.S. strategic delivery vehicles were not needed to ensure retaliation, since enough of those in being would be alerted and off the ground during the Badger's approach. The Air Force, supported by Congressional critics of the administration, still urged greater acquisitions of B-52's and of the shorter-range, very-high-speed B-58; but outside the administration, concern had begun to shift to the dangers of the Soviet missile program and the seemingly slow American governmental response to it.

The U.S.S.R. had openly boasted of a medium-range missile capability since 1955, and had brandished this force at Great Britain and France during the November, 1956, Suez crisis. Medium-range missiles of course were not difficult to conjure up on the basis of German World War II accomplishments, but many technical observers had earlier foreseen insurmountable obstacles to any extension of such missiles' range. The preparation and dissemination of the von Neumann report now had altered such assumptions on missile feasibility, however, throughout much of the American defense establishment; formally presented in February of 1954, the report asserted that a militarily significant ICBM was indeed possible now that thermonuclear weaponry was at hand, recommending that special management priority be given to its development.[2] Earlier estimates on the payload and accuracy limitations of such missiles were found to be needlessly pessimistic, but the major change was that the hydrogen bomb eased much of the constraint imposed by such limitations, so far as counter-city weaponry was concerned. The more widely discussed incentive for missile development at this time was still that it would guarantee penetration of all foreseeable defensive systems, that it thus provided a surer countercity or counterindustry delivery system than had been provided by the bomber, especially in view of the prospective development of air defense systems on both sides.

Yet the possibility that intercontinental missiles might be aimed at opposing delivery vehicles (bombers or missiles) lingered in the background, perhaps posing a very severe threat for the strategic balance. Two factors would be significant for estimating the stability of the missile as a strategic delivery vehicle, but neither of these could have been predicted very accurately in 1954. First, accuracies were crucial, for if a five-mile CEP were sufficient against an opposing city, it might not be menacing to a smaller bomber base, or to a minuscule missile site, while a one-mile CEP would be. Second, the physical fragility of missiles on their launching pads would be relevant; a primitive liquid-fueled missile might be blown off its exposed launching pad by even a strong windstorm, and would be thus a far more inviting target for preemptive attack than a solid-fueled missile stored underground beneath layers of concrete.

More or less coincidentally with the presentation of the von Neumann report, development of ballistic missiles within the Air Force was assigned to Trevor Gardner, Assistant Secretary of the Air Force for Research and Development.[3] Over the summer of 1954, General Bernard Schreiver was assigned the management task of missile development, and the highest priority within the Air Force was assigned to such development.[4] At the Department of Defense level, however, no such priority was assigned to missile programs until late 1955. The significance of such "priorities" might be exaggerated; for a given budget allocation of funds between missiles and other weapons, missiles merely would have first claim at the margin for material or manpower resources that had to be rationed (i.e., resources that could not simply be divided or allocated according to the allocation of moneys to the various projects). Thus in 1954 and 1955 the budget for missile development still rested in the millions of dollars (leading to Gardner's resignation),[5] while bombers were being allocated billions. The priority was thus more psychological and marginal than basic.

At the strategic or intercontinental level, an instability might now be imminent, but it might also still be avoidable. Despite the calculations that had been presented earlier on a sneak attack by Soviet bombers against U.S. bomber bases (or vice versa), a modicum of dispersal bases and a radar warning network (as embodied after 1957 in the U.S.-Canadian NORAD agreement) would make it difficult for either power after 1956 to disarm the other totally, thereby escaping retaliation.

If long-range missiles were not introduced at all, a rudimentary equivalent of assured second-strike retaliatory destruction might thus exist, possessing many of the attributes of the invulnerable underwater and underground-based missile systems of the 1960's. Had a transition from bombers to hardened missiles (storable in firing position under layers of concrete) been directly feasible, with the United States remaining slightly ahead—or equal—in number of missiles, no concern for missile gaps or strategic instabilities need have arisen. When enough hardened missiles had been procured on either side to counterforce-target all opposing bomber bases, enough hardened missiles ipso facto would have existed also on that side to replace bombers as retaliatory weapons.

Complications arose, however, because the first feasible generation of intercontinental missiles would necessarily be launched from above ground and hence would be quite vulnerable to incoming missile attacks (or even to bomber attacks). Being vulnerable themselves, and being able to hit bomber bases without warning, the liquid-fueled, above-the-surface missiles might really make victory a function entirely of who struck first. Three types of scenario were thus in question: the existing bomber confrontation where one side (but not both simultaneously) might acquire the ability to disarm the other (only by sizably outproducing the other in bombers); an imminent liquid-fueled missile confrontation where either side might be able to disarm the other if it struck first; and the solid-fueled missile confrontation of the future, where neither side could disarm the other, even if it were far superior in numbers.

If the transition from relatively invulnerable bombers to more clearly invulnerable missiles (passing through a dangerous interim of vulnerable missiles) was now the essential problem facing the United States, then several issues would come to mind. Was it wiser to skip the production of liquid-fueled missiles altogether, only developing them as a stage on the road to solid-fueled missiles; or was it better to produce and deploy at least some of such missiles, to make the first-strike problem more difficult for any opponent who procured the interim model in quantity? If the latter course were chosen, it might by itself force the Russians to invest in liquid-fueled missiles, as a rational precaution or on more psychological motives.

Similarly, how much effort should be committed to accelerating development of the "hardenable" solid-fueled missile? If neither side procured the liquid-fueled variety, there would be less need to waste resources in hurrying up a process that would otherwise mature by itself, sooner or later. Similarly, how much should be spent on augmenting bomber forces, forces that would not need augmentation unless the transition to secure missiles was diverted into vulnerable liquid-fueled missiles? Some might offer other arguments for bolstering the bomber force or for procuring another generation of it, but if secure second-strike retaliation were now left as the only plausible goal, current bomber forces would probably prove entirely adequate, as long as solid-fueled missiles alone were securely deployed at a slow rate on each side. Facing these three issues—procurement of liquid-fueled missiles, development of solid-fueled missiles, and augmentation of bomber forces—the Eisenhower Administration found its calm approach complicated by the criticism of political opponents at home and by the obscurity of Soviet policies abroad.

Inducing a worldwide postponement of the move to missiles might have served narrow American interests. If one still took seriously the question of who would "win" an all-out war (as some in the Air Force clearly did), then a confrontation limited to bombers would bring existing American force and production superiorities to bear. If the Eisenhower Administration did not take this issue seriously any more, given the power of the H-bombs which inevitably would be delivered against some American cities in such a war, it might nonetheless be inclined to preserve and exploit the image of American victory, for the psychological margin it provided in crisis situations. Serious proponents of the war-fighting view favored increased bomber procurement for SAC; less serious administration officials might still welcome a continued worldwide reliance on bombers rather than missiles, at least for an interim.

The Eisenhower Administration thus had the choice of trying to delay the deployment of long-range missiles, in order to preserve the less delicate balance established by bomber forces, or of rushing ahead to keep the United States numerically first even in the crude early generations of missiles. For reasons domestic and external, an attempt to pursue the first course could not really be successful. It was clear that there was some overlap between the intercontinental missile category and any kind of civilian space program. Hopes were thus entertained in the United States, perhaps naïvely, that ICBM development could somehow be blunted or controlled by a diversion of activity into a space research program which might be international.[6] With a view toward a possible internationalization, therefore, the original American Vanguard earth satellite was kept largely separate from military missile development, so that it might be thrown open to outside participation as soon as an American "first" in space had captured world attention. But the premise of a U.S. "first" was not to be realized.

The Russian intercontinental missile tests of 1957, and more crucially the orbiting of the first man-made earth satellite on October 4 of that year, seemed to confirm all the earlier American fears of a Soviet leap into a strategic weapons superiority; the psychological impact on the United States seemed greater than that of the preceding Soviet A-bomb, H-bomb, or long-range bombers.[7] Part of the excitement may have been induced by the apparent physics of the situation, specifically, that the Russians had suspended a device over the head of the United States, in an orbit from which it could seemingly drop at leisure onto any locality. More directly, it may have arisen because this was the earliest instance of the United States finishing clearly second in a technological race with the U.S.S.R. (the Soviet priority in hydrogen-bomb development, after all, had not been made so very explicit). The United States had committed itself to orbit a nonmilitary satellite in 1958, and had begun testing Atlas and Thor military missiles in 1957.[8] Yet while commentators at the beginning of 1957 had expected such tests to be successful, there had still been no unmarred firings of Thor or Atlas by the end of the year; and the attempted launching of the Vanguard nonmilitary satellites, pushed up into December, was also a spectacular failure.

Measuring the depth of genuine American public interest in defense issues over this period is not easy. The larger public probably had only a vague concern for American force survivability, and even an American opinion-forming leadership did not understand concepts as esoteric as the preferability of second-strike over first-strike postures, etc. Public concern and mobilization soon enough focused on other Soviet "firsts" in less military space programs (especially the first cosmonaut), and then very quickly seemed to recede as the United States began to take the "lead" in space research. In the immediate aftermath of the Soviet orbital landings, in November of 1957, some 53 percent of Americans interviewed thought it time to "take a new look" at American defense policy, with 26 percent thinking instead that American policies were satisfactory.[9] Comparable polls by 1960, however, would show much more normal levels of satisfaction.[10] An influential portion of the American public might thus not have been so alarmed about Soviet progress on the ICBM if the news of this progress had not been coupled with the launching of an earth satellite. If the United States had been allowed to launch its satellite first, moreover, such domestic alarm (and overseas loss of prestige, which may have been a more legitimate cause for domestic alarm) might have been substantially avoided.

The initial reaction of the Republican Administration itself to the Sputnik launching was not at all dramatic, since Soviet missile tests had been under observation, both by radar and by U-2 aircraft, since the summer of 1957;[11] thus the first National Security Council conference after Sputnik, on October 10, 1957, reached no drastic conclusions. Yet four factors now combined to shatter this composure. First, of course, was the public's reaction to Sputnik I, for the resultant uproar could not help but upset the administration. Second was the Sputnik II launch of November 3, with its tremendous payload, considerably larger than American intelligence sources had in fact thought possible.[12] Third, there came now intelligence estimates that Soviet missile production could well be much larger than had been thought, with more than 200 Soviet ICMB's in place by 1962 at the latest, and perhaps as early as by 1960.[13] Plausible calculations might be presented that 175 such missiles could suffice to take out all the strategic air bases in North America without any advance radar warning, while the quantities of Soviet MRBM's already available would handle the overseas SAC bases.[14] Finally, a committee had been convened earlier in 1957 to examine Civil Defense Director Val Peterson's request for $30 billion to be spent on blast shelters. Empowered to consider alternative uses of such large sums, the Gaither Committee now presented a report urging greater expenditures to ensure the survivability of American strategic forces.[15]

Presumably the Soviets would build missiles up to full capacity; when they did so, they would at some point be able to target all of SAC's bomber airfields and all of the much smaller number of American missile launching pads, so that a complete disarmament of the United States could be possible. If all Soviet and American missiles were of the vulnerable liquid-fueled first generation, the United States might thus be able to escape defeat at some point only by striking first. Even this most unstable confrontation had disadvantageous asymmetries for the United States, since the bulk of the American first-strike attack had to be executed by bomber aircraft, giving the Soviets more warning, more of a chance to get at least a few missiles off at U.S. cities, if SAC were at all delayed in reaching the Soviet launching sites. Conversely, if the bulk of the Soviet attacks were by missile, less warning would be available for the United States. President Eisenhower afterwards claimed in his memoirs that the Gaither Committee did not have access to all the available intelligence data,[16] data which presented a less pessimistic picture for the United States. Presumably such data might have included that obtained from the U-2 overflights, although it is not clear what such flights could yet have shown about Soviet missile production rates for the coming 1958-1961 period.

American Responses

The picture drawn of American strategic vulnerability was nonetheless probably overly pessimistic for the United States, even assuming that the Russians would produce as many ICBM's as possible. The accuracy and reliability of Russian missiles were still subject to question. If the Soviets were intent on striking at the largest American cities, then their ICBM's promised immediately or within a few years to carry out this mission with no real possibility of American defense; if intent, rather, on taking out SAC's bombers and budding missile force, the Soviet missiles might be less reliable, and the Russians might find themselves depending additionally on whatever bombers they had, with their greater carrying capacities and delivery accuracies but slower approach patterns that would give greater warning.

The provision of early-warning radar sufficient to trigger evacuations of SAC bases had plausibly reduced the counterforce potential of Soviet manned bombers, at least against American bombers; hence, if the U.S.S.R. did not produce enough ICBM's to cover each SAC base reliably, with allowances for malfunctions and aiming errors, the first strike would be less plausible. If the United States were now to augment its strategic force array with slow-to-fire liquid-fueled missiles, these would presumably offer Soviet bombers a more appropriate target. Yet the calculations for such a coordinated Soviet first strike were substantially more complicated, making any attack less likely.

More sober estimates of the ICBM threat thus noted that the investment in the DEW Line was not a waste, as long as some significant part of the Soviet attack might still have to come by means of a detectable bomber force.[17] Radar, moreover, might yet be augmented and improved in time to detect a missile attack, then to plug a warning signal into the communication systems which had been developed for the DEW Line; this signal, if inadequate for the evacuation of cities, might still be adequate to get many of SAC's bombers off the ground to launch a retaliatory strike against the U.S.S.R., especially if the necessary launching time for SAC could be cut to 15 minutes. Thus, even if the Russians had proceeded to build all the missiles they could right from the start, the Eisenhower Administration might have justifiably felt that this made less strategic difference, so that no drastic American response was in order. The Soviet problem of planning for a completely successful counterforce attack was complicated also by any dispersal of American strategic forces. Overseas deployments might somewhat increase the complication, since salvos would have to be fired in combination at North-American based forces and at SAC bombers in Britain; if the warheads aimed at either base impacted first, this might alert and dispatch the other base's bombers.

The Eisenhower Administration did not have such an easy task, however, in reassuring the American decision-making community that a sufficient retaliatory deterrent would always survive to dissuade the Russians from any first strike at the United States. At least some adjustments to existing aircraft and warning systems, and investments in new (if imperfect) missile systems, would be required to remove the anxiety that had emerged so dramatically after 1957. In addition to measures already implemented in 1956 and 1957 to augment the survivability of SAC bomber forces, other steps were taken. In addition to a stepped-up development of solid-fueled missiles for the long run, some number of liquid-fueled missiles had to be procured for the immediate future.

The role of a successful test program in the establishment of a missile delivery system might be somewhat ambiguous. It would be very common for a Western public to draw comfort from a successful U.S. missile test, or alarm from a Soviet test, in each case implicitly assuming that the capability was established immediately with, and not before, the test. More typically, of course, operational capabilities were established some time after completion of a test series; supporting facilities were only then completed in the assurance that they indeed were appropriate to successful missions. Certainly it would seem unwise to deploy a Polaris submarine on station until Polaris missiles had successfully been fired full-range from a submarine. Similarly, there was little reason to assume that the Russians could already have ICBM's on station as their first full-range tests were being conducted.

Conversely, however, since the United States felt imminently threatened by Soviet missile progress, the deployment and erection of any delivery vehicles whatsoever might seem in order, at least to complicate the attack problem of the better-equipped U.S.S.R.; thus, even as the last test firings were still demonstrating persistent malfunctions in minor components, certain of the same American Atlas missiles could already be deployed for what just might be successful retaliatory strikes in the event of war.[18] With each of these liquid-fueled missiles the malfunction rate might have been high (prior to any successful full-range tests, as well as after), and the Soviet kill rate would also have been high, given the vulnerable nature of their deployment. Yet by their very existence on some sort of launching site, the first Atlas missiles complicated the hypothetical Russian attack problem, presumably forcing the programming of bombers or missiles against them and inducing doubts about whether one or two of them might possibly succeed in hitting Moscow or Leningrad.

Even if the threat of a successful Soviet counterforce strike was thus less than it had been conjectured to be, a deterrence based on vulnerable bomber and missile systems required tension and vigilance at often misleading radar screens, a tension that would be unacceptable for the long run. Quite early, therefore, the emphasis shifted to achieving a second generation of missiles that could be protected by layers of concrete, or by concealment and mobility, to make the question of who preempted whom less relevant. Observers have often pointed to the solid-fueled missiles' capacity for rapid firing as their great advantage over those with liquid fuel. The long launching countdown associated with the early liquid-fueled missiles, since their volatile fuel had to be stored separately, seemed to leave no opportunity for a quick firing, on warning that a Russian salvo was on its way. Yet the ambiguous reliability of radar and other warnings made it extremely undesirable that missiles should ever have to be fired before a Russian missile salvo had clearly impacted in the United States, for frightening prospects would thereby have been generated of mistaken preemptive wars. (Perhaps if the approach of Soviet bombers had been detected, missiles would have nonetheless been fired.)

The more important advantage of solid-fueled missiles was that the storability of their propellant facilitated deployment under the solid protection of a layer of concrete, so that one might securely wait days before deciding to fire them. Thus, the first three squadrons of Atlas D missiles (liquid-fueled) had been deployed above ground in erect firing position, destructible by only 2 psi of excess atmospheric pressure, serving merely to force the Soviets to program one more target. Some later liquid-fueled varieties, three squadrons (27 missiles) of Atlas E, were deployed in horizontal "coffins" underground, secure up to 25 psi of excess pressure; however, they would have to be raised into firing position after a Soviet attack, which might create other problems. Finally, in 1961 and 1962 the first squadrons of Titan I (also liquid-fueled) were activated in underground silos hardened to 100 psi, and were followed by Atlas F and then by the solid-fueled Minuteman, similarly deployed.[19]

The value of an investment in liquid-fueled missiles might be debatable; but accelerating the development of securely deployable solid-fueled missiles clearly generated benefits by putting an earlier end to the instability and anxieties associated with vulnerable weapons systems. The acceleration was accomplished at additional material costs, and with the risk that premature decision might turn out wrong on crucial variables, perhaps then requiring a long delay of operational systems, or massive additional expenditures to repair errors and avoid such delays. Fortunately, few such errors were made with regard to both the Polaris and Minuteman systems,[20] resulting in deployable Polaris missiles by 1960 and deployable Minutemen by late 1962.

Submarine-based missiles offered a special sense of security in the Polaris configuration; there was no vulnerability problem at all for the foreseeable future, thus dispensing with the exchange-rate calculations required for the liquid-fueled Atlas and Titan, and even for the land-based solid-fueled Minuteman. Concern for the ultimate vulnerability of all land-based missiles in fact suggested a mobile variation on Minuteman, to be carried on railroad cars. Here, as with highway-runways for long-range bombers, the relative advantage of the United States in a basically civilian category might again be harnessed for military purposes, in an approach which the U.S.S.R. could not duplicate.

A number of writers in the late 1950's commented on the Navy's seemingly paradoxical shift in strategic argument away from its position at the 1949 B-36 hearings. While it then had denounced the policy of strategic bombing as immoral, it now had become enthusiastic about the Polaris weapon, which for the time would be so inaccurate that it could be aimed only at cities. Yet the Navy's position might not have been inconsistent or shallow in its morality. As part of a policy of finite deterrence or as a backup to a larger and more varied strategic force, the Polaris missile represented a kind of deterrent very different from that of the Air Force in 1948. In 1948 war had been thought very possible. Atomic-bomb-carrying airplanes might deter a war, but primarily they would have won the victory for the United States if war had somehow broken out. In fact, the ability to deter war was dependent in large part on the supposed ability to win it. If war was thus likely in 1948, a moral aversion to the civilian suffering in a counterindustry campaign might be quite tenable. The hydrogen bomb had, however, led to different assumptions: that war would certainly be unthinkable no matter who "won" it, that a strategic strike force would no longer be established in anticipation of its use or its military efficiency, but only for its deterrent awesomeness. If Navy strategists were now less concerned that Polaris would have to be used, if they in fact saw no rational or instrumental use of the weapon, then they were not so inconsistent in arguing that Polaris could be justified, even by the standards with which they had denounced the B-36 program. The enthusiasm of Congress for the Polaris submarine was now such as to authorize an increase in the number of such vessels from five to nine,[21] although the Navy's request for another large nuclear-powered aircraft carrier was ignored.

The fear that the United States would soon be decisively vulnerable to a Russian counterforce first strike if missiles caught SAC's bombers on the ground without warning, since the United States had no intercontinental missiles of its own with which to retaliate, was seen by many as a vindication for Air Force spokesmen such as General LeMay, who had been warning that American deterrent power was in danger. Yet LeMay's arguments as late as 1956, and at times even now in 1958, had still been predicated on differing theories of deterrence: that mere destruction of Russian cities would not deter the Soviet leadership, since an additional prospect of military incapacitation and defeat would be required.[22] Russian bomber forces, for this more extended aerial attrition campaign, were perhaps still more threatening than missiles, and LeMay had all along urged greater production of American manned bombers, in addition to or probably ahead of missiles.

Now that the Russians were claiming to have moved on to missiles, after their unexpected shortfall in intercontinental bombers, LeMay's response was still to advocate accelerating the acquisition of B-52 manned bombers,[23] with an increase in the number of bases at which to deploy them, rather than any straightforward concentration on missile development. LeMay contended that too much effort was now being allotted to the submarine-based Polaris program (a program which stressed simple retaliation and could make little contribution to "military victory"), to the relative neglect of the manned bomber.

The manned bomber certainly was still very valuable as another vehicle for the retaliatory counterpopulation threat (the threat which the Air Force did not regard as sufficient by itself). Even if antibomber air defenses were continually being improved, both the United States and the U.S.S.R. were developing bomber-launched missiles of cruise (and later ballistic) varieties, accurate enough to hit targets as large as cities; bombers might lend themselves, moreover, to an airborne alert procedure which would always keep some H-bomb-laden B-52's aloft, where no Russian ICBM could find or destroy them.

The Soviet Union in the late 1950's and early 1960's showed itself consistently hostile to such airborne alert programs, just as it also expressed opposition to submarine-based deployments.[24] The Russian leadership may have been genuinely far less confident of command-and-

156

control systems than was the United States, perhaps fearing that an American bomber pilot might on his own initiative strike at Soviet cities, as might an American Polaris submarine captain. Sincerity here was presumably demonstrated by the absence of any similar Russian deployments beyond the physical veto of Moscow.

Airborne alert, moreover, seemed precarious to various parties if it required periodic flights toward and then away from Soviet borders, flights which would be monitored on Russian radar screens, with an accompanying increase in tension. All the bombers of airborne alert might have to be flown toward Soviet targets if war seemed imminent, since the bases to refuel them, if the bombers were held back, might not survive a Russian attack expected on the basis of some blips on a radar scope. This by itself might set up tension enough to force the Soviets to launch an attack if they had not yet done so; submarine deployments, on the other hand, required no such adjustment of posture. The physical visibility of airborne deployments was great in any event, with bomb-laden aircraft periodically crashing to earth, hopefully with no detonation of the weapons on board, but with radiational hazards nonetheless. By contrast, submarine deployments did not thrust themselves so constantly, or so precariously, before the international public eye.

Over the three remaining years of the Eisenhower Administration, the greatest and most persistent Air Force pressure would be devoted specifically to the airborne alert proposal, even ahead of missile programs, but the proposal would never be strictly implemented. Weapons were put on board some B-52's already almost always aloft on training flights, but a full-scale program was precluded by the disadvantages cited above and by the wear on aircraft subjected to such endurance flights.

American or Russian bombers might also have constituted a significant counterforce threat, through the early missile era, against widely dispersed, slow-reacting missile sites (while the ICBM was the necessary counterforce weapon against collections of fast-evacuating bombers on air bases). But the threat of a few bombers coming through on so-called "trucking missions" to destroy missile sites at their leisure became considerably less real as SAM air defense missiles were introduced around or close to such sites. If bomber aircraft now had to rely on air-launched missiles to deliver their warheads for the last 1,000 miles to target, this would reduce accuracy too much for reliable counterforce strikes. The desirability of such counterforce instruments was, moreover, not always so clear.

The Russian missile tests might now have decisively outmoded the original view of active defense systems as population-protecting systems. Missiles could not be intercepted by any means at hand, and could reach the United States in a very short time; even if a missile-detecting BMEWS radar were thus procured, the warning so generated could not really suffice for an evacuation of cities. Yet while considerable effort was now expended to give SAC warning of a manned bomber attack (and ultimately of a missile attack), work still was not terminated on other systems intended to shoot down a certain number of Russian bombers before they reached their population target. Interservice disputes on interception weapons were allowed to drift on without decisive adjudication within the executive branch, and Congressional committees sometimes intervened to arbitrate disputes, between the Air Force Talos and the Army Nike-Ajax, and then between the Air Force Bomarc and the Army Nike-Hercules.[25] The SAGE system, designed to direct the interception of bombers detected by the DEW Line, was inaugurated in 1958, although its control centers would never be hardened against missile attack.[26]

Interim Adjustments

If absolutely secure solid-fueled missiles could not be immediately available, interim devices might be relevant. From 1955 until 1963 the U.S. Navy had deployed a submarine-based strategic retaliatory system, the 500-mile, surface-launched Regulus cruise missile. Some 17 such missiles were deployed on five submarines,[27] with plans made for additional atomic-powered submarine Regulus carriers should the Polaris system not come along on schedule. Regulus missiles were also placed on board several surface ships, and one could have argued that something of a sea mobile force already existed throughout the "missile gap," presumably capable of hitting Leningrad from the Baltic Sea with at least a fission warhead. Similar cruise or rudimentary ballistic missiles, submarine-based but surface-launched, were identified as prototypes in the Soviet inventory by 1959;[28] but the Russians apparently were to take much longer in developing and deploying a full Polaris equivalent, capable of being launched from below the surface at greater than 1,000-mile range.

Another American cruise missile now considered for deployment was the 5,000-mile-range Air Force Snark,[29] but only 30 of the Snark missiles were ever procured and deployed into launching sites. Compared with manned bombers, the Snark had a few advantages in terms of stabilizing any Soviet threat. The cruise missiles did not need runways for takeoff, so that they might be deployed far enough apart to force the Russians perhaps to program one missile or more for each Snark site. The speed of attack was similar to that of a manned bomber, making interception of the missile in flight very possible, but perhaps never sure. The attack would be slow, so that Russian bombers could be alerted and evacuated from a base threatened with attack; the Snark thus could not serve as a plausible counterforce weapon, and perhaps might remove any Soviet need for preemption. But the likelihood of at least one Russian city being hit on retaliatory strike would remain high, no matter how good the Soviet air defense was.

One could argue also that Navy aircraft, capable of delivering nuclear warheads deployed on board aircraft carriers, could similarly execute retaliatory missions if other systems did not, thus again deterring a Soviet attack. The carriers of course were extremely vulnerable to missiles, bombers, or submarines, if any such Soviet attack systems could locate all the carriers on the day of the grand first strike. The warheads on board the carriers also were likely to be smaller atomic bombs, rather than the still bulky but more frightening H-bombs. Whether or not the Soviet problem in locating U.S. aircraft carriers was as insoluble as the American President somewhat offhandedly assumed it to be,[30] the existence of such forces at least complicated the Russian calculations necessary for any first strike, and thus made the strike less likely.

Finally, vulnerable U.S. liquid-fueled MRBM's were to be deployed to Europe. The decision to request a basing of MRBM's in Western Europe at first glance represented a significant departure from the American role in NATO; the United States might now become a "consumer" rather than "producer" of security, if the missiles were seen as intended to deter attacks on North America. The SAC bases in Great Britain had of course already served this purpose for over nine years; but these antedated NATO and could be seen as a product of the "special relationship" between the United States and the United Kingdom, in exchange for which the United States had supplied the British with B-29 bombers, and later with assistance on nuclear development. B-29's had also been based in West Germany, until they had been replaced with longer-range and higher-performance bombers based in Spain, Great Britain, and French Morocco. The French basing agreement had similarly contributed to U.S. security, but had also occurred on territory outside the protective jurisdiction of NATO. In any event, bomber bases prior to 1957 had served as an insurance, but not as an indispensable prerequisite, to American strategic air potential; just as importantly, perhaps, they had served as pledges of American commitment to the defense of other countries.

Viewed in the context of the most extreme "missile gap" analysis of 1957 and 1958, the MRBM deployment seemed to be the administration's panicked admission that its retaliatory capacity was obsolete.[31] European powers (on this analysis) would be reluctant to help supplement a retaliatory instrument that was of such doubtful efficacy; Denmark and Norway at the 1957 NATO meetings clearly ruled out any deployment onto their territory, while even West Germany seemed reluctant to accept the vulnerable liquid-fueled missiles being offered. Yet the immediate need for a physical deployment was not as pressing as many commentators assumed, since MRBM's would not be available in quantity for some time. What the United States delegation led by Secretary Dulles perhaps now wanted most was a NATO endorsement in principle for such deployments, as an affirmation to European publics and to the world that the value of the American alliance had not really come into question.[32] The acceptance by Great Britain, Italy, and Turkey of liquid-fueled MRBM's thus was more than sufficient from the American Administration's view of military requirements, as long as Russian missile forces were not as awesome in potential as some had conjectured them to be. A few medium-range missiles would complicate the Russian strategic problem enough to weaken any major threat, and even these missiles would be produced and deployed only after some time had passed. The important problem may have been, rather, to avoid any great resonance in Europe of the doubts being expressed in the United States, and here the Administration was largely successful.

Forward deployment of medium-range missiles is sometimes presented as establishing an absolutely insoluble planning problem for an attacker, since he must coordinate his strikes to destroy both ICBM's and forward-deployed MRBM's. The forward MRBM's will be hit too soon, the argument goes, giving warning to launch the ICBM's; or else the salvo aimed at the ICBM's will have to be fired earlier, allowing intermediately located radar to order the firing of intermediately located missiles. On closer analysis, of course, it might seem that radar could be located by itself at forward locations, and coupled to command posts back at the ICBM sites, with the same result.[33]

In effect, the argument more simply becomes one for multiplying

160

and dispersing offensive weapons per se, regardless of location, for as long as the weapons are vulnerable. The Soviets already had a surplus of MRBM's, so that the deployment of American MRBM's would not tax their short supply of ICBM's; but the deployment of such American weapons made it more difficult for the Soviets to contemplate and execute a successful counterforce strike at American strategic forces. Deployment of soft American ICBM's would be preferable, if they were available, since the Russians might lack enough ICBM's to target all U.S.-based weapons satisfactorily; but even overseas deployments complicated the Soviet attack plan, not so much in straining Soviet arsenals as in straining probability tables.

Soviet Motivation

The most widespread American reaction to the new Russian missile force saw it as a move for a dominant counterforce capability, intended some day to catch the entire bomber force of SAC on the ground and thus decisively defeat the United States in one grand strike. Perhaps the requirement that the United States be alert to prevent such a development made American observers inevitably premature in attributing this intent to the Soviet Union. In any case, the Soviet procurement of intercontinental missiles (as of bombers) was so limited as perhaps to rule this out as the real Russian motive for the missile move. The compensatory actions taken by the United States in the fall of 1957 and spring of 1958 of course may have upended any Soviet hopes for a grand disarming strike, but Soviet disclosures and claims of missile tests do not then fit with such a strategic plan either, if compensating steps were so easily available to an aroused American government.

United States discussions of strategic-level surprise attacks after World War II have often been characterized as obsessive, as deriving from the American experience at Pearl Harbor. Yet much of the speculation cited had surfaced only in 1954 and then in 1958, after the emergence of a known Russian strategic nuclear capability. The experience of Pearl Harbor may, moreover, not have been so irrelevant or misleading, for it had shown that another nation might indeed attempt a coldly calculated but desperate reversal of a United States position of advantage. The cast of mind required to attempt a grand disarming strategic strike in 1959 or 1960 might not have been very different from that of the Japanese decision-makers of 1941, and American cautions here may not have been so wildly misplaced.

A more plausible explanation for the Soviet missile claims and tests was an intention merely to cultivate a general impression of power; moves on Berlin might then meet less resolute and unified resistance, not because the U.S.S.R. ever hoped to execute the grand disarming strike, but because the debilitating idea had occurred to Western viewers that perhaps she could. Coupling the public announcement of Soviet ICBM tests with the launching of the Sputnik satellite may have seemed only a logical step to the Russian regime, since laymen and others tended to lump accomplishments of rocketry together into a continuum of sorts. Yet it seems clear that the Russians thereby intentionally or otherwise made an impact on the American public that could have the most serious effects on armament decisions. Had the Russians launched Sputnik first and then some months later made their ICBM announcements, the effect might have been less. Alternatively, the Russians could have announced their ICBM tests in the spring, when they were conducted, and then launched Sputnik on schedule, with the two news items being not so clearly coupled.[34] As it was, the Sputnik satellite, as it circled the earth over the United States, almost acquired the image of a missile on its way to targets in the United States, with an American public reaction unmatched in the postwar period.

By 1957 Khrushchev had admitted that nuclear war would be very painful for the civilian populations of both sides (after ousting Malenkov in 1955, in part for making a similar admission). Now, with the publicity derived from Sputnik, Soviet generals began to talk of "decisive" weaponry at the strategic level, for the first time admitting that strategic weapons might themselves be able to reverse the outcome of a war.[35] Soviet propagandists had always claimed that Communism would survive a nuclear war while capitalism would not, but now the additional explanation was offered that the Soviet Union had the superior weapons which made bombers obsolete.

Really to exploit their professed superiority in new strategic weapons, the Russians would have to reverse their doctrinal position again, to deny that all-out war would hurt the Russian people so much as to make any recourse to war unthinkable. The Chinese Communist leadership, which had not joined in the earlier admission of the countervalue problem, now seemed to be pressing the Soviets to push their supposed advantage, with the "east wind prevailing over the west wind.[36] In 1959 and early 1960, the Russians showed some signs of being tempted toward this position—not, like the Chinese, by denying the destructiveness of nuclear weapons per se, but by asserting that anti-aircraft defenses might now keep most SAC bombers from reaching

Soviet cities. Yet there was not any great push toward making a Soviet first strike seem credible; such a push probably would have entailed more real scoffing at nuclear devastation, again on the style of that proclaimed by China in 1959, or at least a well-publicized Soviet civil defense program.

In the year after Sputnik, Khrushchev's claimed missiles might indeed have seemed a startling strategic-level breakthrough intended to support new tactical-level adventures. The year 1958 saw the first application of pressure to West Berlin in 10 years, the coup in Iraq, and unrest in Lebanon, and the Quemoy crisis. But by hindsight Russian instigation of the events in the Middle East seems difficult to substantiate, and it is widely held now that the Quemoy crisis also was not ordered from Moscow (although the lack of Sino-Soviet coordination during the crisis may not be so clear).[37] Yet at any rate, there was Khrushchev's threat of a separate peace treaty with East Germany still to be considered.

A third major explanation exists for the Soviet intercontinental missile program, such as it was: the Russians may simply have been reinsuring their countervalue capability for leveling some minimum number of American cities. Since the 1950's, it has often been commented that the Russians do not seem to have done much to beat down the air defenses erected against their bomber aircraft, either in procuring new jet bombers in great numbers, or in giving them the ability to bypass the radar and interceptor screens erected. Yet it would be dangerous to draw any conclusion that the Soviet Union has thus acquiesced in an attrition of its countercivilian capability; the Russian shift to missiles indeed provided an absolute ability to "penetrate" the defensive screen that the United States had erected.

The Russians apparently had begun to develop such rockets as early as 1950 (aiming for very large payloads in the face of prevalent doubts that hydrogen warheads could be miniaturized, or that missile accuracies could be improved);[38] this perhaps demonstrates that the Soviet Union would not have reconciled itself to a mutual superiority of defenses over offenses for the two home fronts, even if the intent of the liberal American scientist advocates of air defense had not been perverted at the United States end. The launching of the Soviet hydrogen bomb program, apparently before that of the United States, similarly casts doubt on any assumption that the Russians might have accepted a mutual rejection of overkill. Conversely, one might argue that the American intent here never seemed to be clear (indeed never

163

was very clear), and that this forced the Russians to reinsure a countercity strategic offensive capability which American air defenses threatened to eliminate. Especially if steps went ahead to shield Europe on the ground, some such Soviet deterrent might be required.

The Russians indeed produced MRBM's in great quantity, unlike their shortfall in ICBM's. The medium-range missiles can be rationalized as illustrating a special fear of West Germany, now that more powerful and longer-range nuclear weapons were stationed on German soil, and/or of France and Britain, the other two independent nuclear powers; yet if the U.S.S.R. had forgone the status of a missile force, Bonn might have done the same. Mass production of medium-range missiles also contributed marginally to keeping the "missile gap" illusion alive, especially in Europe, which might feel the weight of one form of missile inventory as much as another, or amongst those who could count missiles but could not as easily distinguish ranges or strategically significant missile characteristics. Finally, several hundred MRBM's aimed at America's friends in Europe might deter the United States almost as well as a hundred ICBM's aimed at American cities.

Tactical Issues

European doubts about American commitments, and hence a supposedly heightened fear of Soviet invasion, might easily be traced on some logical basis to the American strategic vulnerability issue raised in 1957; yet European fears of Russian aggression in fact seem to have declined steadily over the period, and an explanation for this may not be so straightforward. Reassurances that the Russians would continue to be deterred may now have come from the American compensatory actions taken after Sputnik, especially the deployment of MRBM's to Europe, or may have been even more natural by-products of the supposed American predicament.

One effect of the Soviet missile demonstration had been to shift attention from the United States limited-war deterrence problem to that of security at the strategic level. Somewhat paradoxically, the Soviet missile force may even have erased doubts about U.S. commitments to massive retaliation. Soviet missiles had to have nuclear warheads to be of any use, and thus tended to legitimate the use of nuclears in general. If missiles were a weapon which favored preemption, moreover, so that he would triumph who used his combination of missiles and bombers first, then most crises in Europe or in the Far East might very logically force the United States to strike at the Soviet Union itself.

164

Absolute security for the U.S. interior would at one time have made escalation to general war plausible. There may have been a middle position making an American commitment to massive retaliation less credible (e.g., vulnerable population but secure strategic forces); but any insecurity of SAC might suffice to link America again to other regimes and to make escalation (preemptive rather than self-assured) very plausible. It is thus not quite so surprising that the administration seemed to have lost interest in establishing local war options, nuclear or conventional, after 1957. The American acceptance of a nuclear test moratorium in 1958 was seen in the U.S. Army as an abandonment of tactical nuclear weapons development;[39] testing presumably could have produced smaller warheads with smaller yields or less fallout. A more esoteric possibility existed in the neutron bomb, which could produce a deadly but local flow of neutrons, with little or no blast or lingering fallout, perhaps an ideal weapon with which to defend German territory without destroying it.

Some might even argue that instability in the strategic force confrontation was desirable, as a deterrent to minor outbreaks of limited war. Some of the public rationale for massive retaliation had earlier cited a need to preempt a Soviet attack on the continental United States, any smaller invasion of Europe being seen as a signal that such an attack was coming. If it ever became clear instead that strategic forces and targets had become secure, so that neither side would normally find it advantageous to strike first in order to preempt the other side, then this argument for massive retaliation would lose its punch.

One might argue, alternatively, that the instability of a strategic force vulnerability might make Soviet aggression more attractive, since the United States would not dare to use tactical nuclear weapons in defense when the dangers of escalation were so great. Yet there would be so much uproar connected with any Soviet attack on Europe that escalation was likely in an unstable strategic atmosphere, whether or not the nuclear threshold had been crossed. And U.S. deployment policies in the wake of Sputnik certainly did not reduce the likelihood of tactical (and strategic) nuclears coming into use, particularly since more of such weapons were deployed now to the European continent. There were, however, other means of coupling massive retaliation to the defense of Europe, including simple "pledges of American honor" and on-the-spot deployments of retaliatory weapons; a hair-trigger strategic force confrontation might not be required in addition, and only a few advocates of the "abolition of all war" would adhere with any vehemence to arguments for instability. The Eisenhower Administration probably saw itself as party to a more stable confrontation than its domestic critics contended, and until 1960 generally moved only under some prodding to restore or reinsure this stability.

While still arguing for a total ban on nuclear weapons in 1955 and 1956, the Soviet Union now seemingly shifted its arms control strategy somewhat. The U.S.S.R. still claimed that a war using even tactical nuclears could not be kept limited, thus of course reinforcing any world objections to the new NATO defensive strategy.[40] It further contended that even American deployments of such tactical weapons should be condemned, since they made escalation to the nuclear level more likely in any European "brush fire" war; this last argument might over time make a nonnuclear war in Europe less possible, however, especially if the Americans both accepted the analysis and persisted in the forward deployment. The Soviet line on already deployed tactical nuclears, which had at one point been consistent with a drive to denuclearize war, thus may now have become consistent with just the opposite result; Soviet propaganda had seemingly shifted from stressing that the desirable option of nonnuclear war was possible (if and only if the United States behaved properly) to suggesting that improper American actions had now made the option impossible.

The original Soviet statements that use of tactical nuclear weapons would mean automatic escalation to general war had plausibly reflected Soviet deficiencies in this type of weapon, or a desire to frighten the West into agreeing to nonnuclear war in Europe (a form of war which the Russians presumably had all along been anxious to launch). The new statements, that even a nonnuclear war in Europe would soon escalate to the use of all weapons on targets everywhere, upset this interpretation of Soviet intentions, however. The shift could be seen simply as a candid recognition of reality, for a number of Western commentators genuinely held identical views; the Eisenhower Administration had at least been professing similar beliefs (its deployment of tactical nuclear weapons in fact could have made the hypothesis self-confirming). Other observers might interpret the new denial of the conventional-war option as reflecting Soviet acquisition of tactical nuclear weapons, perhaps the natural boasting of any armed force that had just received new equipment.

Yet even if the Soviet tactical nuclear arsenal was not yet established, it may now have served Russian purposes thus to rule out the conventional war option, since pressure had to be applied to West

Berlin. Just as the Soviet H-bomb was making a Russian conventional threat against all of Western Europe less necessary, West German sovereignty was making a threat against West Berlin more necessary, if East Germany were not to slip out of Communist control at some point in the near future. Deterrence of American escalation to air attack now would become secondary to the securing of East Germany, and different statements on ground warfare strategy were required for this new objective, stressing rather than debunking the likelihood of local wars escalating and going nuclear. In the fall of 1958, therefore, the Russians reopened the Berlin question that seemingly had been closed nine years before, with an announcement by Premier Khrushchev that a separate peace treaty would soon be signed with the East German regime, a treaty presumably terminating Western rights of access to Berlin. For the next four years, the threat of such Soviet action would loom as a major factor in Soviet-American relations, at least until the Cuban missile crisis seemed to remove it.

If American tactical nuclear weapons had served the purpose (intentionally or otherwise) of making escalation to the nuclear level credible for any Russian attack on West Germany, these same deployed American warheads might couple such escalation to (and deter) any American move down the Autobahn to aid a blockaded West Berlin. If Russian triggers were not yet available, American weapons could perhaps serve as plausible triggers, this time for a Russian deterrent. The American deployments, of course, could have been more precarious. No American tactical nuclear weapons were deployed in West Berlin, or even within some distance of the frontiers of East Germany. Yet the danger was present that any probe down the Autobahn might embroil some larger segment of West Germany along the frontiers, so that tactical nuclears might come into use on several different arguments, so that escalation to all-out war was at least plausible, so that the United States might not risk the move.

The most urgent Soviet concern thus may now have pertained to East Germany. One could ask why the East Germans or Russians had not resorted to the erection of a wall through Berlin much earlier, to stop the outflow of refugees which was now so destabilizing to the D.D.R. regime. From the Communist point of view, one could always have hoped that the flow would cease of itself; on the other hand, rumors of any move to erect a wall would leak out in advance, inducing an even greater exodus. The propaganda costs of admitting the unpopularity of the Pankow regime would also have been great at any time, and greater perhaps at earlier stages, when less of the world had begun to ponder and accept the idea of two Germanies. The reaction of the United States, moreover, was an imponderable, since American statements continually and repeatedly asserted the four-power status of all of Berlin; unless the wall were erected between East Germany and East Berlin, a clearly unacceptable solution for the Communists, the threat remained that the United States would go far to keep the exit to West Berlin open. Walls had been erected between East Germany and West Germany, and even on three sides of West Berlin where it touched on East Germany, but a barrier through the city would have to counter a tough Allied legalism. Until the border were erected, however, the D.D.R. lacked an important aspect of sovereignty, one that a dictatorial regime needs much more than ordinary regimes do.

Aside from the open intracity boundary, the existence of West Berlin compromised the sovereignty of the D.D.R. in several other ways, all potentially destabilizing. The mere existence of a corridor of access along the Autobahn, over which national sovereignty could not be fully exercised, was a potential irritant to the regime in trying to settle its population. Even if the land access routes could be effectively cordoned off, the pattern of aerial overflights was even more visible to the East Germans, and such overflights could also be used for photographic and radar reconnaissance. The latter substantive possibility, or the general need for a sense of fully legitimate procedural sovereignty, had induced the Russians to insist on a ceiling limitation on flights to Berlin of 10,000 feet, a ceiling which the United States declined to accept formally, violated once, and then proceeded to accept tacitly, somewhat at British behest.[41]

It may thus seem paradoxical that Khrushchev was unilaterally announcing sizable reductions in conventional forces into 1960 while maintaining pressure on West Berlin, but the policies may not have been so inconsistent. While the Soviet forces were being reduced numerically, Khrushchev stated that they had greatly been augmented in "firepower,"[42] which very likely meant tactical nuclear weapons, again with the risks of escalation. The Russians over this period did not very often hint at any strategic superiority over the United States sufficient to allow the U.S.S.R. to escape unscathed from a nuclear war; while the Chinese perhaps had urged such statements on the Russians after the 1957 missile demonstrations, Khrushchev more typically stressed the inevitable and horrendous destruction that would befall all parties in an escalation to general war, destruction that no first strike or strategic superiority could prevent.

168

While the West often saw the problem of West Berlin to be one of Russian conventional military superiority, the Russians may well have seen their superiority to lie in the presence of tactical nuclears, and in the geography which forced the last clear choice of military action onto the West; Berlin could be cut off by nonmilitary Soviet actions, while the Allies would have to drive a 100-mile military probe through East Germany to relieve the situation. With a blockade, with nonviolent interference with air passage, a situation might be created where the Allies could hold the city only by launching the first overtly military operation. If such a military operation seemingly could not be kept limited (or, just as bad, if the Russians seemed to be mistakenly convinced it couldn't, so that they would probably attack preemptively when escalation was thought unavoidably imminent), then the Americans might allow West Berlin to fall.

After Berlin had been recovered in this manner, thus restoring the significance of the Elbe as clearly separating West from East, the Russians would have time to decide whether to play down escalation again and to reopen the possibilities of territorial limited war, nuclear or nonnuclear (with the hope of thereby gaining more territory by military means), or whether instead to maintain the higher probability of escalation and settle for the frontier of the Elbe. The escalation argument, in any event, for the time bolstered a division along the Elbe, including the transfer of Berlin to Communist control.

Outside of Europe, however, the Russian strategy seemed still to be the more traditional reverse, straightforwardly aiming to avoid any American deployment or use of tactical nuclear weapons. Here the Soviet line did not contend that every war would necessarily see all the most modern weapons come into play, but rather that only the first use of nuclear weapons would then escalate to general war. A local nonnuclear war presumably could be fought without risks of escalation anywhere but in Europe, a war which Communist forces presumably would win, given the lack of American conventional preparations.

Eisenhower's critics thus were fond of listing countries that would fall to subtle Communist limited-war and sublimited-war aggressions, as a result of dangerous tactical nuclear deployments; yet at the end of two terms of office, the administration's record did not look so bad here at all, given the turmoil of decolonization and the many inherent grievances the Communist bloc should have been able to exploit. In the Far East, the atomic threat plus naval and air strength apparently were sufficient to hold Japan and Taiwan, and perhaps also even the islands of Quemoy and Matsu, while reductions of U.S. ground forces did not induce new aggressions against South Korea, but in fact saw Communist Chinese forces leave North Korea in a well-publicized move in 1958.[43]

The Eisenhower Administration would still show itself suitably cautious about deploying nuclears into the most marginal combat areas, as in the 1958 American intervention in Lebanon; tactical nuclear weapons and even the special equipment to fire them were held back,[44] since a small conventional intervention apparently sufficed. Yet by contrast, there came slightly later the deployment of atomic-capable artillery to Quemoy during the 1958 crisis,[45] which may have illustrated a far greater importance attached by the United States to the standing of the Nationalists on Taiwan, or a feeling that the Chinese should be confronted more directly than either Nasserist Arabs or their Russian instigators. The 1958 Chinese Communist shelling of Quemoy raised serious issues for the United States, because Communist artillery was generally more efficient now than it had been in 1954 (threatening to prevent delivery of supplies to, or evacuation from, the island), and because the Nationalists had in the interim moved about one-third of their army, the presumed defenders of Taiwan, to Quemoy.

Whatever practical arguments had applied in 1954 for Nationalist or American air strikes against the mainland (against artillery positions, air bases, or troop concentrations) were thus much more valid in 1958, even if no Communist amphibious assault on the island were to be launched. The atomic-capable American eight-inch howitzers were deployed amid open discussion of conventional or nuclear air strikes against China, but also with a public statement that nuclear weapons could not be used without the expressed approval of the President. In any event, no American air attacks had to be launched, since even the Chinese Nationalists were required this time to withhold their bomber forces;[46] a way was found instead to throw the initiative back once more to the Chinese Communists, by extending American naval escort to within three miles of the Nationalist-held offshore islands. Rather than attack U.S. vessels, the Communists did not press their continuous shellings, and the crisis subsided.

Laos and Vietnam would continue to present problems, but the 1950-1952 Korean pattern of overt and clearly aggressive use of Chinese military forces was not to be repeated there. India commenced having border difficulties with China, but even here there was to be no real military engagement until 1962. By 1961, the United States had lost only Cuba to the Communist bloc, while other countries often

170

written off, such as Guinea, Iraq, and the U.A.R. did not disappear behind the iron curtain. Arguments for greater American limited-war capability may still have been correct, but they hardly seemed to have been proved so in the areas outside Europe from 1953 to 1961. Some combination of massive retaliation, a thin conventional threshold, and perhaps good fortune still sufficed to "contain" the Communist world.

The Proliferation Question

The U.S. Government's attitude on nuclear proliferation from 1957 to 1960 might seem very ambivalent today. Rather than being opposed to the development of national nuclear forces per se, the Administration seemed concerned to bolster the credibility of nuclear retaliation after any Russian ground-force aggression and to maintain a sense of unity amongst the member nations of NATO; the release of nuclear weapons or technology from American control might either serve or hinder these purposes, and would be controlled on a largely ad hoc basis. To the extent that it mattered, the American public now also had become more ambivalent on issues of forward deployment of nuclear weapons; whereas 81 percent had opposed such deployments in 1949, if they were likely to give allies access to such weapons, only 37 percent were opposed in 1957, with 44 percent being in favor.[47]

The relative tolerance of Eisenhower for nuclear proliferation, where it contributed to alliance solidarity, was amplified in the field by military and civilian officials charged with implementing weapons programs. Congress (especially the Joint Committee on Atomic Energy) had apparently expected that tactical nuclear weapons would be deployed into lockers physically guarded by American troops; but they were instead more widely dispersed, with only the most nominal American custody exercised by a soldier or two at the spot, or perhaps none in the case of weapons carried by fighter-bombers.[48] Similarly, greater control had been expected over warheads for the MRBM's deployed to England, Turkey, and Italy, but the warheads were kept mounted on top of the missiles, rather than being stored separately. In each case considerations of combat feasibility, and of the allied morale which was derived from combat feasibility, prompted American officers in the field to interpret their authority broadly. But in each case also, relatively little force was required for foreign nationals to seize control of the nuclear warheads involved and to use them. Until the Kennedy Administration introduced permissive action links, devices which made it physically impossible to fire weapons without some sort of signal relayed from higher authority, this de facto proliferation would persist.

The American Congress, especially the Joint Committee on Atomic Energy, remained much more clearly opposed to proliferation, although the Committee typically alluded to the special characteristics of the would-be nuclear power in question, rather than to proliferation as an abstract issue. Yet hinging the objections to nuclear sharing on such particular issues as the political unreliability of a nation, or its lack of internal security, or its supposed lack of native scientific prowess might make politically intolerable the otherwise acceptable semiproliferation which Eisenhower was attempting, and thus drive a nation (e.g., France) to reject all American assistance that did not lead to explicit nuclear independence. The results were particularly irritating when the United States was forced to retract offers of assistance the administration had already made, as with Dulles' offer of technology for an atomic submarine in 1957, or Eisenhower's press conference endorsement of supplying nuclear weapons to NATO countries in February of 1960.[49] With a free hand, Eisenhower seemingly hoped to take the political tensions out of the explicit proliferation question; without a free hand, he was in any event unsuccessful.

The ascendance of General De Gaulle to power perhaps inevitably presaged an assertion of French national prerogatives in opposition to supranational or alliance considerations. De Gaulle, moreover, would have a problem of placating and appeasing the French Army when the Algerian war was terminated, and a nuclear weapons program was a means of diverting the energies and attention of the French military to a new sphere. French nuclear physicists had been preparing a weapons option, either deliberately or accidentally, since 1955, and the results of their efforts now required a formal validation in an actual weapons production program, or a formal rejection.[50] Such progress, moreover, raised an issue in France of equal treatment with the United Kingdom, in terms of technological assistance and data sharing by the United States. The American Atomic Energy Act was amended in 1958 to allow assistance to nations that had already made progress on their own; the question now emerged whether this had established a new general principle, or merely had resurrected the Anglo-American "special relationship" in a new disguise.[51] Finally, while the United States was seeking to deploy MRBM's to reinsure its strategic deterrent, the buildup of tactical weapons had also reached a stage requiring stockpile sites outside of West Germany, especially for new warheads for the tactical fighters already based in eastern France.[52]

172

The French government in 1958 thus demanded unconditional assistance on nuclear warhead and delivery system production, as a prerequisite to the granting of MRBM and tactical stockpile sites; and it required the redeployment of American atom-bomb-equipped fighter-bombers to West Germany and Great Britain when French control over these stockpiles was not granted. Fears expressed for the vulnerability of land-based MRBM's, or for the danger of being drawn into some war between the United States and the U.S.S.R., do not really explain the French rejection of bases and stockpiles for U.S. nuclear forces. The real issue was probably not nuclear deployment or proliferation per se (to which De Gaulle and Eisenhower were both more indifferent as an abstract issue), but rather the degree of visible French political stature, and freedom of action outside of the American-dominated Atlantic Alliance.

De Gaulle's rejection of American tactical nuclear stockpiles on French territory would forgo the gradual de facto proliferation process described earlier, as would his later rejections of Jupiter and land-based Polaris deployments. The French Government thereby probably also passed up more substantial prospects of American nuclear assistance, comparable with that given the United Kingdom, given Eisenhower's willingness to forward some aid, and the likelihood that the Congressional Joint Committee would have gotten over its suspicions of French internal instability and weakness, as it became accustomed to the impression of a resolute and steady De Gaulle. The absence of American nuclear technological aid must thus largely be traced to French insistence on a very explicit and formal nuclear sharing and to French actions designed to force it.

American policies on EURATOM, on assistance in the development of nuclear propulsion plants, on dispersal of tactical nuclear weapon stockpiles and deployment of hydrogen-warhead medium-range missiles, and on the sharing of atomic information in general thus might seem vacillating and inconsistent, except when seen in the light of Eisenhower's and Dulles' concern for maintaining the alliance, and Congress' continuing fears of foreign internal softness. Largely at the level of retaliation for specific French political actions, the United States excluded France from agreements on the sharing of information on nuclear weapons effects and characteristics, agreements entered into in July of 1959 with Turkey, the Netherlands, Canada, and West Germany;[53] these agreements were not extended to France until the Berlin crisis of 1961 and the redeployment of French troops from Algeria to the European continent. Yet as the French Government moved ahead to test its first nuclear device in 1960, the United States nonetheless voted with Britain on France's behalf in November of 1959, against a U.N. General Assembly resolution asking France not to test, while informally urging the French government to suspend the detonations for the sake of the test moratorium.[54]

Disagreement will persist over whether the policies of the United States on nuclear weapons sharing might not have been better formulated after 1958, and after 1960, especially with regard to France. If France was intent on appearing to be the source of its own ultimate deterrence, so much so that it would expend large sums of money developing weapons and delivery systems, a generous American policy of assistance might well have rebounded to the interest of the United States. French policy does indeed seem to have had an accretion of French political stature and influence as its goal. While the Force de Frappe almost always is discussed in terms of its ability to reach its targets in the U.S.S.R., there is not really any doubt expressed in France about the ability or willingness of the United States Air Force to do the same: while marginal situations can be raised in which French massive retaliation would be more likely and credible than that of the United States, the real issue may have been one of credit—that the source of French independence and security should be physically French. Had the United States been willing to reconcile itself to the loss of relative prestige involved (and to the precedents being set), it seems quite probable that the French Government would have responded with less rancor, and that the question of American reliability in a crisis would have been discussed less openly and searchingly.

Despite French (and American) overstatements of the argument that America might want to avoid a nuclear escalation in defense of Europe, it at no point has seemed very plausible that a major war in Europe would occur with American nuclear weapons not coming into use, when and if the Red Army made any territorial gains. European claims to fear the opposite must thus often be regarded as propaganda for the national nuclear force position, and the United States might have spared itself the deluge of such propaganda if it had been tolerant of the "one more nuclear power" that France represented. Perhaps the analysis of nuclear proliferation has also too often discussed "nth" powers without specifying who the "nth" power would be. If Nationalist China might someday use a nuclear weapon where the United States would certainly not, it was less clear that such a direct discontinuity of interest would ever arise with France. At the very worst, abstract arguments might picture France attacking the United States with nuclears; more commonly, the French nuclear force would be striking at Moscow on an issue too trivial for the United States, thus slaying the common hostage and exposing New York to Soviet counterattack.

At the French end of the discussion, the issue has also from time to time been phrased rather abstractly. President De Gaulle and other French spokesmen have normally been careful to portray an independent French nuclear capability specifically as augmenting the West, as being capable of striking at Russian cities. Yet some of the logic advanced for independent national forces has not lent itself to such clear commitments to one set of national targets over another, and De Gaulle has on occasion even allowed himself to portray the proposed Force de Frappe as a more general threat, capable perhaps of striking at any country, perhaps even those now allied with France.[55] Since the French statements here have not been made so explicitly, or have not been caught up for discussion in the American press, they have as yet had little real impact. Were the French Government to decide upon a deployment of nuclear forces to the Western Hemisphere for any reason (e.g., strategic missiles based in French Guiana, or Mirages plus tankers based in Guadeloupe or Tahiti), then some more serious issues might arise, especially in view of the posture taken and established by the United States in the Cuban missile crisis.

British statements on the role of independent British nuclear forces have always stressed the RAF's coordination and cooperation with the United States, thus not allowing the issue of independent or conflicting use to become at all salient. The deployment of American strategic forces within Britain itself has of course served as a superb pledge that no conflict is in any sense conceivable, and periodic visits of British "V-bombers" to the United States may similarly have served to neutralize the issue in the other direction. Both the British and the French efforts to induce American nuclear weapons sharing could thus be interpreted at least in part as moves to bolster national prestige. But the requirements of such prestige differed significantly for Britain and for France, and this accounts for at least a part of the divergence of the two nations' policies toward American leadership and toward explicit nuclear proliferation.

Britain came out of World War II with a reputation for having been a major partner in the Axis defeat, for having a strong strategic air potential of its own, and for having shared in the development of the atomic bomb. As long as even the most informal agreements persisted with the United States for some sharing of strategic technology, the image of British parity might persist. France, having been defeated and occupied in World War II, did not emerge after 1945 with any parallel image of military prowess. Informal agreements as proposed during the Eisenhower Administration thus preserved a different psychological status quo, one far less acceptable to France; hence the French Government had to turn down arrangements which Great Britain had been able to exploit to its prestige advantage. What was a "special relationship" and "implicit partnership" for Britain would have been implicit satellite status for France, for few would interpret strategic weaponry in French hands as anything but a grant from the United States. Very explicit statements of French independence were thus required, or a truly French independent strategic nuclear program in place of it. American Congressional and Administration policies which seemed (if only perhaps temporarily) to discriminate against France of course made the situation all the more difficult.

In part because of Congress, the British had not been able to maintain the partnership illusion without some independent effort of their own. It had been necessary to develop and test the A-bomb, and then the H-bomb, before Congress would amend the Atomic Energy Act in 1958 to sanction the transfer of weapons technology to the United Kingdom. Similarly, the British had developed their own jet bombers (in part also to support the British aircraft industry) and had made moves toward missile development, even though the United States was willing to supply copies of its own vehicles (as with the B-29 in 1950, the Thor missile after 1957, and the Nautilus-type atomic-powered submarine after 1958).[56] For as long as no absolute British dependence on American-produced weapons and delivery systems became apparent, the United Kingdom could rely substantially on such American research and production to maintain an image of being a first-rank strategic power. At some later date, perhaps at the time of the Skybolt affair, this dependence would at last become more apparent, and British options would be constricted here.

Great Britain's first real strategic force, jet bombers coupled to the new hydrogen bomb, came onto the scene just as Russian missiles were casting the value of bomber forces into doubt. The three "V-bombers," Victor, Valiant, and Vulcan, were procured and deployed over the period from 1955 to 1958,[57] while Soviet medium-range missiles presumably were targeting American and British bases in the United

Kingdom. To dispel notions of vulnerability to such preemptive attack, a four-minute alert (to be compared with the 15-minute alert of SAC) was widely advertised for the bombers of Bomber Command,[58] and aircraft were occasionally deployed overseas to Malta, Cyprus, and Malaya. However believable or reliable the four-minute alert may have been, it was clear that the survivability of the British deterrent force depended largely on the fact that the Russians could not consider a preemptive attack against British forces alone. American forces were still presumed to need bases in the United Kingdom in 1957, now for medium-range missiles as well as B-47's. For this reason alone the British Government would be reluctant to pursue a line of argument advanced earlier by some advocates of a British H-bomb:[59] that an independent deterrent could allow Britain to terminate the American Air Force presence in the United Kingdom. The interspersion of American SAC bases with bases for British V-bombers made the British force more secure against preemptive attack by Russian MRBM's; rather than an argument for American departure, the V-bombers seemed to make a continuation of American bases worthwhile.

Other proliferation possibilities now emerged. From the start of the hydrogen bomb era, the United States had not allowed this most awesome of strategic weapons to become interspersed in "potential battlefield" environments where its use might become subject to the physical influence of Allied troops in the vicinity. Out-and-out strategic bombers were not stationed in West Germany after 1950, and the H-bomb-carrying B-47's and B-52's were kept in Spain, Morocco, and Great Britain thereafter. Distinctions on range of operation similarly seemed to be in effect, since aircraft capable of carrying large nuclear weapons as far as the Soviet Union were not at first deployed in any numbers to Germany after the resumption of German sovereignty, or transferred to the German forces. Apart from aircraft, delivery systems such as artillery and tactical rockets were limited in range, incapable of reaching targets beyond Poland at the furthest.

By 1958, however, technology had begun to complicate the problem in several ways. The second generation of jet fighter-bombers programmed for the West German and other NATO air forces would indeed be capable of delivering newer and smaller models of tactical nuclear bombs, thus for the first time giving nonAnglo-American forces direct access to atomic weapons usable against Soviet territory itself. More directly, a short-term need to deploy medium-range missiles to Italy and Turkey, and perhaps to Germany, would place hydrogen bomb warheads aimed at Russian targets in close proximity to non-American military forces. In each case, problems could emerge which would not have arisen with the SAC bomber bases in Spain and Morocco. In the earlier cases, American crews were still required to destroy any Russian target, with the crews subject to in-flight recall. In the new situation German pilots might complete a weapons delivery, or perhaps Turkish button-pushers would, neither being subject to a veto from Washington in mid-mission.

After 1959, moreover, a deployment of medium-range missiles seemingly became more acceptable to the West German regime, which at first had remained noncommittal.[60] The prospect had emerged of a solid-fueled missile, perhaps a land-based version of Polaris, a missile not so vulnerable to Soviet preemptive attack or so slow to fire. The apparent growth of the Soviet medium-range missile force seemed to supply another excuse for such deployments, at the general level of fairness and parity, and on the specific argument that such Soviet missiles would take out the NATO tactical air forces, thus requiring other Allied weapons to interdict Soviet supply and reinforcement columns moving across Poland. Solid-fueled missiles might be made mobile, and thus constitute a secure interdiction force—a force, however, whose range could all too easily be pushed across the borders of the U.S.S.R. In 1960, the United States thus began tentatively to offer fixed land-based deployments of Polaris on the same terms that had controlled Jupiter and Thor, while General Norstadt suggested the establishment of NATO as the fourth independent nuclear power,[61] with a mixed-manned system of mobile land-based medium-range missiles. As an alternative to the land-based mobile force, the possibility of a mixed-manned submarine force was also put forward.

The H-bomb MRBM was the kind of weapon that Russian (and many Western) observers should presumably have been most reluctant to see moving into German hands. A Soviet sensitivity to the hydrogen bomb/atomic bomb distinction had already shown up in 1956, when the U.S.S.R. apparently had tried to preclude the British H-bomb tests scheduled for February, 1957, with a proposal for a worldwide moratorium on thermonuclear tests,[62] rather than atomic tests in general. Once again the hydrogen bomb may have constituted the terroristic weapon, an order of magnitude greater in impact than the A-bomb.

If the U.S.S.R. was now really opposed to nuclear (especially hydrogen) weapons spreading into the control of West Germany, the stimulation of the missile-gap reports should have been a move which it quickly regretted and tried to reverse, given the American precautionary response of seeking to deploy MRBM's to Europe. Yet while the U.S.S.R. expressed vehement opposition to such deployments over the months after September of 1957 (also for the first time calling for a formal halt to proliferation), Khrushchev would continue to make claims for the superior quality and quantity production of Russian missiles. Soviet endorsements of a test ban might now also seem appropriate as a general antiproliferation device, but this would be much less directly effective against West Germany: the Federal Republic would presumably acquire any nuclear weapons gradually from some other power, rather than developing them itself, and thus would not have to test (nor be able to, given its geographical limitations).

The Rapacki Plan for a nuclear-free zone,[63] presented by the Polish government and then endorsed by the U.S.S.R., might have seemed more seriously intended to preclude a German national nuclear force, especially if one feared that the Eisenhower Administration might not keep full control over its own weapons in West Germany, even with all the publicity given to "two-key" arrangements; the Rapacki specifications of a full withdrawal of all nuclear weapons from West Germany (and from East Germany, Poland, and Czechoslovakia) seemed most directly related to a fear of the Bonn regime.

Commentators thus often interpreted the relatively consistent Russian demands for a denuclearization of West Germany as evidence of a real Soviet commitment here, but the strategic pronouncements debunking any possibility of a European nonnuclear war may contradict this. If the Russians had been interested solely in denuclearizing West Germany, certain threats or offers could have been made over the latter 1950's to encourage the United States in this direction. Rather more consistent with Soviet behavior over this time were the pressing requirements for maintaining East German autonomy; a Western deployment of tactical nuclears to West Germany might in fact contribute to establishing this autonomy, and all Soviet plans for denuclearization thus included enough implicit and explicit recognitions of East German independence to satisfy the prior Soviet goal, but also then to make the plans unacceptable to the West. Had the NATO alliance accepted any of the Soviet-endorsed disengagement proposals, of course, the Russians could have had East German autonomy and West German denuclearization too; as it was, they had to make a choice, and the choice was for Pankow's survival. The Russians thus may have been willing to denuclearize Central Europe, which would have relieved some of their strategic pressure on Berlin, but only on terms that in effect promised to solve their Berlin problem in another way.

It was not so clear, furthermore, why Poland and all of Czechoslovakia had to be included merely to achieve the benefits of mutual nuclear disengagement. The latter may, of course, have been thrown in merely to sweeten the exchange for the West, or to give the world an impression of excessive reasonableness on the Communist side. Alternatively, it is possible that the Polish and Czechoslovak Governments desired the nuclear-free zone more than the Russians did, and obtained reluctant Russian acquiescence. If this were the case, it perhaps demonstrated that the fear of nuclear war in one's own front yard, a fear which had been so mistakenly imputed in advance to the West Germans and to other Europeans in the late 1950's, might in fact have installed itself in Eastern Europe. The inclusion of Poland and Czechoslovakia in the nuclear-free zone thus would indicate a desire not only to keep weapons out of German hands, but also to avoid being targeted preemptively by NATO tactical air forces. Soviet nuclear weapons presumably had already been kept out of the satellites (except for East Germany)[64] but might be moved into the area in the event of military operations, if there were no agreement banning the use or deployment of nuclears within the zone. The Russians in fact now broadened the nuclear-free zone proposals at several points to include more countries, shifting the issue somewhat from Germany[65] and making the chances of ratification seem less; other Soviet programs, in any event, still tended to induce further proliferation to West Germany.

If the U.S.S.R. could be credited with any general aversion to proliferation, it nonetheless now also failed to endorse safeguard plans for reactors distributed to various underdeveloped nations,[66] safeguards designed to prevent the diversion of plutonium to military purposes; here the Russian Government, rather, seemed intent on winning some quick propaganda points in India and other nations, at the risk of encouraging a greater spread of atomic weapons.

There also is evidence that the U.S.S.R. was willing to give nuclear assistance of some sort to Communist China after 1957. The exact nature of Russian assistance to Peking until 1960 may never be absolutely clear. The Chinese regime has suggested that Khrushchev broke his promises and failed to deliver a sample atomic bomb together with details as to its manufacture;[67] despite this claim of Soviet nonassistance, the Chinese apparently acquired an ability to produce weapons-grade uranium, to the surprise of a world which expected the first Chinese detonation to come from a plutonium bomb. It is possible that the Russians intended to supply the Chinese with a nuclear capability in exchange for China's adherence to a test-ban agreement; since the agreement was not in fact negotiated in time, China was then presumably denied further assistance but was able to use what help it had received to go on to a uranium capability. The reputation for weapons of course might always be more important than possession of weapons per se, and a Chinese nuclear capability not subject to test might have been neither credible nor politically effective. If the Soviets had been offering assistance to the Chinese in exchange for adherence to a test ban, this might thus have served as a trap for the Chinese, a trap unsprung only by Western opposition to the ban. Yet the Chinese regime surely would have discovered some way to demonstrate its nuclear capability once it had received it from the U.S.S.R., test ban or no test ban, perhaps by some temporary violation of the treaty followed by an immediate return to the fold, or by a "peaceful detonation."

The trap into which the Russians could have been luring their ally might not have kept China from becoming a nuclear power but, rather, might have increased Peking's reliance on the U.S.S.R., thus weakening its challenge to Russian leadership of the Communist world. Here the Russian problem clearly was similar to that of the United States—namely, to deliver aid in ways that increased political cohesion or subordination on the part of the recipient—while China's problem was that of France—partially how to get weapons, but more importantly how to assert political independence in the process. France's exclusion of American nuclear weapons might have passed up some access to such weapons, and China's denial of military bases to the U.S.S.R. similarly seems to have relinquished the earliest possibility for proliferation; in each case the requirement of political independence came first.

A second possibility is that the Russians may have given the Chinese a diffusion plant capable of enriching uranium sufficiently for use as fuel for power reactors,[68] and that the Chinese instead coupled this diffusion plant to an electromagnetic separation process to make weapons-grade uranium. In this view, the Chinese would have promised to use such facilities for electric power production (perhaps with a small residue of weapons-grade plutonium), but instead decided to consume large amounts of electric power in the final production of weapons-grade uranium (which, unlike plutonium, lends itself more easily to production of a hydrogen bomb).

The Nuclear Test-Ban Issue

One other Russian arms control or propaganda initiative emerged in the mid-1950's. In response to an American H-bomb test of 1954 exposing several Japanese fishermen to harmful amounts of radioactive fallout, a number of Asian nations had begun to object to the testing of nuclear weapons in general; the Soviet Union, perhaps sensing the unwillingness of the West to accept this plea, now began gradually to endorse the proposal, perhaps thereby to embarrass the United States. By 1955, it had come to request test cessation as part of a substantial disarmament proposal;[69] in 1956 it went on to advocate a general test cessation independent of any disarmament proposals, a proposal endorsed in the United States by the Democratic Presidential candidate, Adlai Stevenson.

Stevenson made the test ban one of his major campaign issues against President Eisenhower, who continued to oppose it, citing difficulties of supervision and inspection. The U.S.S.R. contended that tests could easily be detected by external sensors and that no internal inspection was required; however, the real U.S. administration fear may not have been inspection difficulties, but rather that a test ban would make any use of nuclear weapons psychologically less acceptable over time. The Soviet position on arms control up to 1956 had fairly consistently sought to undermine the American commitment to using nuclears in the event of a war in Europe, and the test-ban proposal seemed still consistent with this. Aside from the direct issue of nuclear legitimacy, further testing might within four or five years produce a hydrogen bomb generating very little radioactivity, a weapon which the United States might then have been less inhibited from using;[70] tactical nuclear weapons of small battlefield size similarly might be developed, increasing the Army's ability to defend Europe without escalation to all-out war.

The United States responded to the Soviet test-ban proposal by suggesting a fully policed ban on nuclear weapons production, rather than any unpoliced ban on testing.[71] This of course would serve to win some neutral support for the United States if the Russians rejected it, and if accepted would have left the Soviets with a stockpile presumably much smaller than that of the United States. In some ways it was the ideal American propaganda proposal, for production could be monitored and would have to be, whereas stockpiles could no longer be monitored adequately and test bans in truth might not have to be monitored. As another propaganda counter to the Russian proposals,

182

the British and French Governments in 1957 offered a test ban as part of an inspected general disarmament scheme. The U.S.S.R., in response, seemed willing to consider the presence of inspection teams on Russian territory to police a ban, but as yet offered to tolerate only a very limited number of inspectors under somewhat restrictive rules.[72]

On March 31, 1958, the Soviet Union with great publicity announced a unilateral moratorium on nuclear weapons testing, at the end of a very substantial series of Soviet detonations and shortly before an American test series was scheduled to begin. To offset international criticism of a continued test program, the United States in turn announced its willingness to participate in an experts' conference on the detection of surreptitious nuclear detonations. Surprisingly, the Russians agreed to the conference.

From July 1 to August 21, 1958, a meeting of Eastern and Western experts was convened in Geneva, producing a report which at first glance showed great agreement and promise on new forms of policing for a test ban. Underground tests, the only type that might otherwise not easily be detected (and the type that certainly produced less of a fallout hazard), might, according to these experts, be monitored by seismic detection systems, perhaps requiring no physical-inspection access to the country itself.[73] In purported response to the report, the United States on August 22 announced its acceptance of a trial test moratorium, to run for one year, beginning with the convening of negotiations on a permanent control system for such a test ban. This would allow the United States to complete a test series that the U.S.S.R. might perhaps have been intending to head off. Khrushchev denounced the U.S. contention that further discussions were required on the monitoring requirements for a test ban but agreed to begin negotiations on the subject on October 31, even while labeling them as unnecessary, in view of the Geneva experts' report. No American tests occurred after October of 1958; after a very short test series in November, the Russians also resumed their moratorium, which was in fact to be observed by the United States, Britain, and Russia until September of 1961.

The full explanation of why the Russians had come down so hard in favor of a test ban in 1958, enough to put the United States on the spot by launching a unilateral test moratorium, is not so easy to disentangle. There was of course the standard argument that the Soviet Union was trying to invalidate the use of nuclear weapons for any event of war. As pointed out above, however, the move to a missile capability had tended to legitimize the use of nuclear weapons more than ever. If the Russians, moreover, had desired to make an introduction of nuclear weapons less credible for war scenarios prior to 1957, this interest could no longer be so clear, if West Berlin were the object of their pressure. When and if the U.S.S.R. would feel a need to stress the risks of escalation surrounding the Berlin situation, a resumption of Soviet testing might in fact become very appropriate, if no other considerations decisively favored continuing the moratorium.

Second, a test ban might have inhibited further development of nuclear weapons in a manner strategically satisfactory to the U.S.S.R., and might have imposed less pressure on the Soviet economy. If the closed nature of the U.S.S.R. allowed for some clandestine underground testing, then this might be marginally exploitable to improve the relative Russian strategic weapons position, while still dampening down the arms race. But the option of clandestine testing, so often alluded to by the United States, may not have been essential to the Soviet position, and may not have been so readily available. Even without illegal tests, it was plausible that the U.S.S.R. would find it easier than the American AEC to keep its scientific staffs together and at work. If this were so, then the Soviet Union might still be able to remedy some of its weapons inferiorities in the absence of an all-out development race. If this were so, moreover, some Americans would raise objections to a formal test ban even if the inspection issue were not as directly crucial as it was made out to be.

The American AEC might have a vested interest in continuing a large development and testing program, and might thus exaggerate the demoralizing effect of a test ban on its staff; yet it was plausible that such an effect was there. The Russian equivalent of the AEC might also have an interest in a test program, and in internal debates thus tend to belittle the advantages for the U.S.S.R. of a continued moratorium, also citing the demoralization of its laboratory staffs; yet it was plausible that this demoralization would be less in the U.S.S.R. than in the United States, if only because American physicists had freer access to a larger selection of alternative opportunities.

Even if the U.S.S.R.'s laboratories could not remain active indefinitely without testing, it was possible that the Russians had all along set a date when testing would be resumed. With such a date in mind, Soviet physicists presumably would make great progress in weapons design, leaping ahead of their Western counterparts, who had no such assurance that their efforts would be proved in the field. By such a one-time moratorium betrayal, the U.S.S.R., in this view, might catch up to or surpass the United States in nuclear weapons, after which the nuclear arms race would be resumed in a bilateral fashion. Yet this interpretation may exaggerate the Soviet dependence on testing. The Russians, furthermore, would have to accept some significant prestige costs by terminating the moratorium; and it would have seemed to the Russian advantage to wait for the United States to resume testing first, if only underground, if there were no outside strategic considerations to make a continued moratorium run counter to the Soviet interest.

A third possibility, of course, was that the Russians had put forward a proposal slightly unacceptable to themselves, but which they interpreted to be substantially unacceptable to the United States, and thus likely to be rejected in the West, with the resulting propaganda disadvantages all falling onto the Western side. The United States, in conditioning its delayed acceptance on the convening of a conference to discuss monitoring techniques, apparently had expected the Russians to refuse or to sabotage the conference, thus perhaps relieving the United States of responsibility for vetoing the moratorium. Yet President Eisenhower had now become convinced that the risks of a moratorium had to be accepted if Russian destruction of the conference did not give the United States a clear excuse to cancel it.[74]

The U.S.S.R., presumably surprised by the American move into a moratorium, may yet have been hoping to provoke the American government into a cancellation of it through the short series of Russian tests that followed the American Hardtack series. Hence, the way the moratorium was launched made it plausible that both powers were halfhearted about it. The last series of Russian tests, alternatively, may not have been a provocation to induce American withdrawal, but simply a recovery of the Soviet political position of having been the last nation to test. Psychologically, one begins a moratorium by "stopping testing," by being the last one to test. Had the American Hardtack series gone unchallenged, then it might have been the United States that was seen afterwards as having established the moratorium.

World opinion and propaganda aside, it is thus not at all clear that either major power could have remained unambiguously in favor of a test ban. In certain forms—for example, as it materialized in 1963—a ban could be a lever of détente for the major powers, allowing each to reduce the pressures of propaganda and resource allocation imposed on the other. In the latter 1950's, however, it was not clear that both powers desired such a détente, and in any event other means of détente could have been brought to bear with less complication and fewer technical implications. In terms of reducing the costs of an arms race, the ban might or might not have held advantages for either side. Military establishments desiring higher budgets in both the U.S.S.R. and the United States almost uniformly would oppose the test ban, while civilians doctrinairely opposed to weapons expenditures would normally favor the ban. Yet an astute civilian leadership intent on cutting its military expenditures might well harness progress in nuclear weapons development as an excuse to cut spending on conventional forces and weapons, as Eisenhower in fact had done since 1953, and as Khrushchev seemingly would attempt to do in 1959 and 1960.

The rapid development and introduction of missiles might have suggested a bilateral advantage in postponing a test ban, since smaller warheads with larger yields would be required to equip secure second-strike retaliatory forces, deployed either in underground silos or aboard submarines.[75] The hydrogen bomb, moreover, had been in production for only a year or two when the moratorium went into effect; while the U.S. Government commonly assured all parties that there was no risk of accidental explosion in the bombs being produced and deployed, the intricacies of the designs involved induced at least some physicists to desire further test assurances that accidental explosions were indeed impossible.[76] Aside from arms race implications, therefore, some other more peaceful rationales existed for continuing testing.

A formal test ban might have offered one clear bilateral advantage, if it were agreed upon early enough: inhibiting other powers from acquiring nuclear weapons. In 1957 or 1958 it might have been quite difficult for Communist China to refuse to sign a test-ban treaty, more difficult certainly than it would be five years later. A formal treaty would have had more impact than the informal moratorium that was to replace it; the informal moratorium simply required negative participation, each nation not detonating any devices for the moment, while the formal treaty would have pressed on each nation the positive act of declaring it would not detonate. Once induced to sign such an agreement, a Chinese Government might have found it somewhat more embarrassing to withdraw from its terms. Yet the French Government had announced as early as 1958 that it would not sign a test-ban treaty in the absence of more general disarmament arrangements,[77] and the Peking regime might well have behaved similarly.

Until 1958, a need to maintain the legitimacy of nuclear escalation had seemingly forced the United States, on balance, to reject a test ban, despite the clear objections of the neutral world to further detonations; the U.S.S.R. had therefore been able to impose certain prestige costs on the United States by proposing the ban while itself continuing to detonate new weapons. After 1958, the United States, on balance, preferred to adhere to a cessation of tests, since nuclear escalation could no longer be in doubt, since world opposition to testing had grown stronger, and since the inspection problem might be less real. If neutrals might yet be convinced that an inspection system was reasonably required for a test cessation, however, the United States could now in turn impose propaganda costs on the U.S.S.R. by continually demanding negotiations and concessions on the inspection issue, by proclaiming deadlines after which tests might be resumed with blame falling on the Russians.

The entire process of "negotiations" on nuclear testing before and after the beginning of the moratorium of 1958 can thus be interpreted as a propaganda exchange. The presence or absence of testing was determined by the relative weights of the various factors involved; once this was determined, one side would clearly be vulnerable to the propaganda offensive of the other. On balance, the world's aversion to nuclear testing had probably hurt the United States more than the Soviet Union, both before and after 1958. Before, it gave the U.S.S.R. a superior propaganda position; after 1958, the test moratorium induced by neutral opinion would generate a slight Soviet advantage in bomb development, even if there were no clandestine testing, an advantage for which the United States might now partially compensate by taking the propaganda offensive on the inspection issue.

De facto, the United States after 1958 seemed to have accepted a comprehensive test ban of unlimited duration; one can only speculate as to whether the United States would ever have resumed testing if the U.S.S.R. had not done so in 1961. De jure, or officially, the United States did not commit itself; while this can be interpreted as a failure of the United States and the U.S.S.R. to "agree" on a test ban, it might rather be seen simply as a campaign to focus embarrassing pressures of world opinion onto the Soviet Union. The various Soviet responses up to 1961 on the inspection and test detection issues thus reciprocally amounted to counterpropaganda designed to take the heat off; whether or not the Russians ever believed that the United States would really resume testing unilaterally, the American demands for detection facilities would at least have to be rebutted. Aside from propaganda, a moratorium with an uncertain American commitment and duration might be a more effective deterrent to Soviet cheating, since the United States would not have to prove its suspicions to the world as decisively to be released from its side of the bargain; alternatively, the American reservation of leeway might even deter extensive Soviet laboratory efforts independent of clandestine detonations, or at least any great Russian boasting about new discoveries in the nuclear weapons field.

The United States thus open-endedly extended its original one-year deadline for the moratorium, but President Eisenhower explicitly retained the option of resuming testing at some later point. In January of 1959 the United States dropped its last demands that a permanent test ban be linked to other disarmament steps (e.g., a policed cessation of nuclear weapons production) and concentrated specifically on the inspection issue, expecting that Soviet recalcitrance could be shown to be unreasonable to neutral eyes. The U.S.S.R. could not easily have ignored American demands for negotiations on inspection, for fear that the world would blame a resumption of testing on Russian intransigence; the process of proposals and counterproposals thus continued from 1958 into 1961, with Russian concessions always difficult to assess for significance. The claims of the super powers would differ on how small a detonation might escape seismic detection, on the proper manning of inspection posts, on the need for vetos over on-site inspections, on whether the number of such inspections should be proportional to the unexplained seismic signals, or whether there would be a fixed number per year. By the summer of 1961 the Russians had agreed to accept three on-site inspections per year, although the lag until inauguration of the inspection system was unclear, while the United States required over 20 inspections. In response to an American stress on the differences between underground and open-air detonations, the U.S.S.R. proposed a nominal distinction, i.e., formal ban on above-ground tests and continued moratorium on underground tests, which amounted nonetheless to a continued across-the-board suspension of all detonations.

Whether or not the test cessation was giving the Soviet Union an advantage in nuclear weapons research, the United States thus might still have hoped to force the Russians to accept some inspection; on-site inspection would more decisively discourage clandestine detonations, would inhibit military research in general by the mere passings through of inspectors, and otherwise might open Soviet society in a literally unprecedented fashion. If American demands did not force any Soviet submission to inspection, however, a neutral public might still thereby be shown some legitimate distinctions between open-air and underground testing. Underground tests were difficult to detect and monitor, but less hazardous to health, and might thus escape condemnation at some future point if the message could be gotten across now. While American officials responsible for nuclear development might prefer open-air testing as less expensive, underground testing might supply the morale booster needed to get American laboratories working up to the pace expected from Soviet laboratories.

In April of 1959, President Eisenhower sent a letter to Bulganin suggesting a formalized cessation on open-air testing, with allowance of underground tests for the time. The U.S.S.R. refused thus to legitimate underground tests, and the United States under Eisenhower would not attempt even a partial resumption. The President is reported to have contemplated such a resumption (perhaps of open-air tests also) if Nixon were elected in 1960,[78] but except for the French detonation of 1960, the moratorium was handed to President Kennedy in 1961 unbroken. For as long as a wider international acceptance of underground testing had not been achieved, the United States would on balance prefer to continue its total adherence to the ban, rather than opening itself to Soviet propaganda attack.

An uninspected partial test-ban treaty, by clearly binding the United States not to resume open-air detonations, would have relieved inspection propaganda pressure on the U.S.S.R. while requiring the Russians in turn to acknowledge a legitimacy for underground testing. Yet such a treaty now might still have been of doubtful acceptability for both sides. First, open-air testing might for many purposes be preferred to underground by the American AEC; second, the hope remained that the Russians would yet have to accept some inspection if attention was kept focused on an inspected comprehensive treaty, or at least that the Russians would be politically inhibited by the prestige setbacks suffered in continuing to reject inspection. Hence President Eisenhower never explicitly proposed even a partial test ban without some inspection requirements; in effect, American propaganda pressure might continue even if the Russians agreed to tolerate American below-ground testing. If the Russians, moreover, were technically inexperienced in the techniques of underground testing (as Americans may have been to a lesser extent), a resumption of such detonation might have threatened to give the United States an unacceptable advantage in relative progress on nuclear weapons development. (No Soviet underground tests were in fact clearly detected in the United States throughout the moratorium, and only a few thereafter.)[79]

End of the Missile Gap

The "spirit of Geneva" presumably had ended with the Suez and Hungarian crises of 1956, and a détente would not recur until after the Middle East and Quemoy-Matsu crises of 1958 and the Khrushchev Berlin ultimatum of that year. In 1959 there came a reopening of discussions on arms control, a Russian proposal for an exchange of visits between Khrushchev and Eisenhower, and then Khrushchev's suspension of the Berlin ultimatum during his visit to the United States, in the "spirit of Camp David." As before, this détente led to waves of Soviet-American good feeling at the publicity level, waves which made cultural exchange more possible, waves which presumably also made neutral Africans think more highly of both Russians and Americans. Yet the same period also saw a very intense diplomatic struggle between the Russian and American governments over the international status of Berlin, with each side attempting to push the other down a slippery slope of concessions, to resolve the status of the city's Western sector in its favor.[80]

When the conflict broke into the open with the downing of the U-2 and Khrushchev's abrupt cancellation of the 1960 Paris summit conference, the "détente" was over, but one could express skepticism as to what its real political extent had been. Khrushchev in fact delivered fewer real ultimatums on Berlin immediately after the breaking off of the Paris summit, when relations presumably were very "bad," than he had before, when relations were supposedly "good." The remaining months of the Eisenhower Administration saw less diplomatic pressure than at any time since 1958, a lull which would be terminated soon after the accession to office of President Kennedy, about whom Khrushchev was nonetheless prepared to be more complimentary. There is perhaps some element here of the Soviets attempting to lull American and Western Europeans into a false sense of security while the struggle was actually escalating at the less visible levels, but this would be a very incomplete picture, since the escalations typically were quite visible to the relevant decision-makers on the Western side. The "détentes" thus more likely were determined primarily by considerations other than deception, and may always be.

The ambiguity of the détente was reflected in some minor developments on the arms control front. Ever since 1945, the implicit aim of both major powers (at least for the benefit of neutral observers) had been a complete elimination of and need for armed forces. Real international understanding presumably would place little or no limit on how far disarmament could go, until at last only small police forces were left.

In 1959, Premier Khrushchev elected to give this implicit ideal an explicit dressing-up, in a General and Complete Disarmament Proposal[81] which presumably would schedule the entire process from the start. The move indeed caught the attention of the outside world, ultimately forcing the United States to respond with similarly elaborate explication in 1960 and 1961, but it was not clear that the move had any other significance except that it caught attention. Once the neutral world had been exposed to this new format for disarmament proposals, neither power could safely abandon the style without being labeled as pessimistic or cynical about the long term; hence, both the U.S.S.R. and the United States would now remain indefinitely committed to general and complete disarmament, which meant exactly as much or little as it had meant ever since 1945.

The Chinese Communist regime did not join in the 1959 détente, preferring to continue to denounce the United States roundly while Khrushchev was prepared to sound complimentary. Over this period, however, it was not clear that the Chinese were imposing great costs on the United States at anything but the "attack on reputations" level. Russian missile programs had forced the Eisenhower Administration, even during the détente, to appropriate at least some additional funds for the maintenance of credible and viable strategic forces; over the same period the Chinese were perhaps encouraging Hanoi and the Viet Cong to press on with the guerrilla war against the Diem regime (although the causal impact of such "encouragement" is always a little difficult to assess), were presumably backing the Pathet Lao in Laos, and were attempting to humiliate the Indian regime with their bargaining tactics on the Sino-Indian border question. While all these touched areas of potentially great interest to the United States, the extent of Chinese physical influence would in fact remain small. After the termination of the 1958 Quemoy and Matsu crisis, it was only the imminence of a Chinese nuclear detonation that would again really rouse the United States to any significant alteration of resource allocation vis-à-vis China, and this would not come until 1963 or 1964.

The Soviet-American agreement on the demilitarization of Antarctica, a part of the 1959 détente, has at times been ridiculed by arms control skeptics as epitomizing the triviality of subjects on which agreement was possible. Given the lack of military significance for the continent, the agreement perhaps was very obviously to the advantage of all parties concerned, perhaps in particular to the heading off of some sort of a regional weapons deployment race between Great Britain and Argentina. Yet the agreement did commit the U.S.S.R. to accept inspection of its facilities to ensure compliance with the agreement, and this concession might perhaps have significantly weakened Russian objections to inspection under any other regional or general disarmament agreement;[82] in fact no significant modification of the nominal Russian position emerged, but inspection of a sort now existed at a much more serious level, making weapons procurement détente possible if it were to happen at all.

From 1956 to 1960, the United States apparently conducted some 30 series of U-2 overflights across the U.S.S.R.;[83] similar overflights of Communist China were begun in 1957, although here one could always assert the sovereignty of the Nationalist Chinese regime as the legal justification for such operations. The Soviet Union was not only aware of such flights, but apparently was unsuccessful in some early attempts at intercepting them. Protests were privately delivered to the U.S. Government,[84] as they may have been with earlier RB-36 overflights, but with various moves toward détente in 1956 and again in 1959, the Russians seemingly would not make such overflights an insuperable barrier to cordial relations with the United States.

We know now that Soviet intercontinental missile production was never to be what Western observers had thought it might be in the last years of the 1950's; the explanation most probably is to be traced to Russian economic constraints, or to a discovery of the inadequacies of the first generation of liquid-fueled missiles. The more precise claims that Soviet missiles would seriously outnumber those of the United States by 1961 or 1962 had in fact emerged only from critics of the Eisenhower Administration in the United States and from cautious CIA estimates of what the Russians might be capable of producing in a desire to go all-out. Khrushchev's original intentions with regard to missile tests and Sputnik may well have been to demonstrate Soviet qualitative expertise, and also to hint at a vague qualitative growth of Soviet strategic power. Under prodding by American commentators and reporters, he had gone further and had begun to talk of assembly-line quantity production of missiles.

Yet American administration estimates of Soviet capability and production had more to go on in this period than Khrushchev's statements. Since U-2 photographs obtained in 1958 and 1959 showed fewer deployments of Soviet missiles than had been expected, these might adjust American intelligence estimates of future Soviet missile production on two arguments. Even if one still assumed that the Russians would hereafter produce all the missiles they could, the failure to produce expected numbers of missiles to date presumably reduced the maximum inventory they would be able to have for all future dates. Second, the Soviet failure thus far to produce up to known capacity suggested a lack of intention to produce at full capacity, and this intention might also be projected forward, again reducing estimates of likely inventories for specific future dates. Presumably on a combination of such plausible assumptions, the Eisenhower Administration in 1959 felt itself justified in reducing prognoses of future Russian missile inventories,[85] so that drastic American compensatory actions were even less required.

If certain reports are to be believed, by late 1959 the Russians had already perceived the disadvantages of premature procurement and deployment of liquid-fueled ICBM's; the very large rockets developed could not easily be moved about in the U.S.S.R., but instead had to be deployed along the Trans-Siberian Railway,[86] making the monitoring of their sites relatively simple for United States U-2 flights. Perhaps the large rockets had originally been designed on an assumption that hydrogen-bomb warheads could not so soon be significantly miniaturized; while the Russians thus had a superb set of boosters for space ventures at hand, the design may have proved even more vulnerable, in its extreme lack of maneuverability, than the early American designs. Two kinds of vulnerability questions thus could arise with regard to liquid-fueled missiles: susceptibility to enemy attack and fragility in normal deployment and operations. Even the latter unreliability of systems would force added expenditures on each side for desired amounts of military capability and strategic insurance, thus again making the liquid-fueled option look more and more like a bad buy.

The failure of the Russians to deploy many missiles by late 1959 or early 1960 had thus presumably made some downward revision of intelligence estimates appropriate, but caution still required that the Russians perhaps be credited with a 300 to 80 ICBM superiority over the United States by 1962. Yet the real question of balance would always be distorted if seen only in a comparison of missile forces, for throughout this period the United States retained as many as 1,400 B-47 medium bombers, and more than 500 B-52's. Considerations of economy, and of avoiding provocation of the Soviets, might thus plausibly shelve the procurement of American first-generation intercontinental missiles, with a more orderly development of the solid-fueled second generation. With occasional accelerations of effort when intelligence on Soviet production seemed especially threatening or obscure, the Republican administration would in fact basically tend to adhere to this stance.

President Eisenhower's assurances that the new Soviet missiles presented no deterrence problem would, however, still be upset several times by leaks of information from within the administration itself. Intelligence forecasts of likely Soviet missile production were prepared over this period by the CIA, by the Joint Chiefs of Staff, and at times apparently also by the individual military services (especially when a service had held a minority position in the "voting" within the Joint Chiefs of Staff).[87] Further confusing the picture was the existence of estimates both of "likely" Soviet production and of possible production in a maximum-effort "crash program." Perhaps one should not be surprised at widely varying estimates of an opponent's force levels, especially when one remembers the estimates of Russian ground force levels ranging from 50 to 150 divisions; at the strategic force level, the numbers might seem more critical, but exact numbers would always be hard to measure or to agree upon.

As it was, such intelligence estimates, especially those bolstering the Air Force's case for more rapid augmentation of various strategic forces, were several times made available to Congressional critics of the administration's preparations; had tighter control been held over the disclosure of such estimates outside the executive branch, the public demand for procurement of liquid-fueled missiles might have been less. The Administration, moreover, felt obliged at various points to concede that pessimistic assumptions might prove correct; Secretary of Defense McElroy, in a background briefing in 1959, apparently estimated that the Russians would in fact develop a 3 to 1 ICBM superiority early in the 1960's,[88] an admission which quickly stoked the flames for administration critics.

One should thus not underestimate the value of the U-2 flights in allowing the U.S. Government, over this period, to forgo a drastic strategic adjustment in response to Russian strategic force propaganda. In effect, they supplied the inspection which kept the Eisenhower Administration from expending the funds and deploying the forces its critics demanded. And as a result, perhaps, they allowed the Russians to fail to fulfill their missile claims, since no clear first-strike potential was emerging in the United States. If the Soviet leadership had any conception of the accuracy of the monitoring equipment aboard such U-2 aircraft, it must have seen that its posture of missile superiority would not be believed in the executive in Washington. Yet the U.S. Administration could not easily spell out the nature of its sources of information without giving the Soviets a propaganda issue for the neutral world; the Russians thus could in effect have their cake and eat it too, fostering an impression of missile prowess in the larger uninformed world while tacitly showing the Republicans in Washington that there was in fact no reason to begin running an arms race.

When a Soviet surface-to-air missile first intercepted a U-2 in 1960, the accuracy of the airborne cameras may have come as a surprise to the Russian leadership. The Kremlin might already have understood that the U.S. Government generally knew it was not faced by any unfavorable missile gap; but on the evidence of the downed U-2, SAC planners knew very exactly how many missiles there were, and where they were deployed, dispelling any site-location secrecy promised by the closed society of the U.S.S.R.[89] At least a part of the Soviet objection to inspected missile disarmament programs—that inspection aided aggressors by disclosing locations for counterforce attacks—was thus outmoded. It is often contended that the U-2 incident was merely used procedurally to break off the Paris summit conference, because of Chinese pressure or because Eisenhower's assumption of responsibility for the flight seemed to be a slap in the face of the Soviet leader; but it may also have been a moment of truth for Khrushchev, indicating that his forces were less clearly secure, and his bargaining position less strong, than he had expected.

The Russians might have been able to shoot down a U-2 earlier, but may have deliberately decided to do so only on May 1, 1960; it has even been suggested that this was a decision of the Soviet military, at odds with Premier Khrushchev.[90] From Khrushchev's later deposal and from other evidence, it might indeed be inferred that the Soviet leader's power was never absolute, and that he was engaged in a continual tug of war with other factions in the U.S.S.R., including the military, on a host of questions. The various troop-reduction proposals Khrushchev had advanced, the latest coming publicly in January of 1960, had received unenthusiastic and guardedly negative reactions from the military, as had any cuts in the military budget,[91] cuts for which Khrushchev apparently felt considerable need in face of his economic difficulties.

If the U-2 interception was thus intended to embarrass Khrushchev into a tougher line, forcing him to break off the summit, it may have succeeded. Yet the break-off of the summit is difficult to interpret as a victory for a hawkish Soviet position, because it produced no American concessions (while going through with the summit conference might have produced some), and because it was followed by a relaxation of Soviet pressure on Berlin. Even Khrushchev's announced troop reduction was not rescinded until 1961, after Kennedy had come into office in Washington. One might thus have to amend the above argument to read that the Soviet military selfishly feared Khrushchev would win too many satisfying Western concessions without any obvious reliance on military power, thus making the armed forces' position within the Soviet Union all the weaker.

The United States pledged to suspend U-2 flights over the Soviet Union after the 1960 incident, but reconnaissance of a very similar quality would soon be made possible by reconnaissance orbital satellites; at the abortive Paris summit, President De Gaulle had suggested to Khrushchev that the U.S.S.R. might already be photographing France by the use of such a satellite, and the Russian leader had responded that no one could object to this form of aerial espionage.[92]

The strategic arms race from 1957 to 1961 thus had imposed some serious psychological burdens on the United States. Because the Russians were interpreted as being less of a status quo power, or as having inherently greater conventional capabilities, segments of American public opinion would chronically need to be reassured that the United States was ahead of the Russians strategically, or that it had reached some conceivable strategic plateau, in the form of solid-fueled ICBM's or submarine-based Polaris missiles; yet the Republican Administration had failed to get the United States onto this plateau early enough to prevent a certain sense of distress which did not abate until well into the first year of the Kennedy Administration. Above all this made intellectually credible the spectacle of a Russian "splendid first strike" designed to wipe out American military potential in a single blow, a spectacle which might in fact have been less plausible than in some earlier periods; the Eisenhower Administration sought to suppress this spectacle, but could not to do so completely without some greater Russian restraint in missile development and propaganda.

It remains somewhat unclear why the Eisenhower Administration could not make more convincing use of its intelligence data to bolster its domestic political position, before or especially after the revelation of the U-2 flights in 1960. To the academic world, which had enormously increased its interest in defense after 1956, the response of the Eisenhower Administration to the "missile gap" threat had seemed too complacent to be convincing or reassuring;[93] yet the greater majority of citizens may still have been willing to defer fears of Russian military accomplishments. The Republicans perhaps could not have improved their campaign position by more crisply denying Russian progress; to spell out a Russian failure to produce a maximum of missiles might simply have "awoken" more people to the possibility that there could indeed have been a missile gap. Prior to 1960 one can also cite the government's need to protect its source of information in the U-2, not because the Russians did not know of the flights, but because admitting American flights publicly, while continuing them, might have insulted the Soviet Union enough to force it into some more drastic action.

As it was, Kennedy beat Nixon by a very narrow margin in 1960, with the television debates perhaps having the greatest impact, and with little evidence that the differences in the two defense platforms had won more votes for Kennedy. By 1960 only 21 percent of Americans polled thought "too little" was being spent on defense, while 18 percent thought "too much."[94]

If the Republicans had wished to eliminate the defense or "missile gap" issue in 1960, it is also not clear why the candidate Kennedy was denied full intelligence data available to the Government on Soviet nonproduction of missiles.[95] The Administration may have judged the defense issue to be insignificant to the voters in any event; alternatively, it may have been feared that access to the data would tempt the Democratic candidate to exploit and compromise it somehow, or to set up a stronger defense issue (perhaps unilateral disarmament) than had yet been developed.

The Eisenhower Performance

President Eisenhower liked to see himself as a man of peace. His critics tended to indict Republican foreign policy as unresponsive to any explicit accommodations with the U.S.S.R. The two interpretations may not have been so contradictory, for tacit bargaining need not be explicit (or perhaps even conscious) to be effective.

At any rate, Eisenhower and Secretary of Defense Wilson, in formulating their defense budgets often showed a concern for their impact on Russian military appropriations, or at least so rationalized such budgets' shortfalls of what American domestic critics had desired them to be. If Eisenhower's connection of superdestructive all-out war to small Soviet aggressions was disturbing, this was after all almost identically the line endorsed by the U.S.S.R. after 1957: that war was too horrible to be considered and that local wars were likely to escalate. If, for the purposes of military balance, Eisenhower relied overly much on his strategic forces, few could accuse him of overly expanding them. Had Eisenhower's opponents held office, it seems plausible that their arms budgets would have run a race imposing more of an economic and strategic strain on the U.S.S.R.'s economy. A little bit of this is perhaps brought out most clearly (or bizarrely) in a dialogue between Secretary Wilson and Senator Jackson at the 1956 Air Power Hearings:

> Senator JACKSON. Why did you try to create the impression to the American people and to the world, an impression which obviously the Communists can use, that the Soviets are building a defensive air force?
>
> Secretary WILSON. Because it was the truth.
>
> Senator JACKSON. Would you tell the committee how many Tu-4's they had, and if the Tu-4 is a defensive aircraft or an offensive aircraft?
>
> Secretary WILSON. They put their emphasis on fighters. They put their emphasis on submarines and not on carriers. They built bombers and, as far as we know, without any tankers.
>
> Senator JACKSON. Did they have any long-range bombers at the time you made these statements in 1953 and 1954?
>
> The so-called Tu-4 I am referring to, it is a . . . .
>
> Secretary WILSON. We don't call that a long-range bomber.
>
> Senator JACKSON. That is the B-29 bomber. Did it not have the capability of making one-way atomic missions against the United States?
>
> Secretary WILSON. None of our military people really think that it is a feasible military operation. We talk about it a little, once in a while, but I suppose we got the idea from the Japanese Kamikazes, or something, but . . . .
>
> Senator JACKSON. So . . . .
>
> Secretary WILSON. It is not a military operation.
>
> Senator JACKSON. It is your opinion that up until when, then, was the Soviet Air Force purely a defensive buildup?
>
> Incidentally, all the Russian leaders have been saying that they have been building up defensively, and you are here to corroborate what they have been saying; is that it?
>
> Secretary WILSON. The emphasis was on defense. That is what I said.

Senator JACKSON. Therefore, when you make that statement, you, in effect, are corroborating the Soviet charge that our Air Force is offensive and theirs is defensive. What other inference could you logically come to?

Secretary WILSON. I would like to point out that President Eisenhower at the Geneva meeting tried to put their mind at rest . . . .

Senator JACKSON. I am not talking about Geneva.

Secretary WILSON. Prior to Geneva, and that was a change, and they accepted it, and I think for about the first time, that we really were not aggressors, that were going to try to destroy their communism as such, with a military operation.

I think they told their people that, and I think they first built up their defenses, and what they did speaks louder than what they said. They did build up their Migs first before they built any bombers. They did build submarines and built no carriers.

Senator JACKSON. Mr. Secretary . . . .

Secretary WILSON. They did build their first bombers with no tankers.

Senator JACKSON. Mr. Secretary, isn't there a very simple answer to why they built all these fighters? Isn't it a fact that they were building these fighters during the time when we had an air atomic monopoly?

Secretary WILSON. They were afraid of our monopoly, they were afraid we would use it on them, I suppose. They shouldn't have been, but I think they probably were.

Senator JACKSON. Isn't the reason they were building . . . .

Secretary WILSON. We started with our bases to ring them around. What if . . . let's just be fair about it, now, and give the devil their due. What if they had done the same thing to us that we have done? We rattled the atomic bomb too much, incidentally.[96]

At the material level of détente, perhaps the most significant, the Eisenhower policies thus did not challenge the U.S.S.R. as much as the weapons procurements of Truman or Kennedy. At the verbal level, the détente would be less evident, suggesting either that the Republicans did not realize what they were doing, or that they had good reasons, domestic or external, for disguising this accommodation with the Russians.

Outside the military balance, the Republican Administration had inherited or amplified an assumption that a great political threat remained in the naiveté of various parties and nations towards Communism. In 1948, after all, the fear had been that Italy might vote

Communist, or that France might go Communist in some largely nonviolent process. If the Red Army could now be deterred as well or better by massive retaliatory threats, if a major arms race with the U.S.S.R. could be avoided with perhaps even some improvement in the Soviet outlook, then it would still be essential, in the Republican view, to mobilize European and Asian publics into a staunch resistance to Communism. The threat may have been exaggerated, since Egyptians, Iraqis, Cambodians, and Guineans proved to be unexpectedly sophisticated in dealings with their Communist parties, but it nonetheless suggested a need for verbal confrontations at times more hostile than the military weapons-procurement confrontation.

As argued earlier, Soviet moves toward détente were also too often accompanied by disarmament proposals which might have erased even the meager military force triggers left in the NATO area as a pledge of American commitment. Given that the Republican posture did not call for high military force levels at either the tactical or strategic plane, greater forces than in 1949 nonetheless had to be maintained, and Soviet verbal softenings coupled to further disarmament had to be rejected. Aside from this, the American "moral commitment" to massive retaliation in defense of Europe or Asia might have to be premised on strong moral aversions to Communism, which in turn precluded any extravagant American endorsements of peaceful coexistence.

The Eisenhower Administration was also often criticized for not pursuing the possibilities of disengagement on the European central front, but it is not so clear what the real advantages of such disengagement would have been. The Administration's successor would come into office intent on greatly increasing NATO conventional force strength, thus moving still further from any full disengagement. Even if the Republicans consistently overrated Russian inclinations toward an assault on Western Europe, one might argue that such qualms were resolved more assuredly over time in a highly armed confrontation by which surprise attack and "workers' coups" became totally implausible. Forty divisions on each side of the line might thus ease tensions more quickly than four on each side; after tensions had been eased, after Russian aggressiveness per se had at last become decisively implausible, then mutual troop reductions might occur naturally.

The Administration nonetheless complicated the problem during this time by its continued verbal pressure for German reunification, as embodied in the nonrecognition of East Germany, and the maintenance

200

of Allied privileges in and around West Berlin (although critics of Eisenhower did not normally promise any less hope for German reunification under disengagement). If the United States did not make concessions to bolster the East German regime, that regime might be forced to choose between collapsing and trying to seize West Berlin. The existence of a West German Army might be justified by the requirements of a precautionary defense of Western Europe, but it also bolstered the dignity of the Federal Republic to the disparagement of the D.D.R., and implicitly threatened or promised intervention in the event of another outburst of revolution or rioting in East Germany. Perhaps without large German or NATO forces in West Germany, pressure could have been applied for reunification without risk of warfare, but probably also with no hope of success. With a moderate level of West German and NATO armament, this pressure might have greater hopes of success, but would indeed induce risks of Communist military action. Pressure for reunification thus made the higher level of conventional armaments more dangerous, or vice versa, and this problem remained unsolved as the Kennedy Administration succeeded to office.

As it was, the Republican conventional contribution to the confrontation along the Elbe was more often criticized as too small than as too large. The divisions established under NATO may have served primarily as tripwires for escalation and as pledges of commitment. If the potential of Soviet ground forces had been grievously underrated, then the NATO force might have been menacing in itself; yet this level of forces along a hostile frontier would not normally have seemed highly provocative or conducive to mutually unwanted war.

Aside from East Germany, one might discover another Republican commitment to territorial revision in the 1950's: mainland China. In a legal sense, American recognition of the Taiwan regime as governing all of China might have suggested support for a Nationalist return to the mainland; practical policies, however, were more realistic. The Nationalist retention of the offshore islands had gone unnoticed or tolerated in the last years of the Truman Administration and into 1954, but Communist pressure on the islands soon forced the Eisenhower Administration explicitly to circumscribe its interpretation of their significance to the "defense of Taiwan" rather than the liberation of the mainland.

Very much at the margin, American nonrecognition statements might have made the Peking regime less secure in the mid-1950's if a pro-Nationalist revolt on the mainland was at all possible, one sufficient to allow Chiang's forces to try to come ashore again. But aside from this unlikely prospect, the U.S. military threat was almost entirely one of retaliation by bomber forces in the event of Chinese Communist aggression, since Republican reductions in amphibious forces hardly suggested an American-sponsored landing on the mainland.

The American commitment to Nationalist sovereignty over all of China was thus primarily relevant to legitimating U.S. protection of Taiwan; such Chinese Communist resentment as would emerge related largely to this defense of Taiwan, and only very marginally to any implicit Western offense back onto the mainland. If the nonrecognition policy nonetheless still illustrated any American reluctance to contribute to stabilizing the Communist mainland regime, it was not because the Maoists had demonstrated any clearly independent hostility to the United States. Precisely because Chinese Communism was thought to be under Moscow's control, it seemed all the more intolerable and frightening for a great people like the Chinese to be consigned to alien rule, to some sort of "Slavic Manchukuo."

The German and Chinese situations were thus superficially similar; in each case the United States would have to legitimate its attachments to "half" of a divided country, thus implicitly threatening the other half and poisoning future relations with it. But the implicit threat to Peking was trivial in comparison with the threat to Pankow. Alienating Pankow might be trivial when compared with the costs of precluding better relations with Peking, but Peking might inevitably be alienated as long as it was denied Taiwan.

Finally, the apparent Republican looseness and indifference to strict nuclear controls would also occasion criticism. Clearly, if a threat of conventional outbreak were to persist because of Berlin or East Germany, the relative dispersion of nuclear weapons around potential battlefields might have been thought unwise. Yet this dispersion had to be defended as part of the general strategy for maintaining an American position in Europe, i.e., never to be very explicit about nuclear control or about the sources of the commitment to West Berlin, thus making plausible an American column on the Autobahn even if it was very likely to force escalation to general war. If Russian strategic pronouncements over the latter 1950's coupled the escalation threat to any American military support for Berlin, the Republicans would respond by reechoing the pronouncements and feigning relative indifference to the escalation.

One can also argue that the seemingly blissful Republican approach was as likely to inhibit unwanted independent national nuclear capabilities as the more explicit logic of the 1960's, and that a gradually increasing toleration of French weapons programs (Germany, after all, had already renounced the manufacture of weapons) might later have led to less French independence. If the Republicans were unwilling to draw explicit lines as to who could and who could not join the "nuclear club," this surely did not indicate that they were prepared to have everyone join. Consciously or otherwise, an "antiproliferation" policy was followed in the Eisenhower Administration; the policy has still not been proved clearly inferior to its successor, and it might have been even more "successful" if the American Congress had been behind it.

5   The Kennedy Administration: 1961-1963

Revised Preferences

The Democratic Administration of President Kennedy came into office enunciating several distinct and potentially conflicting themes relevant to national defense. First, the Democratic Party prided itself on not being averse to government spending; the American economy could afford such governmental expenditures, in the Democratic view, and might even benefit from such expenditures if the economy were underemployed. The temptation had been strong, therefore, to accuse the Eisenhower Administration of indulging in "false economies" with regard to national defense, as well as in other areas of government.

The Democrats also prided themselves on being less doctrinairely opposed to Communism, on being more attuned to possibilities of international organization and accommodation, leading perhaps at some future point to substantial disarmament. Prospects for any serious disarmament agreements with the U.S.S.R. did not seem very bright, however, at the beginning of the new Administration, in light of the scare the West had received in the previous four years. Having attacked the Republicans for underexpenditures on both strategic air forces and tactical ground forces, President Kennedy did not come into office a convinced advocate of major disarmament measures;[1] for the time it seemed, rather, that larger standing armed forces would be required, at least until the Russians had given up their claims to West Berlin, and that a significantly larger missile force would be required until Soviet forces were shown to be less numerous and threatening than had been assumed.

205

Perceptions of mutual accommodation might thus fall under the rubric of "arms control," and might even require an increase in military spending in certain cases (e.g., the hardening of missiles);[2] yet if any substantial disarmament were to occur, over the longer range, it might lead to force reductions not easily distinguishable from the "economy" reductions the Republicans had favored. President Kennedy in any event now felt that the United States should advance some disarmament proposals to counteract the propaganda impact of those offered by Khrushchev; there emerged, therefore, an American general and complete disarmament scheme, which again faced many of the inherent obstacles which had precluded broad schemes before, specifically the problem of inspection.

Involuntary submission to inspection had not been terminated forever with the U-2 incident. While President Kennedy had given his pledge that the U-2 flights would not be resumed over the Soviet Union, the United States had by January of 1961 launched its first Samos reconnaissance satellite,[3] part of a photo-inspection program which would continue at an accelerated pace indefinitely thereafter. While Soviet pronouncements on this form of reconnaissance tended to be somewhat contradictory, there had been statements that the U.S.S.R. did not in principle object to this type of reconnaissance; by March of 1962 the Soviets in fact had reciprocated by launching the first of their Cosmos series, a satellite launched in a shallow orbit to take very effective reconnaissance photographs of the United States and of the entire world.

If the termination of U-2 flights in the spring of 1960 had left the United States at all uncertain of its intelligence estimates until the first reconnaissance satellite was operational about a year later, such uncertainty could prove unfortunate from the Soviet point of view if it induced the incoming Kennedy Administration to augment its missile program more than it might have otherwise. Holding back on strategic weapons augmentation might have been difficult for the new administration in any event, in view of the electoral campaign it had waged; but the absence of highly reliable intelligence information reduced the chances for any early reversal of emphasis.

Perhaps most important, the new Administration also seemed to have a greater and more enunciated aversion to risks of nuclear war in general, and to any escalation to an exchange of strikes between the United States and the U.S.S.R. in particular. This may have stemmed from a greater liberal preoccupation with the dangers of human suffering, or from a more careful analysis of all the possible mechanisms of involuntary and misguided escalation; the result was a general desire to "put the nuclear genie back in the bottle," by avoiding the development of foreign national nuclear forces and also by more closely controlling American forces.

Aside from any policy dichotomy between a Republican aversion to spending and a Democratic aversion to risks of war—a dichotomy which it is perhaps easy to exaggerate—changes in the objective environment might have caused either American party now to wish to deal more explicitly and carefully with general-war escalation risks. The stockpiles of the two sides after 1960 made it plausible that all-out war would threaten the very social fabric of nations; it would no longer be a question simply of massive physical destruction or human suffering, for the restoration of society might prove impossible even after the longest period of postwar recovery. The qualitative distinction suggested here could be very hazy, and had been alluded to by some commentators ever since the first atomic bombs; the writings of sober analysts such as Herman Kahn, moreover, had tended to be skeptical as to the full extent of the calamity that would be produced by all-out general war.[4] Yet the debate over Kahn's *On Thermonuclear War* may have combined with Soviet missile tests and the disclosure of nuclear stockpile figures finally to erode the Eisenhower-fostered "war of attrition" image, making the horrendous-total-war scenario more credible and salient than it had ever been before.

The vast variety of weapons now deployed, and the secure second-generation missile systems about to be acquired, raised the parallel issue of which forms of command-and-control system should be chosen over which others. A vagueness had survived on such issues in the past, in part because the explicit questions had not been asked; if permissive-action links were now to become technologically feasible, however, the questions would ask themselves—e.g., why shouldn't the President retain the ability to prevent certain nuclear weapons from being fired, so that he can veto such firings if he judges them counter to the national interest? Similar issues arose on the conduct of any general war, once escalation into it had occurred. Would not the extreme destruction that the Soviet Air Force could deliver now—as opposed to earlier periods—require different targeting policies on the part of SAC; would not the increased options available to SAC—in part also due to the changed nature of the Soviet target—require a new assessment of these options?

The Democratic Administration thus prided itself generally on greater rationality, on a greater willingness to explore all the strategic ramifications of a military posture or of a policy statement.[5] One wanted to establish rational options for even the most awful scenarios, Soviet attacks on Europe or North America, options which would allow the United States still to pursue clearly beneficial ends instead of some passionate spasm of retaliation merely serving a vague moral commitment. Yet to prepare to be rational in even the most unlikely military scenario could make that scenario seem more likely to the other side, and might therefore make it more likely. If the Soviets were as rational and understanding as one might hope (not to speak of the West Germans or French), such discussion of options might be viewed as a peaceful gesture. But an equally likely response might be confusion or distrust on whether the United States now expected to need or use such options more than before.

The Berlin Problem

The Kennedy Administration had come into office thinking that it had two military problems, one at the strategic level and one at the tactical. Deterring an attack on the continental United States would apparently turn out not to be so difficult as the missile gap became more and more clearly illusory, and as American strategic-force augmentation programs, stepped up after the election, began to show results. The tactical problem seemed still to be present, however, as Russian pressure on West Berlin persisted. An important question now concerned the reality and form of the tactical threat the U.S. Government perceived.

The United States in 1961 made significant additions to its own conventional force strength, increasing the number of combat-ready Army and Marine divisions, restructuring Army units that had been made overly dependent on tactical nuclear weapons in the Eisenhower years, and augmenting the Navy and Air Force tactical support units required for effective nonnuclear battlefield operations.[6] It was this buildup, in part, that made possible the dispatch of 40,000 American troops to Germany as a Berlin crisis seemed to be approaching in the summer of 1961.

Fears of Soviet ground attack in Europe had emerged and receded numerous times since the beginning of the cold war. A threat had emerged in 1948 after the Czech coup, and then receded with the end of the Berlin blockade in 1949. It had emerged again with the Korean War, and receded with the death of Stalin and the liberalization and thaw commencing thereafter. The next clear threat of aggression in Europe had arisen in 1958, with Khrushchev's demand for a peace treaty in Germany which would end Western access to West Berlin. For the next four years deadlines were imposed and relaxed repeatedly on such a settlement, deadlines after which a new blockade might be imposed, coupled perhaps with an interference with air traffic and the threat of hostilities this represented.

Where else the threat would be felt now, besides Berlin, was not so clear. Khrushchev in a speech of 1961 had again contended that any serious local war would escalate to general war, which seemingly suggested a general stability for the territorial status quo.[7] The weight of this statement was undercut, however, by Khrushchev's definition of "wars of national liberation" as a distinct nonescalating subtype in which the U.S.S.R. felt itself duty-bound to assist rebel forces, since direct conflict between the two major powers was avoided. The Khrushchev statement thus was widely heralded in the West as signaling a new wave of Soviet-supported nibbling actions around the world, a wave which critics of the Eisenhower Administration had been predicting since the later 1950's. While the statement did not now suggest any Russian limited-war attacks in Europe, the Soviet privilege of defining which were "wars of national liberation" and which were "local wars" seemed just as threatening.

On its face the Soviet statement did not differ much from Chinese Communist statements urging support for guerrilla insurrections around the world. But the Russian prerogative of definition would in fact be turned against the Chinese, apparently as much as against the West. The Russians did not now encourage or support any great wave of guerrilla operations around the globe, but chose instead to define "national liberation" somewhat more closely while at times, as in the early Laos and Vietnam crises, warning that such "local wars" could escalate.[8] But a problem seemingly remained in Europe, with regard to West Berlin.

If Soviet foreign policy after 1957 was aimed primarily at stabilizing the East German regime by altering the status of West Berlin, then it would seem that the Russians had indeed been making progress in compromising the status of the enclave; indeed, the geographical position made it likely they would if only enough pressure were applied. While the threat of war seemed to drop in 1959 with the "spirit of Camp David," the modifications induced in American position statements at the time might well have had the longer-range impact of delegitimizing the Western rights of access.[9] American attempts to undo the damage later in 1959 and in early 1960 probably inclined the Russians to discontinue the détente, following the U-2 incident and the breakup of the Paris Conference.

It was with this Russian drive to alter the status of Berlin that the Kennedy Administration came into office in 1961, a drive which might make the reestablishment of some military balance in Europe particularly urgent, rather than simply an abstractly desirable goal for the future. It might prove difficult to rebut Soviet pressure, however, if Khrushchev still could carry off any reputation for superiority at the strategic missile level; alternatively, Kennedy himself might be interpreted by the Russians as lacking resolution because of his youth and inexperience, or because of his endorsement, in the campaign against the Eisenhower record, of doubts on the credibility of massive retaliation. While many subjects were discussed at the Kennedy-Khrushchev Vienna meeting of 1961, the Berlin crisis was clearly regarded as being of paramount importance, and Kennedy received little assurance that the Russians would not go ahead with their threats to impose a blockade.[10]

Soviet pressures on West Berlin were still often seen as an attempt to weaken the credibility of American support for the rest of Western Europe, which clearly is one effect an American surrender of Berlin might have had. Yet the continued existence of West Berlin as an enclave undoubtedly threatened the stability of the East German regime, especially since the most talented portion of the East's population was more and more using West Berlin as a means of escaping to West Germany. If the Ulbricht regime was unable to gain effective control over its populace, it might eventually fall, and the existence of a unified pro-Western Germany was something the Soviets could not so easily accept. Thus the political form of Soviet demands at this stage, like the military strategic forms, seemed generally to be for a stabilization of the Elbe line rather than for any "domino effect" to be triggered across Western Europe; the discussions were still of "peace treaties," "normalization of the situation," "the assertion of national sovereignty," etc.

To Western eyes the plight of the Russians and of the East German regime might have been understandable; doubts might arise as to whether the flow of refugees was entirely to the interest of the West or of Germany, or whether the instability thereby induced might not be the source of Soviet truculence. It might thus be advisable to tolerate some moderate assertion of sovereignty by the D.D.R., as long as it did

210

not interfere with Western access to West Berlin; yet a great difficulty remained in determining how much assertion was really required to stabilize the status quo, and in avoiding any temptation to the Communist side to compound and exploit the momentum induced by partial Western concessions.

In 1961, the Soviet leadership itself could not yet have been certain that a Berlin wall alone could stabilize the situation in the German Democratic Republic, and Soviet pressure may thus have been intended to accomplish much more, perhaps the total neutralization or even absorption of West Berlin. The tension that mounted through the summer was not eased immediately by the East German erection of the wall to halt the outflow of refugees. Minor confrontations of forces along the new wall occurred as token reinforcements of American ground troops were dispatched to West Berlin.[11] Russian hints at more ambitious military activity might afterwards be interpreted as a mere cover for the erection of the wall, but the extent of the Soviet deployment, and the persistence of the threat of the blockade after the wall had been completed, appeared unnecessary for a simple containment of refugees. The end of the summer of 1961 thus still did not see any guarantee that the status quo in West Berlin would be allowed peacefully to persist.

Public suggestions on closing the frontier had been offered in the West even before the East German action by spokesmen such as Senator Fulbright, and these may or may not have been deliberate hints as to what the U.S. Government considered an acceptable adjustment;[12] at any rate, it seems clear that the West had considered this possibility and decided to tolerate it. The relaxation of Allied access rights to East Berlin would be a more debated concession, while the assertion of Communist control over any portion of West Berlin—for example, over a border zone intruding in some distance all along the new wall—was presumably intolerable.[13] Infringements on air or land access to the city were likewise generally threatening, except perhaps on the 10,000-foot ceiling, where the espionage consideration seemed a more genuinely felt grievance.

It is possible that the Administration in Washington disapproved of the tank vs. tank deployment in Berlin now directed by Lucius Clay on the issue of American access to East Berlin.[14] The confrontation might have been justifiable as a boost to Western morale in general, or as a counter to East German claims to a border zone inside West Berlin. The action has been rationalized also as forcing the Russians to commit their tanks, thus exposing their control over events and again casting aspersions on East German authority and sovereignty. Yet American rights to enter East Berlin without submission to D.D.R. passport control were thereafter no longer exercised, after the world had seen a seemingly frightening confrontation of U.S. and Soviet armor.

In any event, the general Soviet threat to Allied access to West Berlin had been peculiar, not fitting the standard model of anticipated Soviet limited aggressions; here alone the West might need an offensive conventional military capability, while the Russians might not. Despite the abstract analysis, any analogy between Korea and Berlin might have been badly taken; the nonmilitary tactics available to the East Germans and Russians in Berlin were potentially effective enough to force the NATO powers to choose between surrendering the city or initiating military hostilities.

The normal Democratic criticism of "massive retaliation" escalation doctrines had been that such doctrines were not credible, that territory would be lost to Soviet military initiatives as the American bluff was called. The Berlin threat under Eisenhower and then under Kennedy, however, illustrated a very different problem with such escalation: namely, that it might indeed be credible all around, in a setting where any military initiative had to fall to the West rather than to the Soviet bloc. If the Autobahn relief-column scenario thus showed up this disadvantage in the escalation mechanism, one could not be certain that it could be removed if the Russians wished to leave their tactical nuclears deployed so as to maintain it.

Ever since the deployment of American tactical nuclear weapons to the NATO front in West Germany, Soviet strategic writings had come more and more to accept the likelihood that any war in Europe would become a nuclear war, that "all the most modern weapons would be brought to bear." If such arguments tended to protect territory west of the Elbe against Soviet attack—as had been the Eisenhower Administration's intention—they now might also protect territory east of the Elbe, including West Berlin, against Western military intervention. Soviet acceptance of an originally American argument (one that Kennedy might now have wanted to reject) thus might show a willingness to settle for Berlin, which presumably did not lessen the immediate threat to American interests, but altered its form.[15] Since East Germany's position remained politically shaky, and since West Berlin remained an upsetting outpost of Western politics and affluence in the middle of East Germany, it may have suited the Soviet position perfectly now to rebut earlier American Democratic Party arguments that a European war could be kept conventional. The similarity of this reasoning to that of the Eisenhower Administration seems clear enough, only now it was being used on behalf of Soviet interests.

With the Soviet pressure on West Berlin now clearly more real, the European allies of the United States showed themselves somewhat more willing to match American augmentations of conventional forces in West Germany: the Federal Republic extended its period of military service to 18 months, and France brought two divisions back from Algeria to the continent of Europe.[16] The special situation of Berlin might prove far more plausible as a cause for conventional arms buildup, to European eyes, than any abstract possibility of a general Russian move westward. For one thing, the Russian need to act on Berlin was more obvious and threatening; for another, it was the only scenario in which the Russians or East Germans could easily apply pressure without immediately incurring a markedly increased risk of nuclear war. At the same time, the United States augmented its tactical nuclear stockpiles on the European continent and, in response to the seemingly cooperative attitude of the French government, opened the agreement on nuclear weapons information, training, and access to French Army units in Germany.[17]

Western augmentations of conventional forces had, however, been matched by similar augmentations on the Soviet side; the Russian military budget was increased and the term of service extended, with maneuvers of Warsaw Pact forces being staged for the first time.[18] One inference that could be drawn from this was that Soviet bloc conventional forces had not been so inherently superior to those of NATO, but rather so weak that any American or NATO buildup might prove specifically threatening to the Communist powers. If one concluded instead that there had indeed still been a Soviet conventional superiority (perhaps in extensive Soviet reserve structures, plus rapid reinforcement capabilities, outweighing anything similar in NATO), the lesson was nonetheless that Soviet forces had not yet reached any upper limit in effectiveness beyond which the Russians would see no advantage in going. Rather, it seemed that any Western force augmentation might quickly induce a matching Warsaw Pact augmentation, perhaps canceling out any nonnuclear military impact of the American move.

If larger NATO conventional forces were thus generated in response to the Soviet menace to West Berlin, it might not so clearly facilitate a nonnuclear defense of the city, given the deployments of both U.S. and

Russian tactical nuclear weapons. Rather, the aggregation of an Autobahn-breakthrough force would make more plausible the Western response that might very well produce escalation to nuclear warfare. An augmentation of a moving tripwire might thus be achieved, but not a conventional option per se. The Russians were again molding the contest for Berlin into a game of "chicken," and the buildup of NATO forces, however widely advertised as changing the game, may in fact have amounted to the West's playing it. If the European NATO powers were willing to augment their conventional forces with regard to a Berlin threat, moreover, it was not clear whether such augmentations could be maintained or expanded for any other threats.

The Impact of Strategic Forces

For the defense of West Berlin, if not for the rest of Europe, it might thus be necessary to allude again to the strategic forces of the United States, forces which a more elegant arrangement might have kept separate from the European conflict. The first two years of the Kennedy Administration would see some uncoupling of the fate of American cities from tactical engagements, but SAC might yet be brought to bear. As the Berlin crisis developed, B-47's originally scheduled for demobilization were retained in service, and the level of strategic alert was generally enhanced.[19] While this may have simply demonstrated the minimum inevitable link between strategic and tactical scenarios, it could not especially be viewed as a move to isolate Berlin as a territorially limited-war problem.

Soviet missile shortfalls also had some influence. Fairly soon after the inauguration of the Kennedy Administration, its spokesmen had been forced to concede that the missile gap did not seem to have been real, although inflated estimates of Soviet missile production still remained in wide circulation; the United States in fact was about to impose such a gap on the Soviet Union, in part because of the accelerations of the U.S. missile program in the last years of the Eisenhower Administration.

At the beginning of 1961 the U.S.S.R. had been slightly ahead of the United States in number of deployed ICBM's, but a deterrence gap now was next to impossible for several reasons.[20] All the ICBM's on both sides were of a soft liquid-fueled variety, while the U.S. MRBM's deployed forward to bases in Europe were similarly vulnerable, in particular to the many MRBM's the Russians had procured. Yet the first two American Polaris submarines were at sea, carrying 16 missiles each, and no Soviet strategic weapon system was capable of finding or interdicting them. The number of ICBM's on each side (perhaps 50 or 70 in the U.S.S.R., 30 Atlas in the United States), moreover, was not large enough to threaten to destroy either existing bomber force on the ground. At least one invulnerable American weapons system (Polaris) thus had been deployed before liquid-fueled missiles could set up any clear Soviet superiority, or any unstable confrontation where whoever struck first wiped out all opposing strategic forces.

Further procurement of Polaris submarines was, moreover, proceeding apace, so that a significant force would be deployed by the end of 1961, even assuming that not all the Polaris submarines could be on station during noncrisis periods. A portion of the liquid-fueled Atlas and Titan force coming into the inventory would be partially hardened, presumably forcing the Soviets to program more than a single missile against any such sites; and work was progressing satisfactorily on the solid-fueled Minuteman missile, promising deployment by the following year, with a force programmed to exceed 1,000 missiles by the mid-1960's.

Having come into office still expecting a "missile gap" in favor of the U.S.S.R., President Kennedy had thus very promptly stepped up the procurement rates for Polaris and Minuteman, although even the Eisenhower programs would probably have given the United States a significant advantage. The possibility now loomed that the United States might have as many as 1,500 rocket vehicles capable of reaching the U.S.S.R. before the Russians obtained as many as 300 targetable against the United States. Regardless of what little such ratios might signify in terms of rational calculations, the political impact of the seeming imbalance might be serious.

As the United States now assured itself that it would not fall subject to a gap in missiles, an issue remained of whether a new generation of manned bombers to succeed the B-52 should be developed and procured. Many arguments could be advanced for acquiring bombers to supplement the missiles now projected. One could always challenge the mechanical reliability of the missile force, although manned bombers had their problems too. The political reasoning was advanced that bombers could be brought to accentuated degrees of readiness in a crisis, or even be sent aloft toward the Soviet frontiers to demonstrate American resolve; conversely, however, if such actions were needed to keep the force viable, then the nation might be forced to provocative gestures where none were intended.

More seriously, one could argue that the bomber provided an American reconnaissance capability and bombing accuracy to facilitate the destruction of Russian missile sites, where American missiles might not locate or assuredly destroy such small targets. In response to this argument, one had to inquire whether such a counterforce capability would be necessary to deter Soviet attacks, or even desirable. Some analysts had argued all along that it was not retaliation against Russian cities that deterred the Soviet leadership, but rather the threat of losing the military exchange and being conquered; for such observers, American missiles by themselves might thus not be a sufficient insurance against Soviet attacks on either Europe or North America. Yet if the Russians proceeded to harden their ICBM's in underground silos, or to deploy IRBM's aboard submarines at sea, it was not clear how manned bombers would long supply a counterforce capability here either.

One could more generally oppose the maintenance or expansion of bomber forces simply because their survival required greater alertness and tension than a pure force of hardenable missiles. If bombers by themselves might have been retainable on two-hour alert against opposing bomber attack, they had to be on 15-minute alert against missile attack, and would thus play a lesser role in any war in which the United States had not gotten to strike first. On some combination of arguments, Secretary McNamara now opposed further expansion of the B-52 force, or extensive development of the B-70, despite repeated Congressional appropriations of funds for such bombers.[21]

In terms of the short-term vulnerability of only the United States and the U.S.S.R., the exposure of the missile gap would perhaps present the greatest American capability yet for a preemptive disarmament of the Soviet Union at acceptable costs. While the advent of missiles in 1957 had seemed to signal the end of all hopes for population protection in any general war, the move to missiles might now have offered the United States tangible if transitory hopes. Antibomber defenses, presumed to be pointless after 1957, had still moved along to promise higher attrition rates against Soviet strategic aircraft; and fewer such aircraft had been procured than had been expected, since the U.S.S.R. had seemingly lost most of its interest in bombers after 1957. If Russian ICBM's also had not been procured in quantity, there might not be any significant Soviet counterpopulation instrument; American ICBM's might be able to catch much of the Russian bomber force on the ground, with the net result that a coordinated American first strike would yet preclude significant damage to North America.[22]

But less noticed in the relief over the disappearance of the ICBM "gap" was the large Soviet accumulation of IRBM's capable of reaching and destroying all the cities of Western Europe. Having little real capability for hitting the United States if American strategic forces struck first, the Russians may now have thought the ground force occupation threat to Western Europe too slow in execution to supply an effective deterrent, so that only a massive rocket assault on European cities would suffice. The buildup of Soviet medium-range missiles aimed at the cities of Western Europe had not lagged at all behind prognoses,[23] and the identification of the United States with Europeans was (and probably seemed to the Russians to be) sufficient to preclude any grand preventive war at such costs. By necessity before 1949, and partly by choice after 1949, the Russians had thus maintained a hold on Europe to balance the American strategic capability.

As the world became more sure that the major Soviet effort had gone into medium-range missiles rather than ICBM's, Khrushchev's statements began quite specifically to point to the Soviet missile threat to Western Europe, making clear that NATO countries would suffer in any strategic exchange between the United States and the Soviet Union.[24] The Soviet bomber force, somewhat neglected or even deprecated in Soviet statements during the American "missile gap" illusion, was now resurrected and assigned some strategic significance, with several new bomber prototypes being demonstrated at the July, 1961, Moscow air show. More privately, as the Kennedy Administration fulfilled its promises to step up American missile procurement and deployment, Russian spokesmen expressed misgivings about the enhancement of the American strategic posture, suggesting that it was both unnecessary and threatening.[25]

The test moratorium was still in effect in early 1961, with the United States on record as demanding some inspection as part of any permanization of it. But as in Soviet foreign policy, American manipulation of the levers of political détente might have become an inverse function of the real hostility sensed by the administration in power. Eisenhower had perhaps seen fewer pressing tensions, and had thus withheld the compliments. Kennedy saw an imminent crisis at several levels, and wished therefore to cut back on propaganda derogatory to the Soviet Union. The Republicans may have sensed a more constant political hostility on the part of the U.S.S.R., a hostility which could be accepted because the power of American weapons would stabilize the confrontation. Because the Democrats had less confidence in this stability, they would step up the arms race and simultaneously seek to alleviate the hostility.

A more reasonable attitude on a permanent cessation of nuclear testing would thus be consistent with both prongs of the new Administration's initial approach: it would reverse the seeming overemphasis on nuclear weaponry as part of the American defense posture, and it would serve as a gesture of accommodation to the U.S.S.R. when such a gesture indeed was needed. The Democrats had come into office more clearly concerned about the spread of nuclear weapons into foreign control; a formal comprehensive test ban might almost amount to a nonproliferation agreement, especially if one assumed that nations had to test weapons openly to turn them to any political advantage. The informal moratorium initiated in 1958 had clearly failed to stop the French, who had "violated" it by testing a device in February of 1960.

Unfortunately, the Soviet position on a test ban now had become less responsive than it had been in the latter months of 1960, with the indication that three on-site inspections per year were the most that would ever be acceptable. In March of 1961, after the U.N. Congo intervention, the Russians backed out of inspection almost entirely, with a demand that the "troika" principle be applied to any control agency, the functional equivalent of a Soviet veto on all of its activities.[26] By the end of the summer it became evident that the Russians no longer held a vested interest in raising the world's hopes for a permanent test ban.

If the Russians had been only marginally in favor of the test ban after 1957, certain strong arguments for terminating it had emerged by 1961. First, the threat might have to be reinforced of massive retaliation escalating out of American resistance to Russian demands on Berlin. If megaton-range H-bomb tests served to frighten people on the consequences of war, no such tests had been conducted for four years, and Americans might have forgotten how large these explosions could be, or how close at hand they might seem in a crisis. Second, the dispelling of the "missile gap" by late summer of 1961 perhaps cast doubt on Soviet retaliatory strength, since Soviet ICBM's were so few in number, and since augmented American air defenses might interfere with Soviet manned-bomber missions; multimegaton bombs might thus be an ideal means of reinforcing the impression of Soviet countervalue retaliatory strength.

As the Berlin wall was erected in August of 1961, the Soviets terminated their moratorium on nuclear testing. The test series included the largest explosion yet detonated, a 58-megaton bomb, but this was only half the news;[27] the Soviet device was unusually free of radio-activity, which indicated that it could easily have been expanded to a "dirty" bomb of more than 100 megatons simply by replacing its lead shield with one of uranium-238.

Both the magnitude of the bomb and its "cleanliness" were designed to impress the West, but the impression was perhaps not quite as startling as the Russians had hoped. Since the destructiveness of any bomb (at least in terms of blast) is proportional not to the explosive force directly, but to the 2/3 power of the megatonnage, it would take far fewer than 100 one-megaton bombs to achieve the destructiveness of one of the Russian giants; and the destructive force of one large bomb could not be parceled out among several targets. Any test-ban-induced deficiency in American destructive inventories would not stem directly from insufficient maximum size of explosions, but perhaps rather from the problems of miniaturizing warheads for Minuteman and Polaris, the less vulnerable solid-fueled missiles now going into deployment.

The United States responded with new gestures of its own. Partially to signal the end of any lingering "missile gap" misinterpretations, but partially also to bring the weight of American strategic weapons superiority directly to bear on the Berlin crisis, Assistant Secretary of Defense Roswell Gilpatric issued the most assertive statement of American posture in a long time, declaring that the American second-strike retaliation after a Russian attack would be greater in volume of explosive power than any first strike the Russians could launch.[28] The conclusion, of course, was based on both the increments of American strategic forces which had been made in the previous year, and on the failure of the Russians to deploy any significant number of ICBM's in the same period.

The Soviet resumption of testing had presumably served the balance of real Russian interest as reevaluated in 1961, but it also might offer the United States an opportunity to impose some propaganda losses on the U.S.S.R., and for this reason alone any speedy resumption of American open-air testing was held back. American underground testing would be resumed first, because it was less obnoxious to the world and more relevant to certain tactical weapons possibilities the United States was interested in. The United States thus waited some 15 days to announce a resumption of underground testing, while holding off on any public decision to resume tests in the atmosphere.[29] Neutral leaders seemed, however, to equate one resumption with the other, which perhaps indicated that underground testing had not yet been separated sufficiently for the world public eye, or perhaps instead that the timing of the American resumption had not been well arranged. The delay in the resumption of above-ground testing may also have confirmed earlier fears that the United States would find it more difficult to keep laboratories of physicists functioning in the absence of testing. The Soviet test series showed much developmental progress since 1958 even without any clandestine detonations;[30] a suspicion emerged that the United States had not made similar progress and thus had nothing really ready to test in 1961.

Tactical Alternatives

The Berlin crisis, with its mobilization of conventional forces on both sides, cooled off in the late fall of 1961; the Russians for the time would apparently settle for the Berlin wall, as attention shifted to the Sino-Soviet disputes aired at the Russian 22nd Party Congress. Once the security of the D.D.R. Pankow regime was established, then the gains of trying to acquire Berlin might be less, perhaps no longer outweighing the risks.

Several distinct interpretations of the 1961-1963 period are thus possible.[31] There may indeed have been a real threat that the Soviet Union was seeking to apply "salami tactics" to Europe, a threat which only some augmentation of the Western deterrent presumably could erase; opinions could then differ on how the augmentation was best to be achieved. Second, the American leadership may have been sincerely exaggerating this Soviet threat, seeking to augment a deterrent which may already have been more than sufficient, and thus causing some unnecessary distress to its European allies. Third, the new U.S. Administration may have been aware that renewed Soviet aggression was unlikely beyond a solution of the Berlin problem, and may thus less sincerely have been describing an imaginary threat, as a means of inducing Europeans to shift from nuclear to nonnuclear deterrence.

Doubts persisted among Europeans on whether limited Soviet military aggression was very likely, on whether an augmentation of limited war forces was really required to restore a balance. If the Russian effort was confined to a simple consolidation of territory east of the Elbe, an economical massive retaliation balance might still be possible; once the threat to Berlin was lifted, perhaps after erection of the wall (or after the Cuban missile crisis), it would not be easy to find another scenario nearly as threatening. The seizure of Hamburg, for example, seemed far riskier from the Russian point of view, and hence less likely, at least if nuclear no-first-use agreements were not tacitly or explicitly entered into. Any augmentation or maintenance of NATO conventional armies was thus difficult to induce. Europeans were reluctant to forgo a continued and still credible threat of escalation to nuclear war, as long as the probability of the threat's ever coming to execution remained so low, and the Administration would have to reverse this European proclivity, or to adjust its own new strategic preference to it.

While it had earlier been argued that West Europeans (particularly West Germans) urgently desired preparations for a conventional defense of their territory (since any nuclear war, however tactical, would devastate the territory being defended), few such sentiments were now voiced in the German ruling coalition or public opinion (albeit some had emerged earlier from the opposition Social Democrats). European demands for a voice on nuclear matters seemed less to mean a "safety-catch" veto over use of nuclears, and more a "trigger" commitment that nuclears would be brought into use early in any Continental land war.

Several options thus were available to the Administration. Partisans of a renewal of the Eisenhower approach could contend that the defense of Western Europe had not presented such a real problem, so that the threat of application of nuclear weapons was still sufficient to preclude a Soviet move westward. The use of tactical nuclear weapons might favor the defense, removing the Soviet advantage in numbers (although arguments could be presented for the contrary position). Even if the use of tactical nuclears did not hold the Russian armies back, it would inflict severe casualties on these forces and destroy the territory lost to them, thus reducing the incentive for such attacks. Finally, the risk of escalation to general was was inevitably high, since a qualitative distinction as to type of weapon had been broken; the advance knowledge of this might additionally deter an attacker. A defender of pre-1960 American and NATO defense policy could thus argue that tactical nuclears made massive retaliation unnecessary, or that they made such retaliation more likely and more plausible; and both arguments could be prevented simultaneously.

The American Administration would, however, still be concerned to reduce the risks of escalation to nuclear or general war, either as a corollary to some real strengthening of the deterrent, or as the primary goal, with deterrence augmentation serving only as an excuse to sell the adjustment to Europeans. Instead of massive-retaliation escalation threats, the incoming Administration might instead have tried a second approach; it could redefine the role of tactical nuclears to stress their battlefield impact (which inevitably would require some increase in the ground forces coupled to them). And it could reduce the plausibility of escalation by elaborating new territorial ground rules, or by hardening and stabilizing strategic weapons systems. Critics might contend that reducing the escalation threat would reduce deterrence, but the Administration could counter that ground forces with tactical nuclears would securely deter ground invasions, even if the Soviets were assured that no immediate jump to general war was likely.

Many military officers agreed that tactical nuclear weapons were useful or essential for a successful theater defense; nuclears thus would at least have to be kept around in case the Soviets introduced them. This judgment would be endorsed not only by West Germans and other Europeans, but by the U.S. Army itself, even as it sought a greater conventional force allocation. Yet if the tactical weapons provided were to be of very short range, they would have to be assigned forward to formations as small as the battalion; this might make it very difficult to limit spontaneous local skirmishes between NATO and Warsaw Pact forces to conventional weapons. If one desired to avoid the forward deployment of nuclear weapons, tactical systems of longer range were required, raising the threat that such weapons might become the nucleus of independent systems capable ultimately of striking at Poland or at the Soviet Union itself.

In a tactical nuclear theater defense, therefore, it would be difficult to reassure the Soviets, or oneself, that the threat of escalation to city-busting had been reduced. In the early 1950's, it had been taken for granted in several discussions that a limited local nuclear war could be fought. By the end of the decade, however, many American analysts had concluded that the problems of maintaining such limits were very serious, leaving too great a risk of escalation; Russian strategic publications over this period of course had generally refused to recognize the possibility of territorially limited nuclear war, contending that any such war would immediately become general.

It seems very plausible, therefore, that Secretary McNamara and President Kennedy ideally preferred a third long-run approach: that ground forces in Europe be gradually augmented so that a substantially nonnuclear defense would become possible, so that the United States could perhaps renounce even the battlefield use of nuclear weapons.[32] This position could not yet be stated too explicitly, however, lest European resistance be encountered even before that modicum of ground force augmentation needed for a plausible local nuclear war. Critics of this new approach, in the United States and most bluntly in France, contended that the Administration was showing too much advance concern for the fate of American cities, explicitly extending this concern into a fear of any form of nuclear warfare because of the risks of escalation. The Kennedy Administration thus was purportedly telling Europeans that they had to raise conventional forces to fill a deterrence gap the United States itself had produced.

In fact the explicit U.S. position was to suggest a need for a conventional gap-filler before conceding the existence of a gap. Statements by the Defense Secretary typically urged conventional force augmentations so that the United States would not be forced to use nuclears (rather than so that the United States "would not have to accept a loss of territory because it would choose at the crucial moment not to use nuclears"). Aiming to achieve the rational alternative of a conventional defense for some or all of Western Europe, the new Administration was still required, at least for the interim, to show an irrational willingness to introduce nuclear weapons where conventional defense was not available. Yet pressures were continued for European force augmentations with several U.S. spokesmen affirming[33] (while none would deny) the advantages of an all-conventional defense.

Reducing the American intelligence estimate of the Red Army's size from 175 divisions to something more like 60 divisions may have been a justified and long-overdue bit of operations analysis in 1963;[34] coming at this time, however, it made European NATO members somewhat suspicious of the motives behind the revision. If the short-term Soviet potential had ever been as great as 175 divisions, the introduction of 15 years of technological complication into Soviet society and Soviet military practice made the maintenance of such a capability highly unlikely. Peasants could perhaps have been quickly mobilized under the Soviet system to constitute masses of infantry, but not modern armored divisions. If Soviet ground forces were to be a real threat to the ground forces of NATO, they would have to possess far greater levels of mobility and firepower than had been possible in 1945 or 1949, and such levels were increasingly incompatible with any rapid mobilization program encompassing 175 divisions.

The higher American estimate had been retained since 1945, because it had seemed a way of frightening Europeans into making a greater defense contribution, or because it might have justified the reliance on tactical nuclear weapons against any anticipated European objections. Now it seemed that Europeans could better be induced to expand their ground forces if convinced that matching the Red Army was indeed a finite and manageable task. The risk remained that Europeans might find the revised American estimate plausible, but would conclude that a Soviet attack was all the less likely, therefore requiring even less of a NATO conventional effort.

A portion of the conventional option question concerned the number of ground troops the United States could induce the West European nations to provide. The other side of the question involved the American willingness to deploy various forms of nuclear weaponry into Europe, some of which had in effect been promised by the Eisenhower Administration. Because the short-run Kennedy Administration argument endorsed the efficacy of a territorially limited nuclear defense, no clear ban on such weapons could be announced. Yet if the move were ever to be made to a conventional defense, tactical nuclear weapons deployed in forward areas might become a nuisance.

The new Administration thus asserted that tactical missions could be handled as effectively with nuclear weapons based at sea, or in the United States, or perhaps in Britain. Europeans conversely contended, effectiveness aside, that these American arguments reflected a reluctance to employ such weapons, a reluctance that might ultimately encourage Russian adventures if doubts were not removed by deployments to Europe. To complicate the picture somewhat more, General Lauris Norstad, the American NATO Commander appointed during the Eisenhower Administration, was still publicly endorsing similar arguments;[35] Norstad expressed skepticism as to whether a conventional defense would ever be viable enough to be effective as a deterrent, especially in terms of the large budget outlays and long military service periods it required of Europeans.

Norstad's proposal for a NATO "fourth nuclear power" MRBM force had remained on the table in the early months of the Kennedy Administration while Norstad himself was left at his post, perhaps as a pledge to the NATO nations that the most abrupt shift in policy was not yet in store. The decision to retire General Norstad ahead of schedule in the summer of 1962 (as part of a shift which brought General Maxwell Taylor, a proclaimed advocate of conventional options, to the Chairmanship of the Joint Chiefs of Staff) was thus an unpleasant sign for European advocates of a clearly nuclear deterrent;[36] it would not be totally reversed by Norstad's remaining at his post through the period of the Cuban missile crisis.

As a move toward tighter control over nuclear weapons, technical permissive action links were now introduced and attached to the American nuclear warheads deployed in Europe.[37] Such links would make it impossible for an American junior officer, or for a foreign national, to fire many nuclear warheads without some special key, combination, or electronic signal passed on from higher authority, perhaps as high as NATO or even beyond. Certain delivery systems which had been designed to be dual-purpose (e.g., the F-104, usable either for nuclear or nonnuclear weapons) had previously come to be understood as earmarked for tactical nuclears. The stress on such systems was now shifted to conventional armament, with whatever structural adjustments this required; such steps could not help but reduce the morale of units which had assimilated the status of being nuclear-equipped forces, only to be dropped from this exalted role.

A strategic "pause" doctrine was now enunciated: that some time would be allowed to elapse, or some marginal stretch of territory be lost, before tactical nuclear weapons were introduced into any local war in Europe;[38] the doctrine could be interpreted in several ways. For some it may simply have seemed responsive to skepticism on the plausibility of American nuclear escalation. Critics had contended that the United States would not go to nuclears in some mere border skirmish, and the American reliance on nuclear weapons thus was a bluff; the answer here might be that skirmishes of course would not bring massive retaliation, but that any more serious war would, since the pause thus represented the time it took to sort the minor from the serious. The pause might thus simply have been a reassertion of an American escalation policy, in a slightly more rational variation designed to rebut the critics of its originally more obscure form.

Alternatively, the concept of pause could be interpreted as a sizable broadening of the threshold that an enemy would have to cross before nuclears were introduced. If the threshold were broadened enough, the pause might be translated into pure bluff, into a continual redefinition of the trigger for nuclear escalation, so that the prospect still entered into discussion but never had to be executed. If provision for an adequate conventional defense could indeed be made, the pause doctrine might be a suitable vehicle for the ultimate transition to a nonnuclear defense—i.e., our side will pause in the introduction of nuclears until it needs them to stop the enemy's attack, which means never. If no such provisions for adequate conventional defense were achieved, however, the pause might seem so extendible to some viewers that all of Europe could be overrun.

The novelty of "pauses" or "thresholds" can easily be overstated, for some such threshold had always existed. Front-line patrols in Korea or Bavaria had never been equipped with nuclear weapons that could be brought into play with every shooting incident along some lonely border. Nuclear weapons were not deployed to Berlin, or directly along the East German frontier, or to Lebanon in 1958. The issue between the Eisenhower approach and the initial Kennedy policy thus was not so clear-cut, but turned on the width of the threshold and on the extent of its explication. If the Republicans were correct that such a threshold was understood, then there might be less point in discussing it very openly, or some costs if it made the threshold seem wide enough to cover all of Europe. Conversely, if one were in real fear of the threat of accidental nuclear war, then some widening of the threshold might indeed seem urgent, if it could nonetheless be kept circumscribed.

The Kennedy Administration thus did not yet remove any nuclear weapons that had been issued to "front-line forces," and in fact made a substantial increase in the tactical nuclear stockpiles deployed to Europe between 1961 and 1963; the number of warheads was stated to have been doubled over this time, with the number of delivery vehicles reaching a total of 2,500[39] (presumably with more than one warhead available per delivery vehicle). Very short-range weapons, such as the Davy Crockett nuclear mortar scheduled for deployment at the battalion level, were, however, withheld lest the danger be increased of some minor imbroglio going nuclear.[40]

Counterforce and Civil Defense

The American willingness to provide tactical nuclear weapons had received some European reciprocation on the conventional side before and during the Berlin crisis. But this had diminished markedly afterward, and any move to a wholly conventional defense, in a clear and qualitative break from the Eisenhower policies, seemed difficult to attain. Having failed to induce other NATO members to match American augmentation of ground forces, the Kennedy Administration somehow had to rationalize a strategic posture which would seem less than ideal.

Shortfalls in conventional troops, with the continuing deployment of tactical nuclear weapons to potential battle areas, made any prolonged nonnuclear war in Europe unlikely. The Eisenhower Administration had been attacked on the grounds that it would have to be reluctant to take necessary military initiatives when escalation to nuclear war was likely. Now, despite its own best efforts, the Kennedy Administration might be burdened by the very handicap it had identified. Since the rational nonnuclear option had not been made available, the available nuclear option would thus somehow have to be made rational (i.e., usable without automatically bringing about the destruction of American cities); this would be required either to beef up the image deterring the Russians (who might have now had their doubts about American responses if they had followed the defense debate since 1957 at all closely), or to make an adequately deterring image more acceptable to Americans.

The Kennedy Administration thus was tempted to couple a renewed and reexamined American strategic superiority to the deterrence of local conventional attacks, despite some seven years of Democratic assaults on Eisenhower, charging that these elements could not be coupled. Since European NATO members had now seemingly accepted the Republican massive retaliation argument of the 1950's, the Kennedy Administration would be led to disseminate an adjusted version of the argument, citing its counterforce superiority in strategic weapons as highly relevant to the possibility of Soviet aggression in Europe.

The 1962 McNamara statement to the Athens NATO Conference, and his subsequent Ann Arbor speech, could have two interpretations.[41] First, they represented a pledge that the United States would not bomb Soviet cities unless and until the Soviet Union had bombed American cities. Second, they implied that the U.S. Air Force might nonetheless find itself striking first at other Russian targets, at Soviet air bases and missile sites in particular, for it was not made clear that this could come only in the context of similar Soviet attacks on American strategic installations. Perhaps the United States could thus again exploit an advantage at the strategic level to restore the balance at the tactical level. As with Truman, but not with Eisenhower, this involved a rational threat (i.e., one that it would make sense to carry out even if the threat had not already been publicized); it no longer, however, involved the killing of people or attrition of industry, but rather a relatively painless military campaign—which skeptics contended the Russians could never agree to. The McNamara speech, in short, offered very rational assurances for one contingency—in the event of an already initiated general war, American targeting policy would seek to avoid extreme destruction of civilian life. It implied a rational threat for another contingency—in a war as yet limited to Europe, the United States might be willing to escalate to counterforce operations at the general-war level. Skeptics might find the rational assurances unconvincing in face of the administration's own doubts on the containability of local nuclear wars, doubts which made a nuclear general war seem at least as difficult to limit or contain.[42]

The issue of a counterforce capability, by which a nation might strike at another's strategic forces with the hope of completely disabling them, had arisen most clearly before in the later 1950's; Democratic spokesmen had then foreseen such a Soviet capability vis-à-vis the United States as a result of Republican aversions to adequate defense appropriations. Only preemptive attacks might save the weaker nation in such a case. Presumably the Democratic remedy would be to aim for secure missile forces that would forever eliminate the mutual vulnerability problem as a potential cause for unwanted general war. For the administration now to brandish a counterforce capability of its own against the Soviet Union thus represented a minor logical reversal from the 1957-1960 argument. Some of the earlier denunciations of SAC vulnerability had asserted that it was bad, not only for the United States, but for the world as a whole. Would not a similar vulnerability on the Soviet side, induced by American weapons procurement, be disadvantageous for the world as a whole?

Critics thus found the McNamara counterforce statement inconsistent with continuing suggestions that secure Soviet strategic forces were ultimately likely or even desirable. Yet there was not necessarily a conflict. The United States might simply be describing its own currently most rational policy when it stated that it logically had to strike at Soviet forces for as long as they remained vulnerable.[43] Such a statement could even be seen as an additional encouragement to the Russians to make their missile forces secure.

Yet if the Ann Arbor speech had been anything more than a straightforward and candid description of logical American policies, critics might see it as a rather short-lived assertion of a special American advantage, an assertion that would be counterproductive once the advantage had passed away. When the Russians had hardened their missiles, they presumably would remember that such missiles had been the only target McNamara had seemed willing to attack, perhaps in response to some Russian move in Europe; what would the United States be willing to attack on the first strike afterwards, if the shielding of its own cities continued to be a clear prerequisite?

By attaching great value to a force which could strike at targets other than Russian cities, Secretary McNamara was also indicting the French Force de Frappe (and perhaps the British V-bomber force) as contrary to the interests of Western Europe and the world: such small and inaccurate forces always implied unwanted escalation to all-out countercity war. Whether or not the speech was intended to arouse European opposition to primitive independent nuclear forces, it was so interpreted in France and Britain, and McNamara's subsequent disclaimer with regard to the RAF[44] did not reduce French vehemence on the question. If French forces were deficient in force survivability and targeting options, the French response logically could have been that the United States should have provided the assistance to remedy these deficiencies.

At least some of the defense intellectuals previously concerned with the instability of vulnerable strategic forces were again concerned; an apparent U.S. ability to disarm Russian bomber and missile forces might make the Soviet leadership tense and trigger-happy, thus increasing the likelihood of mutually unwanted war. There emerged, therefore, an argument for a reduction of U.S. missile inventories to some "finite deterrent," which could destroy enough cities to make war seem unthinkable, but not enough strategic forces to make war seem imminent. Apart from the conjectured increase in the likelihood of war, there might be other costs in any American attempt to maintain a significant counterforce capability. The financial cost would be high in the huge inventory of bombers and missiles procured, more than those necessary simply to insure retaliation for a Soviet first strike. Such procurements might, moreover, induce each side to increase its retaliatory destructive forces, to be on the "safe side" in terms of secure deterrence, so that the probabilities multiplied that more, rather than fewer, people would die if war were ever to occur.

A similar dilemma existed for the Democrats on population defense, for some forms of civil defense (such as fallout shelters) were appropriate only for a counterforce war. One implication of the original force vulnerability problem had been that it offered a more rational wartime use for strategic forces than simply slamming away at large cities. Even if the possibility of war seemed greater, there would now be an inducement to aim and allocate warheads very carefully, in an attempt to catch the other side's strategic forces on the ground. There had therefore been a certain resurgence of civil defense interest amongst "missile gap" critics of the Eisenhower Administration. Such interested parties did not hope so much to prevent infliction of pain by enemy forces, but rather assumed that an attacker would want to avoid inflicting pain (because he hoped to avoid retaliation), so that civil defense in effect was a form of cooperation with a powerful enemy.[45]

In the same period, some American writers had begun to report the existence of a large fallout shelter program for major Soviet cities.[46] These reports were received with some skepticism, however, and the Soviet Government never made a point of announcing any such modified civil defense program. If the Soviets had in fact begun to build fallout shelters, it would have indicated their willingness to observe limits on all-out strategic war similar to those proposed by arms control writers in the United States: namely, that military installations away from cities might be subject to attack, while cities themselves were not (cities thus suffering only a dusting of residual radioactive fallout).

Yet if fallout shelters had been appropriate in 1959, in response to the counterforce threat posed by the new Soviet missiles, would such preparations be as appropriate when each side was presumably assuring itself of a second-strike countercity retaliatory capability? The exact reasoning behind the Kennedy Administration's proposals for a greatly expanded American civil defense program in 1961 and 1962 is thus not so easy to determine.[47] Two somewhat conflicting strands of argument remained in circulation on behalf of civil defense, and each apparently had some effect.

First, there had been the above criticism of Republican planners for contemplating an all-out spasm war in the event of a Soviet attack, with the prospect that civilians would be killed as quickly as possible. One could justify civil defense, as one could a counterforce capability, as simply facilitating more sensible contingency plans for general war, thus responding to a straightforward liberal criticism of what had been portrayed as an unimaginative Republican policy.

Second, the fact that American civilians were protected might make the prospect of an American counterforce first strike more rationally credible, perhaps in the event of a Russian blockade of Berlin. A counterforce war might now (in contrast with 1959) seem largely to the advantage of the United States, perhaps with the hope that the Soviets would be able to slip in only a few strikes at the United States mainland. American threats of countervalue retaliation might induce the Soviets to avoid deliberate attacks on American cities, so that fallout shelters would suffice to protect city dwellers against the radioactive dust from strikes at strategic bases. Even if the Soviets did muster up a vengeful countercity strike, the incoming missile barrage would be considerably less than had once been feared, and fallout protection was worth something for the case of the near miss, of the unhit twin city, etc.

A general awareness of such American protection might, more importantly, redound to the advantage of the United States in the conduct of negotiations on smaller issues. Civil defense, like other forms of population protection, might always be most valuable for the sensations of strength and weakness with which the United States and the U.S.S.R. went into negotiations. The likelihood of general war might be small, but the notion that one power now had less reason to fear for the safety of its citizens might make all the difference during some crisis. It is thus quite plausible that President Kennedy's decision to ask for a large American civil defense program in May of 1961 was a direct response to Khrushchev's toughness at the Vienna summit. The initial funding request was a moderate one, however, and any large program would have taken some time to implement.

If one wanted to look very far ahead to the achievement of an antimissile defense capability, a program of fallout shelters might be a valuable or necessary accessory. Any program requiring such large-scale civic participation would probably take some time to implement; one could thus argue that it should be launched immediately, even if no decision on an active defense program was yet in sight. Yet precisely because a civil defense program would impinge so much on the civilian sector, it imposed more complicated and variegated disutilities, raised more numerous legitimate objections, and was more vulnerable to obstruction and sabotage by individuals opposed to its international strategic purpose. Civil defense therefore did not get very much further than the marking of preexisting buildings judged usable as fallout shelters. No large governmental appropriations for new construction of shelters were forthcoming, but there was a flurry of individual activity which provoked extensive ridicule for the "shelter mentality" which it supposedly embodied.

Other problems would emerge for anyone trying to preclude severe general war casualties amongst the world's civilian populations. If missile launching sites were located close to or immediately upwind from major cities, any counterforce attack on such sites might generate enough radioactive fallout to pose a severe threat to such populations (even in fallout shelters), especially if the sites in question had been hardened enough to require a ground burst to destroy them. In the Congress the physical location of internal U.S. military installations fell under peculiarly detailed scrutiny, whereas authorizations and appropriations on other questions might go through in far more general terms. Given a desire in the Air Force to avoid the excessive support costs imposed by remote locations, and a matching desire in certain civilian communities for the business revenue generated by military bases, the sites approved for the earliest missile sites in the United States tended to be closer to cities,[48] and hence would not serve to uncouple countervalue and counterforce effects in a future general war. Despite the efforts of individual scientists concerned with arms control, moreover, the public response to fallout arguments was small. Either because it was regarded as cowardly for a community to attempt to avoid the dangers undergone by its Air Force, or because one thought it undesirable in general to talk about a "clean" general war, little public feeling was aroused on the matter.

Critics of civil-defense shelter programs could even argue that efforts to humanize or rationalize general war might make such war more likely; these efforts might tempt the President to attack if he thought American casualties could be avoided, or might tempt the Soviet leadership to try a "surgical" preemptive counterforce strike, since it could avoid triggering a retaliatory counterpopulation strike against itself. On such arguments it might even have been advisable to deploy the earliest American missiles in the middle of cities, to assure the Russians that their counterforce attack inevitably would enrage the United States into full-blown retaliation against Soviet cities.

To satisfy the Russians that a defense of Western Europe was still likely, or to satisfy Americans that such a defense would not be tantamount to an honorable nationwide suicide, proposals had been presented for a conventional force buildup in NATO. These proposals having been rejected, the United States apparently had hoped for the same deterrent effect in allusions to its newly discovered strategic level superiority, a superiority which at least for a time might allow the United States rationally to contemplate the initiation of nuclear war with the U.S.S.R. A problem might arise, however, if the Soviet Union were not content to tolerate the superiority which allowed Americans to solve their dilemma in this way.

The Cuban Missile Crisis

Tensions could have many causes, but the two most salient throughout the postwar period had perhaps been general weapons inferiorities and imminent transfers of territory from one bloc to the other. From 1945 to 1962, the clearest threat of the second sort had applied to West Berlin (or East Germany, as one interpreted the momentum of change). Despite the many forecasts of similarly imminent territorial losses, none would clearly occur after 1949 except in Cuba, and here the change was perhaps unpredicted on both sides; regardless of whether Moscow knew that Castro was or would become a Marxist, his material supporters (some of them American) generally did not. While the fall of Cuba to a "Communist" regime thus had occurred so unexpectedly as to preclude much of an interbloc confrontation over the prospect, the possibility had remained that Cuba might be recaptured by a now-awakened West, and this added a second parcel of territory whose status remained in doubt into the 1960's. If one had taken the threat to the East German regime seriously, one could thus have argued that the Communists were on the defensive "status quo" side on both local fronts in 1961.

Many explanations have been offered for Khrushchev's decision to install medium-range missiles in Cuba in the fall of 1962.[49] The Soviet Premier may simply have been attempting to deal a symbolic slap in the face to President Kennedy, to demonstrate an American lack of resolve throughout the Western Hemisphere. Alternatively, Khrushchev could have been trying to establish a deterrent for the Cubans themselves against the possibility of another American Bay of Pigs invasion; if doubts existed about a Soviet willingness to escalate into all-out war in defense of Castro's regime, the presence of medium-range missiles and tactical nuclear weapons in Cuba might make retaliation against Miami or Washington more likely. In such a case, the missile deployment might have come at Russian suggestion, or in response to specific demands from Fidel Castro for such weapons; if the latter had occurred, then the sudden warming of Cuban-Soviet relations in June of 1962 might retrospectively indicate the point at which the Russian deployment decision was settled.[50]

Third, the deployment may have come as a reaction to the inadvertent American achievement of a numerical dominance in strategic weapons. Khrushchev, perhaps fearing that the Soviet strategic force of intercontinental-range missiles would not suffice to deter the United States, may have seen a movement of surplus medium-range missiles to Cuba as a "quick fix" analogous to the American medium-range missile deployment to Britain, Italy, and Turkey in 1958, and intended not so much to deter an attack on Cuba as on the Soviet Union itself. Additionally, the Russians might have seen a first-strike possibility for destroying much of the U.S. strategic bomber force from such a deployment, outflanking the United States radar warning net with greater accuracy and payloads than were possible by submarine launching or some transarctic global missile shot. If there might no longer have been any clear possibility of an all-disarming first strike, there would nonetheless be a prospect of limiting damage to the Soviet Union in the event of some war not directly launched from the Russian side.

Another argument which Khrushchev himself has offered is that he was seeking only to erect a bargaining counter to American missiles in Turkey[51] (obsolete missiles perhaps scheduled to be eliminated sooner or later in any event), but this seems inconsistent with the size of the force deployed in Cuba—more than 40 missiles—while the force in Turkey consisted of only 15.

The Soviet willingness to deploy nuclear weapons so far beyond Russian borders came as a surprise to most American observers, in view of the earlier failure to trust the East European satellites with nuclears of any kind.[52] Russian forces stationed in East Germany (where they far outnumbered local forces) were assumed to possess tactical atomic weapons (without hydrogen warheads), but no other force outside the Soviet Union was entrusted with anything nuclear. The Russians had seemed reluctant to reciprocate the American move to submarine-based strategic missiles, playing up the command-and-control problem and at points even suggesting the abolition of all submarines as an important disarmament step.[53] This caution may have derived, however, from fear of a coup d'état in one of the satellites or in a portion of the Soviet armed forces, by which nuclear weapons might be turned around to threaten Moscow; a deployment of IRBM's and MRBM's to Cuba presented no such problem, and perhaps was acceptable. In any event, any Soviet rule against overseas deployment was now broken.

Whatever the Russian motivation for wanting an established force in Cuba, the timing of the interim period during which the missiles sites were erected was crucial. Khrushchev may have expected a greater delay and time lag on any American decision to intervene. Once any number of missiles were on station, however vulnerable, the decision to act in and around Cuba was presumably much more difficult for an

American President on physical grounds (an air strike might miss its target, giving trigger-happy Cuban or Russian crews time to fire), or on the political ground that a new strategic status quo had been established, which the United States in turn would now be disrupting.

The Cubans could instead have chosen first to erect a substantial belt of air defenses around Cuba, prior to any deployment of longer-range missiles. The illegitimacy of U-2 overflights of the U.S.S.R. had been more or less acknowledged by the Kennedy Administration, and it might not have taken more than a few U-2 downings over Cuba to force the United States to recognize a similar inviolability for Cuban airspace. U-2 flights over Cuba had in fact been curtailed in the month and a half prior to the crisis, after a U-2 was downed over Communist China.[54] While the United States could maintain the argument of Nationalist sovereignty over mainland China to defend its flights there, no such argument existed with regard to Cuba; in any event, only the uproar over the offensive missiles discovered by such flights may have prevented a smaller uproar over the violations of international law embodied in the Cuban overflights. Yet Khrushchev may have been so terribly impatient to get his IRBM's and MRBM's established that he would not wait for the erection of a screen against aerial espionage. Alternatively, he may have been indifferent to or in favor of American awareness of the offensive deployment, on the assumption that the United States would not intervene, but would be enough impressed by this display of Soviet confidence and power to be cowed elsewhere, perhaps around Berlin.

Why the U.S. Government reacted so vigorously to the Russian deployment is also not altogether clear, and possibly a Soviet expectation of American inaction was not so unreasonable. Presumably the Soviet MRBM's in Cuba made an American first strike against the Soviet Union less plausible: even though these MRBM's were not hardened and therefore quite vulnerable, additional problems of coordination and timing might thus be raised, as with the U.S. deployment of missiles to Turkey and Italy in 1958. But while some U.S. strategists might regret this, the American Government had not in principle opposed any enhancement of Soviet power required to make a successful American counterforce first strike impossible. Russian missiles in Cuba were presumably no more objectionable in this context than similar missiles on Russian submarines in the Atlantic.

Particularly aggravating or confusing to American observers may have been Russian statements at the time disclaiming any need for

Cuban missile bases,[55] noting that Soviet rockets could easily reach the United States from the U.S.S.R., so that Cuba and other Soviet interests would be shielded without any overseas strategic weapons deployments. The statement of course can be viewed as deliberate and malicious duplicity, but might also be seen a trifle more sympathetically. To admit a need for bases before one had them, for deterrence of attacks on the U.S.S.R. or on Cuba, might have encouraged some sort of preemption—preemptive war or preemptive exclusion of Soviet rockets from Cuba. To admit the need might have encouraged any Americans contemplating further frustration of the need, if a Soviet confession of weakness might allow the United States too great a freedom of action. Conversely, one could argue that the U.S.S.R. should have cited a need for overseas deployments in advance (for example, that such deployments were designed only to ensure an otherwise threatened minimum deterrent, in a manner similar to submarine deployments), so that a certain sense of legitimacy and symmetrical sympathy could have been induced in the United States and might have dissuaded or prevented the Administration from opposing the deployment.

Most frightening, perhaps, to American eyes was the prospect of the Cuban regime itself gaining control over such weapons, in light of the apparent irrationality of Fidel Castro. Even if the United States were not contemplating another attempt to overthrow Castro, the danger of his taking control of missiles with nuclear warheads seemed very serious. If the United States were contemplating another invasion attempt, of course, the missiles stood in the way; but Kennedy now would almost pledge himself never to make another such attempt in order to get the missiles out. The American desire to push so hard on the Russian missile deployment may have stemmed more simply from the opportunity offered of discrediting and perhaps ultimately deposing Castro, under circumstances where the world would be more sympathetic than at the Bay of Pigs a year and a half earlier; yet the wording of American statements now focused more responsibility on the U.S.S.R., and less on Castro,[56] since Soviet command and control were thought important to maintain and acknowledge.

Had the U.S.S.R. deployed only the medium-range bombers to Cuba, these might conceivably have been allowed to stay, since there had been no significant American objection to similar arms transfers to Indonesia or Egypt. Because the medium-range missiles more clearly suggested nuclear warheads, however, the United States in the end felt required to insist on the withdrawal even of the bombers, which had been legally transferred to the Cuban Air Force (unlike the missiles, which always remained Soviet property). The American Government of course might have chosen originally to draw its line of distinction between nuclear and nonnuclear weapons. This might have been more straightforward than the debatable distinction between offensive and defensive weapons, but would have had several drawbacks. The identification of nuclear warheads per se by convincing aerial reconnaissance was difficult and unlikely; bombers, like the B-52 in Vietnam, can always be "conventional" as well as nuclear (and, a little more farfetched, so can missiles). Raising the nuclear question might, moreover, have opened the issue of nuclear-free zones, at a point where the United States still preferred to retain full freedom of action on the deployment or use of its atomic weapons.

Throughout the discussion of the Russian missiles in Cuba, parallel deployments of American medium-range missiles naturally came to mind. Ambassador Adlai Stevenson was afterwards accused of having quite early wanted to exchange the removal of vulnerable MRBM's in Turkey and Italy for a Soviet withdrawal from Cuba.[57] At a later stage Khrushchev would attempt to achieve such an American concession, at least partially to reduce the humiliation of his decision to withdraw. The vulnerable (and obsolescent) missiles were in fact to be withdrawn from Turkey some months later, when the first American Polaris submarines were deployed into the Mediterranean. According to various accounts, during the crisis President Kennedy asserted that he had previously ordered the removal of these missiles from Turkey, and that his orders had not been carried out.[58] The presence of the missiles presumably was now embarrassing to him. He could not remove them in obvious response to the Russian intrusion into the Western Hemisphere; but any strategic argument against Russian missiles in Cuba might in fairness apply as well to American missiles in Turkey.

Yet the last word Kennedy had issued on the subject of the missiles in Turkey had come only weeks before the Cuban crisis had erupted, and had still not been definitive in the face of Turkish objections to their removal. Since Kennedy had not ordered that the clear price be paid of ignoring Turkish feelings in the matter, he may thus have had himself to blame for his predicament during the crisis. The Turkish reluctance to agree to these missiles' withdrawal might indicate that they were not so obsolete in terms of political impact, playing a role for Turkey in deterring Russian conventional attacks similar to the role the

Russian missiles might play for Cuba in deterring an American conventional invasion. However vulnerable such liquid-fueled missiles might be, they might plausibly come into use in any war involving Turkey (while the Mediterranean Polaris force might not), and thus deter such wars through fears of escalation. Soviet gains from the Cuban deployment might thus not be nil, if the Cuban crisis made Kennedy more determined to withdraw from Turkey.

The Russians could perhaps with justice claim that the United States had "wired itself in" with forward deployments of tactical and strategic nuclear weapons often enough in the past, deployments which also threatened to proliferate nuclear weapons into less trusted hands. Neither the United States nor any other country should now object if the U.S.S.R. wished to increase the credibility of its massive retaliation on behalf of Cuba. But the Cuban deployment was overseas, in what could be interpreted as a salient or enclave in the West's sphere of power, and the United States had, after all, not yet deployed such warheads to Berlin or Quemoy. (A very tentative suggestion that nuclears be deployed to West Berlin was apparently advanced by Robert Kennedy at an early stage in the crisis.)[59]

It may now have been feared in the United States that such Cuban-based missiles would outflank the BMEWS radar screen, and thus catch American bombers on their bases; Soviet submarine-based missiles presumably would have been too inaccurate to execute the same counterforce mission. Yet Polaris was at sea, some Minutemen were underground, and the vulnerability of the U.S. bomber fleet was a subject of declining concern. On the question of whether a significant American retaliatory force could be retained through a Russian first strike augmented by the missiles in Cuba, Secretary of Defense McNamara reported that no threat existed;[60] a missile was a missile, in Cuba or in Russia, surely capable of doing damage to American civilians, already as surely incapable of preventing significant damage to the U.S.S.R. Paul Nitze apparently contended, however, that the Cuban missiles might plausibly take out some significant segment of SAC's remaining bomber force based in the southeastern United States,[61] perhaps opening a bare possibility of a Russian splendid first strike and in any event reducing the American ability to suppress Soviet second-wave attacks on American cities.

Strategic analyses of the Russian missile deployment perhaps focus overly much on the particular numbers of sites and missiles already in Cuba, or presumably on their way, at the time of the American ultimatum. There was, however, no guarantee that the Russians would have stopped sending missiles to Cuba if the first deployment (projected for 80 missiles on 40 launching pads) had gone unchallenged; shipments might have continued until such deployment became economically inappropriate because of Soviet production constraints, or physically difficult for lack of suitable launching sites in Cuba itself. The first contraint did not seem to have been near at hand, in view of the unaccountably large production of MRBM's which turned up after 1961, to be aimed at Western Europe.[62] The choice of sites might have been more of a constraint, since the Russians seemed quite concerned to keep the missiles out of Cuban control; the U.S.S.R.–dispatched perhaps as many as 20,000 troops to Cuba to operate and guard the missiles, troops equipped also with short-range tactical nuclear weapons.[63] If the missiles had to be kept far from Cuban populated areas, and far from each other to preclude leaving four or five missiles vulnerable to a single incoming American missile, then the confines of Cuba might not have offered so many sites. Yet if the number of missiles could be increased, it might still rationally have been thought threatening.

Explanations for the U.S. stand can also be sought in the American political process. The Eisenhower Administration had perhaps mortgaged its future in the 1952 campaign to pledges of economy in government spending, including military spending; the Kennedy Administration had in turn perhaps overcommitted itself to strength in strategic weapons. Where the Republicans might have been able to tolerate a missile deployment to Cuba (which in "countervalue" terms would only duplicate the capabilities of Russian-based missiles, and in counterforce terms probably achieved nothing decisive), Kennedy perhaps could not.

President Kennedy's commitment against Soviet strategic deployments to the Western Hemisphere thus stemmed partially from the pledges and stances of 1960. The rest of the commitment derived from warnings on "offensive" missiles delivered some weeks before the deployment had begun,[64] in response to an apparently sizable buildup of Soviet air defense installations on the island. Kennedy's proclamation on "no offensive missiles" may have represented a "tying of one's hands" to an intervention policy the administration would never have implemented in the absence of such a proclamation; it was thus perhaps designed to forestall a Soviet action which might otherwise have been unhappily tolerated. On the other hand, the 1959 and 1960 attacks on

Republican complacency might have made likely a tough American stand now even without the prior declaration. In either event, it seems clear that Kennedy could not so easily back down or remain quiet after the warning had once been issued.

One of the earliest responses to the detection of a Cuban missile deployment came with the significant step-up of American U-2 overflights.[65] In accounts of the crisis as it ensued, it is often stated that the Russians were not made aware of American mobilization on the issue until the President's speech and imposition of the naval quarantine.[66] Yet the Soviet government had become aware of the efficacy of U-2 photo intelligence in 1960; the number of such overflights now executed clearly might have signaled that the United States knew the exact extent of the Soviet deployment from day to day, and was extremely concerned about it. Had the Russians decided to withdraw quietly at this point, the operation could have been terminated in response to this tacit expression of American concern, with little or no embarrassment to the Russians.

The last conversation between Kennedy and Gromyko before the crisis, in which Gromyko was allowed to deny again the presence of "offensive" missiles in Cuba, could thus be cited for propaganda purposes as an example of Soviet deceit (or by critics of American failure to confront Gromyko openly, as an American agent provocateur ploy); yet this conversation may in fact have served as a very subtle exchange of tacit warnings: that the United States intended to interfere with the deployment, and that the Russians intended to continue it.

Observers skeptical of U.S. policy have questioned the need for a quarantine or blockade on arms shipments, on the grounds that the number of missiles already in Cuba was still not significant, running only to 40 or so. Logically such arguments might seem straightforwardly mistaken, for the quarantine nominally was addressed not to the missiles already in Cuba, but rather to those that might yet come, the number of which was not so apparently bounded. Yet one remembers that the same U.S. Navy warships which prevented further missile importation later inspected the finite numbers of original missiles as they were withdrawn, and there is a link here between the blockade and withdrawal which must be examined.

The U.S. Administration now clearly would not be satisfied with a mere freeze on the number of missiles in Cuba, but seemed intent on reducing the deployment to zero. The possibilities of invasion or "surgical" air strike were debated early in the crisis, but it seemed preferable that the mere threat of such attacks first be used to induce a peaceful withdrawal by the Russians, if execution of the threat could be avoided. If Russian personnel were to suffer casualties on the missile sites, or perhaps be taken as POW's in an invasion, the costs of this to the U.S.S.R. might be too high to supply any assurance that the crisis could be kept under control; escalation to a war involving attacks on the United States was to be avoided if possible.

The basic American decision in the crisis thus has been described as follows: to begin with the quarantine (which would prevent reinforcements and perhaps induce withdrawal of missiles already in Cuba), and then, if necessary, to escalate to air strikes or to an actual invasion of the island. The sequence is portrayed as finally having been presented most persuasively by Treasury Secretary Dillon,[67] on the simple truism that one could always begin moderately and then escalate, while deescalation from an initially vigorous action would be difficult.

Yet this argument, that America had nothing to lose by beginning at a more moderate level of response, does not fully address the missiles already in Cuba and approaching readiness for action. If one was distrustful of Castro's rationality and of Soviet controls on the missiles, and/or if one was really contemplating an armed incursion into Cuba, the activation of even one hydrogen-warhead missile site might make a significant difference. Air strikes at missile sites only nearing completion could be risked; even if the air strike failed to eliminate the site definitively, it would presumably interfere with further progress on the activation of the site. Against sites on which missiles stood already poised for firing, such residual uncertainties of air strikes or invasions might be unacceptable, with the risk that an MRBM might be successfully fired at an American city in the heat of the limited battle. It was incorrect to say that nothing was lost by waiting, that one could always escalate; escalation might be far more risky after days or weeks had passed.

Yet because air strikes might never be accurate enough to eliminate the missiles "surgically" without killing a large number of civilians in the process, or because of the potential stigma of a "Pearl Harbor," or because the Russian missiles were reaching a stage of operational readiness too quickly, the decision was nonetheless made to begin American operations with the imposition of the quarantine. The blockade made straightforward sense in that it at least confined the size of the American problem to the missiles already in Cuba; if it was difficult to persuade the Russians to remove 40 missiles or so, it would have been all the more difficult to induce the removal of 400.

The blockade, moreover, served as an index of American willingness to take risks in a crisis, involving military operations which by some standards of international law constituted an act of war. The initiative, the "last clear chance," on the question of resupply was thrown back to the Russians, since they could avoid physical hostilities by avoiding positive action; the American naval screen thus served immediately to deter Russian behavior rather than to compel it, an important distinction.[68] Yet the willingness of the United States to take even this risk made later air strikes against the missiles already in Cuba seem more plausible; warnings to the Soviet Union, and deployments of troop-carrier aircraft to the southern United States, were made more convincing by what the United States had already done, as an index of what else the United States was prepared to do.

Paradoxically, it might have been more difficult for the United States to impose the blockade on resupply if there were not already some Soviet missiles in Cuba. Neutrals that had to be convinced of American legitimacy might tend to analogize with a domestic criminal law process, where one did not normally interpose police agents in an individual's path to prevent crimes before he had already begun committing them. Ideally a blockade might have caught "half" the components of a missile system inside Cuba, and prevented the completion or erection of any operational missile batteries on the island. This was not in fact to be the case, but such an impression might still be maintained or circulated during and after the crisis.

Had the Soviets decided to challenge the blockade, American options for effective but inexpensive blocking action would not yet have been exhausted. The Soviet ships might have been disabled with little or no damage or loss of life—for example, by shooting away the rudders of cargo ships at close range.[69] The Russian humiliation thereby incurred would have been great, but it would have been a humiliation imposed more by the very nature of the situation than by Western brutality or arrogance. Just as the geography of the Berlin situation naturally allows East Germans or Russians to make Americans look foolish, without the Communist side looking brutal, so the situation was reversed in the waters around Cuba. Whether or not shooting out a rudder would have been as threatening to Soviet national prestige and to world peace as the killing of Russian technicians around a missile site, the United States had fairly clearly committed itself to some such action in the deployment of the quarantine force; the Russians now had to decide whether they wanted to incur the disutility

242

of having one or more of their freighters towed into an American port, where its missile cargo might be disassembled and examined in detail.

The first sign of Soviet surrender during the crisis thus came when ships presumably carrying additional missiles for the island did not challenge the blockade, but turned to head back toward the U.S.S.R. While this brought a certain sigh of relief in many circles, the problem remained of the missiles already in Cuba, which were still hurriedly being brought to a state of readiness. Having succeeded in circumscribing the problem, the Kennedy Administration had several choices. It might tighten the blockade to include civilian goods as well as additional strategic weapons. It might go ahead with an invasion or air strike to take out the remaining missiles. It might announce its toleration of the remaining missiles, on the ground that by themselves they would be a puny and insignificant force, sufficing only to justify an indefinitely continued inspection of Soviet ships bound for Cuba; alternatively, it might for the time intensify signals that air strikes or invasion threatened, while the impact of the already successful naval blockade was allowed to sink in. Within a matter of days the last combination did induce the Russians to begin dismantling MRBM sites already constructed, with an announcement that the missiles would be withdrawn to the U.S.S.R.

The Cuban missile crisis showed the physical location of nuclear weapons to be of great importance for the less committed nations of the world, regardless of the fact that ICBM's would soon possess global range. A part of such concern could of course be traced to the command-and-control or proliferation issue; a missile aimed at Caracas from Cuba might not be so securely deterred as a missile aimed at the same city from Russia. Yet such rational considerations did not fully explain the general support the United States blockade received from Latin American governments, or the cooperation of such figures as Sekou Touré and Ahmed Ben Bella in denying landing rights to Soviet planes that might be carrying atomic warheads to Cuba.[70] Few observers would have dared to predict any such full cooperation from these nations, but the openness of the Russian deployment of nuclear missiles in this case seemed quite brazen (or was astutely made to seem so by the United States), with a saliency to which most nonnuclear nations would be opposed. The Russians were the offending party in this view, not so much because they had tampered with the balance of power as because they had disrupted the illusion of an enduring balance; the weapons had been moved, and were objectionable not only because of where they landed, but also because they had become visible by being moved.

It is always possible that the Soviets had formulated contingency plans for an American blockade before the deployment of missiles had been completed. Such plans might have called for respect for the blockade, with missiles already in Cuba to be brought to combat readiness, the Americans and Russians settling for that much of a deployment. What would have been difficult to predict, however, was the pressures that would be focused on the Soviet Union once the blockade had been interposed and given in to, pressures from all over the world to go ahead and agree to the dismantling of the missiles already deployed. The argument that surrender on one matter induces pressure for similar surrenders on related matters has many times been raised in the West, on considerations of possible concessions to Soviet demands, but here it seems to have been relevant in just the reverse situation. The neutral world had heaved a sigh of relief at Khrushchev's reasonableness in not pushing his missile-laden cargo ships through the American naval force; it would have seemed exceedingly perverse now for the Soviet Premier to insist on going ahead with those similar missiles which had already been delivered clandestinely to Cuba. Because the world vaguely saw the blockade as relevant to the missiles already inside Cuba, it in fact became relevant.

Whether or not the United States would indeed have resorted to violent military activity two or three days later, if the Russians had not announced their withdrawal as they did, must be left at least partially open to question.[71] The need to preempt the erection of operational missiles might have been a persuasive argument, but it might have been even more persuasive earlier, when it was rejected. If Americans feared a possible obliteration of Miami or New Orleans, then it was perhaps too late for preemptive action because the prospect did not exist of surely eliminating already erected missiles. One can argue that an expansion from one to five ready missiles was still worth preempting, or from five to 15, but the exact choice of number is not so easy to determine here, and preemptive arguments clearly depend on the exact figures in the choice; by the Sunday of the Soviet capitulation, from 12 to 18 of the Soviet MRBM's apparently had been readied for action.[72] The option of an intensification of the blockade might thus have been the more logical next step, perhaps with a decisive impact on the Cuban economy, and with less risk of an atomic salvo hitting one or two American cities.

The United States had already been assured by Khrushchev, in confirmation of its own earlier aerial reconnaissance, that the missiles remained under Russian control,[73] which could be interpreted as reducing the risk of their being fired during an American surgical air strike, and/or as reducing the urgency of such strikes. The possibility remains that no invasion of Cuba was really so near at hand, that President Kennedy would have withheld the air strike and invasion, just as he withheld the air strike on SAM sites that he had defined earlier as the response to any U-2 interception (one was intercepted). To leave the Russians in fear of an imminent invasion would perhaps establish and prove American resolve for any later crises, especially in Berlin, where the Communists could do the "quarantining," and would contribute to inducing a complete withdrawal of the missiles; to describe the crisis afterwards as if preemptive arguments and haste had been operational at the U.S. end might confirm this impression, but these may not have had so much reality.

An alternative impression also achieved some circulation. As it was, the Russians consented to dismantle and withdraw without further American action. To at least part of the world, the impression would remain that the blockade had by itself somehow prevented the deployment of missiles to Cuba, as if the Russians had indeed been caught in the act. Such an inference, confirmed perhaps paradoxically by the photographs of Russian ships submitting their missile cargoes to naval inspection as they left Cuba, also would redound to the benefit of the United States by showing with what ease the United States could upset a major strategic move of the U.S.S.R. The impression that the United States can shake the world without really threatening world war might be an important one to disseminate and might even have been valid, at least in part, for the Cuban case. Advocates of tactical conventional and of strategic nuclear strength could thus find support for their position in the Cuban crisis, and insofar as their arguments are more complementary than contradictory, perhaps with equal justification.

The United States could not state positively after the crisis that all the Soviet missiles had been removed, but the issue of a few clandestine missiles being retained in Cuba was probably never so serious as many laymen in the United States supposed. While it turned out that U.S. aerial surveillance had detected only 30 of 42 Soviet missiles that the Russians withdrew openly from Cuba,[74] this still seemed to give approximately a two-thirds probability that any particular Soviet missile retained in Cuba would be detected, a high risk to run. As long as the Russians could not claim to have the missiles in Cuba, moreover, some of the political advantage of such a deployment would be eliminated. The vengeance of the United States in the event of a renewed Soviet deception might indeed be serious, although this would conceivably inhibit an American Government from discussing any such intelligence, for fear that public uproar would drive it into an uncontrollable crisis situation. Yet even here leaks in the lower levels of the American intelligence-gathering system might soon enough inform the American public of Soviet violations of the promises just exacted, perhaps more convincingly than had the earlier reports of Cuban refugees or of Senator Keating.

If the Soviets had held an interest in moving against West Berlin right after the 1962 American elections, then the political and strategic implications of a Cuban missile force might have strengthened them considerably. A blockade of Berlin might, moreover, have seemed the logical counter in many ways to the American blockade of Cuba if it were not for the overwhelming strategic superiority in bomber and missiles now assumed for the United States. Had the Soviets attempted such a deployment of missiles in Cuba in 1959 (when Castro had just come to power and had perhaps not yet demonstrated his political complexion), then the tough American reaction might not have been nearly so likely, especially when the Soviets were assumed to hold an advantage in a missile gap. As it was, the Soviets may now have been trying to remedy a strategic inferiority, and it was that inferiority which in turn may have prevented them from remedying it.

While the early Kennedy Administration strategic discussion had stressed and implemented city-shielding notions of general-war "rationality" and conventional war "options," as epitomized perhaps in the Ann Arbor speech, American actions in the Cuban crisis weakened any notion of general war without annihilation of populations. During the crisis, which had erupted so soon after the Ann Arbor speech, U.S. B-47 aircraft were deployed to civilian airdromes (thus perhaps denying the Soviets a counterforce "no-cities" option),[75] and President Kennedy had threatened a "full retaliatory strike" against the Soviet Union,[76] seemingly if any missiles from Cuba were fired at any target. The declaratory policies which had seemed desirable when general war was a more abstract question appeared to have lost their appeal when a contest of wills had gotten under way. Critics of the new logic of defense might have contended that Kennedy and McNamara had fallen back onto city-risking declaratory and deployment strategies that had not worked so badly for the Eisenhower Administration, after an earlier departure that might in fact have emboldened Khrushchev to try a deployment to Cuba. European critics would interpret the Kennedy position as rather more consistent, ever ready to risk all-out war for hemispheric interests while declining to do so for European interests.

Finally, one perhaps should not dismiss so lightly Khrushchev's rationalization that the Cuban missile deployment had been primarily intended (and had worked) to preclude any American invasion of the island.[77] The United States, after all, had backed such a liberation attempt in 1961, and President Kennedy had threatened renewed activities in this direction after the failure of the Bay of Pigs operation. With the conclusion of the missile crisis, Kennedy would indeed state that his pledge not to invade the island was nullified by Castro's failure to submit to inspection, but a general impression nonetheless remained that no American-sponsored invasion was likely. Had the Cuban island not been shown to be important to the U.S.S.R., and thereby to the world, some prospects of liberation might not yet have been abandoned. Cuba, after all, was the first real Communist enclave far from the contiguous mass of satellites (or the first since Guatemala in 1954); it might thus have seemed natural for the West to mop up such an isolated Marxist outpost if the missile crisis precedent had not served to make it seem terribly unreasonable for Kennedy to rock the boat once again in a try at the island.

Yet the crisis may also have made the status quo easier to accept for the United States. The fear had been widespread prior to 1962 that Castro's approach would find wide appeal throughout Latin America, with guerrilla wars ensuing from country to country, wherever the existing regimes did not themselves join the Marxist camp. If the threat here had not been substantially disproved by late 1962, Castro's prestige loss in the missile crisis was enormous, having introduced the threat of nuclear war to Latin America; it thus was clear that non-Communist Latin America might yet be preserved without toppling the Castro status quo in Cuba.

Post-Cuban Détente

If the Cuban missile crisis hinged on what some observers would consider to have been pointless issues, it could still be plausibly credited with a considerable effect on the subsequent behavior of the Soviet government. With the exception of some sporadic incidents in the fall of 1963 relating to the counting of Western troops on the Autobahn,[78] the status quo of West Berlin no longer was threatened. One might, of course, have interpreted the post-1962 absence of Soviet-induced tension around Berlin as proof of the stabilization of the East German regime after the erection of the Berlin wall. As time proved the wall's effectiveness, there was considerably less reason for the Russians to fear that some total collapse of the Ulbricht regime was near: the knowledge that one could not escape to the West apparently had the effect of making valuable personnel in East Germany more content with their lot, and plant managers could now count on having their work force in place from day to day. Similarly, as argued above, the world might now have felt more assured that Fidel Castro's regime would survive.

Whether the Russians would have been tempted to seek greater gains after these consolidations, if it had not been for the American response in Cuba, may remain unclear for many years. Other problems emerged for the Russian leadership at this time; domestic demands for the consumer goods which the Soviet economy had not yet supplied, and Chinese challenges to the Russian Party's dominant position in the international Communist hierarchy, might have reduced Soviet initiatives in Germany or elsewhere. Conversely, such problems might otherwise have occasioned the Russians to open newly expansionist initiatives as a diversion if the Americans had not just established a reputation for going to considerable lengths in a crisis.

If one had instead interpreted Soviet inferiority at the strategic forces level as a major source of tension, then this might also be eased, for on two arguments the United States might now stop claiming or seeking strategic force advantages. If the threat to West Berlin were ended, the United States might feel less need for an escalation threat; beyond this, the fuzziness of the American motivation in the Cuban episode might have been interpreted as putting an "honorable" (city-risking) massive retaliation escalation response into effect again, even if no rational options were provided by Soviet numerical inferiorities. President Kennedy's crisis pledge—full retaliation against the Soviet Union if the missiles in Cuba were fired at any Western Hemisphere city, even one outside the United States—was now seemingly matched by the West Berlin speech pledging that America would "risk its cities to defend Europe's cities"[79] Suggestions for rational options continued to be voiced, but less persistently or consistently than before. It was common for Administration spokesmen to extol the Cuban operation as demonstrating the importance of conventional superiority in the immediate threater (i.e., the absolute superiority of the U.S. Navy in the seas around Cuba). But others would speculate that only the President's willingness to threaten an irrational use of strategic weapons had shielded Berlin during the crisis (i.e., where the Red Army perhaps had an absolute conventional superiority).

The swelling of the two powers' arms inventories, moreover, might sooner or later put both onto a plateau where neither could be vulnerable or inferior in any rational sense. Some American arms control writers had long predicted that the Russians would develop a secure retaliatory force, underground or on submarines, to make destruction of American cities inevitable in the event of an all-out war; a few had almost portrayed this as desirable if it would allow the Soviets at last to become less tense,[80] to become more certain that the United States was deterred from cold-bloodedly initiating a war against the cities of the U.S.S.R.

Critics of McNamara's Ann Arbor speech had thus pointed to the supposedly limited duration of the counterforce capability it seemed to be exploiting, and some had argued that the duration should even be shortened where possible. The United States might thus have earlier forgone any large procurement of missiles usable in a counterforce operation against those of the Soviet Union, settling rather for a "finite deterrent" of limited numbers and limited accuracy. Yet such a finite deterrent might never have been surely impervious enough to the other side's counterforce strike, and the policy of deliberate restraint had thus in effect been rejected.

Since missiles were presumably to be acquired in larger numbers by both the United States and the U.S.S.R., however, mutually assured destruction might now become more and more clearly available, if only through the dispersal, concealment, hardening, and multiplication of the two arsenals. One objective of "finite deterrence," to lower total casualties in the event of an accidental war, thus would be lost. The more serious objective, avoiding force-vulnerability incentives to first-strike attack, might be achieved, however, by very large numbers of missiles, rather than by very small, and the United States would now begin to concede this officially.

By the spring of 1963, with the missile crisis substantially settled, Secretary McNamara was testifying that Soviet nuclear forces would imminently be augmented to a point where no American counterforce strike could suffice to shield American cities.[81] McNamara also endorsed doubts as to whether mutual adherence to a no-cities strategy was at all likely in the event of general war, and assured the Congress that the United States was prepared to utilize tactical nuclear weapons in Europe if they were needed.

If the United States were so soon (and perhaps prematurely) to renounce its rational motive for crisis escalations to general nuclear war, this might reflect an early perception of lessened Soviet hostility, and perhaps a sense that discussions of meaningful U.S. superiorities exacerbated such hostilities. Conversely or simultaneously, it might signify the resigned acceptance of an ongoing, nonrational American escalation motive in defense of Western Europe, a motive which now would not so often be denied or explicitly redefined into a more rational form. If the precedent of the American toughness in the Cuban crisis did not depend on a meaningful American strategic superiority, it had not depended entirely on local theater superiorities either. If the coupling of the American deterrent to Europe was now less on the style of the Ann Arbor speech, if there was less talk of an all-conventional defense, then the coupling might simultaneously be stronger and less offensive to the U.S.S.R.

The Soviet move to a secure strategic force in fact came more slowly than had been predicted, regardless of how desirable or undesirable such a move had been thought. The Soviet slowness here can have illustrated economic constraints, or a basic trust of the United States, or technical failings at the level of missile development; but through and after 1963 one might still have retained reasoned doubts as to whether the Soviets could inflict tremendous retaliatory damage on the United States after a well-executed American first strike. While such doubts always would persist longer than predicted, however, the cumulative impact of such Soviet procurements and deployments as were undertaken, and of the repetitious and official predictions themselves, was to wear away any American reliance on a rationally significant superiority at the strategic weapons level after 1963.

Whether or not the aftereffects of the Cuban crisis were responsible for the easing of tensions around West Berlin, both of these now contributed to a new Soviet responsiveness on the issue of nuclear testing. Having implicitly admitted a "wrong" position in the attempted missile deployment to Cuba, the Soviet administration may have felt that its reserves of world prestige had fallen lower than desirable, to such a level that a continued propaganda exchange with the United States might be quite painful. It would therefore be far preferable to cease the exchange, to redirect propaganda pressure against Red China, and in the end to bind the U.S.S.R. to legitimating U.S. underground testing. If no confrontation was now imminent with the West over Berlin, open-air testing was not required as a reminder of the potency of Soviet massive retaliation, of the horrors of escalation.

With the 1958-1961 experience presumably having conclusively demonstrated a Soviet advantage in an uninspected total moratorium, it would have been difficult for an American Administration to agree to such a moratorium again. If the Russians could have been induced to accept some modicum of inspection after 1962, a comprehensive ban might still have been thought preferable by Kennedy, for its opening of Soviet society and likely inhibition of Soviet weapons development efforts, for its greater contribution to détente, and for its more effective inhibition of the proliferation of national nuclear forces. But if the U.S.S.R. could not accept this much inspection, it might be better for the United States to contract for a legitimation of underground testing, and then to sign a treaty, rather than to continue an exchange of propaganda attacks which no longer suited the objectives of either major power.

Any partial or total ban on nuclear testing would have positive advantages for the Kennedy Administration, more than for Eisenhower, who had accepted it mainly because of the prestige costs of failing to do so. Yet paradoxically, it was only under Eisenhower that there has been any prolonged total cessation of American nuclear testing, while the United States under Kennedy acquired and utilized an enduring option for underground testing. Arguing that Presidents are always freer to go against than with their inclinations, that liberals are allowed to be conservative by Congress, and vice versa, does not wholly explain the apparent paradox. Rather, the groundwork laid by Eisenhower in the late 1950's had made the outside world more tolerant of underground testing, testing which the Republicans always would have wanted. And the progress demonstrated by the Russians in their 1961 tests probably reinforced American desires for some testing option, enough so to make a comprehensive ban a very difficult proposal for Kennedy to accept.

American demands for inspection in a comprehensive ban now might have had to be watered down somewhat, as progress was made in long-range detection of underground nuclear explosions. The scientific consensus now seemed to be that permanent manned inspection posts were not required on the territory of the Soviet Union, since seismic stations abroad could identify any really suspicious happenings, which might then require only a certain quota of additional on-site inspections each year. While the United States had at one point sought 20 such inspection visits a year, the demand was gradually lowered in the negotiation process to a minimum of seven, while the Russians were denying the possibility entirely.[82]

The real sequence of communications that ensued early in 1963 will never be fully clear, but certain American arms control experts with close connections to the Administration may have privately told comparable Soviet officials that a Russian offer of three inspections a year would be accepted as a worthy compromise.[83] In any event, such a Russian offer was made, but the United States did not respond with any reduction of its demand for seven inspections. Observers might of course differ on who had compromised the most, and who appropriately should make further concessions to narrow the gap. The United States had moved from 20 to seven inspections, while the U.S.S.R. had only moved from zero to three; but the Russians had acknowledged the abstract need for inspection, a need they had more vaguely accepted in 1959 and then disowned in 1961.

Having thus been caught in a weak propaganda position, the Russians in the summer of 1963 abruptly agreed to an uninspected ban on above-ground detonations, in effect inhibiting themselves from making further propaganda attacks on U.S. underground testing. A direct communications link in the form of a Moscow-Washington "hot line" was also inaugurated with appropriate publicity, followed in October by a U.N. General Assembly resolution banning weapons of mass destruction in space, a resolution receiving the endorsement of both the United States and the U.S.S.R. The propaganda or prestige losses of continuing to resist the partial test ban may thus have become too high for the Russians, after they had been trapped into again accepting the principle of on-site inspection for a comprehensive ban. If the Americans, in exchange for a limited test ban, agreed to stop demanding an opening of Soviet society, then this might be a price worth paying.

A test ban in any event would be a powerful lever for psychological détente, even if it was only partial. Open-air testing attracted notice and suggested large weapons on an open-ended spectrum; underground tests were less noticeable and might be seen as related to a more contained spectrum of tactical or small weapons. Since the U.S.S.R. now desired or required some easing of material and political tensions with the United States, the test ban could supply it. By 1963, the Russians had, moreover, probably acquired more experience and skill in the techniques of measuring weapons effects underground, so that less unilateral advantage now accrued to the United States in a resumption of such tests.

Nuclear Proliferation as a More Explicit Problem

Nuclear proliferation might now also be a more serious issue for the U.S.S.R., since the hope of heading off a Chinese nuclear test, or at least of increasing the prestige costs to the Chinese of testing, may have moved the Soviet leadership to accept the partial test ban. Again, the Russians more typically cited the West Germans as their most feared object of proliferation, but the special circumstances of the Federal Republic still made the test ban less crucial for it than for France or China, however serious the Soviet aversion to a German national nuclear force might have been. A partial ban, on its face, would not amount to the perfect control on proliferation offered by the comprehensive ban, but it still was a significant psychological inhibitor of proliferation if enough signatures could be corralled quickly. Since Communist China was now moving simultaneously to acquire a bomb and to challenge the ideological leadership of the U.S.S.R., a test ban would at least help to win sympathy on the moderate left for Moscow against Peking.

As a détente now emerged with the U.S.S.R., the United States similarly still hoped to make some more general progress in inhibiting the proliferation of independent nuclear forces. If an American nuclear response to a Russian attack on Europe was now as likely as ever, nuclear weapons still might have to be denied to most countries of the world. The proliferation question was now more pressing than it had been earlier: France had tested its first bomb in 1960, and Communist China seemed intent on becoming the fifth nuclear power. The "Atoms for Peace" program had made technology on reactors available to a larger number of countries, so that plutonium atom bombs—if not hydrogen bombs, which required a uranium diffusion plant—might come into their possession soon. And American military policies in Europe, voluntarily or otherwise, were still placing tactical and strategic nuclear weapons into what could easily become national physical control.

If one assigned a high priority to the prevention of nuclear proliferation, there might still be great disagreement on how best to prevent the emergence of national nuclear forces. One approach having many adherents was a clear and forthright opposition to any sharing of nuclear weaponry. A second alternative approach assumed that emerging nuclear forces, like those in Britain and France, might better be undermined by economically seductive technological assistance, assistance which might slowly build a practical American veto into any use of such forces even if the forces were nominally independent.

A control of sorts over the most significant portion of the British nuclear capacity thus perhaps already existed by 1962, since the United Kingdom had reduced its own production of the enriched uranium required for hydrogen bombs,[84] entering into an agreement whereby the United States would trade such material for British-produced plutonium. The costs of maintaining uranium production presumably were high, especially if economies of scale could not soon be achieved. While plutonium production could be accompanied by the generation of usable amounts of electricity, the separation of uranium consumed significant amounts of energy. Having proved that Britain could produce uranium if it had to, by presumably crude and wasteful processes, the British Government thus became content to rely on American supplies of fissionable uranium, which might be construed as giving the United States some option of control.

But such control would presumably be of a delayed-action variety, at best. If some Government of the United Kingdom were to alter its foreign policy approach drastically, to the displeasure of the United States (a highly unlikely event), the United States could cease supplying replacement warheads to the British strategic forces; over some length of time, this might induce a reduction of the hydrogen-bomb stockpile; Britain would have to take time to crank up its uranium separation processes again, and in the meantime would have to rely on plutonium-based A-bombs. Whether such American physical potential for inhibiting British stockpiles would develop into real political control remained unclear, however, since the effectiveness of any such induced control might in fact depend on its never being made explicit.

Almost before the Cuban missile crisis was terminated, moreover, relations between the United States and Great Britain were strained in a seemingly more doctrinaire American opposition to independent national nuclear forces. Arrangements had been made in 1960 for an American Polaris submarine base at Holly Loch, with President Eisenhower simultaneously agreeing to share the Skybolt air-to-surface missile with the RAF.[85] The Skybolt presumably would have prolonged the strategic significance of the RAF V-bomber force, at least as a countercity instrument.

By 1962, however, the United States had found Skybolt to be excessively expensive as a countervalue weapons system, especially now that Polaris missiles were being deployed. Available test evidence did not promise sufficient accuracies to make the air-launched ballistic missile an effective counterforce instrument, and a decision was thus reached to cancel the project. While the poorer accuracies might have been acceptable for the RAF, which desired an independent city-busting deterrent, such missiles seemed undesirable or unnecessary for American strategic forces. The American cancellation was seen as an attempt to eliminate the British city-busting force, but it did not by itself really signal any positive American determination in this direction. The United States had not previously gone out of its way to make retaliatory weapons available to the RAF; in each case the United Kingdom had essentially been offered weapons already procured for American forces, where economies of scale made extra production runs possible at relatively low cost. Skybolt was legitimately redundant for the United States, such that the high development costs were not worth assuming; the affair might thus simply have signaled an end to the time when economic weapons production options would naturally draw the two English-speaking nations together.

But the issue was not quite this simple. U.S. spokesmen professed, somewhat disingenuously, not to understand why the British would want such an inaccurate weapon, thus seeming to want to fool the United Kingdom into giving up its own massive retaliation instrument. Subsequent American statements, by persons as high as the President himself, suggested that Skybolt was "militarily worthless,"[86] thus forcing the British either to give up the weapon or to explicate its value as a crude countercity instrument, and opening the difference between American and British national interests to world review. Secretary McNamara, moreover, was slow to offer Polaris as an alternative instrument for the British,[87] in part perhaps because of legitimate misunderstandings, but in part also because much of the American Government would still have been pleased to have Britain remove itself from the list of independent nuclear powers.

Thus the crux of the Skybolt issue was probably not that the United Kingdom desired a countervalue capability for its own sake, but that such a capability had been made significant by American and French strategic pronouncements identifying it as crucial to nuclear integration or nuclear independence. Until the cancellation of Skybolt, and the ensuing open strategic discussion, most of the world still would have taken it for granted that Britain had such a capability, and could maintain it largely through its own efforts. Secretary McNamara's Ann Arbor speech implicitly had condemned such an independent British capability, but it had then been sanctioned in a following statement, and no clear American ability to deprive the United Kingdom of such a weapon had yet been illustrated. The dialogue of the following fall, however, saw Britain publicly waiting for the United States to grant it such a countervalue weapon in Polaris, clearly disclosing that such strategic prowess on Britain's part was now the result of American largesse. Whether or not the British Government could ever imagine a scenario where it would want to kill Russian civilians and the United States would not, the image of being able to take such independent action counted for something, as it did for France, and the Skybolt affair had moved the British closer to France in terms of the obstacles to attaining this image.

In the end the United States offered Polaris to Britain without any reciprocal commitment that such missiles be kept under immediate multinational control, but it would be some time before such a Polaris force would be deployed, thus perhaps leaving a time gap in Britain's ability to destroy Russian cities. In any event, the impression was strengthened in other countries that the United States was still quite single-mindedly intent on controlling national nuclear forces, presumably so that escalation to general war could come only when it was to narrow American interests, or at least on American signal.

A third antiproliferation approach, perhaps directed more at the countries not yet developing their own nuclear weapons (West Germany in particular), was to offer a greater physical exposure to such weapons, but with a formal U.S. veto on use, as in the double-key systems applied to Jupiter and Thor missiles, and the American veto proposed for the Multi-Lateral Force (MLF).[88] The idea of a mixed-manned or multinational nuclear force went back to the last years of the Eisenhower Administration. Proposals for land-based or submarine-based forces over time were ruled out on technical objections, but a surface vessel force seemed at least physically viable. The exact mission of such a force—strategic assault on Soviet cities, preemptive attack on Soviet MRBM sites, or interdiction attacks on Communist supply lines—was never very clear, since one could argue that the MLF would be redundant for all these purposes. If the issue was the credibility of American responses, then the MLF might be significant nonetheless, if one assumed that a multilateral force with an American legal veto might be a more credible respondent than a purely American force.

Europeans, in any event, might not ponder the veto issue too closely, since the physical proximity of their men to nuclear-armed missiles would produce a psychological if nonrational reassurance, thus hopefully avoiding incentives for a truly independent capability. If, however, one assumed that proclivities toward national nuclear forces were weak in any event (especially in West Germany, which was the major object of concern), then an MLF might be unnecessary, and possibly the source of problems rather than the cure.

A fourth approach, embodied in the analysis of some American proponents of the MLF, was that the American veto should be relaxed once a substantially multilateral agency of control had been established, since any council of six or more European NATO members would be as reliable a guarantee against irresponsible uses of nuclears as would the United States itself.[89] While a few American proponents of the MLF thus hinted at an ultimate relaxation of the American veto, no such promise ever found its way into the speeches of President Kennedy.

One could also have advocated a policy varying among the approaches above from one country to another; yet the example of a legalistic approach in one case might undermine a more ad hoc approach elsewhere, or vice versa. It was argued in the U.S. State Department that support for the British independent deterrent might encourage West Germany to seek the same for prestige or status reasons;[90] thus even if American assistance on Polaris promised to give the United States some substantial control over British deployment of such a force, the United Kingdom would be pressured to pledge such a force to ultimate multilateral control for the psychological benefit of the Germans.

To concede any need for a multilateral force would seem to buffer British and French arguments for independent national nuclear forces; for if the American deterrent was so credible on behalf of Europe, or if national prestige were in fact unrelated to access to nuclear hardware, then there would seem to be no need for the United States to make the multilateral concession.

6   From
         Johnson to Nixon:
         1963-1969

Incomplete Détente in Europe

The uncertain political future of various territories had troubled Soviet-American relations ever since 1945, as strategic weapons alternately served to ease or exacerbate such tensions. Some territorial uncertainties would be lessened now, as Cuba and East Germany were more securely Communist, and (in part because of this) West Berlin could remain tied to the West. But other territorial uncertainties emerged; peace became much more probable in Europe during the Johnson Administration, but became less likely in the Middle East and in Southeast Asia.

It has often been predicted that détente and assured peace in Europe would come about as super powers lost interest in the area, as "alliances weakened" and the world became more "multipolar." Yet we have little confirmation for a prognosis that the superpowers (perhaps out of increased fear of nuclear war) would abandon their alliances and commitments. American strategic commentators in the mid-1950's had been among the earliest to predict that a Russian hydrogen-bomb stockpile would prevent any American escalation to nuclear war in defense of Europe, since the U.S.S.R. thus would at its leisure occupy slices of Europe. Such arguments had been recirculated through several official and semiofficial French sources by 1961, perhaps most clearly in the writings of Pierre Gallois.[1] President De Gaulle also hinted at a vague endorsement of such arguments, but it is not clear that the French Government ever took such fears seriously; it expressed more and more skepticism into the mid-1960's about any Russian expansionism, suggesting that something was still deterring or dissuading the Soviet leadership. West Germans might still regularly conjure up visions of Russian aggression, but other European NATO members showed less concern here.[2]

This disparity in estimates on the likelihood of Soviet aggression might seem paradoxical, for Germans should have convinced their French counterparts, or vice versa, within the exchanges and coordinations of analyses facilitated by NATO and the Common Market. Differences of geographic location might have stabilized a disparity in analysis, however, for Germans could feel Russian troops on what they still were told to interpret as German soil; the Federal Republic would also be the first to suffer in any renewal of "salami tactics," while France could take time to readjust its estimates. A more rational explanation for the divergent professions of security or fear may be derivable from the two governments' preferences on continued American influence in Europe. The primary French desire seems now to have been that the source of European deterrence be European, and that a transition thus be made from a reliance on SAC, a transition all the more feasible because the SAC threat was still clearly effective for the interim. Desire for this transition might lead the French to exaggerate their assurance that the U.S.S.R. would continuously be deterred; opposition to an ouster of American presence and influence, conversely, might lead West Germans to exaggerate their fears for Russian good behavior.

A number of French policies now flowed from De Gaulle's desires to exploit and remold what seemed a reasonably reliable guarantee of peace in Europe: the persistence of the French nuclear program in the face of unexpected difficulties and costs, steady opposition to the MLF proposal, and gradual withdrawal from NATO functions, with a final expulsion of NATO forces and headquarters from France in 1967.

The last French action, if nothing else, made a recourse to nuclear weapons all the more likely for any American defense of Europe. Several options had always existed in abstract for such defense. NATO forces might have withdrawn immediately to a defense in depth if attempts to hold a forward line gave the initiative and casualty advantage to Soviet attackers, and if territory voluntarily surrendered could be recovered soon enough in a liberating counteroffensive. Such a strategy had probably been precluded ever since the accession of West Germany to NATO, however, if only because of the suffering German

260

territory would undergo in the process of occupation and liberation. A second approach would make the attempt at a forward defense, falling back to a still more conventional defense in depth if the forward lines did not hold. It can be argued that this would have become the Kennedy Administration's ideal if European conventional force build-ups could ever have been induced. For as long as ground forces were not yet available for an enduring conventional defense, however, tactical nuclears probably would have to be used whenever Russian forces broke through to make large territorial gains.

The denial of French rear areas, or at least of guaranteed access to such areas for preplanning and ordinance stockpiling, might thus have permanized the requirement that tactical nuclear weapons be used after any Russian breakthrough. Even if other NATO powers could be induced to expand conventional ground forces for a wholly nonnuclear defense in depth, the shallowness of the defense belt without France still might make this impossible. Paris' withdrawal from NATO cooperation can thus be seen as a perception of diminished Soviet aggressiveness, or as a bolstering of an American nuclear escalation threat which may well have contributed to diminishing such aggressiveness.[3]

Aside from any reinsurance of massive retaliation engendered by American tactical nuclear weapons or the French Force de Frappe, other environmental developments also contributed now to reducing the threat of Soviet moves across the demarcation lines. A "grand coalition" of Social Democrats and Christian Democrats replaced the West German Government of Chancellor Erhard in the fall of 1966, and it seemed that the growing economic strength and appeal of the Federal Republic had made appropriate some drastically different approaches to Eastern Europe and East Germany, hopefully lessening tensions and the requirement for military forces in the NATO area still more.

Previously the East German regime had sought the procedural formalisms of diplomatic exchange to legitimize its own existence. Eastern European Communist regimes had recognized the D.D.R. and then demanded diplomatic recognition from the Federal Republic (a giving up of the Hallstein Doctrine) to bolster the D.D.R. For as long as the formalities of diplomatic relations were unlikely to be accompanied by substantial interchange and influence, they might thus redound to the advantage and stability of the Communist East German regime. Developments may now, however, have reversed the likely impact of any relaxation of the Hallstein Doctrine. The liberalization of the regimes in Eastern Europe, and relaxation of Russian influence, meant that some of the natural attractions of West German economics and society would take hold if diplomatic exchanges were launched. Economic exchanges not only increased the income of West Germans, but gave all of Eastern Europe a vested interest in continued peace and respect for Western access to West Berlin, and perhaps even in some marginal satisfaction of German grievances over time.

A renewed threat to East Germany's independence could not go unrecognized in Pankow, Moscow, or elsewhere in the East, and few if any Communist leaders would favor the loss of this independence, other things being equal. Where other things were not equal, however, individual Communist leaderships might be tempted to allow the West Germans prestige gains in exchange for material benefits, or for greater maneuvering space vis-à-vis Moscow. Since the Western threat was no longer embodied so much in West Berlin (except perhaps in the Federal Republic's Presidential election every four years), there would be less counterthreat of a military move against this particular enclave, especially when the economic costs of a Western trade embargo, even for East Germany, were so great.

With the declining likelihood of Soviet aggression, NATO conventional-force levels had begun to fall in the mid-1960's. For the West German regime, and for any of its European NATO allies, maintaining standing armed forces on the Rhine was expensive both on balance-of-payments considerations and in absolute economic terms. Despite its own consistent endorsements of a conventional option, even the United States moved to cut back its deployments in West Germany by some 35,000 men, on economic considerations, if not also because of the requirements of Vietnam. Facilities became available for rapid redeployment of troops to Europe by air in the event of any crisis, as a large American investment in new high-capacity air transport showed results. Battalions or divisions could thus perhaps sit in North America earmarked for NATO, without contributing to pressures on the American balance of payments.

Yet it was less clear that such new systems would always satisfy West Europeans and West Germans on the American commitment. German expressions of fear of Soviet military attack, and desires for continued American troop deployments, had all along described and reflected much more than the simple defense issue. Six divisions of American conventional forces were important to West Germany, not as a means to conventional defense but as a political symbol of American interest and commitment, a symbol which at the extreme might ensure nuclear

262

escalation by the United States. Thus even if the C-141 or C-5A made a battalion in North Carolina the functional equivalent militarily of one on the Rhine, the equivalency might not hold in the political terms that influenced Bonn, East Berlin, Moscow, or even Paris.

From 1965 to the present, therefore, one can see NATO countries reducing their own conventional forces and objecting to their allies doing so. If the diminished Soviet threat allowed West Germany to consider reducing its own force, Bonn still would want to have a full complement of Americans retained in Europe. Similarly, the American Government still complains of any German or other NATO troop reductions as reducing the threshold for nonnuclear defense.

If all troop reductions were to be matched by similar withdrawals by the Warsaw Pact powers, greater NATO agreement on them might be possible, but as yet there has been little evidence of such an intention on the Communist side. Over a longer time, a thinning out of forces might take place on both sides of the Elbe (with or without any dramatic shifts of Russian troops toward the frontiers with China). The atrophying of European conventional-force capabilities over this longer run may be matched by political reassurances precluding any new waves of tension in Germany or elsewhere, any further weakening of the alliance. For the shorter run, keeping troop cutbacks and political confidence in phase across the board may become difficult.

For a time, it seemed that Bonn might be able to extract very great gains from its new Eastern political approaches, with the opening of formal relations with Rumania and Yugoslavia, and similar prospects in Hungary and Czechoslovakia. There was, however, the possibility that the new German approach might be too successful, enough so to threaten the Soviet hegemony over parts of Eastern Europe even outside the D.D.R., and this accounts for at least a part of the Soviet decision to intervene militarily in Czechoslovakia in the summer of 1968. The Soviet decision was obviously a reluctant one; had it not been taken, all would have concluded that the threat of Soviet military aggression into West Germany had been all the more reduced. Increased independence in the Communist states and further West German diplomatic and commercial penetration into the area would have grandly reinforced the NATO-Warsaw Pact military détente while distressing the leaderships of Moscow and Pankow.

Driven to a politically costly intervention, however, the Soviet leadership did more for the moment than to contain this détente, for the momentum of forward-rolling military operations is not so clearly controllable. Having defied world public opinion on Czechoslovakia, the Soviet leadership might feel that it had little more to lose in a further move into Rumania or Yugoslavia; if massive anti-Bonn propaganda were required as an adjunct to any such operations, Bonn in turn might have cause to fear that the military momentum would flow in its direction. The new military tensions of Central Europe in 1968 were thus in part paradoxical. Russian troops in Czechoslovakia might earlier have not seemed so threatening, but only natural, under the Warsaw Pact. Western nonmilitary influences in Eastern Europe might generally have seemed an insurance against Communist military moves westward. Yet when such nonmilitary influences forced a Soviet military move within what was still the "Communist" sector of Europe, the momentum could indeed be threatening. From the immediate standpoint of the NATO area's peace of mind, the Western success-cum-failure in Prague was worse than no change at all. If some sense of normalization and stability could be reestablished, if no military initiatives were taken into Rumania, Yugoslavia, or Austria, then the military relaxation of the mid-1960's might be resumed. Détente was not decisively rebuffed in Prague, but left undecided.

In the immediate aftermath of Czechoslovakia, there would again be some discussion of strengthening NATO forces, but the substantive content of such proposals remained unclear. The North Atlantic Council discussions in November of 1968 could simply be interpreted as part of an orchestrated propaganda indictment of the Russian disrespect for Czech freedom, meant to go along with other public statements reducing Soviet prestige in the eyes of the world. Vague hints of prospective action might also inhibit the Russians from repeating their intervention in Rumania, or, most of all, in Yugoslavia, where older traditions of independence from Moscow had been established. Soviet attacks on Bonn, citing special Soviet rights of intervention under the U.N. Charter, had been particularly threatening after the Czech intervention; talks of NATO force buildups might be an appropriate response, but the option of force reductions in conjunction with the Warsaw Pact was still left open.

As the Johnson Administration drew to a close, it seemed clear that the pattern of the mid-1960's had not yet been terminated. With European decisions that the United States might protest, and American decisions that the Bonn government would protest, the on-the-spot conventional capability of NATO forces had gradually but steadily been reduced by 1969, with any reversal of this trend far from decided. For the moment, the deterrent to aggression across the Elbe demarcation line depends as much as ever on the likelihood of nuclear escalation. Europe still seems so important to both sides that this deterrent is very credible. More than ever, each side seems willing to tolerate the demarcation line as it stands.

From 1964 on, Soviet strategic writings again had begun to acknowledge the possibility that a war in Europe might not have to escalate to the use of nuclear weapons as a matter of course.[4] Changes in official pronouncements here were matched in 1966 with Warsaw Pact maneuvers assuming no introduction of nuclears. Several explanations of the shift in Russian position are possible.

The Soviet pronouncements may simply have come as the response to the earlier series of Kennedy Administration statements stressing the limitation of war, and the importance of the nuclear-nonnuclear firebreak as a line of limitation. Steps taken by the United States to impose central control and a veto over battlefield nuclear weapons may have convinced the Russians that the escalation deliberately or inadvertently threatened in the Eisenhower years would now indeed be withheld. Fears that the United States had already accomplished a de facto proliferation of independent nuclear capability to West Germany, Greece, or Turkey may thus have been assuaged as new policies and new permissive action link devices were introduced. Yet the use of nuclears in any war in Central Europe was indeed as likely as ever.

Alternatively, this change in Soviet pronouncements may have been more calculated. If the success of the Berlin wall now allowed the Russians to forgo the conquest of West Berlin, then a threat of automatic nuclear escalation was not required to deter the Allies from sending an armored column down the Berlin Autobahn, since the Russians no longer were tempted to give the West occasion for such action. Any extreme stress on escalation to general war had a cost for the Russians (just as it plausibly had a cost for the West when the U.S. Administration had been engaging in such a stress); unwanted escalation might occur on some trivial point merely because no groundwork of communication had been laid to limit war. If a blind endorsement of escalation were not required for other purposes, it could be undesirable per se.

A Tenser Middle East

If Europeans were becoming more resigned to the political status quo, this hardly held true for residents of the Middle East in the 1960's. It is indeed difficult to get Arabs to acknowledge any status quo which does not eliminate the state of Israel altogether. In the early 1960's, the presence of a U.N. Emergency Force had helped to achieve a de facto tolerance for boundaries. Yet the stabilizing impact of this force was likely to diminish, with the prospect that the superpowers would be drawn in on opposite sides. To worsen the temptations for preemptive intervention, both the United States and Soviet Union were acquiring naval and air transport capabilities for more rapid and effective entry into the area.

The U.N. had first been used as an intermediary in the 1956 Middle East crisis.[5] Forces from nine nations had been dispatched to cover the Anglo-French withdrawal from the Suez Canal zone, and then were deployed along the Israeli-Egyptian border, informally as part of the Israeli withdrawal from the Sinai Desert, implicitly thereafter to prevent Arab terrorist raids and to keep open the Gulf of Aqaba. The U.N. participation had held joint backing in 1956, when both the U.S.S.R. and the United States favored a termination of the Anglo-French-Israeli invasion, but such agreement on a U.N. role was now eroding. The Cairo regime would thus be tempted to come out from behind the shield of the emergency force, perhaps to reacquire the leadership of the Arab world from the more bellicose Syrians.

Fears of seeming ungrateful to the U.N. might have accounted for an Egyptian reluctance to oust the emergency force earlier, but enough time had perhaps elapsed by May of 1967 to reduce such costs. President Nasser, with at least some Russian backing, would thus now venture to move his forces up to the Israeli border and close the Gulf of Aqaba. U.N. Secretary General Thant proved reluctant, perhaps with the Congo experience in mind, to resist Egyptian demands for the force's withdrawal, as long as the U.S.S.R. did not offer any backing for such resistance.

The magnitude of the Israeli victory in June of 1967 established a new territorial status quo,[6] one which solved some stability problems in the area, but raised others. The new frontiers were easier for Israel to defend against conventional military attack, but perhaps were more penetrable for terrorist groups. The prestige of the various Arab governments in the area was seriously weakened by their obvious territorial losses, making it difficult for them to control or inhibit terrorists even if they wanted to do so. None of these governments displayed any willingness or ability to negotiate with Israel.

Whatever the increase or decrease in territorial stability for the immediate area, the events of 1967 aggravated the cold war in that both the United States and the U.S.S.R. were more definitely drawn into commitments to the opposing sides. The termination of French military assistance forced the United States to become a principal supplier of weapons aid to Israel. The Soviet decision to dispatch a very visible fleet to the Mediterranean just prior to the Israeli victory made it imperative that this fleet remain when the Arabs seemed to need its support more than ever; the situation was similar with Soviet shipments of arms to the U.A.R. The Soviet fleet greatly intensified the confrontation of American and Russian commitments because American naval power had long been committed in force to the Mediterranean, and because the Soviet ships could induce speculation about a "turning of NATO's flank," perhaps relevant to areas such as Cyprus or Greece.

Russian gestures of redeploying some of the fleet into the Black Sea at the outset of the Nixon Administration would only partially relieve such concerns, for the world was now indelibly aware that the Russians were capable of such forward deployments, presumably at their leisure. Similarly incomplete in their reassurance were calculations that the NATO fleet would always far outnumber the Russians in the Mediterranean. For a host of scenarios, ranging from a coup in some North African country to new rounds of the Arab-Israeli war, the presence of Russian ships and landing forces might make a significant difference. When both super powers were reluctant to risk war, three ships getting to a harbor first might outweigh 10 coming later, however capable the 10 might be of outgunning and defeating the three. Commentators might even speculate about confrontations of Western and Soviet naval power in regions "east of Suez," from Yemen, Somalia, and East Africa all the way to Vietnam; however, the events of 1967 (especially the closing of the Suez Canal) paradoxically inhibited the flow of possible conflict, since the Russian Navy no longer could so easily deploy itself to the Red Sea and beyond. One might doubt also whether the conflicts of this region would as easily tempt the super powers into making commitments to opposing sides.

Polycentric Conflict East of Suez

If there had been any validity to the predictions of a breakup of alliance solidarity, these might most plausibly have been directed to what had once been called the Sino-Soviet bloc. The emergence of an open difference of interests between the U.S.S.R. and Communist China, with the launching of clearly counterproductive campaigns at various levels of interaction, might on balance have been a blessing for the Western alliance.[7] If the Russians and Chinese tied up and wasted some of their economic, political, and military strength checking and counteracting each other, then less of such strength might be left to be deployed against the United States and its allies. To the extent that the dispute concerned issues of ideological purity or interparty status, the widening of the Sino-Soviet dispute would be welcome.

On some other issues, however, a difference of interest might be less desirable. It was possible now that the U.S.S.R. desired some sort of détente with the West, and would not so generally condone the launching of guerrilla disorders throughout the world; the Chinese seemed to have opposite interests. Presumably the United States preferred that the Communist powers be in agreement in desiring détente, rather than being in disagreement about it. Conversely, such disagreement would be preferable to an agreement induced by any toughening of Soviet attitudes, whereby the Communist powers would all be opposed to détente.

If the United States were now to face a seriously hostile confrontation with China or any other Communist power, it would at least want to reexamine its earlier assumptions about the military solidarity of the Communist bloc. At the material worst, if one took Soviet pledges of military alliance with China as seriously as before, the Chinese might provoke a war with the West, into which the Russians would semi-voluntarily be drawn. The prospect of a Chinese nuclear weapon, which had been realized all too soon in the fall of 1964, seemed especially ominous, therefore, on the same triggering arguments that had sometimes been connected with the French Force de Frappe. This was not eased by rather frightening Chinese statements of indifference to general war casualties which had been issued in the late 1950's, statements which had been replaced with very moderate "no-first-use" declarations.[8]

The independent attitude of the Chinese and the very development of an independent Chinese nuclear capacity now, however, cast doubt on whether the U.S.S.R. would feel obligated to join any strategic imbroglio they had entered into. For the first time since 1945, it seemed plausible that the United States might have to confront a seriously hostile state not backed by the U.S.S.R. This uncoupling would encourage open speculation about strategic wars with Communist China alone, in scenarios almost religiously rejected earlier;[9] it could even lead to the earmarking of some U.S. strategic forces for use only against China, so that Russians might know that certain missiles, when launched, were not aimed at them. If nuclear proliferation had thus seemingly set up a new "major power" in China to confront the United States, it also helped to uncouple that power from a still far greater Russian military potential. Peking's statements had now ceased to refer to any automatic Russian retaliation for an American attack on the Chinese mainland, and Peking's A-bomb implicitly raised the same question—why would a Chinese bomb be required if Soviet retaliation against the United States were already assured?

If the Chinese could not drag Moscow into a nuclear war, perhaps they still have some leverage on the opposite end of the spectrum, in conventional or subconventional guerrilla war. Each Communist state might have to race to be the most zealous in supporting revolutions against the West. Russian statements generally had dismissed the introduction of tactical nuclear weapons in theaters outside of Europe, echoing the Chinese argument that such weapons could not reverse the outcome of "wars of national liberation." Perhaps the Russians now felt expansionist on their own in various parts of the "third world," or were simply being driven along by the new competition within the Communist bloc. Europe was presumably less subject to such ventures, but Soviet involvements in the Middle East, Yemen, or Vietnam might require assurances to the West that such operations need never go nuclear, that escalation to nuclear warfare in fact should generally remain unlikely. Fears of attempts at territorial aggrandizement for the "Soviet bloc" had thus persisted in the West, if only among those who attached great significance to the guerrilla war threat.[10]

The prospect of substantial American intervention in "counterinsurgency" situations around the world thus emerged quite significantly in the last year or two of the Kennedy Administration. Perhaps this was due to a misreading of Soviet intentions. Perhaps this came instead because the Chinese capacity for fomenting guerrilla insurrections around the world had been exaggerated, a capacity which the Chinese repeatedly announced they would use. But an American desire to confront Peking may simply have come from the form of the Chinese announcements themselves, rather than from any exaggerations of Chinese capability. Peking since 1957 had essentially chosen to engage in a "zero-sum" style of dialogue, first with regard to nuclear war, and then with regard to conventional or guerrilla war. If the Chinese no longer claimed to be callously and rashly indifferent to the loss of 300 million people in a nuclear war, they still persisted in avoiding all acknowledgments of mutual interest with the United States, in a style unmatched by Russian behavior at any time, even in the worst of the Stalinist years. However much one could infer an awareness of mutual interest from Peking's actual behavior, Peking's statements did not reinforce this, and many Americans would still require additional reassurance. However little Peking might actually be able to hurt the United States if it really tried, the United States might thus want to confront the Chinese to force at least an acknowledgment of coexistence, or to discourage any other states contemplating the adoption of a similar style of address.

If Communist China now far exceeded the U.S.S.R. in its desire for anti-American guerrilla war (as it claimed, perhaps in exaggeration of fact), its own capability for inducing such war could not immediately be so awesome.[11] It was difficult until 1963 and 1964 to find many clear anti-Western moves for which the Chinese could be given credit. The source of the Communist moves in Laos between 1959 and 1962 and been ambiguous. The 1962 Chinese humiliation of the Indian government had been very straightforwardly military, such that it would be difficult to replicate elsewhere, and easier for the United States to deter. Only the sharp upswing in the activities and accomplishments of the Viet Cong in South Vietnam now plausibly seemed to support Mao's image as a guerrilla-warfare genius; but even here the Chinese causal role might easily have been exaggerated if the Viet Cong or Hanoi were supplying the bulk of the material and all of the manpower.

It may always be difficult to weigh the "Chinese threat" in specific American decision-making on Vietnam in the mid-1960's. The major vocal challenge was clearly Peking's, and the vocal rationalization of U.S. policy may thus only responsively have come to claim that Peking was the source of all mischief in the area, or of guerrilla threats anywhere in the world. Hence it is very possible that American entry into Vietnam was based on a more complicated analysis of events, assigning Peking all the superficial significance but recognizing that the immediate threat to the Saigon regime emanated from Hanoi or even locally from the Viet Cong. To refute Peking while fighting Hanoi might be reasonable, just as reasonable as Hanoi's policy of allowing the Chinese to claim intellectual credit for a guerrilla war Vietnamese Communists were fighting. If some American officials really thought that counterinsurgency interventions were necessary to prevent Chinese (or Russian) expansion of influence, others may simply have desired to prevent a "local Communist" dominance, however independent it would be of Peking and Moscow. If an insurgent movement was independent, American decision-makers might yet wish to resist it, if it were anti-American in outlook, or antipluralist in domestic tone, or itself expansionist once power had been consolidated.

Discussions of the American Vietnam intervention have tended at great length to criticize or defend "domino theories," or comparisons with Munich.[12] Any loss of Vietnam to the Viet Cong might indeed set a precedent by seemingly confirming Mao's (or Giap's) theories of guerrilla warfare, or by exposing a general American lack of resolve in face of Chinese or other challenge, erasing once and for all the imagery of the Cuban missile crisis. As in other East-West crises, it might be difficult now for either side to concede the small issue without conceding too much more; and it might be impossible for either side to circumscribe itself enough to make possible an opponent's limited concessions. Critics might, however, note that American commitments have several times been deepened by actions described merely as fulfillments of it; there might yet have been ways to ease the United States out of Vietnam without developing any clear precedents, either of Communist guerrilla prowess or of American unreliability. One could argue, in any event, that the war in Vietnam was so special a case, in terms of absence of preexisting political cohesion and stable administration, that no meaningful precedent would have been set by a Viet Cong victory; conversely, the United States may have felt Vietnam to be worth holding for its own sake, if the regime there was threatened, no matter how illusory Communist guerrilla potential might be everywhere else.

The American commitment of sizable ground forces, and maintenance of a bombing campaign against North Vietnam, would by design or accident lead to a continual and hostile confrontation in some ways less intense than Korea, in some ways more so. The Korean War had involved larger armies in explicit combat with each other, including the army of Red China, but Russian participation had been more clandestine, not exposing any specifically American-Russian physical hostilities to the world. The war in Vietnam now saw Russian SAM missiles being fired regularly at American aircraft over North Vietnam, however,[13] while American planes regularly attempted to destroy SAM launching sites; Soviet personnel almost certainly were firing the SAM's and suffering casualties in American air attacks, an exchange which might have been thought unbearably unstable five years earlier in Cuba. Yet any more major eruption of Soviet-American hostilities, in Europe or elsewhere, remained remote, as both sides seemed intent on keeping the war limited.

By the end of 1967, American participation in Vietnam had escalated to the commitment of more than 500,000 American ground troops in South Vietnam (together with some 80,000 Americans deployed in Thailand and on ships at sea), and to a campaign of bombing extending to targets within the confines of Hanoi itself. If the prospect of an early Communist (Viet Cong) military victory had now been eliminated, no solution more favorable than stalemate was clearly within sight.

As American involvement in the war reached its peak, several interrelated prospects were seemingly being offered by the administration in response to critics at home and abroad. The bombings of North Vietnam perhaps might weaken Communist military forces in the south, and/or impose enough disutility on the Hanoi regime to dissuade it from continuing the war. Little clear evidence had emerged to support such hopes, as visitors to Hanoi repeatedly reported high morale among the North Vietnamese regime and populace,[14] and as the interdiction accomplished by such raids apparently touched only a small fraction of troops and supplies being dispatched toward the south. Yet one could expect the Hanoi regime to put up a brave front even if it were seriously distressed by the bombings, even if it were considering asking for negotiations at some future date. The Soviet Union at least placed great stress on the American bombing campaign as something it would like to see terminated, while Communist China continually disparaged any significance for bombings or for bombing pauses.[15]

Apart from the bombing, American ground operations against "main-force" Communist units might inflict similar losses and disutilities, denying the enemy the initiative of attacking more populated areas and liberating areas long held by the Viet Cong. In mid-1966 a hope was still being offered that large-scale American encounters with the main force would erode the strength of such units significantly in a year or two; fewer men and resources would then be required for such major military encounters, and more could be devoted to pacification programs. On such optimistic assumptions, the "war" itself would terminate either because the Viet Cong sought an explicit cease-fire, or because it had been debilitated to the point where it would quietly have to cease firing. A year more of intensive operations did not seem to confirm any such optimistic assumptions, however, and some military officers in the field predicted American involvement in substantial combat operations for as long as 10 years.[16]

With the decision of President Johnson not to seek reelection in 1968, it had become clear that the Vietnam War had less popular backing within the United States than had been usual for American military operations in the past. The suspension of bombing over most of North Vietnam in April, followed by a total suspension in November just prior to the election of Richard Nixon, suggested at least the United States would now have to consider outcomes appreciably less than total victory in Vietnam. The coming into office of Defense Secretary Clifford had on parallel lines placed a ceiling on the commitment of American ground forces to Vietnam, at approximately the 535,000 troops that had already been programmed as of the beginning of 1968. Negotiations with North Vietnamese delegations in Paris moved quite slowly, as neither side seemed yet decided on how much it was prepared to concede. Yet demands for substantial American concessions had clearly become more audible domestically in the United States, with some likely effect on the incoming Nixon Administration.

Barring any American operations which would be too directly humiliating for the U.S.S.R., the impact of Vietnam on Soviet-American relations was hard to measure. The U.S.S.R. would at times profess to be highly incensed by American participation in the war (for example, participation in a track meet was canceled in 1966, only to be resumed in 1967, with the payment of an indemnity for the previous year's cancellation). It seemed that Vietnam at times was driving the Russians to cut back on verbal détente, when solidarity with the Communist regime in Hanoi urgently demanded it; yet at other times (as at Glassboro) the war may have generated even more flattering exchanges, since the U.S.S.R. was concerned that material differences with the United States should not completely erode the détente. Real conflicts, including Vietnam and some other issues, thus were driving the two major powers into a moderately hostile confrontation, but the U.S.S.R. seemed uncertain as to whether to amplify or mask this hostility at the verbal level, and in sum apparently would do neither. As Americans and Russians were shooting at each other in the skies over North Vietnam, tourists and visitors from each country continued to find a welcome in the other, thus perhaps pushing to an extreme the limited-war model which first had emerged in Korea.

273

It had also been predicted that the Vietnam War would severely exacerbate American relations with Communist China. Here the trend was equally difficult to determine. As American air raids spread closer and closer to the Chinese border, the willingness of Peking to abstain from active intervention was presumably being sorely tried. The Cultural Revolution now saw the United States (and the U.S.S.R.) denounced in ever more vitriolic terms, suggesting little possibility for an improvement of relations; even friendly foreigners were insulted and excluded from China. Yet the Cultural Revolution also had the apparent effect of inducing substantial internal turmoil in China, such that military or political initiatives abroad seemed less likely. As the Vietnam War went on, therefore, the American public statements more often pinpointed Hanoi as the chief aggressor and enemy, rather than Peking. Chinese Communist hostility to the U.S.S.R. now at times even seemed to include actions helping the American effort in Vietnam, as with obstruction and delay of Soviet shipments of SAM equipment across China to Hanoi.[17]

The experience of the United States in Vietnam has had profound effects on American willingness to intervene to resist guerrilla movements elsewhere. The costs of the war have been high, and too many optimistic predictions have gone unfulfilled. The object of fear has shifted from Mao and China to guerrilla warfare in general, and then to Hanoi in particular; many commentators are thus convinced that the "domino theory" was exaggerated with regard to guerrilla warfare and Vietnam.

Yet in a more muted form, considerations of dominoes will influence the Nixon Administration, as it would any American government. As the United States disengages itself from Vietnam, the most important considerations for the President will be timing and momentum. It will be important that any Communist victory not be seen elsewhere as the wave of the future, and that enough American commitment remain so that other Communist forces will not sense an invitation to duplicate the Viet Cong's campaign. Too explicit a commitment to withdrawal will make the American operation seem like a surrender, with harmful consequences for the American image in other theaters in the future. Too subtle a commitment, however, may let bureaucratic inertia pull the United States into new campaigns which could prolong the war indefinitely. The President thus will face a series of choices, choices between earlier withdrawal and more convincing American resilience.

The Vietnamese Communists could make this choice easier or more difficult for the Nixon Administration. To respond to American moves by matching deescalations of violence will allow Nixon to withdraw troops faster, and this would reduce the casualties that Hanoi's forces suffer. Yet a quiet American withdrawal gives less of an impression of Communist victory and American defeat, and thus sacrifices momentum that could be applied to Laos, Cambodia, or Thailand. It also runs some risk that the Viet Cong's control of South Vietnam itself might be cast into doubt, for guerrilla cadres can melt when there is no war to wage, and the South Vietnamese Army must still be overcome even after American forces have been withdrawn.

Resignation to Strategic Parity

President Lyndon Johnson had inherited from his predecessor what might once have been thought an overwhelming offensive striking power; but in 1963 it was already unclear whether such an accumulation could remain strategically significant, if missile forces everywhere would soon move into new orders of magnitude. The meaningful American superiority of the early 1960's was likely to end (even if it was several times prolonged beyond American official hints that it was over), since the U.S.S.R. would sooner or later develop an ability to produce ICBM's in quantity at bearable costs. Any acceleration of American production then would have to be enormous to lower the Soviet second-strike capacity to what it had been before. Quantity production of Russian silo-based ICBM's, or simple qualitative perfection of submarine-based IRBM's, would force the United States to produce its own missiles in the thousands (and to accomplish enormous breakthroughs in antisubmarine warfare), or to accept an end to its meaningful counterforce option; now American cities might suffer horrible devastation even if the United States had chosen to strike first.

If it had been intended only to insure that the U.S.S.R. would not outpace the United States to some threatening degree, the projected American missile buildup was excessive. It had become clear well before the assassination that the United States probably did not need all the Minuteman missiles programmed, and this objective was cut back to 1,000 of such ICBM's plus 656 Polaris sea-based IRBM's, a few Titan missiles retained in the arsenal, and a supplementary bomber force whose life-span would remain uncertain. If the original assumption had been that Russian missile production over the 1957-1963 period would rival such figures, the Russians had seemingly lagged far behind, perhaps at times further behind than was healthy.

275

Several transitional proposals were now exchanged on strategic force issues, at least in part to maintain and expand the sensation of détente; it might be possible to justify some mutual gestures even where their substantive arms control implications were not so clear. Reciprocal announcements in April of 1964 of American and Soviet reductions in nuclear weapons material production may simply have been intended to serve as a psychologically reassuring first step;[18] the overkill thus forbidden could not have perceptibly increased the level of destruction in general war, but would reinsure such destruction (perhaps desirably).

In a follow-up to the negotiation of the Test-Ban Treaty, American negotiators had similarly proposed mutual destruction of obsolescent medium-range bombers (American B-47, Soviet Badger), presumably on something like a one-for-one basis.[19] If the bombers really were so obsolescent as to be phased out of use shortly in any case, the American proposal was simply another substantively meaningless move intended to extend the climate of détente.

More serious concern, however, would have to be directed to the emerging balance in the missile field; despite occasional allusions to a vaguer American "superiority," Secretary McNamara still seemed resigned to an imminent invulnerability of the Soviet strategic force, an invulnerability precluding any meaningful American "damage-limiting" preemptive strikes. Yet if the U.S.S.R. were to be conceded a deterrent, this would not leave the United States indifferent to all possible augmentations of the Soviet strategic arsenal. The stability of ICBM vs. ICBM confrontations was assured for the moment, but certain technological developments might upset this stability. Very extensive Soviet procurement of missiles would also make American and Western publics uneasy, regardless of the immediate invulnerability of the U.S. deterrent force. And a move towards ABM defensive missiles, capable of intercepting incoming ICBM's, might seriously complicate the calculations of mutual deterrence.

Perhaps to avert force augmentations that might thus threaten strategic stability, the United States in 1964 proposed a freeze on the quantities and characteristics of bomber and missile forces in the major powers.[20] The freeze would often be described as an attempt to permanize American superiority, and it is plausible that some of its support within the American government derived from such an interpretation. Although Soviet strategic forces had already reached a level where a whimsical American first strike would not be credible, such escalation might still be expected in very serious circumstances. Holding

Soviet strategic forces at their numerically inferior level would at least bolster the public credibility of American toughness in crisis situations, as well as reducing wartime damage to the United States for some scenarios. On such calculations, especially if the calculations were publicized widely enough, the U.S.S.R. might be expected to reject a freeze at 1964 weapons levels.

Yet the United States in such a freeze would similarly agree to forgo several years of Minuteman and Polaris procurement, and the Russians might value the economic savings of a frozen numerically asymmetric confrontation, especially if it seemed to deter a U.S. attack as surely as a costly arms race. The freeze might not commit the U.S.S.R. publicly to inferiority, if the exact numbers of missiles on each side were not written into the treaty for all to see. Problems would persist, however, because the United States still required some inspection as a part of the freeze and, perhaps more importantly, because the freeze extended beyond offensive weapons. For apart from any technological break-throughs which might tempt the U.S.S.R. to accumulate a destabilizing form of offensive missile force, the freeze proposal precluded deployment of ABM missile defense systems, now seen as most threatening by the Johnson Administration.

Soviet Moves to ABM

Some serious objections could be raised to ABM. The population protection offered by antimissile defense might reduce expected general-war casualties enough to make such a war seem desirable for one or both of the major powers. This argument had first seemed appropriate with the deployment of vulnerable liquid-fueled missiles, where each side might have been better off militarily striking first, where only the damage suffered by the civilian sector during the exchanges of strikes would deter everyone from racing to be the first to attack. Reducing general-war casualty figures to 20 million might make war likely even on less calculated motives; even if no nation would launch a war deliberately at that price, the risks of marginal escalatory steps might seem more acceptable, with a danger, therefore, that general war would ultimately result. Allegorically, the argument could be stated roughly as follows: in a room full of men armed with machine guns, the first to invest in a bullet-proof vest might be a source of tension.

If other factors kept down the likelihood of escalation to strategic war under any circumstances, one might have found ABM to be less of a threat in this regard. With the deployment in the early 1960's of solid-fueled missiles which could be "hardened" under layers of concrete, it had seemed for a time that this instability had been eliminated, so that the overkill deterrent might no longer be required. If more than one attacking missile were required to destroy one missile in its silo on the other side, whoever struck first would consume more of his own missiles than he destroyed of the enemy's; logically the scenario would thus never arise where both sides could be militarily better off in striking first, where whoever struck first would win.

The assumption of secure missile forces, able to ride out the other side's counterforce attack, came into some doubt by the middle 1960's, however. Even large amounts of concrete would not protect a silo against attack if a very accurate incoming ICBM with a large warhead landed within 600 feet; and "clusters" of warheads might be carried on a single missile, such that a single missile on either side might now threaten to take out five or 10 missiles on the other. Both these developments might make the first strike very attractive in military terms, so that large amounts of population overkill would be required to deter such an attack with any reassuring certainty; population-protecting ABM might thus again be objectionable because it was destabilizing.

ABM was not, however, thought threatening by all commentators.[21] An establishment of protection against missile attack on each side, by some combination of mutual agreement and defensive technological advantage, might be justified on several grounds. In what is possibly a trivial case, such protection would guard against accidental misfires of single missiles, or against unauthorized firings by a lone military commander who has gone berserk or rebelled against higher authority.

ABM might similarly keep minor powers from inflicting any damage on cities of the major powers, thus perhaps discouraging such powers from developing nuclear weapons or delivery systems. Even if such systems were developed (China detonated its first H-bomb in 1967), the existence of ABM protection for the major powers might make their beneficent intervention more credible in minor conflicts, since the "nth" nuclear weapons system presumably could no longer deter major powers from such intervention. "Light" ABM systems, costing only a few billion and effective only against powers other than the United States and U.S.S.R., might thus be construed as an antiproliferation step. But ABM development could also generate new difficulties in curbing the spread of nuclear weapons, especially if the ABM's warhead itself had to be nuclear. If other powers began requesting ABM protection for themselves, it might be difficult for the major powers to resist such demands, even if the warhead of an ABM was easily convertible to a counterpopulation device, even if the rocket of the ABM might serve as a medium-range surface-to-surface rocket.

ABM, moreover, could be justified in that the Russians seemed to want it, that this alone was a weapons system which could be deployed without Russian objection, or even with Russian approval; if continuation of détente were desirable, ABM would not stand in the way.

Russian claims emerged repeatedly in the middle 1960's that substantial progress was being made on ABM development, claims which could be explained in a number of ways. Some commentators referred simply to a traditional Russian tendency to stress defense, and pointed to the presumed Russian overinvestment in air defenses at various points in the late 1940's and early 1950's.[22] If the Russian military had a tendency to define its role as shielding the fatherland, perhaps with the experience of Napoleon and Hitler to set the stage, it might be politically and psychologically necessary for the Russians to do "all they could" to build a missile-defense system, even if that system could never be effective. Aside from any military foibles, one could argue that the Soviet government would more easily be able to exploit even an imperfect ABM system, in terms of convincing its public that it should indeed run the risks of some crisis. While cynics in the United States might delight in debunking the reliability of any antimissile defense erected, together with any passive defense measures required to supplement it, a Soviet society, with control over news media, might be able to reassure its public that it could survive World War III if it had to.

A more suspicious interpretation of Soviet behavior might fear grand strategic aspirations, especially if the ABM deployment could be coupled with markedly increased inventories and accuracies of Soviet intercontinental missiles. If Soviet missiles or missile clusters could plausibly target all of the Minuteman sites in the United States, with likely CEP's shrinking enough to allow a fairly good kill rate, then only the American Polaris submarine-based missiles would remain to constitute a retaliatory force; for the short run, moreover, it seemed that any ABM system would be especially effective against submarine-based missiles, given their slower incoming speeds and lower trajectories. The risk of another possible Soviet splendid first strike might thus emerge.

A general explanation perhaps most favorable to Soviet intentions would take such strategic pronouncements on missile defense at face value: that the world will be more attractive if the maximum destruction the two superpowers can inflict on each other is reduced. If only 10 to 20 million deaths could be threatened on each side, rather than 100 to 150 million, deterrence of major war perhaps would still be assured, but the fabric of society itself might no longer be perpetually in question. Reduction of the strategic threat might reduce social tensions in the societies involved even if the war were never to occur, since the prospect and possibility of total destruction would be convincingly removed, perhaps allowing individuals to contemplate long-run plans without the conditional disclaimer "as long as there isn't any war." Similar sentiments had emerged somewhat earlier in support of air defense programs in the United States at the start of the 1950's. Soviet statements until recently have not labeled any matching U.S. move to ABM development or deployment as hostile, but almost as desirable. Weapons which destroyed incoming missiles were pictured as straightforwardly opposite to weapons which destroyed people.

But Americans could note that more casualties, rather than fewer, might result in a general war after an arms race in ABM and offensive weaponry had run its course. If either or both of the powers wanted to be absolutely sure of killing 75 million civilians on the other side, given the uncertainties of untested defensive missiles and untested offensive penetration aids, then offensive strikes might be programmed to remove uncertainties, i.e., most probably to kill many more than 75 million if war ever put the probability calculations to the test. The Russians might have responded by questioning the need for a large assured destruction capability, arguing that political pressures for the acquisition of offensive penetration aids could be avoided if the issues were stated properly on each side.[23]

From 1964 to 1968 a peculiar sort of debate thus ran its course, with Soviet spokesmen uniformly defending ABM missile defense systems, and most but not all American commentators opposing them. For the time the U.S.S.R. had apparently become the apostle of defenses, and the United States the spokesman for overkill. Despite objections repeatedly voiced in the United States, the U.S.S.R. moved ahead with some kind of ABM deployment in the mid-1960's. Reports of such a deployment in 1963 had been disproved, but satellite reconnaissance confirmed that the Russians had subsequently begun erecting a missile-defense around Moscow, similar to systems considered and rejected by the United States earlier in the decade, systems not too difficult for U.S. missiles to penetrate.[24]

While the major Soviet threat seemed to lie in the ABM area, the United States response remained moderate. Despite strong pressures from Congress and from the Joint Chiefs of Staff, Defense Secretary McNamara avoided any commitment to a full ABM deployment in the United States, thus still offering the U.S.S.R. an option of mutual abstention. Rather, the major American response came with the development and procurement of penetration aids designed to fool and bypass Soviet defenses: Polaris missiles now were gradually replaced by Poseidon, and Minuteman I and II by Minuteman III. The totals of American missiles would not be increased as part of the reinsurance of retaliatory capabilities: penetration aids were applied to a fixed number of delivery vehicles to renew their ability to destroy Soviet cities. Furthermore, McNamara in September of 1967 approved a limited deployment of ABM,[25] costing only about $5 billion and presumably ineffective against any serious Soviet countercity missile attack.

Soviet Offensive Missiles

While such a "light" deployment was extensively described as shielding American cities against a primitive Chinese attack, another option applied in the anti-Soviet context: shielding Minuteman silos against increasingly accurate Soviet offensive missiles, an objective which McNamara alluded to less strongly in his statement but which was fully consistent with his stress on assured retaliatory destruction. By 1968, the picture of the strategic weapons "ABM vs. overkill" debate between the U.S.S.R. and United States had to change in any event, for a significant expansion of Soviet offensive missile forces became apparent, attracting considerably more attention than the rudimentary Moscow ABM deployment.

Quantitatively the number of Soviet rockets aimed at North America was projected to rise from 350 in 1965 to about 850 by the end of 1968 (of which 700 were intercontinental ICBM missiles, and the rest launchable from submarines). Launching sites for 1,000 Soviet ICBM's have been detected by American photographic reconnaissance satellites, and the Russians might soon have this number of such missiles, to equal the American total in the category (the United States, however, possesses an additional 600 or more submarine-based Polaris missiles). Clearly the unanswered question was whether the Russians would be content with 1,000 ICBM plus 200 submarine-launched ballistic missiles, or whether the rapid rate of increase would continue. Unlike the United States, which remained committed to 1,000 Minutemen and 41 Polaris submarines with 16 missiles each, the U.S.S.R. had not announced any levels at which it would level off.

The weight-carrying capacities of Russian ICBM's are greater than those of the American Minuteman missile, moreover, so that the total "throw-weight" at the U.S.S.R.'s disposal might already have matched that of the United States. Russian nuclear warheads had also been tested at larger explosive megatonnages than those of the United States, so that there would soon be a "megatonnage gap" in which the U.S.S.R. could deliver more total explosive power to the United States than the United States could deliver to the Soviet Union.

The increase in numbers of Soviet missiles came at a time when technological developments were generally casting greater doubt on the invulnerability and stability of all land-based missile forces. Especially disturbing is the development of multiple warhead clusters (MIRV) for missiles, such that one of the larger Soviet missiles might be fired to take out 10 or more U.S. cities, or missile sites. The development of MIRV has not come unilaterally from the Soviet side. Indeed, some of the earliest work on multiple warheads came as part of American efforts to counteract anticipated Soviet progress on ABM defenses. Yet if both sides move ahead with MIRV, this may not cancel out the impact on the strategic balance, but may worsen it. As Soviet missile numbers approach those of the United States, the prospect of multiple warheads threatens to restructure the mathematics of the force exchange again, so that whoever strikes first will come out ahead, with a consequent risk of unwanted general war.

Accuracies of intercontinental missiles, moreover, continue to improve, so that destruction of even a well-protected missile silo might become highly probable for any war scenario. Some reversion to concealment and mobility may thus be required for any second-strike invulnerability, to maintain a strategic balance that has been so confidently taken for granted since the 1961-1962 move to solid-fueled missiles. Increased submarine basing may be required, or perhaps mobile land basing like the railroad-based Minuteman program which was canceled in 1961, for cement hardening will not ensure the survival of a siloed missile if an atomic or hydrogen warhead impacts close enough to it.

In all fairness, the Soviet Union may have every right to seek to match the number of American missiles, although it as yet gives little assurance that this is all it intends to do. Yet if Moscow had remained content with less than this, MIRV as well as ABM might not have forced as much caution on the United States. The world in 1963 had learned to live with a strategic balance in which the United States could meaningfully threaten to strike first. It could be very comfortable in 1966 with a balance in which neither dared strike first. But how much balance would there be in 1972 if both the United States and Soviet Union could plausibly anticipate advantages in initiating nuclear war?

If MIRV is the major culprit in that it threatens to facilitate counterforce attacks on missiles in Siberia and Montana, the situation may not be beyond remedy. It is possible that insufficient testing has been accomplished to count multiple warheads as a reliable weapons system; such tests, when conducted, are fairly easily detected. A ban on testing thus seems a useful arms control checkpoint, since neither side could dare use such a complicated device otherwise, and could hardly cash in on it very much politically.

If testing cannot be halted for some reason, this does not necessarily doom the world to war. The calculations on preemptive war for the moment ignore submarine-based missiles on either side, against which MIRV or any missiles will be ineffective. If MIRV eliminates the ICBM's in Montana or Siberia as viable deterrents, it also magnifies each Polaris submarine as a deterrent by multiplying the targets it can hit from 16 to 48 (someday to 160).

Holding firm at current American offensive force levels in the late 1960's thus ran a risk that the U.S.S.R. would continue the rapid expansion of its strategic arsenal, with psychological and perhaps military costs for the United States. Yet it also remained plausible that the U.S.S.R. was only seeking a nominal parity, perhaps at the level of 1,600 launchers, so that any American move to procure additional offensive missiles would upset a balance that might otherwise be maintained. The ABM prospect had already threatened a new "arms race," and "new round" of spending on strategic weapons, when such spending had fallen off in recent years; a new procurement of offensive weapons would increase this threat all the more. The Johnson Administration thus remained disposed to hold the numbers of missiles constant, while increasing their destructive power and certainty of penetrating to target. The numbers are easily noticeable, and perhaps more provocative if one alters them; the characteristics of each missile are more difficult to notice or monitor, so that restraint here would be unlikely in any event.

Through 1968 the two superpowers exchanged hints of being willing to negotiate on both ABM and offensive missiles. These indications to some extent may have been intended for the satisfaction of other states dragging their heels on signing the Nuclear Nonproliferation Treaty, states which demanded some "equality of sacrifice" from the United States and U.S.S.R. Yet they also showed a more open-minded Soviet view on the ABM question. Had the Czech intervention not occurred, such negotiations would already have been commenced before the elections of 1968; as it was, the attitudes of the new American President and Secretary of Defense left their prospects somewhat unclear, and the Strategic Arms Limitation Talks (SALT) were postponed into the fall of 1969.

The issue has thus become less abstract; both powers have in effect embarked on limited deployments of ABM, with the American deployment being officially described as limited, while the Russians hint they are going much further. Both sides are developing multiple warheads for their offensive missiles and are improving the accuracy of such missiles. The U.S.S.R. is continuing to add to the number of its missiles. Officially the United States has come to stress a ban on ABM and a freeze on the number of offensive missiles on each side. Officially the Soviet Union objects to improvements in offensive missile capabilities while only beginning to acknowledge that ABM might also be limited as part of good arms control.

If an impasse were to result, support might grow again in the United States for the image of an across-the-board "superiority," encompassing both full ABM protection against Soviet missiles, and new offensive weapons to threaten horrendous casualties on the Soviet population. Fears that the Russians were seeking the political advantages of a similar image of across-the-board superiority would strengthen the arguments for such an American effort; a seriously stepped-up arms race would then result, with large sums of money being spent in a fashion which may not leave the Soviet-American détente undisturbed.

If the U.S.S.R. desires détente, for its own sake or for an avoidance of defense spending which can be channeled instead into consumer goods, the SALT negotiations may yet head off a major renewal of the strategic weapons procurement contest. Soviet statements have become less doctrinaire on the desirability of ABM. If Vietnam and Middle East tensions, or the special desires of the Soviet military establishment, instead necessitate a heavy investment in offensive missiles and ABM, the arms race may be on again. Similar results apply if the United States military demands investment in a series of new strategic weapons systems, or if the President feels that such investments are necessary to prove American resolve in political contests with the U.S.S.R.

For each side, it will be important to signal that it has something to give up in strategic weapons procurement, if and only if the other gives up something. Critics of American policy might thus lament that testing goes ahead on a possible MIRV system; defenders of this policy will argue that only thus can the U.S.S.R. be motivated to want to halt deployment of ABM, or production of additional ICBM's. It is probably a mistake in any event to worry about MIRV research causing World War III. The major considerations are avoiding wasteful military expenditures and avoiding the process of mutual political insult that inevitably attaches to such expenditures. Doing so will be difficult, because history since 1945 indeed suggests serious political advantages that can be reaped from temporary images of superiority in strategic weapons. Yet achieving an agreement is not yet determined to be impossible, and will not be qualitatively more difficult after MIRV tests, as compared with before.

Nonproliferation

If strategic weapons cause part of Soviet-American tensions, they alleviate other parts. Yet the effect of such weapons can certainly change if they spread into the hands of many more powers. It thus comes as no surprise that the closest Soviet-American cooperation one has seen in the post-1945 world came in the negotiation of a Nuclear Nonproliferation Treaty.

The problem is not new, but of late it has become much more real. Imminent nuclear proliferation has been predicted often enough in the past, but nuclear technology again and again has turned out to be less practical and more expensive than had been so optimistically assumed in 1945. Yet nuclear reactor technology by 1967 was at last catching up with predictions. Even a nation indifferent to weapons capabilities might soon stumble into them as it pursued the civilian projects which had finally become feasible; powers less indifferent to such weapons could now plausibly use civilian economic development as a covering excuse.

The United States had of course been devoting attention to the proliferation threat for some years now. A rationalization for the multilateral force (MLF) proposal had been that it would preclude German desires for a nationally independent nuclear force. Physical proximity to weapons, even where the United States retained a veto on use, presumably might satisfy the status and prestige hungers of Germans and other West European NATO members. This rationalization had been premised, however, on a quiet acceptance of the plan by most NATO members, with little open resistance and no need for American pressure, and no detailed explications of the exact significance of the American veto. The premise had been proved quite wrong by late 1963: the MLF became an objectification of American-French disagreement, an embarrassment to the West German government, and an undesirable financial burden in the view of other NATO members. As part of the general move to decrease the flow of charges and countercharges between the American and the French Governments, President Johnson now directed that the United States no longer stress the MLF scheme and slowly reduce such commitments to it as had been made.[26]

Abandoning the MLF might do more than ease relations with De Gaulle, however, for the proposal had seemed a major obstacle to any nonproliferation treaty with the Soviet Union. Yet the U.S.S.R. now again seemed more intent on embarrassing the West Germans than on denying them nuclear weapons, since it demanded a very explicit renunciation of the MLF proposal and a ban even on long-standing "two key" arrangements and on "nuclear consultation" within NATO.[27] Western suspicions of Soviet motives here may well have been justified; yet Soviet suspicions might also have been aroused by earlier discussions of MLF schemes which only normally had specified a clear American veto, but occasionally had suggested eliminating it after a time.

An explicit withdrawal of the MLF proposal was not easy for the United States to arrange. Individuals within the American State Department were still intent on pushing the scheme, but the major obstacle to its open abandonment came now from West Germany. The Bonn Government had been coaxed out onto the MLF limb by the United States, at the price of worsened West German relations with France; it thus saw any abandonment of the MLF as just one more embarrassing Soviet-American accommodation indifferent to any voice for the Federal Republic, even though the substance of the MLF had never been valued very highly in Germany.[28] It was not in fact until the emergence of the "grand coalition" of Christian Democrats and Social Democrats at the end of 1966 that the United States would more clearly be able to escape the MLF snare, since the German Socialists were in principle opposed to any German possession of nuclear weapons. West German objections to the nonproliferation agreement remained, but would be expressed on other grounds.[29]

With a surer implicit American abandonment of the MLF, Russian demands on the scope of a nonproliferation treaty were reciprocally eased over time; the broader issue of an ultimate multilateral force (if Europe were ever to unite politically and inherit the nuclear weapons of one or more of its components) would be left vague so that each side might interpret a treaty draft in its own way. If Russian statements on proliferation to Germany had heretofore been largely propagandistic, the summer of 1967 may at last have seen a real Soviet concern on areas much more immediately unstable than Central Europe: the Middle East and the Indian subcontinent. Thus by January of 1968 the United States and the Soviet Union had agreed on the terms of a nonproliferation treaty to be offered in turn to all other nations for their signatures.[30] Yet the major power alignment here may unfortunately have come late.

Several different factors may cause various nations to resist the Nuclear Nonproliferation Treaty.[31] The asymmetrical form of any such treaty might seem politically humiliating; it has been argued, perhaps seriously, that the current treaty bestows an unacceptably inferior status on nations still outside the nuclear club for as long as the current five members are not required to make greater sacrifices themselves. To remove such formalistic objections, the major powers of course might submit to more stringent arms control agreements, perhaps to a comprehensive test ban forbidding underground tests, to a production cutoff on fissionable material or a bomb stockpile reduction, or to some sort of freeze on strategic weapons inventories. Yet none of these proposals is clearly acceptable in substance to both the U.S.S.R. and United States for the moment, nor would they all be so clearly conducive to the interests of world peace. It might be argued, for example, that a meaningful Soviet-American guarantee to India against Chinese attack (to make an Indian national nuclear weapons program unnecessary) would be enhanced by increasing these two powers' nuclear stockpiles and by procuring ABM, both forbidden under the above proposals.

For a nation not particularly deficient in political or economic prestige, such as Canada, Sweden, or West Germany, nuclear weapons might seem less immediately attractive, at least while the list of countries acquiring such weapons has not yet become so long as to induce humiliating comparisons. For India, perhaps undergoing a more immediate disparagement by other states, nuclear weapons ownership might conversely seem a shortcut to international self-respect; French and Chinese self-respect have clearly been enhanced in similar acquisitions of nuclears, and the image of Britain as a great power has not been shortened thereby.

On the question of military security arrangements, India may feel threatened by a combination of Communist Chinese conventional and nuclear power, a threat which recurring Chinese no-first-use declarations diminish only slightly. The Indian government might feel deterred in some future Himalayan confrontation, whatever the declarations, from massing troops in a way vulnerable to Chinese nuclear attacks, even if Peking's troops were massed similarly just across the frontier. In this interpretation Indian nuclear weapons would deter the Chinese from so massing their troops, or at least deter any Chinese threat of tactical nuclear attacks on Indian positions. Similarly, the latent threat of air attack against Indian cities would be made less salient.

Outside guarantees against Chinese attack might be undermined by the subtlety with which Peking could exploit marginal Himalayan tactical situations, with Peking thereby intending perhaps only to subject the Indian government to international humiliations, or to tie up forces during some Indian internal unrest. India's commitment to neutrality between the United States and the Soviet Union might also be upset by any guarantees: insurance from either power may alienate the other, while a joint guarantee may be politically impossible to arrange.

Israel in turn will have to fear the ultimate conventional military potential of the Arab states, even if an Arab atomic capability is unlikely for the near future. Outside defense assistance in the event of an Arab attack might someday not come quickly enough to repulse or to deter such attack. Outside retaliatory punishment might never be executed if all of Israel had already been overrun; Israeli submarines carrying nuclear-armed missiles under the Mediterranean could ultimately constitute a more effective guarantee.

West Germany's security problem has been significantly different from that of India or Israel; Bonn might have found a continuance of earlier arrangements entirely satisfactory, with recourse to national nuclear capabilities seeming neither necessary nor desirable. An American response to any assault on Western Europe has been fairly continuously understood since 1945, since it has lacked the drastic shifts of focus which occurred in South Asia and the Middle East. If one ever came to believe that America was deterred from escalation to nuclears in the event of a European war, then a West German desire for nuclear weapons independence might become very salient; for the time Bonn's fears will be more tentative. Yet the Soviet-American Geneva negotiations on a nonproliferation agreement might seem symptomatic of a growing American divergence of interest from Europe, thus causing German concern. If the nonproliferation treaty were not accompanied by recurrent pressures toward American troop withdrawal, and by the diversions of Vietnam, Bonn's objections to the treaty might have rested more narrowly on the possible negotiation points vis-à-vis the U.S.S.R. being gratuitously surrendered, on considerations of prestige, and on a few real fears of industrial handicaps. As it was, the Federal Republic seemed ready to foresake some of this negotiator's legalism it had stockpiled so long, but fears of American changes of attitude emerged nonetheless to establish new resistance to the treaty.

Hopefully, the military requirement for nuclear weapons might be limited to one or two states at the most, or perhaps totally eliminated. If Israel's victory in the summer of 1967 had decisively dissuaded the Arab states from thoughts of a war of eradication, then atomic deterrents might not have been needed any more; yet this was yet far from certain, and opposite arguments might be generated now in Israel in face of an apparently weak Western commitment to the country. If Indian requirements for prestige and self-respect could be satisfied in other ways, the Chinese military threat might not require an Indian nuclear force on military or strategic grounds; yet the peace of the world, on the other hand, might not have seemed so threatened if India nonetheless moved to get a bomb.

Yet the most significant argument will perhaps have little to do with military strategy per se. Nations can oppose a strict nonproliferation treaty on economic grounds, not merely because of inspection procedures possibly opening one's facilities to industrial espionage, but because there may be inherent economic sacrifices in any halt whatsoever to weapons proliferation. To be full competitors in the commercial nuclear energy field, countries may have to be free to wander into research areas that might constitute de facto bomb capabilities. Older technical assumptions might have seen any production of weapons-grade material as a resource allocation clearly deviant from a maximization of civilian benefits; current developments, however, dictate that electric-power reactors, and the separation plants to purify spent plutonium for reuse in such reactors, will generate bomb material almost as a matter of course. Soon only the time needed to pack such material into a bomb may be left to keep a nation "nonnuclear"; if that time lag is now a matter of years, knowledge of weapons-assembly techniques might soon reduce it to a matter of months.

A less strict control (as with the Soviet-American treaty presented in 1968) would at least preclude all testing of bombs in all environments and the insertion of weapons-grade materials into actual bomb casings; but as long as the plutonium was kept away from such casings (casings perhaps already designed and preassembled), it is not clear what inspectors could denounce. To discourage nations such as India, Israel, and the U.A.R. from rushing to develop bomb-casing designs, and from accumulating weapons-grade material, it might be necessary to provide much tighter guarantees of substantial great-power policing and intervention that would be very difficult to achieve. Alternatively, civilian nuclear programs might have to be circumscribed to erase mutual suspicions and to prevent the generation of weapons-grade materials; but this would require a different nonproliferation treaty, and probably some pledges of great-power economic compensation for the economic sacrifices of those who would have to dump their plutonium rather than enrich it.

A treaty simply pledging nations not to produce "weapons" might, however, become a stabilizer, sufficient to halt any rush to actual weaponry, even if bomb-producing technology thus came into many nations' possession by roundabout means. Much would depend on the way proliferation was discussed during and after the negotiation of the treaty. If nations were still tempted to brandish de facto weapons under a euphemism of "parcels of reactor fuel," then the treaty might become another irrelevant Kellogg-Briand Pact. If the nonproliferation pledge is taken more seriously all around, however, the cycle of arguments can snowball in the opposite direction, with each near-nuclear nation seeing its rivals to be sufficiently inhibited by the treaty. Inspection requirements might thus in the end become only symbolic, or even dispensable, as the halting of proliferation depended on the generation of a climate of confidence rather than on physical obstacles.

The threat of proliferation in a sense has to terminate the cold war aspects of strategic weapons confrontations. If proliferation is halted, it will only be through the active rather than the passive cooperation of the United States and Soviet Union. If proliferation is not halted, there will be many more than two states capable of the horrendous destruction we have expected from the Soviet and American air forces since 1953.

Figures

Figure 1

Military Spending, United States and U.S.S.R., 1945-1968

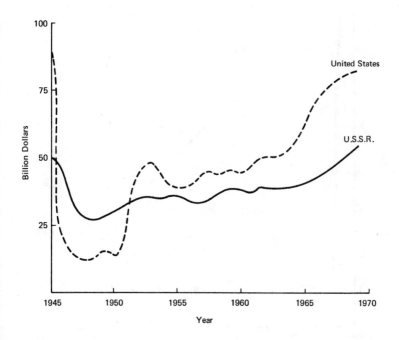

Note: Soviet spending is nominal defense category, plus defense-related research and development. Figure is given in dollars, converted from rubles at ratios of domestic purchasing power, rather than legal exchange rates.

293

Figure 2

Effective Ground Forces, United States and U.S.S.R., 1945-1968

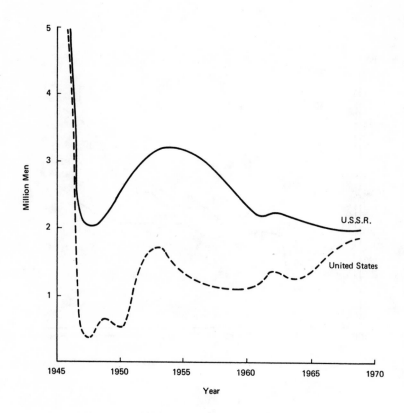

Note: U.S. estimates include Army and Marine Corps. Totals reflect men in militarily functional units, i.e., as opposed to units simply being processed for discharge, etc.

Figure 3

Atomic-Capable Bomber Aircraft, United States and U.S.S.R., 1945-1968

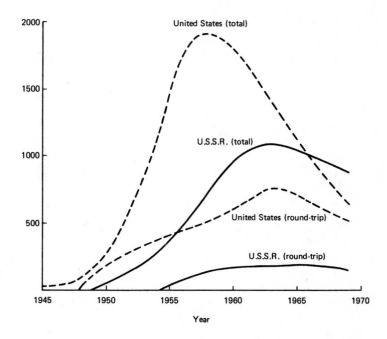

Note: For early years, figure is limited by number of nuclear weapons presumed available. Lower line for each country indicates bombers capable of unrefueled round-trip missions.

Figure 4

Missiles Capable of Striking at Opposing Homeland, United States and U.S.S.R., 1956-1968
(ICBM, submarine-based IRBM, and land-based IRBM when deployed forward)

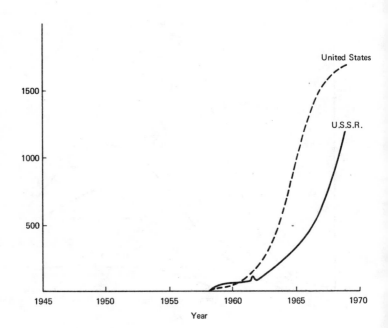

Note: Figures above compare with those presented in Samuel P. Huntington, *The Common Defense* (New York: Columbia University Press, 1961); William Kaufmann, *The McNamara Strategy* (New York: Harper and Row, 1964); Lincoln Bloomfield, Walter Clemens, and Franklyn Griffiths, *Khrushchev and the Arms Race* (Cambridge, Mass.: MIT Press, 1966); and Institute for Strategic Studies, *The Military Balance* (London: Institute for Strategic Studies, various years).

Notes

Notes to Chapter 1

1. See P.M.S. Blackett, *Fear, War, and the Bomb* (New York: McGraw-Hill, 1948), pp. 9-39. See also reviews in *Bulletin of the Atomic Scientists,* v (February, 1949), 34-44; and for a differing interpretation, review by Carl Kaysen, *Bulletin of the Atomic Scientists,* v (December, 1949), 340-43.

2. Casualty figures for bombing campaigns in World War II are to be found in W. Craven and J.L. Cate, *The Army Air Forces in World War II* (Chicago: University of Chicago Press, 1950-1953), Vol. III, p. 801; Vol. V, pp. 722, 725, 749, 754.

3. Blackett, op. cit., pp. 40-47. For an alternative, more farsighted, view, see Bernard Brodie, *The Absolute Weapon* (New York: Harcourt Brace, 1946), esp. pp. 28-34.

4. "The Balance of Military Power," *The Atlantic Monthly,* clxxxvii (June, 1951), 21-27.

5. Ibid.

6. See Blackett, op. cit., pp. 55-60; and Vannevar Bush, *Modern Arms and Free Men* (New York: Simon and Schuster, 1949), pp. 48-112.

7. John L. Chapman, *Atlas: The Story of a Missile* (New York: Harper and Bros., 1960) pp. 25-38.

8. Neville Brown, *Nuclear War* (London: Pall Mall Press, 1964), p. 70.

9. David E. Lilienthal, *The Atomic Energy Years* (New York: Harper and Row, 1965), pp. 119-20; Harry S. Truman, *Years of Trial and Hope* (Garden City, N.Y.: Doubleday, 1956), p. 302.

10. U.S. Atomic Energy Commission, Hearings *In the Matter of J. Robert Oppenheimer* (Washington: U.S.G.P.O., 1954), p. 366.

11. Brien McMahon, "Should We Reveal the Size of our Atomic Stockpile?," *Bulletin of the Atomic Scientists,* v (March, 1949), 66-68.

12. Lilienthal, op. cit., pp. 198-99.

13. Richard Hewlett and Oscar Anderson, *The New World: 1939-1946* (University Park: University of Pennsylvania Press, 1962), pp. 624-31.

14. Earl H. Voss, *Nuclear Ambush* (Chicago: Henry Regnery, 1963), p. xi.

15. Lilienthal, op. cit., pp. 184-85, 423.

16. Ibid., pp. 453-54.

17. See Blackett, op. cit., pp. 45-49.

18. James R. Shepley and Clay Blair, *The Hydrogen Bomb* (New York: David McKay, 1954), pp. 118-19.

19. "The Balance of Military Power," *The Atlantic Monthly,* cvii (June, 1951), 21-22.

20. Vincent Davis, *Postwar Defense Policy and the U.S. Navy: 1943-1946* (Chapel Hill: University of North Carolina Press, 1966), pp. 250-51.

21. Polls reported by Helen Gaudet Erskine, "The Polls: Atomic Weapons and Nuclear Energy," *Public Opinion Quarterly,* xxvii (Summer, 1963), p. 177.

22. See U.S. House of Representatives, Committee on Armed Services, *Investigation of the B-36 Bomber Program* (Washington: U.S.G.P.O., 1949), pp. 48-50. For a similar view expressed by Secretary of Defense Forrestal, see Lilienthal, op. cit., p. 377.

23. For example, see special issue "Civil Defense Against Nuclear Attack," *Bulletin of the Atomic Scientists,* vi (August-September, 1950), 226-78.

24. See Herbert Feis, *Churchill, Roosevelt, Stalin* (Princeton: Princeton University Press, 1957).

25. Paul Kecskemeti, *Strategic Surrender* (Palo Alto: Stanford University Press, 1958), pp. 119-54.

26. Herbert Feis, *Between War and Peace* (Princeton: Princeton University Press, 1960), pp. 6-9.

27. Bernard Law Montgomery, *Memoires* (New York: World Publishing Co., 1958), pp. 297-98.

28. For a standard view on this period, see Feis, *Between War and Peace;* for a very detailed presentation of a "revisionist" view, see Gar Alperovitz, *Atomic Diplomacy: Hiroshima and Potsdam* (New York: Vintage Books, 1967).

29. Feis, *Between War and Peace,* pp. 163-80.

30. See Alperovitz, *op. cit.,* pp. 188-225.

31. For a detailed study of nuclear developments in the U.S.S.R., see Arnold Kramish, *Atomic Energy in the Soviet Union* (Palo Alto: Stanford University Press, 1959).

32. Ibid., p. 76.

33. Ibid., p. 78.

34. *New York Times* (October 9, 1945), 1, cols. 4-5.

35. Hewlett and Anderson, op. cit., pp. 408-530.

36. See Alperovitz, op. cit., pp. 50-61; Hewlett and Anderson, op. cit., pp. 590-606.

37. Henry DeWolfe Smyth, *Atomic Energy for Military Purposes* (Princeton: Princeton University Press, 1945).

38. Margaret Gowing, *Britain and Atomic Energy* (New York: St. Martin's Press, 1964), p. 364.

39. On the decisions to produce and use the atomic bomb, see Michael Amrine, *The Great Decision* (New York: G.P. Putnam, 1959); and Robert Batchelder, *The Irreversible Decision* (Boston: Houghton Mifflin, 1962).

40. Lilienthal, op. cit., p. 198.

41. On the Japanese decisions at the end of the war, see Herbert Feis, *The Atomic Bomb and the End of World War II* (Princeton: Princeton University Press, 1966); Robert Butow, *Japan's Decision to Surrender* (Palo Alto: Stanford University Press, 1965).

42. See Samuel P. Huntington, *The Common Defense* (New York: Columbia University Press 1961), pp. 35-36.

43. On the Baruch Plan, see Hewlett and Anderson, *op. cit.,* pp. 531-619. For a critical analysis of the plan, see Blackett, op. cit., pp. 143-94.

44. Lilienthal, op. cit., pp. 27-28.

45. Hewlett and Anderson, op. cit., pp. 548-51.

46. U.S. Department of State, *Documents on Disarmament 1945-1959* (Washington: U.S.G.P.O., 1960), pp. 17-24.

47. John W. Spanier and Joseph L. Nogee, *The Politics of Disarmament* (New York: Praeger, 1962), pp. 76-82.

48. Davis, op. cit., pp. 244-46.

49. Hewlett and Anderson, op. cit., pp. 581-82; Davis, op. cit., p. 337.

50. Erskine, op. cit., p. 189; Hewlett and Anderson, op. cit., pp. 580-84.

51. U.S. Department of State, op. cit., p. 176.

52. George Kennan, "The Sources of Soviet Conduct," *Foreign Affairs* xxv (July, 1947), 566-82.

53. See Huntington, op. cit., p. 34.

54. See *New York Times* (March 6, 1946) 1, cols. 4-5, for speech and American reactions.

55. See Lincoln Bloomfield, Walter Clemens, and Franklyn Griffiths, *Khrushchev and the Arms Race* (Cambridge, Mass.: MIT Press, 1966), pp. 100-01; Huntington, op. cit., pp. 35-36.

56. Raymond Garthoff, *Soviet Military Policy* (New York: Praeger, 1966), p. 136.

57. For the most comprehensive account of the economic problem, see Joseph M. Jones, *The Fifteen Weeks* (New York: Viking Press, 1958).

58. See Coral Bell, *Negotiating from Strength* (London: Chatto and Windus, 1962), p. 27.

59. Joel Larus, *Nuclear Weapons Safety and the Common Defense* (Columbus: Ohio State University Press, 1967), pp. 46-47; Lilienthal, op. cit., p. 106.

60. Lilienthal, op. cit., pp. 424-25.

61. "Air Defense of North America," *Air Force*, xl (August, 1957), 250-59.

62. "Strategic Air Command: The Deterrent Force," ibid., 242-49.

63. Ibid.

64. Ibid.

65. Hewlett and Anderson, op. cit., p. 500.

66. Shepley and Blair, op. cit., pp. 9-10.

67. Ibid., p. 13; Bush, op. cit., p. 86.

68. *New York Times* (November 7, 1947), 1, col. 8.

69. Report of the President's Air Policy Commission, *Survival in the Air Age* (Washington: U.S.G.P.O., 1948).

70. Ibid., pp. 3-22.

71. U.S. Strategic Bombing Survey, *Overall Report* (European War) (Washington: U.S.G.P.O., 1945).

72. U.S. Strategic Bombing Survey, *Japan's Struggle to End the War* (Washington: U.S.G.P.O., 1946).

73. For basic surveys of Soviet strategic pronouncements in this period, see Raymond Garthoff, *Soviet Strategy in the Nuclear Age* (New York: Praeger, 1958); Herbert Dinerstein, *War and the Soviet Union* (rev. ed.; New York: Praeger, 1962).

74. See Evan Luard, ed., *First Steps to Disarmament* (London: Thames and Hudson, 1965), pp. 9-20.

75. Asher Lee, *The Soviet Air Force* (London: Gerold Duckworth, 1961), pp. 51-67.

76. Ibid., p. 131.

77. Ibid.

78. Ibid., pp. 131-35.

79. Garthoff, *Soviet Strategy in the Nuclear Age,* p. 230.

80. Melvin Conant, *The Long Polar Watch* (New York: Harper and Bros., 1962), p. 33.

81. James Forrestal, *Diaries*, Walter Millis, ed. (New York: Viking Press, 1951), pp. 157-58.

82. For the development of the first Berlin crisis, see W. Phillips Davison, *The Berlin Blockade* (Princeton: Princeton University Press, 1958), pp. 3-22.

83. See Bernard Brodie, *Escalation and the Nuclear Option* (Princeton: Princeton University Press, 1966), pp. 45-46.

84. For a comprehensive account of this period, see Warner Schilling, Paul Y. Hammond, and Glenn Snyder, *Strategy, Politics, and Defense Budgets* (New York: Columbia University Press, 1962), pp. 1-266.

85. Ibid., pp. 135-41.

86. Ibid., pp. 144-48, 192; Forrestal, op. cit., pp. 453-56.

87. See Edward A. Kolodziej, *The Uncommon Defense and Congress* (Columbus: Ohio State University Press, 1966), p. 72.

88. "U.S. Bases in Britain," *The World Today,* xvi (August, 1960), 319-25.

89. "Strategic Air Command: The Deterrent Force," *Air Force* xl (August, 1957), 242-48.

90. Lilienthal, op. cit., pp. 400 ff.

91. Ibid.

92. See Walter Millis, *Arms and Men* (New York: G.P. Putnam, 1956), pp. 323-24.

93. Davis, op. cit., p. 256.

94. "Air Defense of North America," *Air Force,* xl (August, 1957), 250-59.

95. See Marshall D. Shulman, *Stalin's Foreign Policy Reappraised* (Cambridge, Mass.: Harvard University Press, 1963).

96. Milovan Djilas, *Conversations with Stalin* (New York: Harcourt, Brace and World, 1962), p. 181.

97. Millis, loc. cit.

98. See Huntington, op. cit., pp. 309-12.

99. "Strategic Air Command: The Deterrent Force," *Air Force,* xl (August, 1957), 242-49.

100. U.S. House of Representatives, Committee on Armed Services, op. cit.

101. Ibid., pp. 127-28.

102. Ibid., p. 217.

103. *New York Times* (March 3, 1949), 1, col. 6.

104. U.S. House of Representatives, Committee on Armed Services, op. cit., p. 76; David Wise and Thomas B. Ross, *The U-2 Affair* (New York: Random House, 1962).

105. Thomas R. Phillips, "The U-2 Incident," *Bulletin of the Atomic Scientists*, xvi (June, 1960), 222.

106. U.S. House of Representatives, Committee on Armed Services, op. cit., p. 531.

107. Joseph and Stewart Alsop, "Is This Our Last Chance for Peace?," *The Saturday Evening Post*, ccxxv (June 27, 1953), 17.

Notes to Chapter 2

1. James R. Shepley and Clay Blair, *The Hydrogen Bomb* (New York: David McKay, 1954), pp. 11-18.

2. Ibid., pp. 3-5; Charles J.V. Murphy, "The Hidden Struggle for the H-Bomb," *Fortune*, xlvii (May, 1953), 17.

3. See Arnold Kramish, *Atomic Energy in the Soviet Union*, (Palo Alto: Stanford University Press, 1959), pp. 120-23; Jeremy J. Stone, *Strategic Persuasion* (New York: Columbia University Press, 1967), pp. 113-14.

4. David E. Lilienthal, *The Atomic Energy Years* (New York: Harper and Row, 1965), p. 571.

5. Warner Schilling, Paul Y. Hammond, and Glenn Snyder, *Strategy, Politics, and Defense Budgets* (New York: Columbia University Press, 1962), pp. 282-85.

6. Lilienthal, op. cit., pp. 570-71.

7. Ibid., p. 583.

8. For a comprehensive account of the composition of NSC-68, see Schilling, Hammond, and Snyder, op. cit., pp. 267-378.

9. James L. Richardson, *Germany and the Atlantic Alliance* (Cambridge, Mass.: Harvard University Press, 1966), pp. 18-20.

10. See Morton H. Halperin, "The Limiting Process in the Korean War," *Political Science Quarterly,* lxxviii (March, 1963), 13-39.

11. Harry S. Truman, *Years of Trial and Hope* (Garden City, N.Y.: Doubleday, 1956), pp. 410-11.

12. Bernard Brodie, *Strategy in the Missile Age* (Princeton: Princeton University Press, 1959), pp. 319-21.

13. Thomas Whiteside, *An Agent in Place* (New York: Viking Press, 1966), p. 39.

14. See Robert Osgood, *NATO: The Entangling Alliance* (Chicago: University of Chicago Press, 1962), pp. 77-81.

15. Edward A. Kolodziej, *The Uncommon Defense and Congress* (Columbus: Ohio State University Press, 1966), pp. 157-66.

16. Schilling, Hammond, and Snyder, op. cit., pp. 401-03.

17. Shepley and Blair, p. 18.

18. Alfred Vagts, *Defense and Diplomacy* (New York: King's Crown Press, 1956), pp. 329-33.

19. Ibid., p. 333.

20. Warner R. Schilling, "The H-bomb Decision: How to Decide Without Really Choosing," *Political Science Quarterly,* lxxvi (March, 1961), 24-46.

21. Ibid.

22. Omar Bradley, "This Way Lies Peace," *The Saturday Evening Post,* ccxxvii (October 15, 1949), 32-33.

23. See Murphy, op. cit.; Shepley and Blair, op. cit., pp. 176-82. For a contrary interpretation, see Robert Gilpin, *American Scientists and Nuclear Weapons Policy* (Princeton: Princeton University Press, 1962), pp. 112-35.

24. Shepley and Blair, op. cit., p. 179.

25. Ibid., pp. 114-33.

26. Murphy, op. cit.

27. Shepley and Blair, op. cit., p. 177.

28. See Samuel P. Huntington, *The Common Defense* (New York: Columbia University Press, 1961), pp. 326-41.

29. Robert Frank Futrell, *The United States Air Force in Korea: 1950-1953* (New York: Duell, Sloan and Pearce, 1961), pp. 376-80.

30. See Murphy, op. cit.; U.S. Atomic Energy Commission, *In the Matter of J. Robert Oppenheimer* (Washington: U.S.G.P.O., 1954), p. 760.

31. "Air Defense of North America," *Air Force,* xl (August, 1957), 250-59.

32. Ibid.

33. Ibid.

34. Associated Universities, Inc., *Report on Project East River* (New York, 1952).

35. *Chicago Sun-Times* (October 14, 1950), 1, col. 6.

36. See Huntington, op. cit., pp. 326-31.

37. See Walter Millis, *Arms and Men* (New York: G.P. Putnam, 1956), p. 351.

38. For an example, see "The Balance of Military Power," *Atlantic Monthly,* clxxxvii (June, 1951), 21-27.

39. J. Robert Oppenheimer, "Atomic Weapons and American Policy," *Bulletin of the Atomic Scientists,* ix (July, 1953), 202-05.

40. Shepley and Blair, op. cit., pp. 123-33.

41. See Futrell, op. cit., pp. 370-86.

42. "Strategic Air Command: The Deterrent Force," *Air Force,* xl (August, 1957), 242-49.

43. Ibid.

44. Charles J.V. Murphy, "The New Air Situation," *Fortune,* lii (September, 1955), 86-87.

45. "Air Defense of North America," *Air Force,* xl (August, 1957), 250-59.

46. Arthur Schlesinger, *A Thousand Days* (Boston: Houghton Mifflin, 1965), p. 450.

47. Earl H. Voss, *Nuclear Ambush* (Chicago: Henry Regnery, 1963), p. 34.

48. Ibid.

49. Helen Gaudet Erskine, "The Polls: Atomic Weapons and Nuclear Energy," *Public Opinion Quarterly,* xxvii (Summer, 1963), p. 174.

50. Leonard Beaton and John Maddox, *The Spread of Nuclear Weapons* (London: Chatto and Windus, 1962), p. 66.

51. "U.S. Bases in Britain," *The World Today,* xvi (August, 1960), 319-25.

52. R.N. Rosecrance, "British Defense Strategy: 1945-1952," in R.N. Rosecrance, ed., *The Dispersion of Nuclear Weapons* (New York: Columbia University Press, 1964), p. 76.

53. Ibid.

54. Lilienthal, op. cit., p. 282.

55. Beaton and Maddox, op. cit., p. 68.

Notes to Chapter 3

1. A comprehensive account of the formulation of the "new look" is to be found in Warner Schilling, Paul Y. Hammond, and Glenn Snyder, *Strategy, Politics, and Defense Budgets* (New York: Columbia University Press, 1962), pp. 383-524.

2. Ibid., pp. 406-10.

3. Ibid., p. 409.

4. See Dwight David Eisenhower, *Mandate for Change* (Garden City, N.Y.: Doubleday, 1963), pp. 486-89.

5. Curtis LeMay, (with MacKinlay Kantor), *Mission with Lemay* (Garden City, N.Y.: Doubleday, 1965), p. 481.

6. Arnold Kramish, *Atomic Energy in the Soviet Union* (Palo Alto: Stanford University Press, 1959), p. 127.

7. Charles J.V. Murphy, "The New Air Situation," *Fortune,* lii (September, 1955), 86-87.

8. Schilling, Hammond, and Snyder, op. cit., pp. 390-91.

9. Kramish, op. cit., pp. 125-27.

10. Earl H. Voss, *Nuclear Ambush* (Chicago: Henry Regnery, 1963), pp. xi-xiii.

11. James R. Shepley and Clay Blair, *The Hydrogen Bomb* (New York: David McKay, 1954), p. 18.

12. Schilling, Hammond, and Snyder, op. cit., pp. 406-10.

13. Ibid., pp. 388-89.

14. Address of January 12, 1954, in *Department of State Bulletin,* xxx (January 25, 1954), 107-12.

15. John Robinson Beal, *John Foster Dulles: A Biography* (New York: Harper and Bros., 1957), pp. 181-82.

16. Philip Windsor, *City on Leave* (New York: Praeger, 1963), pp. 156-57.

17. See charges by Khrushchev, reported in *New York Times* (March 1, 1963), 1, col. 8.

18. See Eisenhower, op. cit., pp. 459-83.

19. Schilling, Hammond, and Snyder, op. cit., pp. 400-06.

20. Robert J. Donovan, *Eisenhower: The Inside Story* (New York: Harper and Bros., 1956), pp. 183-93.

21. Ibid.

22. Shepley and Blair, op. cit., p. 161.

23. Voss, op. cit., p. xiv.

24. Helen Gaudet Erskine, "The Polls: Atomic Weapons and Nuclear Energy," *Public Opinion Quarterly,* xxvii (Summer, 1963), p. 162.

25. H.L. Nieberg, *Nuclear Secrecy and Foreign Policy* (Washington: Public Affairs Press, 1964), pp. 78-85.

26. Ibid., p. 88.

27. Ibid., pp. 85-88.

28. Schilling, Hammond, and Snyder, op. cit., pp. 420-21.

29. Steven Rivkin, "The Decision-Making Process for National Defense Policy" (unpublished Harvard honors thesis, 1958), p. 143.

30. Charles J.V. Murphy, "The Wild Blue-Chip Yonder," *Fortune*, lii (July, 1955), 52-57.

31. See Gershon Cooper and Roland McKean, "Is Dispersal Good Defense?," ibid. (November, 1954), 126-27.

32. Glenn H. Snyder, *Stockpiling Strategic Materials* (San Francisco: Chandler Publishing Co., 1966), pp. 189-223.

33. Ibid., pp. 223-37.

34. See Samuel P. Huntington, *The Common Defense* (New York: Columbia University Press, 1961), pp. 340-41.

35. John L. Chapman, *Atlas: The Story of a Missile* (New York: Harper and Bros., 1960), pp. 72-73.

36. See testimony of Trevor Gardner in U.S. Senate, Committee on Armed Services, *Study of Airpower* (Washington: U.S.G.P.O., 1956), p. 1109.

37. See development of European and other views reported in polls cited in Helen Gaudet Erskine, "The Polls: Defense, Peace, and Space," *Public Opinion Quarterly* (Fall, 1961), p. 481.

38. U.S. Department of State, *Documents on Disarmament 1945-1959* (Washington: U.S.G.P.O., 1960), pp. 365-72, 427-28.

39. See A. Doak Barnett, *Communist China and Asia* (New York: Harper and Bros., 1960), pp. 292-93.

40. U.S. Department of State, op. cit., pp. 431-33.

41. Ibid., pp. 456-67.

42. Ibid., p. 513.

43. Ibid., pp. 486-88.

44. David Wise and Thomas B. Ross, *The U-2 Affair* (New York: Random House, 1962), pp. 40-59; Charles J.V. Murphy, "Khrushchev's Paper Bear," *Fortune* lxx (December, 1964), 114-15.

45. Comprehensive accounts of the development of NATO policy are in Robert Osgood and Klaus Knorr, eds., *NATO and American Security* (Princeton: Princeton University Press, 1959).

46. *New York Times* (May 29, 1953), 6, col. 2.

47. Osgood, op. cit., p. 107.

48. Huntington, op. cit., pp. 78-79.

49. Osgood, op. cit., pp. 102-03.

50. Ibid.

51. Ibid., pp. 105-06.

52. James L. Richardson, *Germany and the Atlantic Alliance* (Cambridge, Mass.: Harvard University Press, 1966), p. 40.

53. Ibid., pp. 49-50.

54. Lincoln Bloomfield, Walter Clemens, and Franklyn Griffiths, *Khrushchev and the Arms Race* (Cambridge, Mass.: MIT Press, 1966), pp. 24-25.

55. A complete analysis of the fixed inspection post proposals is in Johan Jorgen Holst, *Arms Stability in the Cold War* (Kjeller, Norway: Norwegian Defense Research Establishment, 1965).

56. Bloomfield, Clemens, and Griffiths, op. cit., p. 100.

57. Holst, op. cit., p. 173.

58. Gerald Freund, *Germany Between Two Worlds* (New York: Harcourt Brace, 1961), pp. 144-50.

59. Richardson, op. cit., pp. 42-48.

60. Hans Speier, *German Rearmament and Atomic War* (Evanston, Ill.: Row Peterson, 1957), pp. 182-83.

61. Richardson, op. cit., pp. 42, 45-47.

62. Ibid., pp. 47-48.

63. Ibid., pp. 59-62.

64. Speier, op. cit., pp. 75-83.

65. On the disengagement issue, see Michael Howard, *Disengagement in Europe* (Hammondsworth: Penguin Books, 1958); Eugene Hinterhoff, *Disengagement* (London: Stevens and Sons, 1959).

66. See, for example, the *Der Spiegel* article on "Fallex 62," translated and reprinted in *Survival*, v (January-February, 1963), 14-22.

67. See Henry A. Kissinger, *Nuclear Weapons and Foreign Policy* (New York: Harper and Bros., 1957).

68. For arguments stressing the risk of escalation, see James King, "Nuclear Plenty and Limited War," *Foreign Affairs*, ccclv (January, 1957); 238-56; William Kaufmann, "The Requirements of Deterrence" and "Limited Warfare," in William Kaufmann, ed., *Military Policy and National Security* (Princeton: Princeton University Press, 1956) 12-38, 102-136. A full account of the development of limited war theory is presented in Morton Halperin, *Limited War in the Nuclear Age* (New York: John Wiley, 1963).

69. See Eisenhower statements in *Documents on American Foreign Relations: 1956* (New York: Council on Foreign Relations and Harper and Bros., 1956), pp. 255-60.

70. See Charles J.V. Murphy, "Washington and the World," *Fortune*, lv (January, 1957), 78-83.

71. *Department of State Bulletin*, xxix (September 14, 1953), 339-43.

72. Roscoe Drummond and Gaston Coblentz, *Duel at the Brink* (Garden City, N.Y.: Doubleday, 1960), pp. 121-22.

73. John Foster Dulles, "Policy for Security and Peace," *Foreign Affairs*, xxxii (April, 1954), 353-64.

74. Eisenhower, op. cit., p. 477.

75. Chalmers Roberts, "The Day We Didn't Go to War," *The Reporter*, xi (September 14, 1954), 31-32.

76. John Foster Dulles, "Challenge and Response in United States Policy," *Foreign Affairs*, xxxvi (October, 1957), 25-43.

77. See, for example, Charles J.V. Murphy, "The U.S. as a Bombing Target," xlviii *Fortune,* (November, 1953), 118-21.

78. A.J. Wohlstetter, F.S. Hoffmann, R.J. Lutz, and H.S. Rowen, *Selection and Use of Strategic Air Bases,* RAND Report R-266 (Santa Monica, Calif.: The RAND Corp., 1954). For an account of the preparation and impact of the report, see Bruce L.R. Smith, *The RAND Corporation* (Cambridge, Mass.: Harvard University Press, 1966), pp. 195-240.

79. Wohlstetter, Hoffmann, Lutz, and Rowen, op. cit., pp. 31-32, 365-69.

80. Robert A. Kilmarx, *A History of Soviet Air Power* (New York: Praeger, 1958), p. 251.

81. Ibid., p. 252.

82. Joseph and Stewart Alsop, "Is This Our Last Chance for Peace?," *The Saturday Evening Post* ccxxv (June 27, 1953), 17.

83. Raymond Garthoff, *Soviet Strategy in the Nuclear Age* (New York: Praeger, 1958), p. 178.

84. Allen Dulles, *The Craft of Intelligence* (New York: Harper & Row, 1963), pp. 162-63.

85. Asher Lee, *The Soviet Air Force* (London: Gerold Duckworth, 1961), p. 134.

86. Neville Brown, *Nuclear War* (London: Pall Mall Press, 1964), p. 21.

87. Kilmarx, op. cit., pp. 253-54; Bloomfield, Clemens, and Griffiths, op. cit., p. 95.

88. Herbert Dinerstein, *War and the Soviet Union* (rev. ed.; New York: Praeger, 1962), p. 230.

89. For an interesting example of such an interpretation, see James M. Gavin, *War and Peace in the Space Age* (New York: Harper and Bros., 1958), p. 241.

90. Arnold L. Horelick and Myron Rush, *Strategic Power and Soviet Foreign Policy* (Chicago: University of Chicago Press, 1965), p. 52.

91. Ibid.

92. See testimony of General LeMay, in U.S. Senate, Committee on Armed Services, op. cit., p. 101.

93. Testimony of General LeMay in U.S. Senate, Committee on Armed Services, *Inquiry into Satellite and Missile Programs* (Washington: U.S.G.P.O., 1959), pp. 405-06.

94. See Huntington, op. cit., p. 110.

95. Institute for Strategic Studies, *The Military Balance: 1962-1963* (London: Institute for Strategic Studies, 1963), p. 28.

96. Charles J.V. Murphy, "The New Air Situation."

97. U.S. Senate, *Study of Airpower,* pp. 1713 ff.

98. For example, see Thomas K. Finletter, *Power and Policy* (New York: Harcourt Brace, 1954).

99. See, for example, Nathan Twining, *Neither Liberty nor Safety* (New York: Holt, Rinehart, and Winston, 1966); Thomas Power, *Design for Survival* (New York: Coward-McCann, 1964).

100. Garthoff, *Soviet Strategy in the Nuclear Age,* pp. 170-79; Dinerstein, op. cit., pp. 28-36.

101. Dinerstein, op. cit., pp. 65-82.

102. Kramish, op. cit., pp. 121-132; Jeremy J. Stone, *Strategic Persuasion* (New York: Columbia University Press, 1967), pp. 112-15.

103. Dinerstein, op. cit., pp. 65-82.

104. Horelick and Rush, op. cit., p. 27.

105. Garthoff, *Soviet Strategy in the Nuclear Age,* pp. 84-87.

106. See "The Economic Consequences of Going on," *The Economist,* clxxxi (December 15, 1956), 447.

107. Osgood, op. cit., p. 222.

108. See Harvey A. Deweerd, "The British Effort to Secure an Independent Deterrent: 1952-1962," and Ciro E. Zoppo, "France as a Nuclear Power," in Richard N. Rosecrance, ed., *The Dispersion of Nuclear Weapons* (New York: Columbia University Press, 1964), 87-101, 113-56.

109. Voss, op. cit., p. xix.

Notes to Chapter 4

1. See Allen Dulles, *The Craft of Intelligence* (New York: Harper & Row, 1963), pp. 253-54.

2. John L. Chapman, *Atlas: The Story of a Missile* (New York: Harper and Bros., 1960), pp. 70-73.

3. Ibid.

4. Ibid.

5. *New York Times* (February 8, 1956), 1, col. 7.

6. See Dwight David Eisenhower, *Waging Peace* (Garden City, N.Y.: Doubleday, 1965), pp. 208-10.

7. See Charles J.V. Murphy, "The White House Since Sputnik," *Fortune*, lvii (January, 1958), 98-101.

8. Charles J.V. Murphy, "America's Widening Military Margin," ibid., lvi (August, 1957), 94-96.

9. Helen Gaudet Erskine, "The Polls: Defense, Peace, and Space," *Public Opinion Quarterly* (Fall, 1961), p. 485.

10. Ibid., p. 483.

11. See Charles J.V. Murphy, "The Embattled Mr. McElroy," *Fortune*, lix (April, 1959), 147-50.

12. Murphy, "The White House Since Sputnik."

13. Ibid.

14. See George E. Lowe, *The Age of Deterrence* (Boston: Little Brown, 1964), pp. 179-86.

15. Morton H. Halperin, "The Gaither Report and the Policy Process," *World Politics*, xiii (April, 1961), 360-84.

16. Eisenhower, *Waging Peace*, p. 221.

17. Charles J.V. Murphy, "The Polar Watch," *Fortune* lvi (December, 1957), 118-27.

18. See Murphy, "The Embattled Mr. McElroy."

19. Jeremy J. Stone, *Containing the Arms Race* (Cambridge, Mass.: MIT Press, 1966), pp. 131-34.

20. See James Baar and William E. Howard, *Polaris!* (New York: Harcourt Brace, 1960).

21. Edward A. Kolodziej, *The Uncommon Defense and Congress* (Columbus: Ohio State University Press, 1966), pp. 284-85.

22. U.S. Senate, Committee on Armed Services, *Study of Airpower* (Washington: U.S.G.P.O., 1956), p. 163.

23. See Lowe, op. cit., pp. 220-21.

24. See Joel Larus, *Nuclear Weapons Safety and the Common Defense* (Columbus: Ohio State University Press, 1967), pp. 55-59.

25. Kolodziej, op. cit., pp. 303-07.

26. Jerome Wiesner, *Where Science and Politics Meet* (New York: McGraw-Hill, 1965), p. 290.

27. Institute for Strategic Studies, *The Military Balance: 1963-64* (London: Institute for Strategic Studies, 1964), p. 11.

28. Institute for Strategic Studies, *The Military Balance: 1959* (London: Institute for Strategic Studies, 1959), p. 5.

29. *New York Times* (January 13, 1959), 14, col. 5; ibid. (January 30, 1959), 1, col. 1.

30. Eisenhower, *Waging Peace,* p. 140.

31. Murphy, "The Polar Watch."

32. Ibid.; Coral Bell, *Negotiating from Strength* (London: Chatto and Windus, 1962), pp. 170-71.

33. See Albert Wohlstetter, *On the Value of Overseas Bases,* RAND Paper P-1877 (Santa Monica, Calif.: The RAND Corp., 1960).

34. See Jeremy J. Stone, *Strategic Persuasion* (New York: Columbia University Press, 1967), pp. 123-25.

35. Herbert Dinerstein, *War and the Soviet Union* (rev. ed.; New York: Praeger, 1962), pp. 227-28.

36. Alice Langley Hsieh, *Communist China's Strategy in the Nuclear Age* (Englewood Cliffs, N.J.: Prentice-Hall, 1962), pp. 84-109; Arnold L. Horelick and Myron Rush, *Strategic Power and Soviet Foreign Policy* (Chicago: University of Chicago Press, 1965), pp. 74-75.

37. See Morton Halperin and Tang Tsou, "The 1958 Quemoy Crisis," in Morton Halperin, ed., *Sino-Soviet Relations and Arms Control* (Cambridge, Mass.: MIT Press, 1967).

38. Charles J.V. Murphy, "Khrushchev's Paper Bear," *Fortune,* lxx (December, 1964), 114-15.

39. See testimony of General Maxwell Taylor, in U.S. Senate, Committee on Armed Services, *Hearings on Major Defense Matters* (Washington: U.S.G.P.O., 1959), p. 58.

40. See V.D. Sokolovsky, ed. (U.S. editors: Herbert Dinerstein, Leon Goure, Thomas Wolfe), *Soviet Military Strategy* (Englewood Cliffs, N.J.: Prentice-Hall, 1963), pp. 289-93.

41. Jean Edward Smith, *The Defense of Berlin* (Baltimore: Johns Hopkins University Press, 1963), pp. 200-01.

42. Carl A. Linden, *Khrushchev and the Soviet Leadership: 1957-1964* (Baltimore: Johns Hopkins University Press, 1966), pp. 92-93.

43. *New York Times* (February 19, 1958), 1, col. 3.

44. Lowe, op. cit., p. 152.

45. Hanson W. Baldwin, "Limited War," *The Atlantic Monthly,* cciii (May, 1959), 35-43.

46. *New York Times* (August 15, 1958) 2, col. 4.

47. Helen Gaudet Erskine, "The Polls: Atomic Weapons and Nuclear Energy," *Public Opinion Quarterly* (Summer, 1963), p. 174.

48. Larus, op. cit., pp. 80-83.

49. H.L. Nieberg, *Nuclear Secrecy and Foreign Policy* (Washington: Public Affairs Press, 1964), pp. 193-95.

50. For a full account of the evolution of the French nuclear program, see Lawrence Scheinman, *Atomic Energy Policy in France Under the Fourth Republic* (Princeton: Princeton University Press, 1965).

51. Nieberg, op. cit., pp. 180-84.

52. Leonard Beaton and John Maddox, *The Spread of Nuclear Weapons* (London: Chatto and Windus, 1962), pp. 88-89.

53. Ibid.

54. Ibid., p. 91.

55. Ibid., p. 87.

56. Nieberg, op. cit., pp. 169-70.

57. Beaton and Maddox, op. cit., p. 75.

58. Ibid., p. 76.

59. See Leon D. Epstein, "Britain and the H-Bomb," *Review of Politics*, xxix (August, 1959), 511-29.

60. Nieberg, op. cit., pp. 177, 188.

61. Ibid., p. 192.

62. Lincoln Bloomfield, Walter Clemens, and Franklyn Griffiths, *Khrushchev and the Arms Race* (Cambridge, Mass.: MIT Press, 1966), p. 154.

63. Text in Eugene Hinterhoff, *Disengagement* (London: Stevens and Sons, 1959), pp. 402-07.

64. See Roger Hilsman, *To Move a Nation* (Garden City, N.Y.: Doubleday, 1967), p. 172.

65. See Hinterhoff, op. cit., pp. 436-442.

66. Nieberg, op. cit., pp. 123-28.

67. *Peking Review* (August 15, 1963).

68. See Morton Halperin, *China and the Bomb* (New York: Praeger, 1965), pp. 78-82; Arnold Kramish, "The Great Chinese Bomb Puzzle—and a Solution," *Fortune*, lxxiii (June, 1966), 157-58.

69. See Bloomfield, Clemens, and Griffiths, op. cit., pp. 151-58.

70. Freeman Dyson, "The Future Development of Nuclear Weapons," *Foreign Affairs*, xxxviii (April, 1960), 457-64.

71. Harold Karan Jacobson and Eric Stein, *Diplomats, Scientists, and Politicians* (Ann Arbor: University of Michigan Press, 1966), pp. 41-43.

72. Ibid., p. 17.

73. Ibid., pp. 72-73.

74. Ibid., pp. 45-53.

75. See Donald Brennan and Morton Halperin, "Policy Considerations of a Nuclear Test-Ban," in Donald Brennan, ed., *Arms Control, Disarmament and National Security* (New York: George Braziller, 1961), pp. 234-66.

76. Larus, op. cit., p. 31.

77. Jacobson and Stein, op. cit., pp. 104-05.

78. Ibid., p. 263.

79. Ibid., p. 353.

80. Smith, op. cit., pp. 181-234.

81. U.S. Department of State, *Documents on Disarmament 1945-1959* (Washington: U.S.G.P.O., 1960), pp. 1452-74.

82. Ibid., pp. 1550-56.

83. Murphy, "Khrushchev's Paper Bear."

84. Ibid.

85. Murphy, "The Embattled Mr. McElroy."

86. Murphy, "Khrushchev's Paper Bear."

87. See Lowe, op. cit., pp. 148-229.

88. Ibid., p. 194.

89. See P.M.S. Blackett, "Steps Toward Disarmament," *Scientific American,* ccvi (April, 1962), 34, 45-53.

90. Linden, op. cit., pp. 68, 90-93.

91. Ibid., pp. 114-15.

92. David Wise and Thomas B. Ross, *The U-2 Affair* (New York: Random House, 1962), p. 155.

93. For the classic statement of the need for concern on strategic

vulnerability, see Albert Wohlstetter, "The Delicate Balance of Terror," *Foreign Affairs,* xxxvii (January, 1959), 211-34.

94. Erskine, "The Polls: Defense, Peace, and Space," loc. cit.

95. Theodore Sorensen, *Kennedy* (New York: Harper and Row, 1965), p. 612.

96. U.S. Senate, Committee on Armed Services, op. cit., pp. 1758, 1760-61.

Notes to Chapter 5

1. Theodore Sorensen, *Kennedy* (New York: Harper and Row, 1965), pp. 518, 612.

2. See Thomas Schelling and Morton Halperin, *Strategy and Arms Control* (New York: Twentieth Century Fund, 1961). For a full discussion of the arms control issues raised at this point, see also Robert Levine, *The Arms Debate* (Cambridge, Mass.: Harvard University Press, 1963); Hedley Bull, *The Control of the Arms Race* (New York: Praeger, 1961).

3. David Wise and Thomas B. Ross, *The Invisible Government* (New York: Random House, 1964), pp. 302-12.

4. Herman Kahn, *On Thermonuclear War* (Princeton: Princeton University Press, 1960). For a discussion of the reactions to this book, see Herman Kahn, *Thinking About the Unthinkable* (New York: Horizon Press, 1962).

5. For an authoritative presentation of the thinking of the new administration, see William Kaufmann, *The McNamara Strategy* (New York: Harper and Row, 1964).

6. Sorensen, op. cit., p. 627.

7. See Raymond Garthoff, *Soviet Military Policy* (New York: Praeger, 1966), pp. 211-12.

8. See Thomas Wolfe, *Soviet Strategy at the Crossroads* (Cambridge, Mass.: Harvard University Press, 1964), pp. 124-29.

9. Jean Edward Smith, *The Defense of Berlin* (Baltimore: Johns Hopkins University Press, 1963), pp. 211-28.

10. See Sorensen, op. cit., pp. 543-50.

11. Ibid., pp. 583-601.

12. Smith, op. cit., pp. 259-62.

13. Ibid., pp. 267-341.

14. Ibid., pp. 318-24.

15. See Raymond Aron, *The Great Debate* (Garden City, N.Y.: Anchor Books, 1965), pp. 221-23. Also see Robert Jervis, *The Logic of Images in International Relations* (Princeton, N.J.: Princeton University Press, 1970), for an elaboration of this argument.

16. James L. Richardson, *Germany and the Atlantic Alliance* (Cambridge, Mass.: Harvard University Press, 1966), p. 283.

17. *New York Times* (September 8, 1961), 1, col. 2.

18. Garthoff, op. cit., p. 152.

19. *New York Times* (August 1, 1961), 1, col. 6.

20. See Stuart Symington, "Where the Missile Gap Went," *The Reporter,* xxvi (February 15, 1962), 21-23.

21. See Kaufmann, op. cit., pp. 217-28. For a good summation of the arguments against manned bombers, see Jeremy J. Stone, *Containing the Arms Race* (Cambridge, Mass.: MIT Press, 1966), pp. 75-123.

22. Sorensen, op. cit., p. 513

23. Lincoln Bloomfield, Walter Clemens, and Franklyn Griffiths, *Khrushchev and the Arms Race* (Cambridge, Mass.: MIT Press, 1966), p. 95.

24. Arnold L. Horelick and Myron Rush, *Strategic Power and Soviet Foreign Policy* (Chicago: University of Chicago Press, 1965), pp. 93-96.

25. Arthur Schlesinger, *A Thousand Days* (Boston: Houghton Mifflin, 1965), p. 301.

26. Harold Karan Jacobson and Eric Stein, *Diplomats, Scientists, and Politicians* (Ann Arbor: University of Michigan Press, 1966), p. 329-33.

27. Ibid., p. 342.

28. *New York Times* (October 22, 1961), 1, col. 5.

29. Jacobson and Stein, op. cit., pp. 278, 283.

30. Ibid., p. 281.

31. For discussions of the NATO defense problem, see Henry A. Kissinger, *The Necessity for Choice* (Garden City, N.Y.: Anchor, 1962); Glenn Snyder, *Deterrence and Defense* (Princeton: Princeton University Press, 1961); Alastair Buchan, *NATO in the 1960's* (New York: Praeger, 1961); Alastair Buchan and Philip Windsor, *Arms and Stability in Europe* (New York: Praeger, 1963).

32. See Richardson, op. cit., pp. 74-75.

33. See Address by Alain Enthoven reprinted in *Survivial,* v (May-June, 1963), 94-101.

34. *New York Times* (November 17, 1963), 38, col. 1; ibid (November 19, 1963), 13, col. 1.

35. Charles J.V. Murphy, "NATO At the Nuclear Crossroads,"*Fortune* lxvi (December, 1962), 84-87.

36. See Edgar Furniss, *DeGaulle and the French Army* (New York: Twentieth Century Fund, 1964), pp. 272, 275-76.

37. Joel Larus, *Nuclear Weapons Safety and the Common Defense* (Columbus: Ohio State University Press, 1967), pp. 94-98.

38. See Richardson, op. cit., pp. 74-77.

39. Institute for Strategic Studies, *The Military Balance: 1965-66* (London: Institute for Strategic Studies, 1966) p. 13.

40. Richardson, op. cit., p. 80.

41. *New York Times* (June 17, 1962), 27, col. 1.

42. For an extended presentation of the reasoning behind the "no-cities" doctrine, see Robert Fryklund, *100 Million Lives* (New York: Macmillan, 1962).

43. See Michael Brower, "Nuclear Strategy of the Kennedy Administration," *Bulletin of the Atomic Scientists,* xviii (October, 1962), 34-41.

44. *New York Times* (June 24, 1962), 5, col. 2.

45. For a discussion of limited general war scenarios, see Klaus Knorr

and Thorton Read, eds., *Limited Strategic War* (New York: Praeger, 1962).

46. Leon Goure, *Civil Defense in the Soviet Union* (Berkeley: University of California Press, 1962).

47. See Sorensen, op. cit., pp. 613-17.

48. Ralph E. Lapp, "Nuclear Weapons Systems," *Bulletin of the Atomic Scientists*, xvii (March, 1961), 99-102.

49. On the Cuban Missile crisis, see Elie Abel, *The Missile Crisis* (New York: Lippincott, 1966); Albert and Roberta Wohlstetter, *Containing the Risks in Cuba*, Adelphi Paper No. 19, (London: Institute for Strategic Studies, 1965); Horelick and Rush, op. cit., pp. 141-56; Sorensen, op. cit., pp. 667-718; Schlesinger, op. cit., pp. 794-841; and Roger Hilsman, *To Move a Nation* (Garden City, N.Y.: Doubleday, 1967), pp. 159-232.

50. See Arnold Horelick, "The Cuban Missile Crisis: An Analysis of Soviet Calculations and Behavior," *World Politics*, xvi (April, 1964), 363-89.

51. Ibid.

52. Abel, op. cit., p. 18.; Hilsman, op. cit., p. 172.

53. Bloomfield, Clemens, and Griffiths, op. cit., p. 103.

54. Hilsman, op. cit., pp. 220-21.

55. *New York Times* (September 12, 1962), 1, col. 8.

56. Hilsman, op. cit., p. 212.

57. Schlesinger, op. cit., pp. 807-08.

58. Abel, op. cit., pp. 190-91.

59. Schlesinger, op. cit., p. 863.

60. Abel, op. cit., p. 51.

61. Ibid., p. 52.

62. Bloomfield, Clemens, and Griffiths, op. cit., p. 95.

63. Hilsman, op. cit., p. 159.

64. Statement of September 4, reprinted in *Department of State Bulletin,* xlvii (September 24, 1962), 450.

65. Hilsman, op. cit., pp. 185-92.

66. For an argument that the Russians were not aware of the step-up in U-2 overflights, see Hilsman, op. cit., p. 200.

67. Abel, op. cit., p. 81.

68. See Thomas C. Schelling, *Arms and Influence* (New Haven: Yale University Press, 1966), pp. 69-91.

69. Sorensen, op. cit., pp. 707-09.

70. Schlesinger, op. cit., p. 815.

71. See Abel, op. cit., p. 201.

72. Hilsman, op. cit., p. 191.

73. Abel, op. cit., p. 187.

74. Albert and Roberta Wohlstetter, op. cit., p. 11.

75. Abel, op. cit., p. 114.

76. Address of October 22, 1962, reprinted in *Department of State Bulletin,* xlvii (November 12, 1962), 715-22.

77. Abel, op. cit., p. 214.

78. See George Bailey, "Again the Autobahn," *The Reporter,* xxix (November 7, 1963), 16-17.

79. *New York Times* (June 27, 1963), 1, col. 8.

80. See Oskar Morgenstern, *The Question of National Defense* (New York: Random House, 1959), pp. 74-77.

81. See Testimony of Secretary McNamara in U.S. House of Representatives, Committee on Armed Service, *Hearings on Military Posture* (Washington: U.S.G.P.O., 1963), pp. 308, 332.

82. Jacobson and Stein, op. cit., pp. 425-35.

83. Ibid., p. 426.

84. Arnold Kramish, *The Peaceful Atom in Foreign Policy* (New York: Harper and Row, 1963), pp. 34-35.

85. Schlesinger, op. cit., pp. 856-64.

86. Ibid., p. 863.

87. Ibid., pp. 859-61.

88. Ibid., pp. 871-75.

89. H. L. Nieberg, *Nuclear Secrecy and Foreign Policy* (Washington: Public Affairs Press, 1964), p. 213.

90. Schlesinger, op. cit., p. 865.

Notes to Chapter 6

1. Pierre Gallois, *The Balance of Terror* (Boston: Houghton Mifflin, 1961).

2. See George Bailey, "Germany Between Two Alliances," *The Reporter,* xxxv (October 6, 1966), 27-32.

3. For a differing analysis, see Brigadier K. Hunt, *NATO Without France,* Adelphi Paper No. 32 (London: Institute for Strategic Studies, 1966).

4. Thomas Wolfe, *Soviet Strategy at the Crossroads* (Cambridge, Mass.: Harvard University Press, 1964), pp. 122-23.

5. See Edgar O'Ballance, *The Sinai Campaign* (London: Faber, 1959).

6. See Michael Howard and Robert Hunter, *Israel and the Arab World: The Crises of 1967,* Adelphi Paper No. 41 (London: Institute for Strategic Studies, 1967).

7. On the development of the Sino-Soviet dispute, see Donald Zagoria, *The Sino-Soviet Conflict* (Princeton: Princeton University Press, 1962); William Griffith, *The Sino-Soviet Rift* (Cambridge, Mass.: MIT Press, 1964); William Griffith, *Sino-Soviet Relations: 1964-65* (Cambridge, Mass.: MIT Press, 1967). On the strategic significance of the split, see Morton Halperin, *China and the Bomb* (New York: Praeger, 1965); D.E. Kennedy, *The Security of Southern Asia* (New York: Praeger, 1965); Alastair Buchan, ed., *China and the Peace of Asia* (New York: Praeger, 1965).

8. See Halperin, op. cit., pp. 34-37.

9. See Thomas C. Schelling, *Arms and Influence* (New Haven: Yale University Press, 1966), pp. 184-89.

10. On the counterinsurgency question, see David Galula, *Counter-Insurgency Warfare* (New York: Praeger, 1964); Sir Robert Thompson, *Defeating Communist Insurgency* (New York: Praeger, 1966).

11. See Morton Halperin and Dwight Perkins, *Communist China and Arms Control* (New York: Praeger, 1965), pp. 28-47.

12. See, for example, Marc S. Fasteau, "Munich and Vietnam: A Valid Analogy?," *Bulletin of the Atomic Scientists,* xxii (September, 1966), 22-25.

13. *New York Times* (November 11, 1966).

14. See articles by Harrison K. Salisbury, *New York Times,* (January 1, 1967), 1, col. 1; ibid. (January 2, 1967), 3, col. 1; ibid. (January 3, 1967), 3, col. 2; ibid. (January 4, 1967), 1, col. 6; ibid. (January 16, 1967), 1, col. 3.

15. See *Peking Review* (October 14, 1966).

16. *New York Times* (August 8, 1966).

17. For summary and denial of these charges, see *Peking Review* (July 15, 1966).

18. U.S. Arms Control and Disarmament Agency, *Documents on Disarmament: 1964* (Washington: U.S.G.P.O., 1965), pp. 4, 165-71.

19. Ibid., pp. 101-05.

20. Ibid., pp. 7-9.

21. See Donald C. Brennan and Johan J. Holst, *Ballistic Missile Defense: Two Views,* Adelphi Paper No. 43 (London: Institute for Strategic Studies, 1967).

22. See Freeman J. Dyson, "Defense Against Ballistic Missiles," *Bulletin of the Atomic Scientists,* xx (June, 1964), 12-18.

23. See N. Talensky, "The Anti-Missile: A Soviet View," ibid., xxi (February, 1965), 26-29.

24. *New York Times* (September 19, 1967), 1, col. 1.

25. *New York Times* (September 16, 1967), 1, col. 8.

26. See Philip Geyelin, *Lyndon B. Johnson and the World* (New York: Praeger, 1966), pp. 159-81.

27. U.S. Arms Control and Disarmament Agency, *Documents on Disarmament: 1965* (Washington: U.S.G.P.O., 1966), pp. 443-46.

28. See Henry A. Kissinger, *The Troubled Partnership* (Garden City, N.Y.: Anchor Books, 1966), pp. 129-86.

29. See Theo Summer, "Germany's Reservations," *Survival* ix (May, 1967), 144-45; Carl von Weizäcker, "Nuclear Inspection," ibid., 146-48.

30. Text in *Survival*, x (March, 1968), 81-83.

31. See Alastair Buchan, ed., *A World of Nuclear Powers* (Englewood Cliffs, N.J.: Prentice-Hall, 1966).